The Crown and the Turban

A Qur'án school pupil and his teacher

The Crown and the Turban

Muslims and West African Pluralism

Lamin Sanneh

WestviewPress

A Division of HarperCollins*Publishers*

Published in 1997 in the United States of America by Westview Press, 5500 Central Avenue, Boulder, Colorado 80301-2877, and in the United Kingdom by Westview Press, 12 Hid's Copse Road, Cumnor Hill, Oxford OX2 9JJ

Library of Congress Cataloging-in-Publication Data
Sanneh, Lamin O.
The crown and the turban : Muslims and West African pluralism /
Lamin Sanneh.
    p.   cm.
  Includes bibliographical references and index.
  ISBN 0-8133-3058-0. — ISBN 0-8133-3059-9 (pbk.)
   1. Islam—Africa, West.   I. Title.
BP64.A4W367   1997
297′.0966—dc20   96-35598
                                                                          CIP

The paper used in this publication meets the requirements of the American National Standard for Permanence of Paper for Printed Library Materials Z39.48-1984.

10   9   8   7   6   5   4   3   2   1

To Sand, K, and Sia

True happiness consists not in the multitude of friends,

But in the worth and choice.

—Ben Jonson (d. 1637)

The rapid changes of recent years have forced us— sometimes painfully— to realize that the world is a much more diverse place than we had previously thought. As well as other countries and nations, there are also other cultures and civilizations, separated from us by differences far greater than those of nationality or even of language. In the modern world, we may find ourselves obliged to deal with societies professing different religions, nurtured on different scriptures and classics, formed by different experiences and cherishing different aspirations. Not a few of our troubles at the present time spring from a failure to recognize or even see these differences, an inability to achieve some understanding of the ways of what were once remote and alien societies. They are now no longer remote, and they should not be alien.

—Bernard Lewis

Contents

Part Two
Islam, Africa, and Colonialism: Religion in History   67

Part Three
Education and Society: The Roots of Muslim Identity   117

Acknowledgments

Some of the material assembled here had appeared in earlier forms in scattered places. I have hunted and gathered it into what I trust is a permanent home and in so doing reworked and supplemented it within an integrated framework. In doing so, I discovered that the task to reconstruct amounted to a separate, entirely new enterprise going beyond mere rewriting and rectifying of details. For example, the essay style allows for the staged development of an idea or theme characterized by closure and final integration. However, such a style would be inappropriate for chapters in a book, for then the chapters would become stray pieces in want of anchorage, with the whole being less than the sum of its parts. As it happens, one major focal point that emerged in the course of recasting the material is the ideas of Ibn Khaldún, which are transfused throughout this book.

Thus it may be said that the demand to produce a work dealing with the social, political, and intercultural dimensions of Muslim Africa has provided the motivation for a fresh synthesis, reconstruction, analysis, and reflection, and I took advantage of that reassessment to introduce new materials and to readjust everything else. For that opportunity I am grateful to the Pew Charitable Trusts for a grant to undertake an assessment of current needs and concerns in Muslim and Christian Africa. I am also indebted to colleagues and friends in Procmura in Africa, whose dedication to interreligious issues has encouraged and guided the inquiry represented in this book. I owe a huge debt of gratitude to a long line of teachers, mentors, supporters, colleagues, students, and friends who inspired and guided me to embark on the study of Muslim society, first in the Middle East and then in West Africa; people such as John Crossley, John Taylor, Henry Ferguson, Ted Lockwood, Hans Haafkens, J. Spencer Trimingham, Tom Beetham, Thomas Hodgkin, Hugh Thomas, Johann Bauman, Kenneth Cragg, John Taylor, Humphrey J. Fisher, Patrick Ryan, Trine Paludan, Andrew Walls, Richard Gray, John Carman, Wilfred Smith, Bill Burrows, Jim Tully, and in Africa the numerous individuals, men and women, Muslim and Christian, who over the years steadied my hand when I was new to or uncertain about the subject, and who, equally invaluably, deepened and corrected my understanding. I owe them all more than words can express. A draft of the book was first developed as the Henry Martyn Lectures at Cambridge University, England, and I am grateful to the Trustees of the Henry Martyn Trust and to David Ford and Graham Kings and their colleagues for the invitation. But it goes without saying that I alone take responsibility for the views expressed here.

I am aware of numerous people who have helped me in this work and in other ways clarified my ideas and understanding of the subject. But most of all, I pause to acknowledge the help of my family. I shudder to think of the many sins of omission and commission that are mine in any case but am further disturbed by the time and resources taken away from family responsibility in order to write this book. I am encouraged by the reminder that this book will always stand in relation to my family like the perishable before the imperishable, for what is even a clamorous literary distraction compared to love's tranquil scope? May I, nevertheless, offer this book as a token of appreciation, however inadequate as evidence of my deep indebtedness to them, and gratefully acknowledge that I simply could not have done it without their much abused forbearance.

I may, perhaps, be indulged in the hope that this work will revive interest in what was once a growing field of academic inquiry, namely, the historical exploration of religion in its social, political, and intellectual dimensions, and do so in the context of the pluralism of contemporary society. I have tried to deal with this pluralism in two fundamental ways: first, in terms of continuities and parallels, and, second, in terms of contrasts and divergences. In the first case I have shown the responses and convergences between Islam and indigenous African traditions, and in the second, I have indicated where the Muslim demand for Islam to be buttressed by the state conflicts with modern Christian and secular beliefs. However, even in the case of Muslim political militancy there are areas of potential fruitful convergence, so that the Muslim insistence on the relevance of religion to political life may be reconciled with that form of political liberalism that is hospitable to religious freedom. I have, therefore, been profoundly affected by the argument of the advocates of temporal Islam that religion without political relevance is worthless, and this understanding has led me to the view that, given the claims of Islam for divine providence in history, it would be a fatal compromise of those claims to entrust the religion to state supervision and vice versa. Religion may be too important for the state to ignore, but it is too much so for the state to enjoin it. Similarly, the state is too central to human interests for it not to overlap with the religious domain, but it is too contingent for it to behave as revealed truth. On both counts, that is to say, on the grounds of religious interest and of political contingency, we are left with a version of separation of church and state and thus with the fruitful convergence between religious voluntarism and political liberalism. In any case, that is the view put forward in this book. Thus the theme of continuities and parallels pervades the general outlook of this book and has influenced its conclusions.

Lamin Sanneh
New Haven, Connecticut

Orthographical and Bibliographical Note

I have followed in the main the *Encyclopaedia of Islam, New Edition,* in transcriptions from the Arabic, except in a few details. I have indicated the *tá' marbútah,* as in Qádiriyáh instead of Qádiriyya, except where it is quoted. In a few exceptions I have yielded to prevailing practice, as in *salát* instead of *saláh.* I have disregarded the French *dj* and *k* of the *Encyclopaedia* for the English *j* and *q* respectively, and I have omitted the ligature. I have followed the Flügel verse numbering of the Qur'án and Arberry's translation.

On the bibliographical front, I have used several untranslated local Arabic chronicles obtained in the field from clerical family archives. The major ones used in the book are as follows:

TBI = Ta'ríkh on the Silla clan of Baní Isrá'ila, obtained from al-Hájj Khousi
   (Ar. Khawth) Silla of Brikama.
TKB = Ta'ríkh on Karamokho Ba of Touba, obtained from al-Hájj Shaykh
   Sidiya Jabi of Brufut.
TKQ = Ta'ríkh on the Kabba-Jakhité clan, obtained in Kuntaur-Fulakunda
   from the estate of al-Hájj Kemoring Jakhité.
TSB = Ta'ríkh on Sálim Gassama (Karamokho Ba) of Touba by al-Hájj Mbalu
   Fode of Marssassoum, Casamance, Senegal.
TSK = Ta'ríkh on the Suwaré clan, obtained from Al-Hájj Banfa Jabi, Macca-
   Kolibantang, Senegal.

Introduction

The perspectives offered in this book arise from a relatively simple theme, namely, the Muslim encounter with the peoples and societies of West Africa, and especially with their religious traditions and political institutions. Islam is both religion and state, and in that combination it has penetrated several societies in Africa, advancing on both fronts where possible, typically with the religious yogi preceding the state commissar. In that combination, too, Islam has encountered Europe in its African empire, an encounter fraught with the tension between Western secularism and Islamic "politicalism." The Muslim encounter may in this sense be set within four broad contexts: (1) the quasi-quiescent traditional African communities and their laissez-faire practice of toleration and inclusiveness; (2) the Muslim West African tradition of clerical pacifism running parallel to Muslim militant theocratic activism; (3) the European colonial dispensation and its momentous legacy in the virile national secular state; and (4), not insignificantly, the emergence of an African Christianity shorn of any doctrinaire political blueprints but now set to engage Muslim "politicalism" on rules alien to its life and self-understanding.

I use "Islam" here in three interrelated senses: as a religion prescribed in Scripture, law, and tradition; as a "territorial" civilization with its own historical development, much like "Christendom"; and, finally, as the faith practice of persons and communities.

Muslim Africans demonstrate political confidence based on classical Islamic sources and reinforced from the tradition of Muslim rule in precolonial Africa, whereas, for their part, modern Christian Africans have no comparable political experience to draw on and consequently, they feel on the defensive. This disequilibrium constitutes a major factor in the tone and weight of the religious subjects treated in this book, divided into four parts: Islam and the African context: social and religious synthesis; Islam, Africa, and colonialism: religion in history; Muslim education and African society: religious formation and the public order; and finally, Muslims, Christians, and the national secular state: public policy issues. This last section develops the major theme of the book, which concerns contemporary projects affecting religion and politics, with the public sphere as the setting. The effects of Western political and missionary influence are considered in all these themes.

In the encounter with non-Muslim societies, to take a historical theme, Muslims possess the advantage of being African, although as new converts such Muslims may be minorities with little vested interest in indigenous cultures. Such advantage has sometimes been successfully deployed to leave Muslim groups entrenched in society. They preserve their difference, adopt an exotic culture, and reject assimilation. Yet they are never alien or unconnected to the communities concerned. The situation of such Muslims in non-Muslim societies, however, tells us a great deal about indigenous principles of toleration and inclusiveness, which are rather different from the Muslim *sabr*, the forbearance and tactical prudence that is urged in classical sources. Had non-Muslim Africans been able to express themselves on this point, they would have spoken about the *zongo* and *ardo* tradition of welcoming and giving succor to the stranger in their midst and how that fosters genuine tolerance and diversity. Muslim Africans have certainly benefited from that tradition.

The engagement of Muslims with European colonial authorities shows considerable divergence from the Muslim encounter with indigenous Africa. European ascendancy was inimical to the interests of both Muslim and non-Muslim Africans, for the logic of colonial rule was to suppress and dominate, with or without consent. Even though colonial administrations might in the end have been willing to co-opt amenable African Muslim leaders and reward collaboration as a condition of administrative stability, the arithmetic of white colonial intrusion targeted centers and persons of influence for "pacification," a euphemism for calculated military suppression.

However, Muslim perception of colonial overlordship was itself very complex. Colonial authoritarianism might have achieved for Muslims the felicitous result of abolishing godless institutions, banishing pagan customs, what the French would include in "native feudalities," and might for that reason have been welcomed by Muslims. Furthermore, colonial policy might itself have welcomed Muslim cooperation in quelling indigenous African resistance, as happened in Senegal or north Nigeria. Yet colonial administrations might have adopted a version of metropolitan anticlericalism and gone on the offensive against maraboutic Islam, which would then have antagonized even the most committed of Muslim allies.

Conversely, some administrations favored a less confrontational approach and justified their action by prevailing romantic notions of enlightened paternalism. As one nineteenth-century colonial governor expressed it, "The Negro plays his part/Within Nigretia's virgin heart." Muslims were idealized as architects of the civilization that is appropriate to the African genius, and they should for that reason be promoted as Africa's natural moral tutors. Contrasted to this position was European civilization, which was viewed as too refined and alien and, therefore, as deleterious to Africans. On that basis Christian missions were denounced as forms of Western cultural alienation, and those Africans educated in mission schools tagged as bamboozled victims of the West, cooperating in their own captivity out of an inborn perfidiousness. Pride and prejudice had attained the high-minded refinement of cold fusion, but it was a process that spared Muslim Africa in its role as tutor to, and as prototype for, the noble savage.

These flights of romantic fancy, refined to an art in the focused intensity of antimissionary sensibility, were no substitute for sound policy, as everyone knew. Colonial administrations and European commercial houses, for instance, continued to depend on mission-educated Africans to keep their books, teach in their schools, operate their machinery, write their correspondence, and translate their orders. It was such rising demand for educated Africans that showed the limits of a pro-Muslim policy, for Muslim communities were unable or unwilling to make Muslim education tools of Western-inspired social and economic development. For a time, administrators thought all that was required to remedy the problem was funding and the requisite supervision, not realizing Muslims set far more store by education than merely viewing it as a passport to a career. For the Muslims learning cannot be separated from religion, because both are tied to their idea of God. For colonial administrators, by contrast, education was a secular matter, for no one claimed, even in mission schools, that the medium of instruction, not to speak of the subjects of the curriculum, had a revealed status. Therefore, mission education clearly contributed to the secularization process and was consequently less doctrinaire than religious propaganda might pretend. In any case, colonial policy pitted avowed support for Muslim institutions against the logic of gender and nonconfessional access in Qur'án schools. Colonial authorities, and missions for that matter, assumed that ability was the key to educational success and that it mattered not a whit about the gender or religion of pupils. Muslims, by contrast, gave gender and religion a normative status. The two views could only clash. Thus the level at which Muslim education exerts its profoundest impact, the level, that is to say, of religious identity and moral commitment, is the level also of the sharpest ideological Western resistance to it. Islam continued to be a major factor in the terms the West demanded for its hegemony in traditional Africa.

We need to understand something of the nature and power of Muslim education, its ambition to redesign society from the root up and leave a permanent imprint on young minds, in order to appreciate its pervasive influence and enduring strength, and, concomitantly, its resistance to Western secular predominance. This can be done in at least two ways. In the first we can look inside and see the tradition from the point of view of Muslims themselves. The example of a childhood Qur'án school education provided here is intended to perform that function. The second way is to look at the matter from an outside engagement with it, in particular, the implications of government attempts to integrate or else develop a semiofficial status for Muslim education. The two aspects are interconnected at the point where the resilience of Qur'án schools adds muster to Muslim demands for a requisite national policy to support Qur'ánic education. Those demands in turn confront the secular national state with trying to find a modus vivendi between education for personal and social growth and education for truth and moral obedience.

Western and Muslim attitudes to education differ. As colonialism set it up, education was a public commodity to be rationalized and dispensed so as to advance specific social goals. For the Muslims concerned, education belonged with their holistic worldview. It may help us if we can see education in the context of other subjects that are equally of religious interest to Muslims. The material in Part 3 on the role of clerics takes up this issue. In that connection prayer, dreams, and healing, and, controversially, slaves and slavery all fill a role in Muslim society, with professional clerics performing in these fields and providing necessary justifications for them.

Here again Western colonial policy was unsympathetic to Muslim values, and, in the specific issue of slavery, for instance, the West demanded as a price of including Muslims in the colonial empire a drastic alteration in the rules of engagement. The West moved to outlaw slavery and to place it beyond the pale, whereas Muslim clerics were absorbed with hedging it with the assurances of divine injunction. It did not mollify Muslims to be told that slavery was unacceptable by Western secular values when Muslim revelation sets out the matter differently. For example, in 1824 the British Consul General in Morocco approached the sultan on the matter of the abolition of the trade in slaves. The sultan expressed amazement, which any West Indian or Southern Christian slave-owning family would share, at the idea, saying that "the traffic in slaves is a matter on which all sects and nations have agreed from the time of the sons of Adam . . . up to this day." The sultan said he was "not aware of slavery being prohibited by the laws of any sect, and no one need ask this question, the same being manifest to both high and low and requires no more demonstration than the light of day."[1] A hundred years later, the French were still seeking the cooperation of the sultan for the same cause.

The question is: How can we describe the institution of slavery in Muslim society with understanding but without condemnation or defense of it? Also, which is the trick, how can we recognize as legitimate the justifications offered by religion, law, and custom without necessarily accepting them for ourselves? In that sense Muslim slavery is a good test of the standard by which we study and understand other cultures, and that test may be defined as follows: How do we say something that is conceptually and "essentially" characteristic of religion without taking out of our analysis religious persons who are historically and descriptively representative of it? The assumption in this procedure is that we do not have to be religious "fundamentalists" in any but the most innocuous sense of the term in order to give pride of place to those persons who are themselves religious by conduct, claim, and intention.

In the fourth and final section, which is concerned with the political sphere, we look at Western secularism, in particular the unitary autonomous state as the heritage of the Enlightenment secular tradition that separates the church as a subordinate sphere from the state as the superior realm. We contrast with that secular tradition Muslim views on the unity of religion and politics, of the appropriateness of Caesar crowned and turbaned. In its encounter with the Muslim world, the West has been nowhere more durable and decisive than in the institution of the unitary secular state, and we would be naive to pretend that there is anything on the horizon, other than cosmetic changes, that can compete with the state as instituted by the modern West. Yet it would be equally obtuse to ignore the forces that contest the hard-core ideology of the secular state, including Muslim contentions. Hence the crucial need to consider the response to the secular state among Muslim and Christian Africans, and, especially, the religious sources in the West itself of secularism. That is the concluding grand theme of our study, and its importance is to be measured by the growing repercussions stemming from the Muslim encounter with the Western secular political tradition.

Part One

Islam and the African Context: Social and Religious Synthesis

When Islam first appeared in African societies, people were intrigued, curious, puzzled, perhaps even bewildered, but seldom hostile. The welcome Muslims received allowed them to flourish as a minority community, usually strategically nestled along important trading arteries where their usefulness to their non-Muslim hosts was assured. In time such Muslim commercial enclaves would grow in size and influence, attracting converts from the local population. The converts would keep one foot in the old traditions and draw on their new faith in terms that are congruent with earlier custom and usage. Thus Islam begins in continuity with the old, demanding little radical change as a consequence.

However, as knowledge increases and practice becomes less lax and better informed, the reform impulse is stirred and a break is signaled with the old dispensation. This reform phase might take several generations to emerge, if it emerges at all, and when it does it draws attention to prescribed rules of practice and the appropriate sanction in Scripture, law, and tradition. In general, reform Islam breaks out only in spasmodic ways rather than with formal *jihád*. A charismatic Qur'án school master or *sharíf* appears in the land and offers the community the opportunity of regular instruction for their children. The children then become better informed, and their success raises the general standard of observance and conduct. By the time a second generation arrives, the religious tone of society has been considerably raised, with the occasional pilgrimage to Mecca strengthening the reform impetus.

Over a period of time, important Muslim visitors start arriving in the community on visits, some long, some short. Their coming makes an important point of the worldwide nature of religious fellowship, and when they leave they bequeath requisite symbols of Islam's cosmopolitan status, such as an illuminated manuscript of the Qur'án, a legal manual, an embroidered turban or prayer rug, a picture of the Ka'ba (though never of the Prophet), some prayer beads, a silk gown, and so on. Eventually a ruler emerges who decides to embark on the pilgrimage and returns in triumph as a titled, accomplished pilgrim. His personal example inspires respect for Islam and assures the religion the prestige of state backing.

I am interested in the intervening stages before any decisive political triumph of Islam, in how and where Islam engages traditional African religions and what imprint it bears from its close proximity with African materials. Thus behind the public profile of state sponsorship lies the ample terrain of religious accommodation, a terrain Islam elevates with its own prescriptions but one that has been thoroughly worked with traditional tools. Thus the prescribed Muslim prayer coalesces with local rituals to allow the structure of Islam's five daily prayers to fix a regular pattern on local observance, which is brought into line with the unsettling thrust of Islam's lunar calendar system with its antiagricultural bias.

The lunar calendar, not being based on the seasons, is thus free of the predictability and obligations of the farming cycle. Local Muslims might not directly interfere with the seasonal agrarian rites that are based on the solar calendar. Rather they would bring the experience of their daily and weekly prayer observance to dominate the extended intervals between the seasonal festivals, and the more frequent quotidian pattern in time will eclipse the quarterly agricultural cycle. The shift is eased with the retention of the names of the old rituals, with the New Year, rain, harvest, and storage rites, for example, continuing to be known by their local designation though their observance may now feature prayers based on the Qur'án. If we take a long-range normative view, we may say that Islam has rigged the old dispensation and will in due season supplant it. Conversely, if we take a medium-term social view, we can say that the old dispensation has co-opted Islam and domesticated it. Both views are plausible, although the social reality of a domesticated Islam will have become too indelible a part of the religion for it not to perdure into the long term. Thus dreams, dream interpretation, healing, and amulets belong as much to the Muslim religious tradition as they do to indigenous therapeutic culture, and they thus defy any rigid attempt at separation.

Slavery, in spite of its controversial nature, fits, or has been made to fit, into the social and religious life of Muslim Africans. The institution is regulated by Scripture, law, and custom, resulting in its full integration with Islam. However, given the pre-Islamic roots of slavery in Africa, there are indigenous forms of the institution that Islam has not introduced or disrupted and that have survived into the new religion. Thus the progress of Islam in Africa has not conflicted with the practice of slavery. On the contrary, slavery has facilitated the spread of Islam and given it greater range with slave dispersal. It has also been the occasion of some of the most painful encounters between Muslims and the European colonial powers who moved to outlaw slavery.

The clerical Muslim habit of slave-owning clashed with avowed colonial policy to abolish slavery and emancipate slaves, by force if necessary. In theory, Muslim jurisprudence could support emancipation and thus reconcile itself with colonial directives to that end. According to the religious code, slaves are made, not born, with the implication that circumstances producing slavery need not be permanent or unqualified. In practice, however, slavery was too deeply entrenched to dissolve from internal humanitarian impulses, and its persistence placed the clerics on a collision course with abolitionist colonial regimes.

Under normal circumstances, it would be difficult to reconcile slavery and its associations with violence, injustice, and dehumanization with the ethical sensibilities of religion, and when that difficulty is set in the context of pacific clericalism as is done here, then it creates a dilemma bordering on the scandalous. Something of that potential scandal was revealed when the clerics involved in the practice of slavery offered only passive resistance when faced with the colonial measures abolishing slavery. Even though such abolition struck at the heart of the clerical system, the clerics conformed to the demands of their colonial overlords with nothing beyond disgruntled murmurings. Slavery could not have subverted their moral scheme. Thus, if slavery survived among the clerics from the force of habit and circumstance, it could end with external measures without those discrediting the clerical vocation as such. As it is, Islam survived emancipation and adapted and flourished in the new colonial circumstances. Yet the survival of the clerical tradition, which slavery had done so much to promote and with which it was intertwined, suggests the survival of at least vestiges of slavery in aspects of clerical practice, such as in education and farming and in the norms of caste status that attached to the descendants of slaves. In other words, slavery has been of positive value for Muslims.

So to repeat: The dynamic medium-term view we get of Islam and traditional Africa combining, separating, and again coalescing confirms that Muslims are involved in a developing historical process of change and consolidation, of challenge and reaffirmation. Ultimately, Muslim Africa would exhibit much of the confidence and flexibility, the focus and diversity, the commitment and tolerance that have been constitutive of African societies themselves.

1

Muslims in Non-Muslim Societies of Africa

A story is told about the first Zoroastrians, called Parsees, who arrived in Bombay, India, where they still flourish as a commercial enclave. Their Indian hosts, jealous of preserving their religious traditions from the presence of the new immigrants, sent them a full jug of milk as a sign. Their meaning was that just as the Parsees could not add any more to the jug without spilling some of its rich content so would they be unable to add anything valuable to the content of Hindu religious custom without inflicting a serious loss. It was not, we can see, a friendly message. There was genuine fear about the incoming immigrants and their new religion. But the response of the Parsees to this message was equally significant. A committee of local elders, called the Panchayat after the Hindu model, was quickly convened and these elders formulated an appropriate reply, which they sent back with the jug of milk. When the jug arrived it was found to contain a gold ring or, in a variant tradition, sugar. The Parsees had slipped it in as a way of saying that they would still add something precious—or sweet—to the jug of milk, and by implication to the content of Hindu religious culture, without upsetting either. Whether there were also hints of the future renown of Parsees as successful commercial entrepreneurs is not clear, but obviously they had little doubt about the worth of their contribution to their adopted land.

The story, or at any rate its essentials, may act as a paradigm of less boundary-conscious Muslims meeting their non-Muslim African hosts within jealously guarded boundaries. The present writer was told a story about a wave of immigrant Muslims who arrived in Upper Gambia from Bundu, Senegal, in the nineteenth century. They settled among cattle and pastoral Fulbe. Every day at dawn the Muslims congregated at the local mosque for prayer, summoned there by the *adhán*, the canonical call to prayer. The town's Fulbe inhabitants, constantly awakened by the early morning prayer ritual, became worried, for they feared that the Muslims were thus quarreling among themselves and seeking to compose their disputes at first opportunity. For, they reasoned, if the Muslims continued without fail to have "palaver" like this every day, then it was only a matter of time before their disputes spilled over into society and they became embroiled. By a unanimous decision they packed their belongings and, taking their Muslim guests by surprise, abandoned the town to "safety." They had misconstrued the Muslim presence, and, ignorant of the Islamic religious code, they misunderstood the *adhán* as a call to arms. As a story it is today preserved among the Muslims concerned as an amusing historical anecdote, yet it shows with remarkable clarity the dramatic frontline in the encounter between the old tribal dispensation of the land and the new Islamic world order poised to play a defining role in the self-understanding of the people.

The central premise of this book is that Muslims took a favorable view of Africa's religious openness, found affinity with certain practices, capitalized on shared understanding, exploited gaps in local techniques and resources, and then, after enough head of steam had built up, asserted the primacy of Muslim Scripture, law, and practice. It is this dynamic historical theme of affinity and challenge, of accommodation and primacy, that this book tries to develop with the transmission and establishment of Islam in African society. African pluralism and the Muslim outreach thus came to a natural convergence with the implantation of new and diverse Muslim communities, whose life also intersected with the colonial, secular, and Christian forces that were penetrating Africa. The crowning outcome of this complex process is far from assured, but the salient fact of turbaned devotees extending their influence in society by the progressive introduction of Islamic religious and political ideas gives the process its identity and direction.

Religious Impulse

Perhaps a fruitful way to describe and analyze historical stages in the evolution of relations between Muslims and non-Muslims in African society is to define precisely the shifts that have occurred from a social perspective. Two broad categories of Muslims should be studied. On the one hand we have foreign Muslim elements coming to Black Africa and staying there for various lengths of time. Some came clearly to trade. Others passed through as professional travelers, observing, advising, and even admonishing as they blazed the dust trails. Still others came as skilled craftsmen, offering their services to rulers, members of the nobility, and other leading citizens. Some others came in the spirit of the mendicant friars: solitary destitutes who flung themselves on the Samaritanly mercy of local populations. An important group of foreign Muslims also came for specifically religious purposes: missionary agents concerned with the spread of Islam or with its proper observance; traveling scholars and devout clerics who encouraged, and were themselves encouraged by, devotion to Islam. It is fair to say, as will be made clear presently, that these foreign Muslims constituted the minor theme of religious consolidation in African societies. On the other hand there are the local populations who were islamized with varying degrees of success and who subsequently adjusted the faith to the African situation with uneven thoroughness. The first group of Muslims we might call the transmitters and the second group the recipients. Thus we have two agents of Islamic diffusion, and the evidence indicates that the recipients were far more important in the spread of Islam than the transmitters and that something of the nature of the religious process in Africa can be learned from their method and outlook. Given that fact, I am less concerned with matters of technical chronology in this chapter than with an assessment of Islamic impingements on the indigenous process, and vice versa.

Until recently the view was widely held that Islam came to Black Africa by way of military conquest, a view that survives in the popular mind as the spread of Islam by the sword. Legends die hard, and this one has had a particularly resilient life, like the legendary seven-headed python of Soninké tradition. However, Muslims did not relate themselves to non-Muslim societies purely by military means. Islamic militancy is a fact in African societies that cannot be denied, but its dramatic nature should not mislead us into thinking that it was the only way.

Social Roots

'Uqbah b. Náfi' (d. A.D. 683), the military conqueror of North Africa, is regarded by some historians as an ephemeral presence in the islamization of Africa.[1] In one sense this is true. There are, as far as we know, no enduring intellectual monuments to 'Uqbah, and his achievements in matters of effective administration are even less assured. Nevertheless a considerable body of tradition exists in which 'Uqbah is accorded pride of place. The traditions of the Tuaregs, for example, set considerable store by 'Uqbah.[2] The same is equally true of the islamized Serakhullé, known in other sources as Soninké.[3] The Muslim Fulbe elite, the *tcherno*, similarly claim a notional affinity with 'Uqbah.[4] In all these traditions the military theme is absorbed into the religious irruption normally accompanying the establishment of the Pax Islamica. The standard device for representing that religious element is by claiming Sharífian contact, or even descent, and boosting it with appeal to the *ashâb*, the companions of the Prophet, and their followers (*tábi'ún*). Indeed 'Uqbah is surrounded by that kind of distinguished company, a circumstance that finds eager parallels in numerous accounts of the origin of ethnic groups in Muslim Africa. In this way the genealogical system (*nisbah*) of ethnic groups in Africa became suffused with exotic material of oriental vintage to produce hybrid tribal heroes who led the faithful remnant from Pharaonic Egypt and, equally plausibly, became the Prophet's flag bearers.[5] Obviously Muslim groups who reconstitute their heroic legends in this way are asserting an important rhetorical principle of the primacy of indigenous values, though these might be transformed into a vehicle for transmitting Islamic influence. Thus we get hints even in the old legends and myths of the potential importance of the recipients of Islamic influence. The reform tradition in Black African Islam, although concerned to sweep away the ancient deposits of local religion and custom, significantly sidestepped what is clearly a non-Islamic practice of constructing elaborate genealogical lines to preserve contact with the ancestors, a practice that elided naturally into saint veneration, a theme I shall take up in subsequent chapters in this book. Muslim tradition has categorically stated, in circumstances admittedly of an ad hoc nature, that there is no kinship in Islam, whereas in Black Africa kinship is the very sap and fiber of social identity, a truth Islam would ignore at its cost.[6]

The process of the transformation and transmutation of Islam in non-Muslim societies in Africa begins, I believe, at this level of a fictive, ideal relationship with the past. It used to be said of Islam that in a commonsense adaptation to the African environment it allowed itself a wide margin in securing followers, becoming all things to all men and peradventure winning a few genuine adherents. That kind of approach may suit our form of Western religious disenchantment, with the grass greener on the other side, but as an accurate description of the process of religious adaptation in Africa it reflected the real situation only as in a mirror image, for it seems incontestable that more often than not Islam was absorbed into preexisting notions of flexibility and tolerance rather than introducing these for the first time. Where local Muslims succeed in exploiting this tradition of pragmatic flexibility a new flowering of religious life would occur, as if that is the result of Muslim religious materials only paralleling and reinforcing patterns of pre-Islamic custom and practice. Islam in fact tries to restrict the wide margin that the old religions allow to their followers, and in doing so to force a choice, that being the natural reflex of a missionizing religion. For its part the African advantage exists from being on home base, with the ancestors and their protégés within reassuring range. There is only one reasonable conclusion to draw from this; namely, the imported demand for conversion is submerged in a vigorous, living, traditional religious reservoir and is acquired at the price of mutual interpenetrating. Of course the reformers, trading Muslim credentials, objected that this interaction overturned Islamic criteria by subjecting them to indecisiveness, but ironically enough the reform tradition itself benefited from traditional toleration, which gave it an open, public forum. In a later chapter I shall take up the public policy issues in Christian-Muslim encounters, but here I should say only that I have no doubt about the enduring reality of the old tolerance at the very core of the reform movement, at any rate in sufficiently resilient form to allow us to characterize the shift in Muslim attitudes in terms of continuities and operative flexible local options. As I shall try to show from contemporary sources, the reform impulse appears to have been sustained by Fulani national feeling even if scruples of faith and obedience guided the movement. In practice it may not be possible to separate ethnic passion from religious motivation, though in the language of doctrinal justification it is prescribed codes that receive prominence over mundane calculations.

Before going further into the African material let me say that the situation I have so far described applies equally well to Christianity, as it must if the African medium is the vital force we are claiming it to be. To test that argument we have to check the weakest possible link in the chain. When Africans were transported across to the Western hemisphere the dislocation of their religious, social, and other cultural institutions produced an unprecedented chaos in traditional materials, and the foreign lands to which they were taken appeared inhospitable. But, as Pierre Verger and Juana Elbein Dos Santos have shown in detailed accounts of African communities in the Bahia province of Brazil, indigenous African religious beliefs and practices survived in their Christian transformation, bearing remarkable similarities to their African originals.[7] Dos Santos was able not only to demonstrate the African genesis of much of local Brazilian religious practice but also to trace numerous cults to their counterparts in specific Yoruba areas like Oyo, in addition to giving precise details in Orisa, Egungun, and Alagba Ile Olukotun.[8] Dos Santos also shows how Portuguese became the ritual language of the cults, later organized into a federal structure under the name Umbanda.[9] Pierre Verger, for his part, shows the fascinating way Muslim Africans in Bahia in the early nineteenth century kept in close touch with developments in Africa by utilizing a sophisticated network of contact and communication. For example, the most serious slave revolts in Bahia, between 1806 and 1826, owed their inspiration and organizational stimulus to the Fulani *jihád* of Sokoto, a remarkable illustration of the extraordinary mobility of people, religion, and ideas.[10] African religious and cultural practices survived in the harsh conditions of plantation slavery, taking in their stride the Sisyphian hurdle of the notorious middle passage, and were no less resilient on African soil, whatever the attitude of hard-line reformers. Islam had not entered a *cul-de-sac*.

Religious Change

The uneven impact of Islam on African societies affords us an opportunity to assess the real process of religious change and to see whether ritual transformation is the traditional religious counterpart to the Islamic legal system. Put another way, we cannot be sure that when local populations observe the Islamic code on performance of the *salát* they are not also extending by means of it their earlier understanding of ritual territory inhabited by spirits. On the surface, the *imám* as leader of *salát* is the representative of a radical new religion, but he performs functions that evoke the old diviner interceding with the spirits and the souls of the departed ones. Thus, even where the stream of faith appears to be in full spate, we cannot know that it is not carrying in its bosom the imperishable deposit of Africa's religious heritage. There would, thus, appear to be a double process of challenge and hospitality in the encounter of religions in Africa.

Some idea of the challenge of Islam, and the hospitality of African culture, can be gained from a detailed look at the apparently hospitable environment of the Nupe of the middle belt of Nigeria, who use Islam as no more than a carriage to mobilize their traditions. Nupe had a dual deity, Soko (sky-god) and Gunnun (earth-god). Nupe ritual activity was concentrated on Gunnun, but with the introduction of Islam the prominence given to Gunnun disappeared (although a disintegrated remnant of Gunnun ritual persisted), while Soko as the sky-god assumed a new importance as a conceptual equivalent for Allah.

Nupe believe that man consists of three principles united in one body (*naka*): his eternal soul, called *fifinge*; *Rayi*, the life-force which leaves the body when death occurs; and *Eshe*, a personal essence that clings to the body after death and that perpetuates the personality of the dead one as an apparition. The *fifinge* is a kind of wandering soul that is active in sleep and manifests itself in dreams.

The tenacity of the worldview represented by the preceding account of religious ideas among the Nupe is extended in two other areas where Islamic influence is noticeable. In their ideas on death and funeral ceremonies the Nupe seem to use Islam as a boost, and where substitution is possible, a parallel path is followed. They believe that after death and burial the *rayi* is sent back into the corpse (*ekun*) and two angels called *walakiri* arrive to test its profession of Islam.[11] This inquest continues for forty days, after which the angels report back to God and the individual is rewarded or punished according to the verdict and then cut off from all contact with the living. *Alijena* is the place of reward, something of a facsimile of a happy family life on earth, and *Emina* the place of awaiting sentence. Despite the forty-day severance rule, Nupe believe in a reincarnation in which *eshe* and *fifinge* are amalgamated with a fresh *rayi*.

An elaborate ritual occurs on the eighth day after death, which is continued with subsequent visits to the graves of departed relatives. The family cult (*nba*) of ancestral spirits (*dako*) involves the offering of libations and prayers. There are also the cults of water spirits (*kpanka*) and twin spirit (*bakomba*). The feast of mourning that forms the climax of the eight day ceremony is marked by prayer with libation, called *ebala*. Muslim Nupe adopt the Islamic parallel of *aduwa* (*du'a*) in its place, though retaining the ritual features of the traditional ceremony.

In the organization of religious life the Nupe have assimilated Islamic elements within an existing framework. There are two dichotomous areas presided over by religious authorities. Important chiefdoms have a leading diviner called *ndazo* who is dedicated to rituals concerned with *Gunnun*, whereas smaller rural centers are presided over by a village priest called *zigi*, who also fills an intermediary role between *ndazo* and *Gunnun* and then between the spirit forces called *kutizi* and the people. There is a clerical group among the Nupe called *ena Manzi*, and it is from their ranks that the Mallams of Islam are recruited. The chief cleric, called the *manko*, becomes the *imám*, and his deputy the *nayemi* (Arabic: *ná'ib*), *madiu*, and *kitábu* (reciter).[12] The esteem in which Islamic learning is held among the Nupe derives from traditional understandings of the function of the masters of the religious craft. Islam may have broadened the Nupe understanding of what constitutes knowledge to include mastery of the sacred and secular so that the Nupe began to recognize that among the class of the learned are people with knowledge about political affairs and dynastic succession and others with competence in Qur'án reading and amulet making. Such a refinement of the educational process still continues to capitalize on the honor accorded to ancient wisdom.[13]

In an account of the complex cosmology of the Dogon people of Mali we are given fascinating details of their myths about the origin of life and how God and man came to be locked in an intricate love-hate matrix. God created life and the spheres from clay, and by "the first attested invention of God, the art of pottery" He molded and fired the heavens. God is called Amma, and He is one. He took a lump of clay, squeezed it in his hand, and flung it from him. From its scattered pieces came the earth, exuding an amorous fragrance that tempted the God Amma. He approached the earth, now lying face upwards, but found his advances impeded by a protruding termite hill, symbol of provoked masculinity. God the all-powerful cut through this hindrance and forced intimacy, a primordial blunder from which the world has never recovered. It was a defective union and what resulted was a jackal, symbol of the travails of God, not the intended twins. Unsatisfied and unexhausted, God tried a second time and the results were successful. Water, the divine seed, issued forth and entered the womb of the earth, leading to the birth of twins. These became the two spirits, called Nummo, sharing the divine essence and becoming his effective instruments and agents. They are everywhere, like water, which is in fact their visible manifestation whereas speech and sound become their self-realization. By the work of the Spirit, man and woman were created, each with dual sex functions, but the Nummo Pair arranged to have the man circumcised, thus freeing him from the contradictions of his femininity and equipping him with an unambiguous paternal function. From his subsequent amorous exploits came a quiver full of children, from whom the Dogon descended.[14]

The Dogon maintain strong links with the dead members of their community, a relationship sometimes amusingly taking the form of teasing or hurling insults at their souls, a piece of reckless indulgence in which they are emboldened by drinking fermented liquors. The drink is deemed fortified with the life force of the dead, who hover over the millet beer. The life force mingles with the beer, discharging an intoxicating power into it. It also transfuses it with something of its own restless spirit and disturbed wanderlust. The old men who partake of this sacrament imbibe that ferment of disorder and become themselves incoherent. They barrel along the narrow streets, spitting insults. The fermented liquor is infused from a calabash, itself the symbol of a world turned upside down. The life force of the old men resists the "impurities" shed by the souls of the dead, and, under the influence of drink, their sputtering alerts their hearers to build altars, "and that gives satisfaction to the dead. . . . For the old, drunkenness is a duty; it seems like disorder, but it helps to restore order."[15] The malevolence that is due to the sins of the dead is thus averted from the living.

The basic outlines of this intricate worldview have ostensibly contracted under the impact of Islam,[16] although, because of the comparative newness of Islamic influence and the complexity of Dogon cosmology and ritual, the old worldview predominates; scholars like Germaine Dieterlen would say that worldview is indeed indomitable.[17] Whatever the final issue we can recognize the contrasting features of traditional religion with Islam and therefore the kind of change or changes that occur with the presence of Muslims. For example, Muslims would ban alcohol and libations.

The example of the Yoruba of west Nigeria is well known. The detailed description of their religious worship reveals an equally complex world. The Yoruba have come under Islamic influence, and it would appear also in their case that in many ways Islam has not been allowed to override local esteem for ancient tradition, in spite of persistent criticism by the Yoruba Muslim leaders, called *alfa*.[18] In a valuable monograph that was completed for a Ph.D. at Harvard, Patrick J. Ryan, S.J., provides numerous details on ritual practice among local Muslims. In the ceremony of *wonk*, which is the washing of conversion, the convert undresses in front of the *alfa*, the presiding cleric. He washes the convert's right and left hands three times each, his right and left legs three times each, and his elbows three times. All this takes place at 6:00 A.M., and it suggests strong Islamic influence, though the underlying religious outlook is here traditional, too. Cash offerings then follow in a covered dish brought for the occasion.[19] Johnson in his classic *History of the Yorubas* describes how Islam came to Oyo. The Emir of Ilorin, Shitta, required the reigning Alafin of Oyo, Oluewu, to visit Ilorin as a vassal. Oyo refused and lost heavily in the subsequent resistance (c. 1833).[20] But just to show that Ilorin itself was far from being a showcase for Islamic orthodoxy, Shitta's successor, Ahmad ibn Abí Bakr, a nephew of the former, tried to purify Islam in Ilorin. In a significant encounter with traditional religious practices, the early Muslim reformers in Ilorin felt compelled to challenge the authority of *Egungun* when the head slave of the Emir, Jimba, confiscated the dress of the cult and required the citizens to accept the Qur'án and adopt Arabic names in place of the old ones at the pain of the sword.[21]

The turbulent convergence of a self-conscious Islam and an invigorating traditional Yoruba religiosity, merging with the pacific stream of Christianity, produced a rich variety of religious practice. Because both Islam and Christianity are late arrivals in Yorubaland it should strike us as odd that their representatives should feel justified in securing the guilt of local religious stalwarts by calling them infidels. In practice, however, attitudes are more flexible. Ryan has shown, for example, that Christian elements have found their way into Yoruba Islam: Muslim graves in Ijebu, for example, display the Cross as well as portrayals of deceased relatives.[22] The pledge at the marriage ceremony involving modern Muslims is given in the Christian style.[23] I came into possession of a book of prayers designed for use in Muslim schools in Yorubaland. Many of the prayers imitate the stiff dignity of the English Book of Common Prayer, Cranmer's sonorous diction making a not uncomfortable transition into a totally different world.[24] The Ansár-u-Dín Society, a conservative reform movement led by an illustrious Ilorin Muslim scholar, al-Ilúri, had a tradition of organizing Sunday schools for their students where again the Book of Common Prayer and the Bible were evident as sources of influence.[25] Then there is the inevitable phenomenon of secularism and its wide-ranging effects on Muslim life and practice, a secularism that has not spared traditional Qur'án schools and Arabic as a mystical language, as we shall see in subsequent chapters. The Muslim encounter with Christians has to be seen in this wider, secular context. Thus have the secular hosts surrounded Muslim strongholds like the walls of Jericho, making many modern Muslims adopt the strategy of adaptation and adjustment that is just short of surrender, and, if their critics are to be believed, sometimes tantamount to it.

In his account of the Ijesha kingdom among the Yoruba, John Peel has observed the close links between religious affiliation and economic, political, and educational factors. For example, he notes how the leading traders and other pioneers among this branch of the Yoruba "virtually all became Christians (a few, Muslims), though not usually as a result of schooling."[26] On the question of conversion to Christianity and Islam, Peel cautions against proceeding on the basis of a general theory of conversion, such as that advanced by Robin Horton, which says that conversion to world religions can be explained by "the increase in social scale." Peel insists that "the range and diversity of Ilesha's old religion belies any characterization of it as *purely* the cosmology of a closed and static society. While there was much there that was highly specific to particular localities and lineages, the major deities were of 'pan-Yoruba' type and many quite local cult-figures were refractions of them."[27] Thus any claim for conversion either as a mechanical response to world order experience or as a triumphalist break with the old seems unjustified.

Musa Abdul evokes this flexibility theme when he says he feels encouraged as a modern Yoruba Muslim scholar by the prospects of Muslim-Christian collaboration and neighborliness.[28] Babs Fafunwa, another leading Yoruba Muslim, similarly feels confident about the beneficial effects of secular education.[29] Opposite them are men determined to resist the slide into the past of Yoruba religion or a drift into secularism. A. S. Olatunde belongs to this category of Yoruba Muslims. He is forthright in his denunciations of the pervasive Yoruba custom of prostration, of the Eyo masquerade, and of the ritual of offering sacrifices.[30] He is joined in this by al-Ilúri and the members of the Bamidele Society. They also condemn the accommodation of Islam with Yoruba traditional religion, including the adoption of traditional Yoruba names.[31] Al-Ilúri also insists on the retention and encouragement of Arabic as the ritual language of Islam and defends it against the criticism that it is of little secular value. Instead he argues that Arabic should continue to be taught as a linguistic discipline alongside its other functions.[32]

Indigenous Response

So far we have only considered the situation from the viewpoint of the late arrivals. How did the leaders of the traditional religious customs regard this intrusion of their territory? Is there any evidence that they resisted the unflattering picture painted by their opponents, who saw them as misguided? In raising this question we return to the point I made earlier about the underlying firmness of the African religious heritage. In one or two other places we are told that because of the power of militant Islam only faint traces of the old order can be detected, and even that with great difficulty.[33] In what I am now going to say, it should be clear that if we can support such a wholesale destruction of ancient African religious materials then something more than the religion of Islam has to be brought in to account for that. However, that is a separate assignment. The traditional Yoruba religious leaders say that sacrifice to *Eshu* may be waived for those Muslims and Christians whose conscience would not allow them to do so. Instead they may give token alms, called *sara,* or prepare a feast.[34] What is *Eshu*? A modern scholar gives the following description:

> *Eshu* was not the Devil or Satan, although this identification has been accepted by many educated Yoruba. He was a troublemaker who started fights and killed people by toppling trees and walls on them; in this sense he can be considered a divine trickster, the divine counterpart of Tortoise in Yoruba folktales. He was also the divine enforcer who, with a remarkably even hand, punished those who failed to make sacrifices prescribed through Ifa divination, and rewarded those who did so. He was also the messenger of the gods, one of whose roles was to deliver sacrifices to Olorun. Most of the sacrifices prescribed through Ifa divination were placed at the shrines of Eshu, who carried them to Olorun, after keeping a portion for himself, and reported who had offered them. One Ifa verse speaks of Eshu as the one appointed by Olorun to watch what the other deities did on earth.[35]

This attitude of tolerance and reasonableness was in some cases consciously pursued in the interests of greater community harmony. There is the famous example of the Freetown Yoruba community who decided in the nineteenth century that potential friction between Muslims and Christians could be avoided by calling the leaders of the respective communities to a general public meeting under the significant patronage of the Orisas. Those present at the meeting, including the veteran Freetown Muslim leader, Abayomi Cole, hailed it as a great landmark.[36]

Even if these several examples have to be used as a basis, we would still be right to conclude firmly that traditional religions were on the whole favorably disposed towards the presence of Muslims—and Christians for that matter—in their midst. The controversial dimension of interreligious encounter has very shallow local roots. It was an importation constructed on the notion of exclusiveness.

For that reason, among others, I feel a particular ennui from the thrust of the recent book by the Yoruba historian, T.G.O. Gbadamosi.[37] I would be ready in theory to believe that Yoruba Muslims banged away at their traditional religious opponents and beat them into the ground, for thus has pious eloquence always resolved the contest between truth and error. Yet I would still not be certain that in reality traditional religious leaders, brought face to face with a new phenomenon of assertive proselytization, melted away in defeat, as Gbadamosi represents it. For example, at Abeokuta we have an encounter between Muslims and followers of Ogboni, the cult of the Earth God, a cult with important organizational political features, in which Gbadamosi credulously gives the Muslims the upper hand. The same pattern emerges in the Yoruba towns of Ijebu-Ode, Iwo, Ekiti, and Iseyin, among other places. According to Gbadamosi, the *aborisa*, the worshippers of the Orisas, are pitted against Muslims, and, by a suspicious intervention of fate, are confounded and exposed as "pagans" without real spiritual power. Someone Gbadamosi describes as "an eclectic Muslim preacher" was outstanding for "fearlessly denouncing the pagans and the Ogboni as vermin . . . and encouraging all to convert to Islam, the way of salvation."[38] The outcome of all this godly fervor was a predictable triumph for Islam. "The Ogboni soon gave up the unequal struggle, leaving the Muslim group undaunted and apparently invigorated."[39]

Such a treatment of the process of religious change misconstrues an important episode in the history of religions. I confess to a certain professional envy. The admirable works of people like J. Olumide Lucas,[40] E. Bolaji-Idowu,[41] and John S. Mbiti,[42] among others, on the vitality of African traditional religions and the urgent importance of a truly Christian appreciation have still to find their counterparts among Muslim African writers. It is a surprising hiatus given the long history of borrowing between Islam and local religious elements. Something of this surprise led René Bravmann to inveigh against the proponents of an iconoclastic Islam.[43] Keeping people like Gbadamosi in mind, one can perhaps understand Bravmann's impatience when he castigates writers for their preoccupation with the inflexible extension of what he quaintly calls "the orthodox theology of Mecca."[44] Yet a significant earlier study on Yoruba religious carving that treats Islamic materials is not mentioned by Bravmann.[45] Bravmann writes in spirited defense of what today we would call popular Islam, distinguishing that from the religion of the emirs and scholars, convinced that such popular religiosity is closer to the basic ethos of African societies than the august rectitude of word and sword. Allying himself with the work of J. Spencer Trimingham,[46] whose detailed historical and thematic investigations of Muslim Africa opened the field to the modern scholarly enterprise and whom tutorial obligation requires me to hold in esteem, Bravmann states: "The syncretic nature of Islam in West Africa is based . . . on the very make-up of the religion."[47] This assertion suggests that something more besides the established canon could be added to the structure of Islamic juridical authority. It is, admittedly, easy to see Muslim Africans importing non-Islamic customs, some frankly outlandish, into Islam, as the Mouride case illustrates, and in that sense it is true that the "make-up" of Muslim society resembles a patchwork quilt rather than a seamless robe. Muslim Africans, it goes without saying, arrive by many and diverse doors into Islam; yet, without the rubrics of duty and practice, of norm and prescription, we would scarcely know any of those doors, let alone track those entering them. Islam, indeed, is what Muslims make of it, but Muslims include canonical directives in their understanding of Islam, whatever the inadequacies in local expression. I should, however, for the sake of the argument of this chapter, welcome the kind of statement that portrays Islam as essentially syncretist, yet I can only do so with reservations. It is syncretist only as a phase or for want of knowing better, not as a permanent state, or at least that is what reform-minded Muslims would say, and prudence or strategy might make such reformers turn a blind eye to controversial mixing. In the end, however, syncretism is dry tinder to the passion that faithful observance would in time ignite. The relevant issue is that non-Muslim societies may be strong enough to delay or even put off a final reckoning, leaving Muslims with no choice but to acquiesce. I would argue that such a situation does not represent a loss for Muslims, it only stops them from imposing their word on others. In that case, the Muslim gains would be something bequeathed to them by their non-Muslim hosts rather than gains they extracted with the *Sharí'ah*. Flexibility, then, is a good thing, and when Muslim Africans adopt it, it is very good—those facts are not in dispute. However, I would maintain that traditional Africa deserves the credit for much of that flexibility and the tolerance it fosters. I do not see why representative Muslims should anathematize their non-Muslim neighbors for maintaining such a propitious view of religious tolerance. It may come to pass that a growing number of reform-minded Muslims finds coexistence irksome or even offensive, requiring them to pronounce a verdict of guilty on their less scrupulous coreligionists. But that again suggests that Muslims may chose to define the degree or method of change, especially because Islamic identity is such a dynamic phenomenon. I would stress flexibility on the understanding that even the devout may embrace leniency without mortal compromise to themselves.[48] Thus may Islam offer valuable matching tissue without turning into a cadaver.

I assume in this argument that traditional African cultures have intrinsic resources of adaptability and discernment, that they can take from Islam (or from Christianity) what agrees with their values, rejecting or radically modifying other elements that conflict. Some of these populations have continued to resist conversion to Islam in spite of many centuries of sustained contact. Such resistance must carry a deep attachment to the pre-Islamic heritage whose ethos and worldview people find satisfying. The large areas of Sudanic Africa that Islam has cleanly bypassed, such as the middle belt of Nigeria and significant bands in Senegambia, Guinea, and Sierra Leone, suggest that indigenous Africa does not lack the resources with which to withstand Muslim (or Christian) missionary assault. Furthermore, traditional religions have occasionally made deep inroads into the ranks of Muslims and others, a process that Muslims misleadingly term "reversion" on the basis that it is a setback for the truth. Nehemia Levtzion, in his detailed description of Islam in the Middle Volta region of Ghana, shows how, in one area, the Muslim cleric found himself in keen competition with the priests of the powerful medicine shrine and, unable to match their strength, abandoned Islam and joined them.[49] In many other examples Islam survives only by taking shelter under the buoyancy of traditional religious vitality.[50] We are not so much witnessing the flexibility of Islam as the capacity of African religions for subtle response and adaptability. That factor alone explains the cockeyed phenomenon of Islam seeking to rivet the chains of orthodox conformity on people and also contenting itself with nothing more than a mere lip service to its tenets. The Muslim

religious code, if that is the standard, is violated by anything less than the observance of the five daily prayers, and there is nothing in the law as such to enable
people to change that number. Nor indeed is there any substitute for the canonical obligation to perform the worship of *salát* in Arabic. In a historical sense it is
equally hard to see how the tradition of militant reform could be sustained by the
awareness that flexibility commands the same unquestioned authority as the requirements of inflexible conformity. A house cannot be divided against itself in
that fashion and survive.

Reform Islam

However, traditional religions have in certain crucial features, including their organizational structures, benefited from contact with Islam. The centralized features
of local religious cults have often attracted the hostile attention of Muslim leaders,
and perhaps Islam succeeds in dismantling the political basis of these cults. Yet
Muslim competition for such sources of local power[51] testifies to their power and is
a recognition of their strategic importance. At this point we should take up the
question of the Fulani *jihád* in Hausaland. The iconoclastic stance of the Fulani *jihádists* is undeniable. In numerous verses and jurisprudential pronouncements the
Muslim reformers attacked not only the political practices of their non-Muslim
leaders but also customary religious and social practices, sacred and profane, of the
people in general.[52] Usuman dan Fodio (d. 1817), the creator of the Sokoto
caliphate, was unstinting in his efforts to eradicate traditional religious influences
and institute a fresh reform order.[53] Muhammad Bello (d. 1837), his son and heir,
who in fact built the original walls of Sokoto in 1809, stiffened this Philistine resolve. Hugh Clapperton, who met Bello in Sokoto, was attracted there partly by
virtue of his own Calvinistic scruples and was not a little disconcerted to find that
something of the old religious mentality persisted in the popular piety of the city.
He had taken with him a number of astronomical instruments in which Muhammad Bello showed knowledgeable interest. Clapperton, recording the meeting that
took place in March 1824, describes it thus: "I first exhibited a planisphere of the
heavenly bodies. The sultan knew all the signs of the Zodiac, some of the constella-
tions, and many of the stars, by their Arabic names."[54]

Elsewhere in Hausaland Clapperton wrote faintheartedly of the clamorous demands of local people for religious service. "I was," he says, "unluckily taken for a
fighi, or teacher, and was pestered, at all hours of the day, to write out prayers by
the people. . . . Today my washerwoman positively insisted on being paid with a
charm, in writing, that would entice people to buy earthenware of her; and no
persuasions of mine could either induce her to accept money for her service, or
make her believe the request was beyond human power."[55]

In another incident, Clapperton describes how, on a visit to the vizier of Bello
in Sokoto, he found him engaged in arcane study. He writes:

This morning (April 9, 1824) I paid the gadado a visit, and found him alone, reading an Arabic book, one of a small collection he possessed. "Abdallah," he said, "I had a dream last night, and am perusing this book to find out what it meant. Do you believe in such things?" "No, my lord gadado; I consider books of dreams to be full of idle conceits. God gives a man wisdom to guide his conduct, while dreams are occasioned by the accidental circumstances of sleeping with the head low, excess of food, or un-easiness of mind." "Abdallah," he replied, smiling, "this book tells me differently."[56]

Such evidence indicates that the reformers had not done with belief in the power of magic, divination, fortune-telling, dreams, and dream-interpretation, and with the general sphere of invisible powers and forces. Why, then, the reform imperative? Admittedly, religion was a force: The reformers wished to purify the observance of Islam so as to create greater commitment to prescribed rules of faith and conduct. But there was more. Fulani ethnic feelings were to the fore in some of the major cleavages that developed in the reform movement. The reform party included Fulani sympathizers whose Islam was often more questionable than that of their enemies. The population of Kanem-Bornu led by Muhammad al-Kánemí, for example, were professed Muslims against whom the Fulani de-clared the *jihád*, raising embarrassing doctrinal questions about the ethics of drawing the sword against fellow believers. Furthermore, zealous Fulani troops with only a modicum of instructed faith were given sanction to operate as over-lords under the *jihád* banner in districts whose chief offense was to lie on a differ-ent side of the ethnic line. In many such places the *casus belli* was mounting eco-nomic grievances of the pastoral Fulani against the levies, imposts, and poll tax of the Hausa rulers, whose exactions sometimes extended to enslavement of the Fu-lani. The cleavage here is the fundamental one of the values of sedentary popula-tions conflicting with those of a mobile, pastoral people who, without ties to the land and without a stake in established institutions, nevertheless require pasture and access to wells and country routes to maintain their lifestyle. This cleavage runs the entire gamut of life in the Savannah and Sahel regions of Africa. Yet, as the reformers themselves conceded, Muslim Africans at that or other times were equally to blame as their "pagan" rulers. Fulani ethnic claims would in turn not provide any more effective insurance against corruption. Thus the problem per-sists of how to strike a balance in the relationship between religion and political rule, between faith and ethnic advantage.

Having defined the old religions in antagonistic terms and roused Muslims to believe that change would usher in a new age of justice and truth, the reformers were now left to contemplate the consequences of betrayal and failure. The old re-ligions continued to fill an important gap in the surviving worldview in spite of the pressure the *jihádists* brought to bear.[57] In a perceptive analysis of Islam in Manding society, called by him Dyula, the French scholar, Yves Person, has pointed out that as a minority faith Islam came to have a place in traditional reli-gious society. Muslims came to form a religious/social caste alongside other occu-pational castes, such as the *nyamakala*, or artisans' class, without sharing the marriage restrictions of the latter.[58] Living in close physical proximity to traditional religious people, the Muslims came to express their religious worldview through the local idiom. As a rationalization for their own status of non–ancestor veneration, and wishing to keep in step with their hosts, the Muslims said that everyone would come to the same divine end, except that non-Muslims would be sent after death to a place called *Tabakoroni* (*taba* being a tree for which the botanical name is *Storculia cordifolia*), a sort of purgatory. Person is right to conclude that this doctrine was a casuistic device to avoid the explicit call to conversion that Islamic law demands.[59] Louis Brenner, in his study of Islam in Bornu, makes the same point the other way round. He writes: "In practice the exigencies of governing led rulers to depend more on their own administrative devices than the *Sharí'ah*, whose jurisdiction often became narrowly restricted to matters of family law and inheritance. This restrictive tendency resulted partially from the fact that the *Sharí'ah* was too explicit on some matters and therefore difficult to enforce. It also resulted from the need for governors and rulers to compromise with the demands and prejudices of their subjects, who, particularly in the frontier regions of the Islamic worlds, were not always willing to abandon their ancient customs although they claim to have converted to Islam."[60]

Mutuality

The interdependence between Muslims and non-Muslims in many African societies suggests that neither side requires the disintegration of the other as a precondition of its existence. The non-Muslim Hausa, called the Maguzawa, adopt Islamic religious terminology in describing their worldview without feeling that they require the baptism that Islam has long promised them.[61] Conversely, pioneer Muslim clerics have, with equal lack of inhibition, assumed the religious language and methods of traditional diviners and shrine attendants without relinquishing their specific Islamic identity. In many significant ways the representatives of the two respective communities have a lot in common beyond the African medium. That in fact was one of the poignant lessons of a play by an educated modern Muslim in Freetown. The largely Muslim audience who saw the performance of that play reacted by pointing out that the plot was calculated to give pride of place to the traditional religious diviner.[62] There are probably all kinds of internal tension going on within both worlds: within Islam, the tension between the universal claims of Islam and its particular local manifestations and between the centers of religious orthodoxy and the peripheral areas of accommodation; and in traditional religions, between the village inhibitions of small shrines and the expanding reputation of traveling diviners and between the earth cults of particular localities and regional cults of growing townships. But interdependence is bound to raise the level of religious awareness and thus increase the opportunities for a fresh interpretation of the ceaseless human quest for a supernatural identity.

The figurative jug of Africa's traditional religious heritage is ample enough for Islam (and much else besides) to find room in it without being entirely broken down and reconstituted. Islam and traditional religions will at first mingle on the basis of the old practices and ideas, and at this stage of interaction there is little Islamic displacement. Some Islamic elements, such as its legal and linguistic teachings, are weakened, but these are not lost, thanks to Islam's fixed body of Scripture and the learning that sustains it. Islam's compatibility, then, does not deny its difference. In the markets of the old towns, for example, Islam and traditional religions are represented by different professional traders. One set of stallkeepers sells copies of the Qur'án and Arabic legal manuals, while another sells medicinal herbs, roots, horns, and pouches. There may even be a third section of stalls selling printed Western books and school supplies. The lines among these traders may occasionally get blurred, but they are not completely erased. A sacred page of the Qur'án, for example, may be stuffed into a pouch obtained from the traditional stallkeeper and carried around as a talisman, but neither is displaced. Scripture and spirit forces converge on aiding access to occult power. Trimingham is right to stress that what is involved here is a dualism that does not deny interpenetration, that the Muslim African "is not torn between two warring forces."[63] Thus, the outward forms and symbols of the old harmonize with the inner conviction of the truth of Islam, a truth governed not by blood and tribe but by religious injunction.

In his investigations of Islam among the Dyula people of the Ivory Coast, Robert Launay has identified two basic types, the *mory* Islam of the scholars and its undercurrents of Wahhabi reform, and the *tun tigi* Islam of the warrior class with its mixed and lax practice and its accommodation to indigenous religious forms. Behind this twofold division lies another distinction: the difference in *mory* Islam itself between what Launay calls *bayani karamogoya* and *siru* or *siri karamogoya*. *Bayani karamogoya* is religious knowledge based on canonical sources, what Geertz has called Scriptural Islam, and *siru karamogoya* is religion as secret knowledge concerned with personal needs in this world.[64] *Bayani* is the local variant of the Arabic *bayán*, and translates literally as the evidence, or the demonstration, and means the revealed Qur'án. *Siru* or *siri* is a variant of the Arabic *sirr*, secret, esoteric, and is connected with divination, amulet making, and other forms of clerical practice. At the same time it evokes Sufi mystical ideas. Though frowned on by the stalwarts of *bayani karamogoya*, *siru karamogoya* has been the tender bridge linking the world of African religions to unofficial Islam in its Sufi version, offering prospective converts a hospitable niche in which the old and new may be auspiciously blended. This example suggests plural options are available to practitioners, with law and custom giving people the freedom to adopt and adapt, as they have always done. It should caution us against a doctrinaire view of religious change and identity in Africa, as Peel has admonished.

Local Muslim practice places a great deal of stress on ritual and performance as prescribed by the rule books. Thus *kalám*, or theology as rational disputation and apologetic, is of marginal interest to the rank and file and their clergy. Ibn Khaldún defined *kalám* as the science or method by which the dogmas of faith are proved and defended against the skeptics, and understood that way, we can see why *kalám* just never took off in Muslim West Africa. The articulate rational skepticism it assumes as a foil for its powers is missing in standard African religious culture. Conversion or resistance to belief is not, at least initially, a matter of verbal debate but of social custom and convention expressed in such things as dietary and sartorial habits, ritual taboos, and ethnic and residential identity. Even the doctrine of *tawhíd*, of prescribed belief in the divine unity, is transmitted within the indigenous mythological code of belief in the supernatural and the ethical system based on it, rather than by philosophical disputation, as in Avicenna's or al-Ghazálí's treatises. In place of *kalám,* the *hadíth* functions as the mechanism by which local myths and legends are adopted into Muslim practice, thus placing local populations within the new Islamic frame without a violent rupture with the old. Thus, for example, might traditional reverence for nature survive into Islam by the claim that the Prophet in his lifetime used to seek shelter in the shadow of a local sacred tree, and thus, too, might dioscuric beliefs find sanction in reverence toward Hasan and Husayn as the Prophet's twin grandchildren. The *hadíth* culture as such allows mythological freedom, though this freedom is not the same as corruption; more accurately, the *hadíth* offers rhetorical scope for the genealogy-saturated and story-soaked cultures of traditional societies. That is what takes the place of abstract cognitive systems and prevents religious differences from assuming the status of an open, formal conflict. John Henry Newman described the proof of God's existence as the testimony borne to truth by the mind itself, a procedure in which mind is given primacy. Muslim Africans by contrast would stress ritual and social custom, which convey and refract truth.

The final word belongs to the practitioners of the ancient art of interreligious living. In an article published in 1946 Kenneth Little drew attention to the role Muslim holy men fulfill in society, being eagerly patronized by all sections of the community, Muslim, traditionalist, and Christian alike. He recorded the story of an itinerant Muslim cleric, called by the local title, *alfa,* who delivered a public address in June the previous year before the paramount chief of a Mende chiefdom in Sierra Leone. The *alfa* talked about a once powerful chief called Mulku Suliman who fed and clothed a pauper. This pauper started preaching about poverty and hunger in the world and was immediately disowned by Mulku. The pauper returned to God as the archangel Gabriel and reported on Mulku's disobedience and pride. Mulku was then seized while on a walk and carried to heaven on his horse, a flight that brought on excruciating hunger. "It was then," the *alfa* continued, "that Mulku realized what hunger is like." The horse then halted at a place where Gabriel sat on the throne, but Gabriel ignored Mulku when the latter greeted him, a greeting demanded by the rules of chiefly protocol. Not for us to miss its import, "Mulku wept bitterly," the *alfa* said, "and realized that there was a power even greater than his own: that of God, the Omnipotent." Disobedience to God is like one to the chief, and through him to the district commissioner, the governor, and the great king in England. The *alfa* then went on to describe Pharaoh and Moses before coming to the Poro secret society, which he condemned as a society that does not pray. According to him the field of the last judgment was once a Poro bush. He urged the importance of prayer.

He told of a vision of heaven he had once in a dream. In heaven you do not wink, die, or grow hungry. There is no darkness, only pure light. If you want something you simply think of it and there and then it becomes available. You also retain your sexual instinct, and someone automatically appears by your side if you need a sleeping partner. To conclude this session the *alfa* ordered and presided over a ritual offering. He asked the chief to make a sacrifice to ease the way to heaven. The offering consisted of a large quantity of seed-rice, cooked sweet potatoes, an old coat, a pair of sandals to protect the feet from thorn-pricks, two cocks as food, an old mortar and pestle, two buckets for collecting water, and a quantity of kerosene. These items were to be contributed by the rich. The poor were to give a bundle of wood and seven bamboo slats. The *alfa* himself, not to be left out, would give seven kola nuts, one old pot, and three splinters. This sacrifice, known by its local name as *kpakpa,* was duly made in the compound of the paramount chief and left there.[65]

There are numerous themes contained in this fascinating material, such as the obvious appeal for Muslims of the organized political power of the chief and the colonial authorities, the relatively underprivileged position of Muslims in a non-Muslim society, the notion of individual responsibility before a heavenly judge, and the unmistakable Qur'ánic picture of Paradise as a state of sensual bliss. And of course the journey of the chief to heaven, which strongly evokes the *mi'ráj*, ascent, of the Prophet of Islam to heaven and his encounter with Gabriel. However, these themes are enlivened through the pervasive influence of the local cultural setting, explicitly Poro and *kpakpa.* The reference to Gabriel ignoring Mulku's greeting would be appreciated by the audience in the context of the enormous value society places on observing the desideratum of greeting the chief. In formal and informal settings alike, the greeting is the open sesame to social and communal business, the indispensable etiquette of human intercourse. Few things have hindered or hampered the introduction of new religious communities in Africa, especially Western missions, as the neglect or bungling of the rules of greeting and being properly introduced to the chief. Muslims now appropriate it for the final reckoning.

The inspiration of the *alfa* may have been Islam, but he also carries in his occupational saddlebag the traditional medicine man's tools of the trade. And both find welcome in the ritual repast of *kpakpa,* a local sacrifice sustaining the aspirations of a minority Muslim community. The ritual is symbolic of the distributive function of traditional religions, for in this case the wealth of the privileged members of society is spread to others less fortunate, as a part of which Muslims receive their portion through the agency of the *alfa*. Thus Muslims are enriched by appropriating the fruits of traditional religious ethics. For its part, traditional religion discovers an ally in the *alfa,* and the paramount chief can only benefit from the publicity created by the exploits of the ambulating cleric, in addition to having his authority reinforced by divine sanction. The reference to the chief Mulku suffering humiliation in heaven, something of a contradiction of course, is probably designed to secure political recognition for the *alfa* and is an indication of the way in which representatives of organized religion carved themselves a niche in traditional chiefdoms.[66] At this stage the *alfa* is a figure of some curiosity, and the challenge he represents to established religious and political authority is concealed, if not actually neutralized, by the all-inclusive vitality of local religion. But one should not lose sight of the dilemma for the *alfa.* Unless he is going to remain an irrelevant curiosity he has somehow to adopt a locally established hero as part of his spiritual pedigree[67] and gain thereby local credibility for his work. Such local roots may get overlaid with a veneer of Islam, but they are the hidden, and often overlooked, source of religious creativity. That creativity sustains the principle of flexibility and historically allowed Muslims to be incorporated into non-Muslim societies in Africa. All of which represents a considerable achievement for indigenous hospitality and tolerance.

2

Islam and the African Religious Synthesis: Society and the Religious Outlook

The more innocent form of the superstition, in which the mendicant friar could venture to appear as the competitor of the witch, is shown, for example, in the case of the witch of Gaeta. . . . His traveler Suppatius reaches her dwelling while she is giving audience to a girl and a servant maid, who came to her with a black hen, nine eggs laid on a Friday, a duck, and some white thread. . . . They are sent away, and told to return at twilight. . . . The mistress of the servant maid is pregnant by a monk; the girl's lover has proved untrue and has entered a monastery. The witch complains: "Since my husband's death I support myself in this way, and I would make a good thing of it, since the Gaetan women have plenty of faith, were it not that the monks balk me of my gains by explaining dreams, appeasing the anger of the saints for money, promising husbands to the girls, men children to the pregnant women, offspring to the barren."

—J. Burckhardt[1]

Islam arrived in sub-Saharan Africa from North Africa and Egypt beginning from at least the tenth century. By then much of the great Muslim legal and intellectual developments had taken place, with repercussions being felt everywhere in global Islam. Muslims were accomplished masters in realms of trade, statecraft, and scholarship, with Islam furnishing rules for a just society and for personal piety. The distant frontier of Africa would participate in this vigorous culture of Islam as a religion concerned with this world and the hereafter. In its essential nature, Islam threatened no radical secular alienation of African life and custom and was for that reason relatively easy to incorporate into the rhythm of traditional African life. Even in societies with rudimentary political systems, people responded positively to the benefits Islam brought in terms of personal ethics, public order, and religious conviction. In their encounter with African religions, Muslims brought materials from Islamic sources to complement and supplement traditional techniques of divination, oneirology, astrology, and similar practices. Thus the Islamic additions to the stock of African religious and cultural thought and practice "could be absorbed and used, and often were, without destroying the general fabric of traditional society. They modified the fabric, introduced new strands and colors and patterns, and provoked new forms and fashions; yet the overall effect was almost everywhere one of reinforcement and renewal, not of destruction."[2]

However, although Islam threatened no program of radical demythologization, it nevertheless represented something of a radical metaphysical reconstruction of the traditional worldview by furnishing the intellectual and practical apparatus for dealing with present evil and for preparing for life hereafter. Thus Islam strengthened the existential and instrumental tendencies of traditional African religions while introducing a social and public code and a new note of urgency centered in a future eschatology, all of that promoted by Scripture and law.

One of the deeply fascinating facts of the scheme of reality is that human beings, in self-reflection, should stumble on the idea of something ideally different from themselves without which their self-understanding, being in that case merely self-reflexive, would be a tired reiteration of themselves, another outlet for self-repetition and a never-ending déjà vu. In any case, from the tension of being confronted with the potential and progressive alteration of its self-image there arises for society the imperative of transformation, and thus of faith and moral action. Society caught in such tension is society in the act of transcending itself, of making the passage into new habits and forms of consciousness via the sacred-secular combination, without the cost of disowning itself. It would be fruitful for us to probe such matters to account for what might be involved in wholesale cultural shifts and in the subtle transitions human beings make between familiar and unfamiliar idioms. As Muslim Scripture contends, religion stands at the junction of all our beginnings and endings ("in your evening hour/and in your morning hour," "alike at the setting sun/and in your noontide hour"[3]), and rules the natural span of years with its eternal command and restraint. With its injunctions and rules of observance, Islam introduces cumulative social change and a commensurate shift of loyalty. Thus, the religion is equally a matter of words and works, of faith and deeds, of intention and conduct, a pattern of duty and observance. Islam belongs as such with the scheme of historical consciousness.

In the particular case of Muslim Africa, Muslim religious life and practice resonate with many aspects of religion in traditional society. The theme of the first chapter is taken up here again, namely, that Islam may on the surface appear to be a break with indigenous life, but in practice it represents an affirmation and a fulfillment of it, though it may challenge, too.

The Spiritual Life

Islam is deeply enmeshed in practical spirituality, personal devotion, and other forms of popular piety. The structure of the religious life encourages such attitudes. For example, the prescribed *salát,* or ritual obligatory worship, occupies a prominent place in the life of the faithful. The regularity of the worship regime, punctuating the day at five set intervals, helps to fix attention on religion in personal habit. This daily cycle of worship is in turn enfolded within the weekly calendar, culminating in the Friday Congregational worship, what is called the *yaum al-jum'ah.* However, Friday as the Muslim Sabbath is not a day of rest as in the Jewish and Christian traditions, but a day in which secular affairs are consecrated by a sacred pause. After the Congregational worship Muslims resume normal business. The obligatory daily *salát* are five in number: the Dawn Prayer (*salát al-subh* or *al-fajr*), a prayer consisting of two prayer positions (*raka'át, rukú';* singular: *rak'ah, rak'a*) and comes, as the name indicates, just before daybreak; the *salát al-zuhr* (four *rukú'*), which is performed after midday; *salát al-'asr* (four *rukú'*) performed before sunset; *salát al-maghrib* (three *rukú'*), between early evening and bedtime; and, finally, *salát al-'ishá* (four *rukú'*) before sleeping. Muslim tradition has accepted this number of five prayers as binding, although in the Qur'án itself only four prayers are mentioned, and even there in an imprecise way.[4] The *salát* prayers of this category are incumbent (*fard, farídah*) in Muslim Law on all competent Muslims.

There are other forms of *salát* that do not fall into this category but are embraced in a less formal and more voluntary category of supererogatory prayer, called *du'a.* In addition there are times when a prayer ritual is performed, for example, upon first entering a mosque for prayer (such as for Friday Congregation Prayer) or before the commencement of Qur'án recital, or before going to bed. This kind of prayer is called *náfilah,* additional. In Muslim Law it comes into the category of recommended or meritorious acts (*mandúb*).

Du'a,[5] because of its informality and flexibility, is used in varying circumstances and in clerical activity is usually associated with the possession of *barakah,* efficacious virtue, by whoever performs it. Among the clerics it is used widely to include informal and spontaneous calling down of blessings on clients as well as a more rigorous and disciplined practice of religious retreat, *khalwah.* The length of such retreats also varies, from three days to the traditional Qádirí pattern of forty days as practiced by initiates of the Suhrawardí branch of the Qádiriyáh *taríqah.*[6]

Khalwah belongs to a category of prayer activity in which local clerical practice has been most concentrated. The other forms of prayer may also be listed: the *salát al-istisqá,* which is a rite for rainmaking; the *salát al-khawf,* a prayer in time of fear or anxiety, and *salát al-istighfár,* a prayer of penitence, asking forgiveness of God. A prayer similar to *khalwah* but much more specific and better targeted is the *salát al-riyádat.* Another is *salát al-ittiqáf,* a prayer of stillness and silence, undertaken for ten days and devoted to recital of the Qur'án and the performance of *salát* (of the *náfilah* category). Another prayer ritual, *salát al-i'tikáf,* requires fasting and may be spent in seclusion in a mosque. Much shorter and less demanding is the *salát calá al-nabí,* a prayer of memorial to the prophet used in intercessory prayer as well as at *mawlid,* the birthday of the Prophet. This prayer is related to the prayer of greeting to the Prophet (*tahiyáh*) based on the Qur'án (xxxiii:56). A spiritual exercise, called '*ilm al-asrár* ("secret, esoteric knowledge") is usually accompanied by prayer devotions; its aim is to bring miracles to pass.[7] There is a large category of prayers known as *salát al-istikhárah,* prayer of seeking guidance on a choice of action in given circumstances. It is one of the most widely used instruments in African Muslim clerical activity, particularly in the dramatic setting of military action and similar confrontations.

Up to now we have considered the spiritual regime in terms of the daily and weekly calendar, and it might be helpful to summarize the effects of such a regime on African life and thought. The spiritual regime as instituted in official Islam helps to rationalize life on a daily and weekly basis. Muslim Africans and their non-Muslim neighbors who are thus furnished with a calendar allowing them to date events in terms of the daily worship and of the weekly Muslim "Sabbath," acquire the habit of managing their lives on that foundation. Such a way of measuring time involves an implicit break from the old calendar, which is based on the rhythm of the agricultural calendar, with its feasts and seasons regulated by the solar cycle.

This implicit break becomes explicit when the weekly Muslim Sabbath opens the way for the adoption of an annual Islamic ritual that is tied to the lunar calendar, as occurs, for example, with the annual Ramadán month of fasting, followed later by the annual pilgrimage, or *hajj,* festival. Because the Islamic lunar calendar is shorter than the solar calendar, and because as such it does not coincide with the farming, agricultural calendar, it represents a radical break from the old traditional cycle. The old rituals, tied to the solar, agricultural system, are wrenched from their temporal moorings and allowed to float with no fixed footing in the new lunar cycle. These old rituals then have to bid on terms set by the new religious order, and if they survive they do so with a fresh orientation. For instance, the harvest festival as the rite of firstfruits, based on the farming calendar, might in that form survive into the Islamic system, but its content is now filled with observances governed by the Muslim ritual code. In the case of the rite of firstfruits, the rules of *zakát,* of the obligatory tithe, would apply. For example, my mother and other women relatives set apart a fortieth part of the rice harvest as *jakko,* Manding for *zakát.* In time the *jakko* was completely separated from the old thank offering rite over which women presided in the name of the community and became instead an individual assessment on personal produce. It was paid to the *imám,* who might offer a short extempore prayer of thanks in return. What is interesting about the *jakko* is that the ultimate sanction for paying it comes from indigenous ideas of purity and danger: Anyone improperly consuming the *jakko* would, either immediately or as a long-term consequence, bring a curse upon himself or herself and any relatives, and that worked as a deterrence on the conscience of potential delinquents. *Jakko* is bitter fruit and is best got rid of. In one case of a severe drought that I can remember, for instance, the women were caught between paying out *jakko* and starving their children on the one hand and, on the other hand, withholding it to feed their families, though in so doing they would be violating the norms of *jakko*. With grim resolve, they decided to pay it out rather than risk the curse of a breach.

By the nature of his office, the *imám* is ill-equipped to enforce such norms or to prescribe for their infringement, except in asserting the priority of compliance with *zakát* prescriptions, which in any case are no longer bound by calculations of the agricultural calendar. It is as such that numerous Muslim African communities would adopt Islam and its religious system long before they had any inkling of the radical overhaul of the indigenous system of life implied in Islam's call for structural and objective adjustments of local life and thought.

It may be useful at this stage to consider the pilgrimage festival prayers, namely, the *'íd al-adhá*, or Bairam festival. It is rather elaborately and ornately observed. Timed to coincide with the *hajj* to Mecca, it involves the slaughter of sacrificial animals. One traveler gave a description of this festival or a similar occasion in central Guinea. In this instance, all the men were armed with guns, lances, bows, and arrows, which were laid aside during the actual prayers. The chief of the area attended the festival prayer on horseback with a two hundred or three hundred strong escort. The *imám* came later, preceded by one Mamadi Sanici (Ar. Mahmúd or Muhammad Sanúsi), who may have been his *ná'ib* (assistant) but is described as "chief magistrate." The *imám* was ornately dressed in a fine scarlet mantle trimmed with gold lace at the fringes, which had been given him by one Major Peddie at Kakandi (Guinea). Both the *imám* and his *ná'ib* were accompanied by escorts carrying white silk banners that were marked by a red figure, probably a crescent or a star, although the source says it was in the shape of a heart. Music was provided by two large drums. The account continues: "The almamy repeated the prayer with an air of sincere devotion. It was a solemn spectacle to behold so numerous an assembly all kneeling in adoration of their God."[8] At the end of the prayers the congregation waited to hear the *khutbah,* sermon. "Old men formed a canopy with some white pagnes" beneath which the *imám* sat and "read a long prayer in Arabic. . . . After this prayer Mamadi Sanici, the chief, harangued the people—asked them to transfer their trade to Wassoulou, Baleya, and the Futa Jallon, saying the road to Bouré was very dangerous and all dealings in that part must be suspended. Then the crowd dispersed."[9] Women attended on that occasion, but although they joined in the prayers they were seated at some distance from the men. It may be observed that the disquisition on current trade conditions came after the prayer rite proper and did not therefore form any part of the formal devotions. Another festival prayer is the *'id al-fitr* performed at the end of Ramadán.

There are random references in documentary sources to prayer activity by clerics, ranging from the obligatory *salát* to occasions of *du'a* (pl. *ad'iyah*) involving outsiders. This material may now be presented in terms of how it relates to its intersection with everyday life. The seventeenth-century English traveler, Richard

Jobson, refers to Muslim clerics worshipping God, probably a reference to *salát*. He also says that there is no day of abstinence among Muslim clerics and their communities, although Friday is regarded as a day of public prayer.[10] Another story also seems to involve a *salát* prayer. A Muslim cleric arrives at a river bank in the morning, accompanied by his slaves. One of the slaves is carrying a big gourd that he fills with water from the river and takes to the cleric, who is waiting at some distance from the river. The cleric used the water to wash with. Then a second gourd is filled and taken to the cleric, who proceeds to wash his hands. A third gourd is brought and the cleric washes his face and then he kneels to pray. He prays first towards the east (*qiblah*) and then towards the west, after which he concludes the prayer (*taslím*).[11]

In *salát*, obligatory prayer strictly speaking, performed by and required only of Muslims, there is little the professional cleric can do to include outsiders, and as far as these clerics are concerned, living as they do among strangers, this imposes a real restriction. However, ways have been found to compensate for this apparent limitation, largely through the practice of spontaneous or supererogatory prayer in which both Christians and others can be included. By the practice of providing prayer protection for trade caravans, for example, the cleric in general was attempting to infiltrate a buoyant circle of small-scale entrepreneurs with a considerable range of operation. Jobson describes a hazard-fraught river scene in which a cleric was accompanying a cattle caravan during a crossing, and, standing in the canoe in which they were traveling, the cleric offered prayers for the protection of the cattle against attack from crocodiles. The cleric, as an extra precaution, was attended by a man with a drawn bow.[12] An eighteenth-century English traveler, Mungo Park, observed that a schoolteacher and two of his slave merchants sat between members of a trade coffle (caravan) and the townspeople at a public meeting place. They engaged in a long spontaneous prayer, led by the cleric, after which they walked around the coffle three times (presumably for protection), making marks with the end of their spears. They ended the ritual by muttering something "by way of a charm."[13] Examples of prayers for trade caravans can be multiplied, but they do not add much to the general impression that may be formed of clerical involvement with long-distance trade.[14]

The inclusion of outsiders, such as pagans and Christians, in spontaneous or supererogatory prayer is well attested. Park describes one public occasion, this time the appearance of the new moon, when "Pagan natives, as well as Mahomedans, say a short prayer. . . . This prayer is pronounced in a whisper—the party holding up his hands before his face; its purport (as I have been assured by many different people) is to return thanks to God for His kindness through the existence of the past moon, and to solicit a continuation of His favor during that of the new one. At the conclusion, they spit upon their hands, and rub them over their faces."[15]

We have fuller details of the celebration of New Year's Day among a certain group of professional clerics. This celebration falls in the month of Muharram in the Muslim calendar. The New Year celebrations are accompanied by prayer devotions, concluding with a recitation of *súrah al-ikhlás* (cxii) one thousand times. New Year's Day is called by the clerics *Musu-koto salo,* literally "old women's prayer."[16] It is followed by the month of *safar al-khayr,* which is celebrated by another elaborate prayer ritual, called *kekoto salo,* literally, "old men's prayer." Prayer devotions pervade this occasion, and ideas and notions borrowed from the African cosmology are sustained by supporting them on Qur'ánic foundations. The faithful believe that during that time of the year 23,000 dangers descend on the world in the form of material deprivation, disease, or spirit-possession. A formidable prayer structure is erected to provide protection for humans. A *náfilah salát* is performed consisting of four *rukú'.* Each *raka'a* is accompanied by a recitation of the *Fátihah,* the opening chapter of the Qur'án, followed by *súrah al-kawthar* (cviii) ten times, *súrah al-ikhlás* (cxii) fifty times, and *súrah al-nás* (cxiv) and *súrah al-falaq* (cxiii) once each. All these *súrát,* except the *Fátihah,* form part of the earliest Meccan *súrát.* After this sequence a prayer is recited and a part of it written on wooden slates and then washed off; the liquid is subsequently dispensed as an extra precaution against the malevolent forces represented by the 23,000 dangers.[17] The potency of the spirit world is a notion shared with pagan populations, and, thus, in the clerical endeavor to provide preventive or curative prayers, the distinction between Islamic and pagan medical procedure becomes tenuous and indecisive. At a later stage of this chapter the pagan parallel is treated more fully.

Some forms of prayer are particularly valued for their use in dream inducement, a subject of great significance and interest throughout Africa. It would be appropriate to postpone discussion of this subject to a later stage in this chapter. We might, however, refer to a popular manual directed at introducing a wider, nonspecialist audience to the subject, which gives the following description of prayer, with hints at its dream capability:

> Prayer is the shield which safeguards the etheric body, and the sleeper now rests with the knowledge that he is available to receive instruction if such can be conveyed to him at the time. Upon entering the sleep state, a sudden dramatic switch is thrown in the mind. The feeling nature is replaced by the mental nature which becomes a reservoir of potential reception. Mind alone does not have the motivation or will but is influenced by a greater force than it possesses; this force is similar to the life within a flower which sprouts the seed and pushes its new growth upward through the soil.[18]

Sainthood *(Wiláyah)* and the Cult of Saints in Muslim West Africa

The question of saints in Islam, particularly in Súfí Islam,[19] is of cardinal importance, as we shall see in the two chapters to follow, and we should expect the clerics, already familiar with Súfí sources, to pay some attention to it in their clerical life and practice. The traditional attitude by outside students of West African Islam has, however, been to relegate it to an insignificant position. Yet there is incontrovertible evidence that a considerable tradition of saint veneration has been maintained among the clerics, and the problem is to define this tradition in such a way that it is not made to resemble a full-blown cult.

Among the clerics there are strong enough elements of saint veneration to indicate that the notion is familiar and of considerable interest. For example, the burial ground of the cleric, Karamokho Ba, at Touba in Guinea became such a center of pilgrimage. People undertook long journeys to have their various petitions made at the side of his grave as well as those of his relatives. Such veneration of the dead, although it never grew into a cult with special ritual features and an independent religious code, has its source in a similar environment of ancestral worship among traditional religions. Al-Hajj Soriba Jabi describes the pilgrimage scene at Karamokho Ba's tomb and says the *ziyárah* there is another of the miracles vouchsafed to him, of even higher merit: *"Ziyárah darí-hahu fahadhihi hiya gháyah al-karámah min Alláh ta'álá."* ("The pilgrimage to his tomb was established, and this was the utmost limit of a miracle from God the Exalted.")[20]

The tradition of prayers at the graveside of Muslim saints may not be connected with a saint guild in the technical sense of that term, but it is part of the phenomenon of saint veneration and wonder working widely diffused in Muslim West Africa. A well-known case is that of the *qádí* 'Uthmán Daramé of Tendirma. His tomb became a popular religious center where prayers were offered for the cure of various ailments. The author of *Ta'ríkh al-Fattásh* says that an active devotional life continued at the tomb, which was located behind the main mosque of Tendirma: All wishes made there were fulfilled and diseases cured.[21] It would appear that 'Uthmán Daramé acquired a strong religious following in his lifetime, represented in one instance by a miracle that occurred when uncooked rice left for him by his mother in a dish was later discovered changed into a cooked meal enhanced with various spices and condiments, and that after his death people still continued to believe that some spiritual efficacy attached to his tomb.

The tombs of founders of clerical centers are consistently venerated. The site of the grave of al-Hájj Sálim Suwaré, a thirteenth-century religious personage and the founder of the Jakhanké Muslim clericalism, became a treasure of religious feeling and devotion at Diakha-Bambukhu.[22] The grave of Mama Sambou, or the one alleged to have been his, was a center of attraction for successive clerical generations at Sutukho. Clerical sources claim Mama Sambou was a contemporary of al-Hájj Sálim Suwaré. It is claimed that the *sultán* Muhammad Rimfa (of Kano) asked to be buried at the site of the grave where 'Abd al-Rahmán Jakhite was buried so as to benefit from the latter's *barakah*.[23] Karamokho Bekkai's tomb in Nibrás continued as a center of pilgrimage for private religious groups. Muhammad Sanúsí Silla, the founder of Kounti, was buried on the left side of the *mihrab* on the outer verandah of the main mosque, and prayers are offered at his graveside.[24] Such holy gravesites were invariably visited and prayers offered before any important project or venture was undertaken, or for health, blessing, protection, and guidance. Acceptance into professional clerical communities, an easy matter in general, was facilitated by the presentation of guests and visitors at the tomb of the original founder, for the belief is held that even after death the spirit of the pious patriarch continues to keep guard over the center to preserve it. This reverence is also related to the notion of sainthood (*wiláyah*), for clerical patriarchs are held to be saints whose intercession on behalf of their members is sought and prayed for.

The clerical view is contained in a section of Soriba[25] that goes into considerable detail on the qualifications for sainthood, and since this discussion follows closely on an earlier one on the miracles of Karamokho Ba it is relevant to an understanding of the prayer power attributed to holy men. One of the important qualifications is the man's capacity for inner spiritual reform evidenced by his headship of a Súfí order (*istiláh al-tá'ifah al-súfiyáh*). A saint must consequently be prominent in divinely attested works to be distinguished sharply from acts of revolt or rebellion (*ma'siyah*). The second requirement is to shun all works of violence and causing harm and to rely solely on God, the true reality, keeping in mind and being on guard about things that concern His praise. He must have unimpaired capacity for distinguishing between various classes of wrong and disobedience and be unwavering in his resolve to conform to divine norms.[26] The saint is required to do this in consonance with the Qur'ánic verse that says: "God is the protector of those who believe" (ii:258). His third quality is that he makes common cause with the upright (*al-sálihína*), following the verse in the Qur'án: "Thou art our Protector. And help us against the people of the unbelievers" (ii:286). Both Qur'ánic verses contain the root *walí* (pl. *awliyá*), or saint. Some stress is put on the fact that God is on the side of the faithful, and the saint is a leader among such people. Furthermore, a saint is expected to be in close communion with God if he is to benefit from the numerous spiritual gifts bestowed on the *awliyá*.[27]

Trimingham writes that the veneration of saints, so prominent among Jakhanké clerics, "is a different thing from the power of *barakah* and on the border line with magic."[28] But this distinction does not exactly fit the case. The example of Shaykh Fanta Madi Kabba (1878–1955), a Jakhanké cleric popularly ascribed the honorific "Sharíf of Kankan" and of wide religious renown throughout the western Sudan, is a well-attested instance of a man who rose to the status of a saint to whom numerous miracles and wonders were attributed.[29] The clerics themselves encourage visits to the tombs of saints, usually founders of flourishing clerical centers. The evidence is that all the outward forms of a cult of saints are maintained even though the full-blown doctrine or practice of cult worship appears missing. What is therefore surprising is not the presence of vestiges of a cult, but that, given the bridge of such close resemblances, the clerics do not seem to have gone over completely to the cult. All the necessary criteria for the emergence of saint cults exist in clerical Muslim society except for a predilection for saint worship among adjacent populations. This is crucial, for there is little doubt that the clerics, so conscious of good public relations and alert to the advantages of rendering religious or clerical services, would have exploited to the full a commodity that they have in abundant supply. "But with Negroes in general, although public opinion canonizes devotion, learning, or manifestation of power in the living, no account is taken of these same men when dead. This is perhaps related to the fact that pagan Sudanese pay little attention to the graves of ancestors once the full ceremonies have been accomplished. This is connected with their idea of the personality of man which is severed from the disintegrating corpse, whereas Islamic belief links the soul with the corpse, one day to be resurrected, which it visits and to which honour can therefore be paid."[30]

The Power of Prayer to Curse

A category of prayer for which the evidence is very weak indeed among the clerics is prayer used as a curse, that is to say the exploitation of prayer to harm, or threatening to harm, thus inducing fear and respect for the cleric. There are many examples of this category in other parts of Muslim Africa, but many clerical communities oppose such use of prayer.

The *curse* as such fits into the larger framework of misfortune and evil, a subject on which traditional religious resources are heavily concentrated. Islam's reputation in significant part depends on what it can offer to deal with evil. The potent curse contained in appropriate Scriptural and arcane sources is the answer, and individual clerics suitably equipped are the personified mediums qualified to deal with the enemy. Sometimes popular demand for such expertise is so great that canonical practices, such as ablution, recitation of the Scriptures, and the call to prayer, are deemed to possess extra special effect.

In one example, the prayer ritual performs exactly this kind of function, applied to the regulation of relations between religion and the secular sphere. The goal was to preserve a clerical community from political interference, a form of protection against the harmful effects of associating too closely with the state. In the time of the Mali empire, the corporate clerical integrity of the clerics in the holy town of Gunjúr was not only safeguarded but became the basis for receiving political deference. On the night of the twenty-sixth Ramadán, the king would visit Gunjúr and make a food offering that he gave to children. The food would be consumed, and afterwards the children would pray and call down blessings on the king. This prayer ritual was the only occasion on which the king would enter the clerical town; for the rest of the time he would act through the *qádí* of Gunjúr.[31]

Dreams and Dream-Interpretation

Although dreams are a subject of universal skepticism in the modern West, in Muslim society, it happens, dreams are resplendent with religious truth, images imprinted on the mind by a higher prompting, envoys of tidings poured out from the shining ivory gate normally kept at bay by daylight preoccupations. The prophet without dreams is without honor, for dreams uphold the exalted office of prophecy. Bukhárí (d. 870), the magisterial compiler of canonical tradition, states that sound dreams are the anchor of divine revelation: The Prophet's inaugural revelation came through that channel.[32] The Prophet assures the believers that if they see him in a dream, then that is guarantee of its truth, because the evil one cannot imitate the image of God's messenger. Thus sanctioned, the dream is established as a fount of ethical teaching and made available to the righteous for guidance, instruction, and encouragement. Through sound dreams, according to the revered Bukhárí, the upright in heart receive messages from high, and thus favored, they gaze with astonished eyes upon signs of God's work. Consequently, the message of dreams is received as vital injunctions and directives to be acted upon. Let us examine dreams, as we have done with prayer, from that point of view, paying attention to the social and historical effects.

Prayer and dreams overlap to a considerable extent in clerical religious activity and, as we have seen, in *salát al-istikhárah* the two are inseparable. In that context prayer is the medium through which dreams, particularly "Prospective Dreams" (ones in which the dreamer receives messages of the prospects of a venture) are incubated.[33]

Clerical notions about dreams derive mainly from the definitive Islamic work on the subject, *Ta'tír al-Anám fí Ta'bír al-Manám* by 'Abd al-Ghaní al-Nábulsí (1641–1731). This is a two-volume manual of nearly seven hundred pages. There is a smaller, more popular work, *Ta'bír al-Ru'yá*, attributed to Muhammad bin Sírín (d. 728). Bin Sírín is also quoted as the author of another popular work on dreams that appears to be widely used in Black Africa.[34] Al-Nábulsí quotes a tradition attributed to the Prophet to provide normative support for dream activity. According to al-Nábulsí, "the Prophets used to think of dreams as divine inspiration (*al-wahí*) and to see them as concerning sacred laws (*al-yuhimmu fí shará'i al-ahkám*): 'thus Prophecy has passed, and only the envoys of glad tidings (*mubashshirát*) remain—sound dreams which a man sees or which are shown to him in sleep.'"[35] Al-Nábulsí makes a distinction between different types of dreams, which provides the accepted orthodox framework for dream classification. There are three broad types: dreams of good news from God, which are sound dreams recorded in the Hadíth; dreams of ill-omen from Satan; and finally, dreams that originate from autosuggestion or from the self (*ru'yá mimma yuhaddathu bihi al-mar' nafsihi*).[36]

Al-Nábulsí gives a detailed account of the origin of dreams (and visions) in Islamic thought, and although the tradition goes back to Joseph, the archetypal dreamer (*súrah* xii), the sanction for it is derived directly from the experience of the Prophet himself—a far more convincing argument than pronouncements attributed to the Prophet. In a tradition (hadíth) originating from the Prophet's wife, 'A'ísha (local variant Aisatou), it is reported that the Prophet told Abú Bakr of a dream he once had. He said that he saw Abú Bakr and himself raised on a ladder and then Abú Bakr climbed two steps on the ladder and turned to him and said: "Oh, Apostle of God, God has rushed to your side with His mercy. I shall outlive you by two and a half years."[37] According to the account, this dream experience preceded the granting of the spirit of Prophetic revelation (*al-wahí*), and it is the close connection between *al-wahí* and *ru'yá al-sálihah* that has enabled Muslim authorities to list *ru'yá al-sálihah* as a forty-sixth part of Prophecy.[38] Al-Nábulsí goes even further and claims dreams are an integral part of sound faith: "He who does not believe in dreams does not believe in God and the Last Day."[39] To quote al-Nábulsí again: "The knowledge (or science) of dreams is the first science since the beginning of creation and has never ceased to be bestowed on all Prophets . . . who were instructed regarding the science until their Prophethood was demonstrated by means of it."[40] In the case of the Prophets this science of dreams includes both the faculty of dreaming and the gift of dream-interpretation (*ta'wíl al-ru'yá*), that is, the spontaneous power to penetrate to the heart and meaning of dreams without having to rely on acquired skills, to be distinguished from other kinds of dream analysis (*ta'bír al-ru'yá*) by means of acquired or mechanical skills.

Dreams played a significant role in clerical Muslim communities, similar in fact to the role they played in the general Islamic Súfi tradition. A vast subject in itself, its serious investigation is only just beginning.[41] Trimingham says that dreams form an important part of the formation of a new Súfi *tá'ifah*, order, and observes that among the Khalwatiyáh the members "cultivated the practice of dream-interpretation (*ta'bír al-ru'yá*), so much so that some of the leaders have said that it is the pivot (*madár*) upon which their Path rests."[42] He also quotes ibn 'Atá Alláh's definition of what seems to be a visionary experience.[43] In this connection, a vision of al-Khadir (cf. Qur'án xviii:64–81), "the spirit of Islamic gnosis," is important with respect to sainthood and the founding of a new *tá'ifah*. People who dream this way can equally have a vision, the former experienced while sleeping and the latter while awake.[44] The ethical theologian, Abú Hámid al-Ghazálí, was under the instruction of his guide and master (*murshid*) Yúsúf al-Nassáj in Tús when, in his own words, he "was vouchsafed revelations (*wáridát*) and saw God in a dream."[45] No hard and fast line seems to be drawn between dreams and visions, both being central to the practice of Súfi brotherhoods as well as to the religious experience of the clerics.[46]

In the dream that 'Á'isha reported from the Prophet, in which the missionary character of Islam is described, Abú Bakr is said to have remarked to the Prophet that the black and white figures that appeared in the dream indicated that the Prophet's following would embrace the Arab race and non-Arab peoples as well. Two remarks may be made about this statement: first, that the intimation of the death of the Prophet in the dream is now further strengthened by a reference to the success and completion of his mission, and, second, that the phrase about God's mercy is now expanded by including in that a universal submission to the

Prophet's message. Both that dream and the notion of a missionary enterprise find parallels in clerical tradition. The cleric al-Hájj Sálim Suwaré is said to have left Mecca on his last pilgrimage and embarked for Black Africa on a proselytizing mission following a dream (*ru'yá*).

Religious Healing

Dreams, prayer, and healing are interconnected in general clerical practice. As in certain aspects of prayer and dream activity, in healing the clerics have served a wide religious constituency. Although they have operated in the same area as the traditional herbalists, professional clerics have not penetrated this area of traditional healing in any depth. They have for the most part limited their activities to utilizing the sacred language of the Qur'án, a province within which they are safe from competition from local non-Muslim priestly clans.

Periapts

A general, ill-defined area of healing activity is the provision of amulets. Trimingham has indicated the role Islamic amulets played in preparing pagan cultures for the greater infiltration of Islamic elements by weakening the earlier pagan traits. For example, among the pagan Bambara, the phrase *bisimilay* (Ar. *bismilláh*, "in the name of Alláh") is used in sacramental invocations and magical incantations because it is believed to be a phrase of power. The word *sadaqah*, freewill offerings, is used for offerings to the gods. Similarly amulets are accepted from Muslim clerics, who also transmit other aspects of the material culture of Islam, without any observable shift of allegiance away from the pagan religious culture.[47] Since the adoption of amulet-use is several stages removed from an articulate Islamic faith, it bears more of the characteristics of pagan culture than Muslim. What distinguishes Islamic amulets from pagan ones, apart from the sacred Arabic language, is mainly the procedural elements employed to decide whether the means, not the ends, are lawful (*halál*) or unlawful (*harám*). Muslim clerics will in the main try to determine whether or not their therapeutic procedures are sound, not whether or not such procedures are justified in the circumstances. Nevertheless, this exercise does not change the aims or goals for which amulets might be intended, and what the Muslim cleric offers in its making is a regularized procedure rather than a completely different substitute. The cleric is not denying but rather borrowing and inflating a pagan idea and tradition of spirit-power and control.[48] *Tasríf*, which equips him in this matter, is the means by which the cleric works out an accommodation to a pagan practice. The path of transition that pagans may eventually adopt is thus facilitated by the cleric.

The clerics use the term *hijáb*, plural *hujúb*, for an amulet. It is also used to mean any phrase from an Islamic ceremony or prayer devotion that is believed to be infused with *barakah* and that is efficacious when retained on one's person, either in the form of a memorized formula or as an amulet. Such *barakah*-charged formulae can also be written down on Qur'án slates and washed off, the mixture serving as medicine. As a rule, such amulets serve an all-purpose function. Jobson, visiting the Senegambia region, describes in some detail the function and nature of amulets, which he calls "Gregories." He says:

> The Gregories bee things of great esteeme amongst them, for the most part they are made of leather of severall fashions, wonderous neatly, they are hollow, and within them is placed, and sowed up close, certaine writings, or spels which they receive from their Mary-buckles [clerics], whereof they conceive such a religious respect, that they do confidently beleeve no hurt can betide them, whilst these Gregories are about them.[49]

Jobson goes further to tell of the medicinal value of these amulets: "They are used for all sorts of maladies and for any swellings or sores on the body; for protecting horses and other animals; men also adorn their weapons with them."[50] Amulets are also used on drinking occasions, and Jobson describes the custom of the king of Casa (whose religion is not stated) of pouring a small quantity of liquor on one of the amulets.[51]

Mungo Park provides numerous details on the many uses to which amulets (he calls them, after the Mandinka word, "saphie") can be put.[52] This is his description:

> These saphies are prayers, or rather sentences from the Koran, which the Mohamedan priests write on scraps of paper, and sell to the simple natives, who consider them to possess very extraordinary virtues. Some of the Negroes wear them to guard themselves against the bite of snakes or alligators, and on this occasion the saphie is commonly enclosed in a snake's or alligator's skin, and tied around the ankle. Others have recourse to them in times of war, to protect their persons against hostile weapons; but the common use to which these amulets are applied is to prevent or cure bodily diseases, to preserve from hunger and thirst, and generally to conciliate the favour of superior powers under all circumstances and occurrences of life.[53]

In practice clerics write the requests of their clients inside these amulets in vague and general language. In one amulet, for example, Paul Marty found the following instructions: "An effective talisman against all earthly evil whether caused by sword, saber, knife, rock, wood, Muslim or non-Muslim chief or chiefs, male or female, without exception. That no one may fear Mamadou Daï. May no evil of this lower world ever touch him. With the permission of God the exalted, and by virtue of the holy steed Bouráq [on which the Prophet mounted to heaven] and the sublime Qur'án."[54] The amulet formula is usually surrounded on the four corners by the archangels: Gabriel, Michael, Ezrael, and Ezrafael. Many have the names of the Prophet and God written at the center, surrounded by Qur'ánic verses. The proximity of amulet therapy to pagan notions is pointed out by Marty: "It is curious to state that the Muslim amulet is considered as a great preservative against the evil spells of the agents of fetishism, which implies belief in the power of these agents and in the reality of their action, whether religious or magical."[55]

Psychological disorders and mental ill-health, including various types of phobia and manic depression, form a significant part of the cases with which Jakhanké clerics deal. Here the cleric is able to relate the Qur'ánic ideas on *jinn*, incorporeal beings inhabiting the terrestrial world, to local notions about spirit power.[56]

Offensive Prayer

Two final issues should be considered: The first is the use of prayer as a weapon to cause disease and death, and the second is the contrast between religious healing and faith healing, with the subsidiary issue of similarities with Christian African examples. As in the case of prayer, the evidence for the use of the prayer to cause disease and death either as a deterrent against hostile acts from anticlerical individuals and groups or as a weapon of punishment is slender. However, there are numerous instances of the use of prayer to avenge an injury or wrong, or as a threat to force reluctant clients into compliance. It is reported that the first Muslims in Kano in the fourteenth century subdued their opponents by praying successfully against them, and they were all struck blind.[57] Walad Abú Sádiq, the saint from the Nilotic Sudan, in what appears to be Muslim infighting, cursed a judge with skin disease because the judge had criticized his marital irregularities.[58]

Faith Healing

The distinction between religious healing and faith healing is in familiar use in clerical practice, although the distinction is not rigid: A person taking part in religious healing can pass into the sphere of faith healing, and vice versa. Faith healing in this tradition requires the client to have an initial attitude of faith that the cleric possesses the power to heal so that he is prepared to repose all confidence in him. Religious healing does not require this attitude, so a schizophrenic or an epileptic in deep coma can be submitted to the methods of religious healing. Whereas faith healing requires the active presence and participation of the client, religious healing does not. A parent can represent his or her child in religious healing but not in faith healing. The prior psychological disposition of trust and reliance on the cleric is essential to faith healing; sometimes that trust and reliance are elicited or prompted by the personal charisma or *barakah* of the cleric, and sometimes they depend on an implicit conviction of the utility of Islam on the principle of *ex opere operata*.

Faith healing, as opposed to religious healing, is known to have played a prominent role in West African Christianity, for example in the Aladura Christian movement. Their founder, Joseph Shadare, was guided in a dream during an influenza epidemic in 1918 to form prayer groups.[59] The West African patriot and Anglican Bishop, James Johnson, approved the early work of the prophet Garrick Braide in Eastern Nigeria, "who for seven years healed the sick without taking a penny in return."[60] In the Independent African Church tradition there is a strict insistence that both herbal traditional and modern medicine should be altogether excluded from among religious devotees.[61] Along with this restriction has gone the insistence that, for a person to receive faith healing, conversion was necessary.[62]

There is for the clerics a further, perhaps secondary, distinction between religious healing and faith healing. Faith healing can be effected at religious shrines, such as the tombs of saints,[63] and, much more pertinent, it is often practiced by clerics because it obviates requiring their clients to be able to manipulate religious symbols. Often a prayer, deeply intoned and whispered into the ear or over the head or outstretched hands of the client is enough. Once the conditions of faith healing are met, the cleric can, and many in fact do, apply the techniques of religious healing to augment the processes of faith healing. A client may approach a cleric on the basis of faith in him, and the cleric then delivers a powerful prayer on his client's behalf. He may go on to prescribe certain procedures for the client in the same way as he would for religious healing. The example of the Senegalese Mouride Brotherhood makes this abundantly clear: a *muríd*, accepting the all-embracing efficacy of his *shaykh's barakah*, is entitled to protection by his *shaykh* from spiritual dangers and to healing in times of illness. At the outset the *muríd* places himself in the hands of the *shaykh* "like a corpse in the hands of the embalmer," as the vivid phrase has it. As a result the *muríd* receives some of the benefits of his *shaykh's barakah* through direct or indirect physical contact.[64] Following this, the *shaykh* can, in the event of an illness, perform the functions of the traditional healer and magician. "Even the Khalífa-General (Head of the Brotherhood) will prepare an amulet under certain conditions, and although payment is not demanded, a gift in return is normal. Others will attempt to cure *tálibés* of various illnesses, both physical and mental, through the use of invocations, certain herbs, and holy water."[65] In view of such evidence, the following comment seems justified: In faith healing the living and the dead can be called upon to cure; in religious healing both client and cleric are in the land of the living.

Conclusion

In the examples we have considered here, clerics do not seem to lack for clients. Expertise in prayer, dreams, and religious healing pays off huge dividends materially and in terms of social prestige. These religious activities bring together two of the most valued and prestigious skills, namely, knowledge or learning, and religion, or a reputation for it. Clerics who possess these skills have at their feet the large mass of the people and a devoted circle of followers for whom the old boundaries have ceased to offer stability and assurance. In spite of their own frailty and failures, the *shuyúkh*, spiritual directors, offer mediatory assurance backed up by a chain of transmission (*isnád*) that is notionally attached to the Prophet's infallibility, though in practice it is to the *shaykh* that the novice is clasped unconditionally. Thus have the *shuyúkh* appeared in society trailing a mass of devotees as pious festoons whose responsiveness to their leadership is as much a reflection of *shaykhly* charisma as of popular hysteria, as the Mouride case, considered in Chapter 5, illustrates.

In the synthesis of Islam in traditional Africa it is important that the clerics should be able to draw upon canonical sources of Scripture, Hadíth, theology, and history to offer a convincing answer to the challenge of "inculturation," of making Africans, steeped in ancient religious practices, feel at home in a "catholic," popular Islam. Consequently, the fundamental similarity between Islam's practical metaphysics and the applied nature of African religious ideas allows for a natural convergence, or at least a convergence at enough critical points to offer a smooth transition.

We shall consider presently the details, character, and nature of saintly devotion as well as the social and historical dimensions of sainted leadership. Suffice it to say here that the religious power of clerics is tied up with popular demand, and sometimes this popular pressure is so great that, in response, clerics improvise, not always wisely or honestly. In the final analysis, however, it is such popular patronage that sustains professional clerics and secures their roots in society rather than allowing them to become an isolated elite guild. Under such conditions, Muslim clerics acquire a professional identity without the risk of fringe autonomy. They are socially connected and yet not politicized enough to risk secular captivity, and not romanticized enough to fall victim to cultural complacency. It must be of considerable advantage to clerics that they can mobilize on so wide a religious front as they guide and instruct their followers caught in the flux and reflux of Africa's encounter with challenges of the sacred and secular.

3

Slavery, Clerics, and Muslim Society

Very often a man purchases a slave with his money, and he serves him till he dies; and notwithstanding this, he is nearer to God than his master, as was the case with the Children of Israel who, in their time, on account of the revelation granted to them, were superior to all other people; yet God gave them in servitude to Pharaoh, with all his arrogance and Heathenism, until the period of the departure of Israel by the hand of his patient and provident servant Moses. . . . Therefore, O men of understanding, be not arrogant over your slave or make yourself superior to him. Seek from him with kindness what God has decreed to you of profit from him, and know that God, who made you ruler over him, is able to make him ruler over you. Thank God for His gift, and be not ungrateful.

—A Mandinka Muslim scholar[1]

The controversial nature of slavery, and the negative image it attracts, makes it difficult to include in any reasoned account of society. Almost everyone agrees that the institution is an infringement on liberty and freedom and an offense to humanity and morality. Our feelings in the matter are deeply colored by trans-Atlantic slavery and its racial dogmatism. Under the circumstances, it is difficult even to describe how slavery, or some forms of it, might belong with the practices of an ethical Muslim society, let alone how it may strengthen and promote religious life and practice. This is the task confronting us here. Although it would be more natural to wait until the facts have been presented before venturing an opinion on the matter, I may be permitted to make an appeal now. In my investigations I was struck by how naturally my Muslim respondents gave slavery an objective legal standing, contemplating it as an institution with its own laws, rules, standards, and conventions, knowledge of which forms part of the expertise that distinguishes learning as a prestigious vocation. Muslim slavery is not based on ignorance, but on knowledge.

In view of this rather unusual attitude on the part of religious masters and their clientele, my appeal is to postpone, though not ignore, engagement with negative sentiments on the matter until evidence of its conception, source, character, practice, and function has been adequately presented.

First, I may be permitted two caveats, one by way of response to questions of humanity and morality. However elaborate and sanctimonious the justifications of slavery might be in the religious code, the institution as such does not rest on any theory of a divinely designated race or culture but rather on circumstances and conditions that are inherently changeable. In other words, slavery is fundamentally qualified by religious norms, law, and social convention, without that foundation in any way denying potential abuses in it. The other caveat is about those at the receiving end, for enslavement is a dramatic, even traumatic, way to be hauled into the Muslim world order. Even the means furnished for receiving back one's freedom leave the slave enmeshed in the moral dragnet of his or her captivity. The manumitted slave merely accedes to the qualified status allowed him or her by Muslim law, with reversion to servitude as the notional alternative to entanglement under the law. Manumission allows the slave to feel that slavery is right, that the system is judicious and just, and that, under religious blessing, a rigorous thoughtfulness has gone into its establishment.

The material considered here is in the nature of a case study of the clerical Jakhanké Muslim families whose religious life I examined in the previous chapter. The social and educational organization of the clerical order demanded a good supply of manpower, and indeed the very continuity of the tradition in the past depended on the availability of extra labor that would free the children of the clerics, another potential source of labor in the family, for a full-time educational career. The acquisition of slaves and their widespread and large-scale employment by clerics were essential to the clerical enterprise. Ritual restrictions as well as the social taboos of inferior status and separate quarters distinguished the slaves from their free clerical masters. After a time slaves not only served an economic function but also a ceremonial one as their masters began to measure the prestige and importance of a clerical order by the size of the slave quarters existing in it. Even when it became uneconomical to acquire slaves, either because of slave overpopulation in one particular center or, later, through the legal penalties imposed by colonial administrations,[2] slavery still continued among the Jakhanké clerics, who had come to attach a special ritual and social significance to owning slaves. For such clerics slavery was justified by social or religious arguments rather than by race, since slaves were the same race as their clerical masters. But in general race continued to determine the nature of slavery, as, for example, among Muslim Berbers in the Maghrib and North Africa, where blackness is still steeped in vestiges of slavery.

The Historical and Religious Origins of Slavery

The origin of slavery is obscure and the date for its appearance in Africa uncertain. It would seem, however, that at a very early date slaves formed an important item of tribute payment imposed by political rulers on their vassals or subordinates. Nubia, for example, had to provide as *baqt,* an annual tribute, to Egypt numerous slaves, many of whom were obtained from its southern neighbors.[3] The black slaves supplied in this way were used as domestic servants, laborers, and troops. The practice was very important as a source of cheap labor during the first two centuries of Islam, giving rise to traditions traced back to the Prophet to the effect that "He who has no friend should take a friend from the Nubians," and "Your best captives are the Nubians."[4] The large-scale importation of such Nubian slaves introduced the black racial factor in a new way into Arab Muslim consciousness. Thus 'Ubaydalláh, appointed by the caliph to the post of governor of Sistán in 671 and again in 697, as a descendant of the Nubian slave, Abú Bakra, was taunted in a satire thus:

The blacks do not earn their pay,
by good deeds, and are not of good repute
The children of a stinking Nubian black—
God put no light in their complexions![5]

The satire had its effect, if a delayed one, with the caliph al-Mahdí (ruled 775–785), who abrogated the acquired Arab pedigree of the descendants of Abú Bakra and compelled them to revert to the status of freedmen of the Prophet.

The penetration of Islam into Black Africa seems to have encouraged the widescale practice of slavery. Although slaves were taken by such means as punishment for economic insolvency, theft, and similar offenses,[6] by far the greatest numbers came from purchase and conquest.[7] The introduction of Islam by the sword further helped to spread the institution of slavery. "With the spread of Islam in negro Africa and intensification of Moroccan pressure in this direction, beginning in the last centuries of the Middle Ages, the question of the legality of subsequent sales had to be put to some great jurists; they answered circumspectly, giving the dealers the benefit of the doubt as to the origins of individuals offered for sale."[8] Trade and war in this context were not mutually exclusive means of acquiring or making slaves. The high demand for slaves, which was everywhere a feature of markets at one time or another, encouraged the forcible capture of weaker neighbors in the event of a dispute.

We shall return later to the wider question of the status of slaves in Islam. We may briefly point out here, however, that although Islamic law considerably ameliorates, some would even say potentially abrogates, the servile condition, nevertheless custom, history, and economic gain have combined to produce an enduring tradition of slavery among the dark-skinned populations of Africa, often on the pretext that the slaves were nonbelievers but sometimes even in flagrant disregard of that pretext.[9] As Ibn Khaldún expressed it, God had made Africa a natural source of slaves, for "the Negro nations are, as a rule, submissive to slavery, because [Negroes] have little [that is essentially] human and have attributes that are quite similar to those of dumb animals."[10]

In Islamic law the effects of slavery are mitigated by three fundamental principles: restrictions on its origin, that is, it can be imposed only in circumstances of
obstinate unbelief and refusal to submit to the *jizyah,* payment of tax; observation
of the legal rights of slaves; and, finally, provisions for and recommendation of
manumission.[11] Although we are justified in pointing to the practice of slavery
among the Jakhanké and other Muslims, it should be borne in mind that when
followed in spirit, the law acted as a solvent on the proliferating slave camps into
which plundered peoples were concentrated. But caution is necessary in thus invoking the enlightened power of the law, for the slave-dealer who suffers its reprimand for taking with the left hand may offer generous ransom with the right and
thus leave his critic without cause for blame.[12]

Such dexterity among slave-dealers is commonplace in African history, for by
placing Black Africa under a mythological curse the slavers were able to quarry
from its ravaged ruins without the fundamental deterrent of conscience. The
whole project became waterlogged with easy gain, and the bursts of humane sentiment we may get here or of genuine kindness there were insufficient altogether
to drain the swelling enterprise. The task of putting in fetters the children whose
Hamitic ancestors bore the original curse proved as little difficult to justify as it
was rewarding. Indeed, although there was a legal prohibition against enslaving
fellow Muslims, this scruple was breached with few qualms when it came to enslaving Muslim Africans. For example, the ruler of Bornu, a Muslim, wrote a letter
to the sultan of Egypt in 1391–1392, saying he was deeply anguished that, in spite
of being free Muslims, he and his people were the target of slave raids by Arabs
from the north. These Arab raiders "have devastated all our land, all the land of
Bornu. . . . They took free people among us captive, of our kin among Muslims.
. . . They have taken our people as merchandise." The Bornu ruler asked the sultan to search out these unfortunate blacks in the various slave markets and restore
them to freedom and Islam,[13] a request that most likely went unheeded. We hear
of no mass return of ex-slaves to Bornu or anywhere else in Africa. Thus Africa
continued as a storehouse of slaves, with the Holy Book to aid and abet.

One story makes this point particularly clearly, and since it also disposes of the
possible suspicion of religious bias in the present writer it bears quotation in full.
Captain Theophilus Conneau records a conversation with Ama-De-Bella ("Ahmadou Billo"), brother of the king of Futa Jallon:

> I desired him to tell me if these wars of devastation commanded by the Holy Book,
> were not more frequently instigated by interest in the great profits his Mahometan
> countrymen reaped from the results. I gently insinuated my belief that he himself
> would not undertake to storm one of the well-fortified Caffree towns if not prompted
> by a successful booty of slaves. After a minute's consideration he replied with some
> humor that Mahometans were no better than Christians; the one stole, the other held
> the bag; and if the white man . . . would not tempt the black man with them, the com-
> mands of the Great Allah would be followed with milder means. Somewhat convinced
> on the subject, I retired from the field of controversy with a flea in my ear.[14]

The Qur'án positively enjoins the taking of slaves in *jihád*:[15] "When you meet the unbelievers, smite their necks, then, when you have made wide slaughter among them, tie fast the bonds [of slavery]."[16] This Qur'ánic injunction on making slaves from religious wars is, however, propounded alongside various rulings on the manumission of slaves, a question that receives elaborate and devoted treatment in Muslim law manuals. Some of that material, in the Qur'án and in the law, may be presented to indicate the extent to which Islam recognizes slavery as a social institution.

In one place, the Qur'án makes the freeing or ransoming of slaves one of the fulfilling obligations of true piety (Ar. *al-birra*), alongside belief in God: "True piety is this: to believe in God, and the Last Day, the angels, the Book, and the Prophets, to give of one's substance, however cherished, to kinsmen, and orphans, the needy, the traveler, beggars, and to ransom the slave" (ii:172).

In a similar vein, the Qur'án enjoins believers to make available free-will offerings for the ransoming of slaves (ix:60). Manslaughter committed by a Muslim against a fellow Muslim can be compensated for by setting free a slave (iv:94). Expiation for perjury can be obtained, among other means, by freeing a slave (v:91). These and numerous other regulations are laid down precisely in Muslim law,[17] and have in the past influenced the conduct of officials as they prepared to extend the frontiers of Islam over non-Muslim populations.

Málik ibn Anas (d. 796) is the earliest systematic legal exponent in Islam and the predominant legal authority for the clerics, as for other West African Muslims. Therefore, his detailed and careful treatment of slaves and slavery deserves a special word. Málik's legal methodology is governed by precedent and prevailing practice, utilizing the principle of general assent (*'ijmá'*) as an important jurisprudential criterion. His standard formula is "the generally agreed on way of doing things among us," or, "according to the way things are done among us." He then proceeds to flesh out that rule with specific citations. Unlike some of the other contemporary Islamic legal authorities, Málik drew his inspiration from the Medina of the Prophet's dispensation, which vested a charismatic quality in the opinions and practices of the community there. Consequently, Málik expressed his legal formulations with the pragmatic flair of orthodox privilege. "My community shall not agree in error," a well-known *hadíth* from the Prophet had said, and Málik's legal school was the endorsement of that. His work, the *Muwatta*, as the first written compendium of law produced in Islam, is at the same time an affidavit of the establishment at Medina.

In his treatment of slaves and slavery, as of other subjects, Málik gives prominence to practical issues, basing his opinions on *Hadíth* evidence and prevailing standards. When he reflects on the great body of material at hand, it is less to philosophize than to classify and categorize. His world is that of the courtroom rather than that of the academy.

Three broad classes of slaves concern Málik. One is the *mukátab* slave, who has been given a contract (*kitábah*) of freedom against stipulated future payment to his master, either a lump sum or by installment. But a *kitábah* need not be a formal written contract and may in fact be inferred from certain duties or responsibilities that the slave has been allowed to perform by his master, such as doing trade or performing the *hajj*. However, a slave cannot demand a *kitábah* from his master.[18] A *mukátab* in law is a qualified (*mahjúr*) slave, that is to say, he is someone whose slave status is attenuated by factors tending towards the restoration of rights. For example, a *mukátab's* property may not be taken by his master, though if he has children the master may claim these.[19] Nevertheless, if the slave in question is a woman and she became pregnant by her master, she has an automatic right to be considered a *mukátabah,* or else an *umm walad,* a subject to be considered presently. In general a *mukátab* slave may not be sold, or, if he is, his right to buy back his freedom is unimpaired, so that no additional legal impediments may be allowed to prejudice his qualified status. Málik says tersely, "That is because his buying himself is his freedom, and freedom has priority over what bequests accompany it."[20] If the *umm walad* is attached to a *mukátab* and he died before the completion of the terms of his *kitábah,* then she forfeits her rights as *umm walad.*[21] In Málik's hands the *mukátab* remains a slave as long as any part of the *kitábah* remains unpaid,[22] though other legal schools take a more lenient view and stipulate that a *mukátab* is free immediately upon the granting of a *kitábah* and that the amount due his master is considered a debt charged to the *mukátab.* In between those two extremes are opinions that compute the *mukátab's* freedom on a pro rata basis, in proportion to the schedule of payments.

The status of the *mudabbar* slave, the second major subject of interest, compares well with that of the *mukátab* and is given considerable attention by Málik. Both are contract slaves, but the *mudabbar* is one given an undertaking (*tadbír*) by the master that the slave becomes free upon the master's death. If the *mudabbar* still owes his master anything it becomes a debt charged to the account of the *mudabbar* after the master's death.[23] Once granted, the *tadbír* may under no circumstances be rescinded,[24] although if slaves are the subject of a general bequest their status may be changed by the master making the bequest, for to allow otherwise would infringe the fundamental right that the master as free agent has over his will (*wasíya*).[25] In this sense a bequest has legal precedent over the rights of a slave, so that even a *mudabbar* is subject to the terms of the bequest after the death of his master, although in theory the portion considered as *tadbír* is not prejudiced. For example, if the master dies in debt and has no other property, one third of the *mudabbar* is regarded as free and the remaining two-thirds reckoned as property of the heirs. "If the master of the *mudabbar* dies and owes a debt which encompasses the *mudabbar,* he is sold to meet the debt because he can only be freed in the third (which is allowed for bequest). If the debt only includes half of the slave, half of him is sold for the debt. Then a third of what remains after the debt is freed."[26] A *mudabbar* acquires certain rights. His master may not sell him or otherwise dispose of him or his services.[27]

Slaves of both genders may come under the category of *mudabbar,* too, but a female slave acquires the status by an additional means, namely, as *umm walad,* which introduces the third category. Slave masters who have congress with their slave women make them *umm walad* if pregnancy results, and an *umm walad* enjoys comparable rights to the *mudabbar*. She is in fact a *mudabbarah*.

Law and religion have combined both to complicate and clarify the position of slaves in Islam. To take *umm walad*, pre-Islamic Arabia already had a tradition of taking slaves as concubines,[28] and the tradition persisted into Islam. An ancient Islamic authority refers to the custom and then cites the Qur'án in support.[29] Concubinage (*istisrár*) was legalized, with no limit set as to number.[30] A further element was introduced by Islamic law: A man may not marry his own slaves, although he could marry someone else's.[31] This rule presumably was put in place to recognize that the norms of marriage conflicted with those of personal property, as slaves are considered. At any rate, having allowed slaves to become Muslims, Málik affords them the full Islamic rule of marrying at any one time up to four women of their kind.[32] As we examine Jakhanké clerical practice we shall see that legal and religious factors have similarly contributed to the understanding and management of the slave institution.

In summary, then, Málik, who sees the law as a convoy of equal parts all proceeding in security under the sanction of orthodox conformity, pursues with the help of anecdotes, citations, reports, opinions, and the other devices of the hunter and gatherer the subject of slavery. His overriding objective is to integrate every aspect of the topic into the framework of established convention and to refine it with religious sentiment as one in the purpose of God and the conduct of believers. Belief and action are for Málik like the fuel and the flame, and he fuses slavery into that integrated formula.

Such data provide incontrovertible proof that a real distinction exists in Islam between bond and free and that such distinction places the class of slaves in an inferior, disadvantaged category. According to these tenets the clerics did not err in recognizing and exploiting this class of bondsmen, and, when pressure was brought to bear by colonial administrations, they only tempered the harshness of a slave condition by reducing the workload and offering various forms of dispensation in observance of the injunction of the Prophet when he urged "kindness to slaves."[33] The rest of this chapter will be concerned primarily with the way the clerics acquired slaves and the role such slaves played in clerical society. Attention will also be drawn to those institutions in which traces of slavery have survived.

Methods of Acquiring Slaves

The clerics acquired slaves through straight purchase, pious gifts, inheritance, and as rewards for clerical service. In their contacts with Samori in the nineteenth century they obtained a substantial quantity of slaves, mostly by direct purchase: Samori would supply slaves and in return he received salt, strips of locally woven cloth, gold, and cash.[34] As we have already noted, the clerics provided prayer support for Samori, and for this service they were rewarded with slaves. Samori's contacts with the clerics in Bundu seem to have been extensive. For example, two prominent clerical centers in Niokholo Samécouta and Sillacounda flourished from the captives that came from Samori's wars.[35]

Prayer support for a warrior in exchange for slaves was not necessarily confined to those instances in which the clerics had no moral objection to the worthiness of the warrior's cause. Whether they identified their clerical interests with Samori's revolution is not certain, but they also provided prayer support for Musa Molo, from whom they obtained slaves, although it was generally known that Musa Molo was fighting not a *jihád* but a political war directed at anti-Fulbé circles, sometimes including local Muslim resistance. Indeed, two of Musa Mulo's implacable enemies were Fode Kabba and Momodou-Lamin, both previously aligned with the clerics. In addition, Molo's stiffest resistance came from sources of Muslim strength, and his own men were for the most part the staunchly anti-Muslim Fulbé.[36] On one occasion Musa Molo came to ask for prayer support for a military expedition he was about to undertake. After a successful expedition he returned to this particular clerical center, Jimara-Bakadaji, and gave a number of slaves as a reward.[37] After his wars with Dikor Kumba at Patta, Musa Molo brought six slaves (three male, three female) to Fode Ansumana. When a cleric was approached by a prospective warrior requesting his clerical services, he was normally paid, after victory, ten male and ten female slaves.[38] Such transactions make it clear that slaves were a staple economic commodity and an indispensable part of a prosperous community. The clerics regarded them in this way and obtained by prayer and other types of clerical activity what other people might obtain through warfare.

One of the largest centers of slave concentration among the Jakhanké clerics was at Touba, where at one point the number of slaves reached 11,000–12,000.[39] Karamokho Ba himself represents the archetypal image of the successful cleric to whom slaves were given as pious gifts.[40] Imám 'Abd al-Qádir Bademba, of the Soriya faction, for example, heaped honors on him and made him a personal gift of seven slaves and a thoroughbred horse, as recounted in the Kabba chronicle.[41] The creation of a separate clerical order in the Khairabaya Jabi *qabílah* was a direct result of the large number of slaves Karamokho Ba's brother, Muhammad Khaira, brought back from his travels and handed over to Karamokho Ba as pious gifts made by the latter's sympathizers and friends.[42] Karamokho Ba is reported to have been so pleased by the unexpected size of these pious gifts that he bestowed a special blessing on Muhammad Khaira, as a result of which the latter and his descendants evolved into a powerful separate *qabílah*.[43] A good supply of slaves continued to flow into Touba under Karamokho Ba's successors for, apart from the voluntary (but numerous) pious gifts important political rulers made to the Touba clerics, it was standard practice for ex-students to make yearly donations. The cleric who undertook a *tournée pastorale* was also likely to acquire a good number of slaves as pious gifts. Karamokho Qutubo, for example, on the one occasion when he traveled from Touba to Mauritania gathered in the friendly places he passed through, in addition to a huge following of students, a number of slaves.[44]

For Karamokho Sankoung more precise details are available. He personally owned some 1,200 slaves, most of them pious gifts from contemporary political figures. Samori is said to have given him many slaves; Alfa Yahya, the nineteenth-century Fula leader from Labé, on one occasion gave him about forty; Modi Sellou, a local Fula leader, once gave him seventeen slaves, and another Fula patron, Tcherno Dama, gave him eight.[45] A successful fellow cleric in Kankan, described in local accounts as an opponent of Samori, Daya Kabba, once gave Sankoung eight slaves as a personal gift, and another local patron was Alfa Álimou from Labé, who is said to have given him many slaves.

A good number of slaves at any one time in Touba were born in slavery, and over a generation or two a significant increase in their numbers resulted from this natural process. Jakhanké clerics inherited the slaves of their fathers, and the possibility of a thinning out of the slave population was removed through the device of a rigid caste system out of which neither slaves nor their descendants could break. The Jakhanké rules applying to the inheritance of the father's property, which included slaves, were very rigid.

Slaves in Jakhanké Traditions of Dispersion

In Serakhullé traditions slaves are mentioned from the beginning of their dispersion. The stories have a legendary flavor but there is no reason to suppose that the slave element was an invention by later Serakhullé communities heavily committed to the slave trade. One version says that when Dinga, the ancestor of the Serakhullé, was on his travels he was accompanied by a slave, Biranin Tunkara, who acted as his bodyguard. From Diakha-Masina (referred to in the source as Dyara-Ba) Dinga went to a country called Darega where he found a well named *kire gede*. In charge of it was a slave woman called Terigabe Senewali. She was under orders from her master not to let anyone drink from the well. But Dinga and his traveling party would not be restrained and a contest of magical powers ensued in which Senewali spat in Dinga's face and blinded him. A leading traveling companion, Suduro, then came to Dinga's rescue and cured him.[46]

Mama Sambou's sister, Tenenkuta Jabi, was accompanied by a slave girl when she fled from Sutukho. She crossed at Fattatenda to the district of Jimara, where she and her slave girl went into hiding in a cave until a hunter came upon them there.[47] Slaves also figure prominently in that most characteristic form of Muslim mobility: the *hajj*. Momodou-Lamin was accompanied home from the pilgrimage by ten slaves who carried his gifts of three hundred copies of the Qur'án. The slaves were sumptuously dressed, marching pompously.[48]

Slaves were of considerable importance in the initial founding of Jakhanké clerical centers. There is scant information on the founding of Sutukho, but Jobson says that when he visited it he found slave quarters into which slaves were strictly segregated by their clerical masters.[49] Many of these were descended from slave families whose origins probably dated back to the founding of the town. Didécoto, a clerical town, included caste families as well as slaves at its inception. Karamokho Ba went to old Touba with a good supply of slaves, and these, and many more who were acquired later, transferred to Touba itself to be utilized in the practical business of helping to build the new clerical center. In a nonclerical context slaves were prominent at Náta, founded by Ba Gassama after a split with the Touba leadership. Náta does not appear to have become a clerical center, and in fact Ba Gassama's reputation was as a slaver and not as a cleric.[50] Nevertheless, his decision to leave Touba and settle at Náta was facilitated by the large number of slaves he possessed. The main force he deployed to found the village consisted of slaves, in the manner and following the examples of other Jakhanké centers. When he returned to Touba he was accompanied by three hundred slaves.[51]

The prosperous Darame Jakhanké center in the Gambia, Jimara-Bakadaji, was founded with slave assistance. The leader of the slave quarter when Fode Ansumana established it in 1885 was Bamba Sise, himself a slave. Other sections were Sidibekunda, headed by Tuman Sidibe, Jakhitekunda, Jallokunda (Fulbé), Dembelekunda, Sankarakunda (Bambara), Konatekunda, Sisekunda II, Tarawarekunda (Bambara), Sanekunda, Susokunda, and Jallokunda II (Fulbé).[52] Sectional heads of the slave quarters reported directly to the general head, who coordinated efforts and organized the slaves into task force units.[53] Fode Ansumana continued to add to the number of slaves he owned through pious gifts and purchase.

When Karang Sambu Lamin migrated to Sutukung, he had a number of slaves in his following. Dembele was the senior slave; his children were Sara, Yahya, and Mama; the others were Kali, Jaydatou, Nyimma, Fode Modou, Wonto, and her son Muhammad-Lamin (the latter named after Karang Sambu Lamin) and a daughter.[54] Sutukung was already a strong community when Karang Sambu Lamin came there, so his slaves were not instrumental in founding the center, but his own clerical practice was strengthened through the utilization of his slaves. Indeed, after he was persuaded to come to Sutukung through what the sources describe as the unanimous and collective pressure of the Sutukung Muslim community, Karang Sambu was given extra slaves to help him to settle down.[55]

The Use of Slaves in Agriculture

The use to which slaves were and are still put in clerical centers follows a standard pattern. A substantial proportion is employed in farm labor. One clerical elder made an explicit point of this pattern when he said that the clerics have traditionally acquired slaves in order to put them to farm work and that way relieve pressure on the children of clerics, who were then put to full-time education.[56] Clerical involvement in agriculture has been extensive, and the attention clerics gave to this aspect of their work is in direct proportion to the size of their educational establishments. Slaves provided the food base of such educational establishments until slavery was banned by colonial administrative decree, when a new form of bondage was grafted on to existing institutions to take up the slack.

Documentary sources give numerous references to the use of slaves on farms. According to one estimate, in the eighteenth century, about three quarters of the population of the Senegambia region were slaves and most of these were employed in agricultural labor.[57] In Niani one account estimates identical figures for slave and free and adds that most of the slaves were employed in farm labor.[58] Another source says that slaves spent two-thirds of the working day on the farms of their masters, and the other third on their own farm.[59]

Qur'án school pupils were used on the clerics' farms in a similar way to how slaves were used, and the practice was widespread throughout Muslim Africa. It was normal practice in clerical schools that when a student enrolled he was regarded as the domestic slave of the teacher. For all practical purposes he followed the same work schedule as other slaves, with the slight difference that he received a modicum of education while in residence. Some idea of the transaction between the parents of students and the schoolteachers is given by Mungo Park. In order to gain the release of the student the parents had to bring a slave or the price of one. If he could not be redeemed by his parents, the student was required to work on the farms of the teacher until the latter decided to release him.[60] Park estimated that the price of a prime male slave ranged from £18 to £20,[61] but periodic fluctuations in the market naturally affected the figure. The following description of the Qur'án school regime in north Nigeria among the Hausa makes the point vividly of the resemblances to domestic servitude.

> I want to explain our relation with our teacher during the years of Koran schooling. The teacher's treatment of us is often so harsh that it causes us to take no interest in our lessons. Besides learning, we are forced to perform hard tasks which are so burdensome that they make us stupid with tiredness. We sometimes do simple domestic work: the teacher making us spin his wife's cotton, grind corn, fetch drinking water, bring bundles of grass from the bush, etc. His wife becomes too proud to do any work besides cooking.
>
> In the rainy season many teachers treat us as harshly at working as slaves. Any idea of learning is put aside and we are led to the bush and made to cut a farm of a great extent for us to work. As the rainy season approaches, he drives us daily to the bush in order to prepare the vast farm. Then we start tilling the soil for growing crops.
>
> We continue doing the same thing up to the time of the harvest. So at the middle of this season the only possible time for learning is during the night when we want to rest after the labours of the day. On account of tiredness you find some of us falling asleep and knowing nothing of the work. We even forget some of our old lessons during this season.[62]

The theory that Qur'án school students were in a state of redeemable servitude gained some notoriety after the institution of slavery was abolished. The clerics did not directly resist the colonial law forbidding them to keep and maintain slaves: They lived in grudging compliance with the regulations but sought to evade the material effect of the law by fostering and exploiting notions of servitude among the people, some of them ex-slaves, to whom they offered Qur'án schooling. Under the innocent cover of their educational institutions they maintained the same degree of control as before over their ex-slaves while simultaneously increasing the range of their clientele to surrounding areas. Thus, while professing their compliance with the will of their political overlords, they put to double effect the legitimate offer of education. They maintained their tradition of cooperating with political rulers, but with slavery they did so with a difference.

Marty has made similar observations, and although he is not a disinterested witness, representing as he does the colonial administration that was attempting to abolish slavery, his account contains elements that are pertinent to the issue. He writes that in all the local villages the old ties that bound slaves to their masters in the days before emancipation tended to repeat themselves, but this time in the guise of the familiar religious set-up. Marty confirms that many Jakhanké slave masters kept in contact with their ex-slaves and began operating Qur'án schools in those areas where liberated slaves went to settle. Whereas previously clerics made only token efforts to provide instruction for their slaves, they now pursued this line of activity with energy and determination, and such services as they rendered were initially provided free. But beneath the seemingly generous nature of such activity they fostered a set of obligations and binding considerations from which the clerics derived material gain and religious power. Marty continues: "One can attest to the fact that the ex-slave has been transformed into a religious client and has adopted again the path of the cause of his master in order to bring him gifts. It is no longer a slave master he obeys; it is a *karamokho* [religious master] to whom he now renders homage."[63]

The extension of educational services to pupils from the class of ex-slaves enabled the clerics to cope with the serious and sudden drain on their economy that emancipation foisted upon them. A number of women slaves were attached to their Jakhanké patrons as concubines and others were formally pronounced free just to become the legal wives of their masters.[64] The practice of redeeming a *tálib* at the termination of his studies with a slave or the price of one was no longer enforced in precisely the same terms, but the concept of ransom (Ar. *fidan*) has survived in another form in that parents are expected to give some sort of remuneration to the cleric according to their means. The unspecified character of the transaction usually means that students, or their parents, live in a state of continuous obligation to clerics. It is not uncommon, for example, for students to render an annual homage to the cleric involving agricultural produce, livestock, cloth, and cash. In addition many send their own sons to their old teachers, and in this sense the bonds are passed from parent to child.

A regular feature in clerical centers is that successors to the leadership tend to be chosen from the younger sons of the clerical leaders. In the context of plural marriages and the wide age differences between clerics and their wives, this practice results in enormous age spans between one clerical dynasty and another. One example is given of a man who, had he lived, would have been aged 120 in 1966, and his son, the incumbent clerical leader, who was 65, and the designated future leader, a son of the incumbent, who was aged 8.[65] Alongside this feature of uneven dynastic chronologies is the extent to which clerical centers will enroll all the male children of the clerical lineage in full-time education, leaving slaves and other students to carry out essential work on the farms. Thus the economic strength of a clerical establishment, deriving in the past mostly from slave manpower, ensures a correspondingly secure clerical genealogy. In the absence of slave labor, many clerics now look for those students who, for various reasons, are willing to place themselves in bondage to the cleric in return for free education. Such students, usually coming from some considerable distance away, may take a longer time than normal to complete their course. In the meantime they supply the cleric with the necessary manpower for supporting a system of full-time education for the children of the center.[66]

In spite of the evident extensive survival of traces of slavery in clerical educational work, the comparison can be taken too far. There is no parallel, for instance, to the numerous legal and ritual restrictions imposed on slaves. As will presently be made clear, slaves constituted a class of deprived members of the clerical community, and the chains of caste inferiority were automatically riveted on their children. Slaves were totally denied juridical status, and their exclusion from responsible office was reinforced by the entire weight of Islamic law, Muslim social practice, and traditional stigma. However oppressed the slave's Qur'án school counterpart may be, a wide chasm still divides him from the restrictions and ritual inhibitions with which the slave was burdened.

The Legal Position of Slaves

Islamic law and Muslim customary practice, respectively *Sharí'ah* and *'ádah*, coincide at numerous points to define the position of the slave in the Muslim community. There are some generalized rulings. Slaves as such do not inherit, and their property remains the property of the owner. Under certain circumstances, such as when a slave has signed a contract (*kitábah*) with his master stipulating the payment of a fixed sum in exchange for freedom, the slave (now called *mukátab*) regains some of his personal rights.[67] I have already examined in the opening parts of this chapter the Scriptural and legal support for slaves and enslavement, and suffice it to say here that clerical practice is fully armed with such impeccable resources.

Thus the clerics observe the canonical restrictions, with some responsiveness to local conditions and historical circumstances. For instance, the *'iddah*, the required waiting period before a divorce becomes absolute, is two months for slaves whereas for others it is three months.[68] Although the *zakát*, the obligatory alms, are mandatory for all free-born Muslims, they are not required of the slave in the same way. A slave's property or the *zakát* due on it is made over to his master.[69] A master gives alms for his slave at the annual *zakát al-fitr*. A slave cannot assume the office of *imám,* which is a general rule in Islamic law and practice, although some *madháhib,* schools of thought, have different rulings on this matter, allowing a slave to lead public prayers provided this function carries no juridical or similar responsibilities.[70] Among the clerics even the descendants of a slave emancipated before his death cannot fill any important religious office. Slaves are also excluded from the leadership of a *majlis,* the school or educational organization. The *hajj* is not enjoined upon them (although, as will be shortly discussed, there is provision in Islamic law for slaves to make the *hajj*), and they cannot make the animal sacrifice at the pilgrimage feast, the *'íd al-adhá.* The matter of oath-taking is of no consequence since among the Jakhanké there is a tradition of refusal of oaths. But a slave cannot qualify as a competent witness before a consistorial assembly. He cannot substitute for the free man. His word against that of a freeborn person is null and void. The tradition that makes the Friday Congregation Prayer mandatory for all Muslims except slaves[71] is observed, and since the class of *mukátab* slaves exists only as a legal fiction this ruling affects all slaves.

The structure of such disabilities is further reinforced by local custom and practice. In one community, where slaves have for more than three generations achieved a statutory emancipation, the appearance of a subservient slave ethos is carefully maintained even today. In this setting slaves provide labor on the farms of their masters; they pound their couscous and thresh their rice; they undertake the building of their houses; they go on errands. The children of these slave families go to study under their parents' masters. At the circumcision ceremony circumcised slaves look after the children of their masters, constantly attending to their needs, bringing them food and presents, and providing all the necessary equipment for the passing out ceremony. The duration of the circumcision confinement varies, but the usual length is about two months.[72] At weddings slaves head-carry the bridal trousseau for which they may receive gifts, carefully distinguished from payment. Slaves may accompany their masters on long journeys and carry the luggage required for the trip. They may not eat from the same dish as their masters, or, in some cases, as any free-born person. After the slaughter of an animal in the community slaves (and leather-workers) do the flaying. The head of the animal and the skin are taken by them.[73]

From a slightly different tradition, an equivalent set of conventions is observed towards slaves. After his master, or his master's wife, has been away on a journey, a slave goes to meet him (or rarely her) and, in the case of able-bodied slaves, he bears his master on his back and brings him home. In cases where a slave is unable to do this, he will nevertheless make a token offer and then carry his master's baggage. Upon reaching home the slave washes the feet of his master as a symbol of his subservience and brings him a calabash of fresh milk to drink. Slaves cannot marry without first obtaining the authorization of their master. They do, however, possess their own compounds and are Muslims.[74]

In discussions elsewhere with the clerics some of these points were repeated. A marriage contract cannot be undertaken without prior authorization (*idhn*) from the master.[75] A slave thus authorized is called a *ma'dhún,* and he may also engage in trade for his master. A slave can apply for the *mukátab* status, but even here he is at the complete mercy of his master, who determines the amount to be paid and the method of payment. He can be asked to pay a prohibitive price, which completely negates any advantages that the right was supposed to have given him in the first place.[76]

Marriage rules are different for slaves. The children of slave parents inherit the slave status of their parents. If a slave man marries a free-born girl the children belong to the owner of their father. If a slave woman marries a free man, their children are free.[77] The clerics can emancipate their female slaves and marry them subsequently, a practice for which support is found in the Qur'án, *súrah al-nisá'i* (iv *passim*). However, according to strict Islamic law slave wives must be someone else's slaves and one's own slaves can be taken only as concubines.[78] Slave women thus married are liable to half the chastisement of free women if they contravene the marriage rules.[79] Although technically a slave woman stands on an equal footing with the free co-wives, she occupies an inferior status in the domestic management of the home. Muslim law allows a man up to four wives,[80] but that number can in effect be increased by taking slave women as concubines. The four legitimate wives of a household take turns in managing the domestic affairs, including the supervision of any female slaves,[81] but a slave woman married in such a household would be given menial tasks and no corresponding responsibility in running the home.[82] For example, she would pound the couscous normally used for breakfast and husk the rice. It was not common, in the days before emancipation, for slave women to own property in the form of rice fields; instead they worked on the fields of their mistresses. In some cases slave women did own fields, but the produce from them belonged to the household in which they lived and was not eligible for the *zakát.*[83] The children of such slave women were, however, free of any legal restrictions.

The Ceremonial Functions of Slaves

The ceremonial role of slaves in clerical centers, which their descendants continue to fulfill, has been touched on. In the circumcision ceremony they take leading parts. They provide the ceremonial robes of the initiates, robes fashioned in the traditional style of a fully fledged hunter. At weddings they carry the bridal trousseau, and they sometimes play the role of matchmaker by running errands. After the slaughter of a sacrificial animal, as at the Bairam festival, it is customary for slaves to be apportioned the head and skin of the animal. A slave goes out to meet a returning master and provides the ceremonial washing of feet, followed by a calabash of fresh milk. When the cleric goes on a journey his slave will usually lead the way, sometimes carrying a staff in his hand. The legal ruling that in certain infringements of the religious code a slave can be freed as legal restitution was not always kept, but instead clerics made pious food offerings for slaves to consume. This offering is done in the spirit of the Qur'ánic verse that enjoins the provision of free-will offerings (*al-sadaqát*) for the relief of the needy, including slaves (ix:60). Normally slaves received only a modicum of education, so that they did not join prayers or hold religious office among the clerics. However, in Islamic law slaves can attend the pilgrimage in the company of their masters and be adorned with the pilgrimage vestments (*al-ihrám*). Having accomplished the *hajj* that way they qualify automatically for enfranchisement.[84]

Information on the ceremonial and similar functions of slaves is provided by outside observers. One incident already described concerns a cleric who came to a river bank accompanied by his slaves. One of the slaves carried a large gourd that he filled with water from the river and brought to the cleric, who was waiting a short distance away. The cleric used the water to wash himself with. A second gourdful was brought and the cleric washed his hands. With the third and final ration of water he washed his face and then commenced performing the *salát*.[85] On the prestige or decorative value of slaves, one writer, a century later than Jobson, gives some details. According to him domestic female slaves not yet fallen into a state of concubinage had an easier life than the average slave. They were lavishly dressed, and sometimes better furnished with clothes and jewelry than their masters' wives. They were known, for example, to have coral, amber, and silver pieces on their person that were reckoned to be worth £20 or £30 sterling.[86] Mungo Park describes the Bairam festival (*'íd-adhá*), called locally *banna salee,* in the Jarra area. The slaves were magnificently attired on that day and provided with lavish meals. They seem to have taken full part in the festivities of the day, and Park reported no constraint on them.[87] It is doubtful, however, that slaves also attended the *'íd-adhá* community prayers, and the expectation would be that they stayed away from that part of the proceedings. René Caillie, who describes the *'íd-adhá* prayer and says that the chief attended the prayer with an escort of up to three hundred, does not refer to slaves forming part of the retinue.[88]

Emancipation and Clerical Attitudes

Slave families, as we have seen, have continued to be attached to their clerical patrons long after emancipation. Local colonial administrations enforced the emancipation decrees of the 1890s through a series of measures. In the Gambia Protectorate the traveling commissioner, Cecil Sitwell, conducted a survey on the south bank of the river and reported on the state of the slave trade in the area. He noted, among other things, that there was a buoyant traffic in slaves, particularly those captives taken from Fode Kabba's *jihád*.[89] In an earlier period, the administrator of the territory, Cooper, estimated that the profits from the trade in slaves amounted to some 500 percent, and in the same period he observed that "there is hardly one single exception where produce is not bought by traders in this river through the medium of slaves."[90] A Slave Abolition Ordinance was enacted in 1906 and put into effect. It provided that if a slave set foot on English soil at Bathurst (now Banjul), Albreda, or MacCarthy Island he was granted automatic enfranchisement, and that slaves anywhere became automatically free after the death of their master.[91] The Gambia colony did not have sufficient police or military force to put many of these provisions into effect, and consequently numerous slave families continued to live in bondage to their masters. In addition, since so much of the effectiveness of the ordinance depended on individual slaves taking the initiative and traveling to Crown possessions to achieve free status, very few did, and most were content to seek relief within conditions of slavery. Under such circumstances clerical slave masters retained their slaves. For many of these clerical slaves the ties with their old masters were too strong to snap by what would amount to a personal repudiation of their servile status.[92]

The slaves of Karang Sambu Lamin, for example, did not begin dispersing before the 1940s, well after the death of Karang Sambu himself. At Bakadaji, slave compounds existed and slaves continued to honor some of the old obligations to their masters' families at the time of writing this book. Slave groups and other castes similarly existed at Bani-Kantora and Bani-Sami, although in the latter case it was the Jouné, Dhahaba, and similar caste families who predominated. Some descendants of slaves lived in Wuli-Bani, a Jakhanké clerical center in the same area as Sandu-Jakhaba. There was also widespread use of the Jola ethnic group, the target of numerous Muslim military operations in the Casamance region, as domestic slaves. In fact one Jakhanké cleric said that the Kujabi and Sambu Jola, two of the most numerous of the Jola families, were originally descended from the slaves of Mama Sambou Gassama.[93]

The disruption of Touba's clerical activity by the mass emancipation of slaves has to be analyzed in the light of the close connection between a strong agricultural basis, supported by slave labor, and a successful clerical enterprise based on family tradition. Clerical distrust of French motives was exacerbated by the rigid French stand on the question of slaves. Two accounts, already given, say that in one day the French, who had a *poste* in Touba, freed some 4,800 slaves. One account says the figure was far greater, involving some 8,000 slaves.[94] Whatever Touba's slave population (and one reliable estimate puts it at 11,000), even the lower of these two figures is a drastic cut for a single day. It is impossible for the outsider to assess the psychological impact of such measures, so that we must rely on al-Hájj Banfa Jabi and al-Hájj Soriba Jabi as insiders to tell the story of how the clerics felt among themselves. The consequences of such a policy for the continued existence of the Touba clerical establishment were swift and far reaching.

Clerical accounts suggest that the French did not make what to the clerics was a crucial distinction between slaves destined for a clerical center and slaves owned and utilized by mercantile interests. Here Banfa and Soriba's attitude to Ba Gassama, who operated as an independent commercial agent in the buying and selling of slaves, was one of mistrust and disapproval. Ba's political intentions were also suspect. As their subsequent readjustment to statutory emancipation showed, the clerics believed that the institution of slavery was itself akin to traditional notions of client status (*mawlá*) and patronage (*ri'áyah*), notions that antedated and survived slavery in the form outlawed by the French. The clerics suspected the French of willful malice, for they could scarcely conceive how emancipation could be justified on any rational basis other than the French desire to flex their political muscle and punish the clerics for their religious reputation alone. The clerics' behavior and conduct at the time confirm this belief, and all the available evidence shows the clerics grasping after reasons that go beyond the particular dénouement at Touba, which they found in alleged French antipathy to Islam.[95] The clerics felt that only that kind of set policy on the part of the French could explain why they came down heavily on the Touba clerics, an analysis that more accurately reflects the confusion of local clerics than the realities of French policy. For that matter, we should now probe the clerics' real attitude on the matter.

The clerics were firmly convinced that the French adopted an anticlerical policy to destroy Islamic social institutions, including slavery and clerical solidarity. Thus they outlawed slavery as the mainstay of clerical practice. Such explanations show the clerics admitting and expounding the paramount role slavery played in the religious life. Once the element of slave labor was removed, Touba's fate was as good as sealed. It could not recover quickly enough to lay unqualified claim to Karamokho Ba's heritage, at least not in terms of a comparable future for it. The clerics turned to student labor as compensation, but that source lacked the stability and servility of slaves as chattel. The eventual arrest and exile of Sankoung, and the repercussions that followed, hastened Touba's decline. Although it was to make a brief and fitful rally after the return of Sankoung from exile, it had lost the basis on which to effect a permanent and stable recovery. So the clerics, no less determined to carry on the tradition they received, looked elsewhere, and in particular to settlements of ex-slaves, where lingering habits of servitude might provide the subservient ethos eminently useful for educational service. The result was further dispersions both in the direction of ex-slave settlements, where previous bonds of servitude were reasserted in less onerous ways, and in other places where student labor was easy to obtain and retain.

We are still left with questions about how the principle of "the priesthood of all believers" that defines Islam's nonsacerdotal view of religion can be made to square with slavery and its stigma of exclusion, or, indeed, how pacific clerics could condone and even profit from an institution that has roots in bloodshed, violence, exploitation, and dishonor. Slaves are made, not born, and making them involves bending them, but, alas! does not require mending them. However, the historian need not wait for morally satisfactory answers to these questions in order to expound the subject of slavery or identify its place and function in clerical Muslim communities. Others more competent than the writer must inquire into motives and judge whether good intentions played any part in what were often deeply personal matters between slaves and masters, to weigh, for example, whether principle or expedience carried the day, though the clerics show instructive enterprise by blending principle and expedience to promote religious moderation.

In this regard I must report that my original inclination was to leave slavery out of all discussion of Muslim society because I felt it to be an unsavory subject and a prickly pear in the hands of infidel outsiders. This inclination was openly challenged at a public meeting in Jimara-Bakadaji where slaves were present. The issue, as put to me, was not whether slavery was good or bad, but whether with my scruples I could be trusted to report reliably on it when evidence for it was so incontrovertible. How could I be a trusted scholar when I wrote only on things I personally approved of? I relented, but still with a bad aftertaste. If my informants made slavery the litmus test of scholarly credibility, then in describing it the scholar must be mindful that his or her standard of scrupulous impartiality does not become an end in itself or an excuse for trampling on the sensitivities of others. For then objective reporting would exempt itself from consequences that would constitute grievous injury to the conscience of those who look for moral accountability. Fortunately, Muslim slavery is sufficiently infused with long-established norms to make intrusive moralizing unnecessary. The historian's task, happily in this case, when complete, does not dispense with the demands for moral scrutiny whose nature, nevertheless, requires different expertise.

To return, then, to the clerics and to the meaning and significance of the acquisition and ownership of slaves for their tradition of political neutralism and military pacifism. They defend themselves by a dexterous combination of principle and expedience: principle requiring them to insist on their traditional independence, and expedience allowing them a tolerable margin of activity in slavery. In this connection, it should be stressed that clerics could get away with such unapologetic involvement in slavery and the slave trade largely because Muslim society accepts the practice as congruent with revealed truth and with the example of the Prophet, whatever spin some conscientized jurists may put on it. It is well to recall the sentiments of Málik ibn Anas, referred to above. Málik has convinced jurists, and all Islam with them, to discover higher insight in the practice of slavery and so bypasses all the otherwise difficult Woolmanian scruples by integrating with felicitous result every aspect of slavery into the framework of established convention, and there refine it with religious sentiment as one in the purpose of God and the conduct of believers. Belief and action are for Málik like the fuel and the flame, and he fuses slavery into that integrated formula.

However, the historical practice of acquiring, disposing of, or maintaining slaves was fraught with hazards that only agile or well-placed clerics could have escaped. It required a cleric of exceptional powers of discernment to be able to avoid the losing side in a dispute or to escape the consequences of defeat. Either could bring the loss of slave revenue and of clerical independence from the threat of political or military action. However, what is clear in much of the historical and dogmatic sources on slavery in Muslim Africa is the successful way Muslim clerics have been able to incorporate slaves into the functions and self-understanding of a respectable Muslim religious order. If we recall that slaves came from populations that Muslim reformers regarded as legitimate pagan booty, it is remarkable that slaves should in turn acquiesce and accept the doctrinal justification their captors imposed on their heritage, a justification that legitimized their enslavement in the first place. Apart from short-lived revolts and rebellions among the slaves themselves, there has been little significant antislavery tradition among the champions of Muslim religious orthodoxy, with the consequence that slave descendants in Muslim society continued to suffer vestiges of the legal and moral stigma first imposed on their forebears.[96] Thus the resilience until relatively recently of institutional slavery in Muslim Africa attests to a wider phenomenon, indicating that those Muslims who incorporated slaves into clerical practice had principle and practice on their side. The clerics, then, need suffer no more compromise of their reputation than a supple conscience would dictate.

Part Two

Islam, Africa, and Colonialism: Religion in History

An important argument in this section is that nineteenth-century colonialism must be placed in its particular historical and cultural context, and that one such context is the rapid change through which Muslim West Africa had been passing. Such rapid change drew colonialism willy-nilly into the eddy of events and thereby imposed certain constraints on it *in situ*.

In the particular case with which Chapter 4 opens, colonial officials took sides in the cleavages created by turnovers in traditional rivalries and alliances. The unstable nature of local political events meant that officials were often unsurefooted, not knowing whether a friend today might be a foe tomorrow, or a foe this time would be a friend next time. So officials cajoled and coaxed or warned and threatened in a mixed pattern of uncertainty.

A crucial feature of the cleavage that was to confront colonial power was the rural-urban configuration. The colonial authorities came on the scene as the champions of metropolitan values into whose refined strands the pacified and grateful native races would in due season be absorbed. Consequently, the new imperial order introduced in the colonies forces that would produce towns and cities and the bureaucracies necessary for order and efficiency. As far as the colonialists were concerned, that was how European society evolved, with urbanization controlling economic activity and with the social permutations and combinations conducive to surplus production, exchange, and distribution. It was that mercantile culture that fired the wheels of civilization and moved humanity forward on the path of progress and freedom. What could be more natural than to attempt to replicate this European model in an Africa that was so scandalously bereft of the material benefits of civilization and the technology to take full advantage of virgin promise?

The problem with this prescription was that in a good deal of precolonial Muslim Africa the overwhelming strength of the local economy was in rural districts where it was controlled by religious masters, or by leaders who were in cahoots with the religious masters. This rural balance of power had shown no signs of weakening when the colonial era arrived. There were many internal contradictions in the rural regions, but these contradictions were resonant with rural priorities and could be resolved with their reconfiguration. In any case Islam's cumulative appeal was concentrated in hinterland regions whose affairs were now intimately tied up with the values and interests of religion. By resolving to draw all the main centers of influence into the unifying net of colonial control, the imperial overlords had committed themselves to pursuing a policy of direct intervention in local affairs even if that meant plunging into the maelstrom in the rural sector.

Chapter 4 describes in detail the robust nature of rural Islam at this time and the strong leadership it generated in the string of centers held together by observances and rituals centered on charismatic personalities. The entanglement of a leading member of this charismatic circle with French colonial officials provides a dramatic illustration of the limits of a metropolitan policy. Tcherno Aliou, the figure in question, had thrown a finely spun web over the whole terrain of rural sensibility, a web that the earlier French support for him had extended and then, in a reversal of policy, had sought to unscramble, since it could not co-opt it. By that stage Tcherno Aliou's range had exceeded French estimates of what he might be capable of. In reaction, officials accused him of bad faith, of failing to hold himself bound to the French come rain, come shine. Before long Tcherno Aliou was tainted with the brush of Mahdism, a hold-all for unamenable religious militants. In fact, Mahdism was an important piece of the general context of colonial involvement in late nineteenth-century Africa. Mahdism was the acute angle that shaped the unilinear discourse of colonial hegemony and pushed it to assume a posture largely unnatural to its literal metropolitan logic. Following the example of Napoleon's invasion in Egypt in 1798 when he announced to an incredulous Muslim population that he had converted to Islam, high-profile administrators elsewhere assumed the posture of notional *muftis* who ensured their directives and pronouncements possessed a moral aura by having them translated into the borrowed tones of the revered Arabic. In that form the new colonial rulers would compete with their indigenous religious opponents in a common register. The aim would be to secure the wholesale transfer of moral obligation, rather than to deny that it existed, and to retail it to willing collaborators. In this way, the sacred resources of religion would underwrite the secular project of colonial overlordship, and the dark-skinned natives, having already been conditioned to submit to Allah as the lord of the universe, would henceforth submit to whites as the master race. One colonial official propounded this view, saying the French should "collaborate with the marabouts in the education of Muslim youths. [However,] Let us make our collaboration serve the development of French influence, otherwise the Muslims will continue to raise their children away from us and left to themselves the Coranic schools will conserve their predominantly religious influence."[1] Thus did the struggle for the hearts and minds of rank and file Muslims become transformed into competition for control of rural power, a struggle that also involved reducing religion to calculations of dominion and authority.

In Chapter 5 I assess saintly authority in its social and historical context. My aim is to establish the roots of the tradition in Scripture and tradition, show its connections and divergences with analogous indigenous categories, and describe its social expressions in personal and communal life. The conclusion I reach is that sainthood and saintship did not lead to the privatization of piety or to withdrawal from worldly affairs. On the contrary, saints and their followers staked their reputation as much on worldly success as on personal charisma and were as enamored of the political crown as of the religious turban, and the combined effect of their dual heritage has been to promote religion as both power and charisma.

Religion in that formulation was difficult for the new colonial authorities to grasp adequately. If they approached Islam as a client religion that could be disarmed with official patronage, they could not be sure that even a quiescent Islam might not erupt into public attention with charismatic personages whom mass devotion would typically incubate. If, on the other hand, Islam was approached as a potential political ally, with provisions made for *qádí* courts, for family law, marriage, and inheritance, for education, and for the pilgrimage to Mecca, then such provisions might promote interests just as inimical to colonial rule. If Islam was ignored as public truth, it might lapse into an enclave mode, using its insulation from public responsibility to stigmatize infidel colonial rule. If, by the same token, Islam was acknowledged and given a public role, it would detract from the doctrine of comprehensive colonial mastery. As one candid evaluation put it, "To suppress the [Qur'án] schools would be dangerous, to abandon them to themselves would be folly."[2]

The authorities were at pains to assure themselves that they were, in their own words, the natural protector of Muslims. To that end they adopted the principle of utilizing Islam as an accoutrement of imperial policy. Xavier Coppolani articulated an approach to Muslim Africans that became the official colonial line. The clergy, he said, was represented "by veritable tribes of learned men," independent, and astute brokers of peace with a reputation for justice. "Their rosary replaces the gun," and their influence on the masses and over the warrior chiefs is considerable. For that reason, they have "become the auxiliaries of our policy and could become the precious instruments of pacification if, bearing in mind the rivalry between warrior chiefs, we combine the various elements and attack the question with determination and unity of views."[3] A good deal of the assertion about the power of the clergy over warrior chiefs was wishful thinking, though the authorities sometimes acted to make reality fit fiction. At the root of the issue is the colonial perception of Islam as inherently untrustworthy, whatever the proximity or distance of Muslim leaders to the colonial power. One official observed that it was necessary to be on guard with regard to clerics who appear supportive, because they "have done everything to exploit the initial profound ignorance of the

French, posing as victims whereas too often they were merely trying to enlist our
support in their illegitimate refusal to pay their suzerains for the protection which
had been afforded them for centuries."[4] Such perfidy stems from an intrinsic antipathy, as described here by one colonial official:

> It is an undeniable fact that in all the regions where Islam is profoundly rooted we are
> held in the greatest scorn by certain marabouts. The biggest danger is there is in this
> country a form of bastardised Islam, a mixture of religion and ridiculous supersti-
> tions, a superficial religion in which the marabouts and the pseudo-marabouts who
> abound in this country are the carriers of malicious rumours, maintain the credulous
> people in sentiments of hatred against us and work towards the brutalisation of the
> race by superstitious practices. This element is perforce hostile to us. The chiefs need
> these marabouts who distribute a thousand *gris-gris* [amulets] for the success of their
> pillages and, in exchange, these marabouts enjoy numerous privileges.[5]

The colonial authorities were resolved that clergy so fleet of feet should not be
allowed to pass unnoticed through the loopholes of uncoordinated official policy.
"Maraboutic propaganda—*the hypocritical façade behind which are sheltered the
selfish hopes of the former privileged groups and the last obstacle in the way of the
complete triumph of our civilising work based on respect of justice and human liberty*—will disappear completely when all its activists, identified and closely
watched, are no longer able to pass through the gaps in the vast network which
surrounds them throughout the entirety of our West Africa."[6]

In different circumstances, popular, superstitious Islam might be preferred to
the pure Islam of the creeds, the uncertainty being due to official reluctance to see
Islam except in terms of its colonial usefulness. The governor-general of French
West Africa, William Ponty, thus reasoned that Muslim West Africa possessed a
special character by virtue of its vigorous syncretism. "Our Muslims," he wrote re-
assuringly, "have not accepted the pure Coran, whatever their devotions they have
wanted to preserve their ancestral customs."[7] A logical policy implication of that
view was that Muslim West Africa must be sealed off from Arab Islam: Specifically, Arabic must be discouraged in French schools and be replaced with French,
the language of civilization and virtue.

Yet even that course of action did not offer long-term security, because for
Muslim Africans even French could not take the place of the veneration accorded
to Arabic. The authorities could not promote Arabic, or allow its continued use,
without fostering anticolonial sentiments. "Even indirectly to oblige those under
our jurisdiction to learn it in order to maintain official relations with us comes to
the same as encouraging the propaganda of the votaries of Islam. . . . The few
Arabic-speaking natives are most commonly religious persons, marabouts often
under surveillance, and people moreover who very often have a mediocre understanding of the language in question. We should not tolerate having to rely on
such 'scholars' for the honest communication of our intentions."[8]

Yet the resilience of Islam, its natural advantages of learning, organization, discipline, duty and devotion, self-sacrifice, its elevated moral and ethical system, its code of personal piety and public order, its strong historical sense, and its cosmopolitan ethos, all of that made it a force difficult to ignore and hazardous to encourage. Very little in the metropolitan calculations of colonial rule prepared the new executive powers for dealing with the religion as a two-edged sword, and that miscalculation was to have long-term consequences both for the West and Africa.

4

Tcherno Aliou, the *Wali* of Goumba: Islam, Colonialism, and the Rural Factor in Futa Jallon, 1867–1912

Setting the Stage

The irruption of the European colonial order into Africa had a deep and long-lasting effect on Muslim society, and especially on the Muslim religious elite. One reason is the assertive and dramatic nature of the colonial order, the sudden way in which it arrived and expected local populations, without much warning or preparation, to fall into line. The effect of the sudden colonial order becomes clear in the example we have chosen as the subject of this chapter. But first, a little background may be in order.

Futa Jallon, the scene of our story, underwent a major Muslim political revolution early in the eighteenth century when Muslim immigrants and their first Fulbé converts staged a takeover of power and reversed the old social order, dispossessing and replacing the old nobility and reducing them to servitude. The movement thus conformed in several important respects to the classical lines of dialectical change, one of the few genuinely successful examples of early grass-roots mobilization and empowerment. Under such conditions Islam acceded to power. However, the Muslim party was far from united, with a major cleavage developing between the clerical side of the revolution and the secular. The clerical faction traced its pedigree to the eighteenth-century founder of the revolution, Karamokho Alfa, after whom the clerical faction was named the Alfaya. The secular party looked to Ibrahima Sori and his program of Fulbé ethnic and economic dominance, hence the name Soriya. The Alfaya and the Soriya, both Muslim but with different agendas, came to an amicable and, by all appearances, a workable arrangement whereby power alternated between the two houses, a procedure

73

based on Islam as equally sacred and secular. Almost two hundred years later European accounts and local chronicles continued to report the Alfaya and the Soriya still taking turns in governing the state, although we need not assume that all was smooth sailing.

Historians have long tried to determine whether religious ideology or secular ambitions were more influential in shaping the affairs of Futa Jallon, but we need not be forced into such a choice. In time, the revolutionary ardor waned while the state continued to expand its territorial base, incorporating several non-Fulbé groups, not always with a concern for how such new groups might integrate with the settled populations. Yet even in its most successful secular phase the state used Islam as the engine of expansion and the banner for rallying the troops. In the most fateful military adventure, the Fulbé authorities exceeded the bounds of strategic self-interest and pursued a vainglorious ideological line of trying to convert the non-Muslim ruling aristocracy of Kaabou. It proved a costly miscalculation, for although Kaabou was destroyed, a destruction maintained in oral traditions as *turubang*, Futa Jallon had itself paid too high a price to come out unscathed. It failed to recover and fell prey to internal dissension exacerbated by tremendous social instability from an overburdened peasantry and to external danger with the inexorable intrusion of the French. The quasi-anarchist Hubbubé movement, described below, erupted at this time, making a vain bid for the inspired mantle of Futa Jallon's dual and bipartisan heritage, but in fact exposing the costly limitations of its own Cromwellian view of affairs. The French, meanwhile, were gathering speed along the coast in their eventual thrust into the hinterland.

The main personality of our story, Tcherno Aliou, made his appearance during this period of internal entropy and external challenge. He himself would lay stake to the true heritage of Karamokho Alfa, if only to censure those clerics of his age who claimed to represent the Alfaya tradition and yet whose growing unpopularity disqualified them from playing any further role in retrieving lost glory. The secular party represented no credible alternative either, because, following Kaabou, it was in disarray, and its leaders, including Alfa Yahya, the king of Labé, were in full flight before the French. Tcherno Aliou might succeed in salvaging something from the general ruins, but before that his course would collide with the rising French demand for total surrender and acquiescence.

Invasion, Reprisal, and Dénouement

At about 6:30 on the morning of 30 March 1911 several detachments of French officers and local troops invaded the village of Goumba, known locally as "Missidi," and became embroiled in sanguinary operations. Two French officers were killed and another two badly wounded. Eleven soldiers also died and nineteen others were injured. The exchange raged for three and one-half hours before the French were able to extricate themselves.[1]

In the attempt to document exactly what happened and to discover whether better military preparations and more effective intelligence gathering could have averted the disaster, French administrators undertook a meticulous investigation. It brought to light a major religious movement in hinterland Guinea of which the affair of Goumba was a significant part, but still only symptomatic. Goumba's ruling personality was Tcherno Aliou, a Shádhilí scholar well connected with Saharan centers of learning, especially Morocco. The village of Goumba, the center of his religious activities, was a small settlement with a population of about two hundred, but it formed the hub of a cluster of similar settlements that together held four times the population of Goumba.[2]

The French military intervention against Goumba was the climax of a series of investigations designed to discover whether Tcherno Aliou was organizing an anticolonial uprising, and in particular whether he was exploiting political sympathy for Alfa Yahya, against whom the French had taken punitive measures.[3] The violence at Goumba confirmed their view that Tcherno Aliou was at the head of a plot to challenge French rule, and they held him responsible for the loss of life on 30 March. Measures were immediately taken to restore French morale and to hunt down Tcherno Aliou, who in the meantime had escaped to neighboring Sierra Leone, aided by his principal disciples.

Not much is known of the early life of Tcherno Aliou. He was born c. 1828 and eventually came to settle in Goumba in 1867. That move coincided with the penetration into Futa Jallon by the French. It was also a period of acute social and religious unrest, as epitomized by the rise of the militant Hubbu movement (see the discussion later in this chapter). Suffice it to say here that Futa Jallon was undergoing epochal changes at this time. The rule of the Almamys, the traditional rulers, was crumbling. The gains and principles of the reform movement initiated by Karamokho Alfa between 1727 and 1767 were being increasingly compromised. The established religious elite, who had wielded great influence, were now rapidly losing moral credibility. European pressure and dominance on the coast compounded the problem by restricting the trade in slaves, on which the wealth and power of the traditional social and political elite were based. To compensate for the colonial squeeze, the old elite tried to eke more revenue and labor out of slave populations and that increased the disenchantment among slave and peasant groups. The arrival on the scene of new religious masters, among them Tcherno Aliou, aggravated the climate of unrest directed against the old religious elite. The new religious leadership offered a rallying point for alienated groups and united them in a common cause against the old establishment. Thus Islamic revivalism, specifically the *diaroré*, combined with imperialism to press the Almamys closer to their eventual demise.

In this social and political ferment the rural factor proved decisive. The economic base of the Almamate lay in its control of sources of production in rural areas—chiefly slaves used in productive labor and as conscripts in military campaigns—as well as its control over the movement of goods. Another important economic source were the levies on produce and livestock and the taxes collected on goods using routes controlled by the Almamys. Political disaffection in that sphere would constitute a major problem for the old elite. In addition, the French, having staked a claim on the coast and the great riverain system of the Rios Grande and Nunez, which carried much of the wealth of an inland power like Futa Jallon, were tightening their grip on events in rural Guinea. This French expansion created a new political climate among the people on the peripheries of Futa Jallon and encouraged the repudiation of the authority of the Almamate, which, after the pyrrhic victory over the state of Kaabu in 1867, was unable to recover its strength, let alone suppress irredentism.

The central issue in the affairs of Futa Jallon at this time, therefore, was the disposition of the authority once held by the Almamys. The French forces were poised to wrest control of the area's economic and political power without the corresponding assurance of control over social systems fostered by new forms of Islam, as they would need to if their authority was to survive. Ultimately this situation brought the two Almamate claimants to power into confrontation. Religion was a significant source of social power that the French could not afford to ignore in their bid to oust the Almamys from control in Futa Jallon. Although the old religious elite had shared the fate of the Almamys as their patrons, a new and more credible class of religious masters had grown up to take over. Tcherno Aliou, as part of this new religious order, thus came to represent a threat to the French. The power of the Almamys had been concentrated in the rural sector, where Tcherno Aliou and his cohorts would make a telling bid for control. As they were advancing into that sphere, too, the French could not bypass Tcherno Aliou, whether as ally or as rival.

From their radically different vantage points, the French and the old aristocracies came to regard the new religious men with an identical fear. For the old religious men the issue concerned the growing power of the Shádhiliyya, a North African religious fraternity emphasizing in devotional exercises the cultivation of inner resources alongside involvement in secular affairs.[4] The fraternity was named after Abú'l-Hasan al Shádhilí (1196–1258), although it was his disciple, Ibn 'Atá Alláh (c. 1250–c. 1310), who was responsible for popularizing the movement in the Maghrib[5] and whose influential work, *Kitáb al-Hikam,* has been published together with an account of his life and work.[6] The man responsible for bringing the order to Futa Jallon was Modi Sellou (1760–1813), the *alfa* of Labé district.[7] Shádhilí teachings and devotional practice spread quickly in the area, with coteries of initiates developing under charismatic *shuyúkh,* whose authority contributed to the irreversible loss of influence of those who upheld Karamokho Alfa's legacy. Tcherno Aliou had established his reputation as a formidable Shádhilí scholar with a strong following and as a proven enemy of the old political elite, against whom he had been engaged in several military incidents. The French, for their part, discovered pretty quickly the inadequacies in their policy of assisting the rising power of the new religious elite as a counterpoise to the declining influence of the old men, for a strengthened religious power, however profoundly opposed to the old establishment, might not acquiesce under foreign rule. The inescapable logic was to pursue this new religious power to its strategic centers, which were all in the countryside. It is, of course, true that in the new conditions created by imperial rule, power shifted from the hinterland to the coast, where urban centers grew up. But before the colonial takeover of Futa Jallon, the great towns of Labé, capital of the district with the same name, and Timbo—together with Fugumba as the preeminent ideological center where the creation of Futa Jallon was announced in 1727—were symbols of political and moral failure, with the emergence into prominence of village congregations in what were called *missidi* (lit. 'mosque'), in other words, retreat centers founded to sharpen the boundary between the old and the new as between the corrupt and the virtuous.

At first the French perception of this inherent contradiction in local Islam was clouded by a preoccupation with efforts to topple Futa Jallon's ancien régime. For that task they secured the alliance of the new religious men without fully understanding the roots of popular disenchantment any more than their religious partners fully understood the logic of imperial conquest. With regard to Tcherno Aliou the French discovered much later the flaws in their reasoning. One source describes it thus: "Local chiefs, jealous of his growing influence, ardently pursued him and tried to chase him out. However, Tierno Aliou repulsed all their attacks, thanks to the foreign protection of the French, [a protection given him] because for a long time the administrators failed to acknowledge the dangers represented by this religious leader, renowned for his holiness, because his prominence shadowed our influence and our penetration into the country."[8]

In the first phase of their dealings with Tcherno Aliou, the French adopted his cause as their own. In one particular incident, the French officer, Lt. Millot, sent a detachment of his troops to put down the Susu in 1893. A little later, the administrator, M. Beckman, intervened in similar circumstances to suppress a local chief on behalf of Tcherno Aliou. With the French intervening to stabilize the military front, Tcherno Aliou concentrated on developing his religious power and organizing his growing following. His reputation for saintliness increased; the socially disenchanted gravitated toward him; disciples enrolled in his cause; stories of his mystical powers circulated widely; and in the general atmosphere of political despondency occasioned by the profound crisis in the Futa Jallon power structure and the approach of foreign rule, the village of Goumba and its *wali* became a focal point of new expectations. In the formative years between 1867 and 1911, Tcherno Aliou built up a considerable reputation, which he increasingly turned to account in educating a strong cadre of disciples.

Before considering in detail the religious movement that was being launched by Tcherno Aliou, we should at this stage try to describe the general religious background from which he came. A tradition in Futa Jallon of the period accorded mystical titles to those religious figures who were unconnected with ruling circles and who also showed unusual marks of spiritual favor. One of the most prominent of these titles was *sirruyanké,* granted to diviners of established reputation; in the Fula language the word is an adaptation of the Arabic *sirr* (secret, esoteric knowledge). As a title it might be exchanged with *walí*, saint, though there was an important distinction. A *sirruyanké* exercised his powers by deliberate and conscious application. The resource he controlled was the technique and the means, and his reputation was based on performing his functions well. The *walí*, by contrast, was possessor of *barakah*, a moral force with inherent virtue, and by that fact was vouchsafed miracles as confirmation of his status, tokens of divine favor of which his type was the single most important repository. Tcherno Aliou was a *walí*, the possessor of a grace that enabled him to accomplish by his word success in this world. Marty recognized this distinction when he wrote:

> The giving of miracles is not something the Foula religious masters do, and they play little role in the reputation for thaumaturgy. All such prodigies are altogether totally accidental. This was the case with the walí of Goumba. A miracle, well known to all of Fouta, is one that was accomplished in the course of the nineteenth century involving Karamokho Alfa. In the course of the aggression he undertook against Timbo, Kondé Buraima, the chief of Oussoulounké, wished to reach the Foula in their affection for the great religious leader, Karamokho Alfa. He went to open the tomb of Karamokho Alfa who had been buried there for a century. He cut off his left hand. At that instant blood miraculously gushed out, and Kondé Buraima closed the tomb and fled.[9]

The precise part played by Tcherno Aliou in this miracle is not very clear, but the impression is allowed to form that he was ultimately the moral guarantor of the reform legacy of Karamokho Alfa, with whose sacred blood his own saintly spirit was intermingled. The moral bankruptcy of the traditional elite entrusted with defending that legacy was at the same time demonstrated by their inability to bar Kondé Birama's way.

Such examples of saintly *barakah* achieving moral victory helped to establish their author firmly in the esteem and devotion of ordinary people, and a certain premium began to be placed on acquiring the marks of saintly distinction. That a whole class of *sirruyanké* practiced the divinatory art suggests that the aspiration was widely shared, encouraging tendencies of charlatanry among a section of the practitioners. Marty notes how quickly contenders for the role can multiply:

> It is generally agreed that the most pious of the marabouts frequently experienced divine revelations. The *walí* of Goumba, for example, had them frequently. In the course of his encounters with the divinity, he would disappear from view and return to earth having obtained not only information about events but also new intellectual and physical powers. These revelations occurred during the nights preceding the two great Islamic festivals, *Juldé Soumayé* [end of Ramadán] and *Juldé Donkiri* [the Mecca pilgrimage]. On these nights there is not a single cleric who does not claim, in the guise of a monkey or some other animal, to have had some communication with God. From such encounters they predict rain and fine weather, the state of future harvests, fat kine succeeding lean, and vice versa. This practice sometimes leads to exploitation or extortion.[10]

Because of popular demand charlatans appeared from time to time, claiming the powers of a *sirruyanké a*nd making apocalyptic promises that proved false. Some of them suffered imprisonment as a result.[11] Such popular distortions we must regard in part as the weakness of the traditional Muslim *'ulamá,* whose outlook had the result of reducing Islam to providing therapy and other forms of therapeutic services for individuals and groups. It left Islam a virtual hostage of unscrupulous men in whom piety and vanity commingled to feign works of *barakah.*

Tcherno Aliou was in a different class, as is shown by the ascription to him of the title *walí,* a genuinely moral figure whose inherent virtue was light-years removed from the acquired skills of a *sirruyanké.* As such, Tcherno Aliou symbolized the renovation of Karamokho Alfa's pious legacy, as well as its value in halting contemporary disenchantment under colonial domination. From his own point of view, Tcherno Aliou would be living proof that Islam was a credible influence in worldly affairs, and that Futa Jallon's classical heritage could be salvaged.

However, a more problematic issue is how the popular perception of *barakah* encouraged the adoption of the militant term *mahdí,* a term with strong political implications. One source for official tetchiness on the *mahdist* idea was the sensational Mahdist movement in the Anglo-Egyptian Sudan (1884–1885) in which General George Gordon, known to history as "Chinese Gordon" from his involvement in the Taiping Rebellion (1863–1864), was killed by the forces of Muhammad Ahmad, the self-proclaimed *mahdi.* The Sudanese Mahdiya set all European colonial officialdom on edge. In 1979, that is, a hundred years later in the Muslim calendar, the West found itself dealing with the doctrinal recycling of the *mahdist* theme as "political fundamentalism" in Iran and elsewhere. As a result the West once again felt itself on edge, its security apparatus scrambled. It had failed to contain the phenomenon at the source but insisted that containment was the answer to its spread, a policy that would not distinguish between bait and fish.

In any case, with regard to Tcherno Aliou, information on his political ambitions is at best sketchy, and apart from circumstantial evidence, a good deal of which is more bait than fish, we are on shaky ground indeed in attempting to support the charge that Tcherno Aliou was also a *mahdí* engaged in a political contest with the French. What is less difficult to sustain is the notion that the *walí* of Goumba had acquired enormous political significance by virtue of the strong following he attracted and from his record of open differences with the Fulbé *mawubé* (traditional political elite). Most of the Mahdist material we possess comes to us from one fateful event: the military engagement at Goumba on 30 March 1911 and the subsequent trial of Tcherno Aliou on charges arising from that battle.

It is clear, once detailed investigations began to be conducted into his immediate past, that Tcherno Aliou would emerge as an important personage with the power to influence a wide circle of people both near and far, and therefore his political significance in the context of popular disenchantment and the decay of traditional institutions would be apparent to the French. It is necessary, therefore, that, in the absence of primary evidence on the point, we understand any Mahdist claims against the wider social and political background. Popular religious figures

like Tcherno Aliou inevitably assumed an importance far out of proportion to
their organizational achievement, and spontaneous groups of devotees, however
haphazardly equipped, would give the appearance of purposeful preparation.
Tcherno Aliou himself appears to have encouraged the adulation of his disciples
by vaguely pointing to a coming apocalyptic war that would signal the defeat of
imperial forces in the land. But in 1910, when most of the Mahdist predictions
were made, the *walí* of Goumba was an infirm octogenarian, lame and nearly
blind. In any future political dispensation, such as a Mahdist state, he could not
have hoped to play more than a symbolic role. The point was conceded by official
reports that described the *walí* in 1910 as so physically decrepit that "everyone ex-
pects him to die soon."[12] It was about all he could do even to remain upright in
his house. Thus, we would have to discount any strong or immediate personal interest on his part. Yet this is not to say that his *barakah* did not compound the political risks by encouraging Mahdist sentiments, for the climate of social disenchantment would have been highly conducive to such ideas. The whole
atmosphere was primed for deliverance and thus for a savior, any savior.

In a public statement concerning the future of French rule in Futa Jallon, Tcherno Aliou declared in 1910 that the French presence would not extend beyond
fifty years and that he and the people were already witnessing the forty-ninth.
However, it is clear in this context that the *walí* was supplying a religious outline
to a discontent whose roots were deeply economic. The new French measures imposing taxes on an impoverished peasantry added to the grievances long held by
rural dwellers. A disciple of Tcherno Aliou wrote to his master, complaining
about the new taxes and urging direct action to relieve the situation: "We are tired
of paying taxes to the French. You must give the signal for revolt." (Nous sommes
fatigués de payer l'impôt aux français, il faut donner le signal de la guerre.)[13] His
response invoked the Mahdist sentiment, but only as an argument against precip-
itate action: "We must not be pressed. The time has not yet come. You will recover
what you have paid to the whites. I hold the keys to Kindia and Conakry. The
Mahdi will appear soon. Continue with your prayers and with amassing arms." (Il
ne faut pas être pressé. Les temps ne sont pas encore venus. Vous retrouverez l'ar-
gent donné aux blancs. Je tiens les clefs de Kindia et de Conakry. Le Mahdi va bi-
entôt paraitre. Continuez vos prières et achetez des armes.)[14]

Tcherno Aliou's transformation from friend to foe has been tied to the Mahdist
issue, with the sources insisting that once he presented the idea of Mahdist rule,
he sought the means for achieving it. Thus, the amassing of arms was conjoined
to the religious obligations of his followers. So at his word his disciples collected
guns, sabers, powder, and uniforms. Bullets were manufactured from local
foundries by blacksmiths of the village of Yara. He proceeded to surround himself
with a tight bodyguard of six to seven men, "'determined and well armed . . .
charged exclusively to defend his person, if need be to the final extreme.'"[15]

Tcherno Aliou, it is alleged, began to prepare his followers for what would be
portents of the imminent arrival of the *mahdí*. He told them that when the rail-

way then under construction by the French reached the town of Kouroussa, signs would be given about the arrival of the expected *mahdi* and that would signal the end of French power. The railway (built 1900–1910) was of course the most aggressive symbol of French power in the economic life of hinterland populations for it threatened to circumvent the traditional channels of trade and to bring rural districts within the administrative orbit of centralized control. That it would mark a watershed in the history of the area is without doubt, but that it would also mark a turning point in the scale of local anxiety was equally predictable. Tcherno Aliou would be expected to pronounce on it, and the evidence shows that he did. He went even further, informing the chief of the district of Massi about the new political forces entering the land and how a Mahdist state would come to replace existing powers. He added the specific detail that the demise of French power would be heralded by the killing of a French officer. A few days after this prediction, the French administrator in charge of Massi, M. Bastié, was assassinated at Kora.[16]

Some eight days earlier Tcherno Aliou had tactically mobilized his men, obtaining official permission for this action on the pretext that he had to put down marauding elephants. The men who heeded his call included those from Simbaya, seventeen kilometers from Conakry, the headquarters of the French in Guinea. That he had a base so close to Conakry was in hindsight considered brazen effrontery by the French. The French inspector in charge of Muslim affairs, M. Mariani, happened to be on tour in the area at the time. Alarmed by the growing movement of men all bound for Missidi, the religious center at Goumba, but unable to fix with any degree of precision the project being undertaken, he informed the administrator.

As a sign of his growing confidence, or perhaps due to the immunity that his great age might have assured him, Tcherno Aliou does not appear to have gone to any lengths to conceal his political feelings, if the accounts are to be believed. According to these accounts, he told M. Basias, the administrator, of his opposition to the French in his country. The point was driven home when, it is claimed, he turned down numerous invitations to appear in Kindia on the occasion of the French governor-general's visit in December 1910. Though he pleaded, it is suggested, his great age, officials were quick to observe, again with the benefit of hindsight, that he had intended a slight, for the next day he went riding for a distance of forty kilometers: "'to demonstrate clearly to his devotees that he is able to defy stoutly our orders and that he was more powerful than we.'"[17] At issue is how the French could tame the *wali's barakah* and neutralize him. It was not enough, as we shall see presently, that Tcherno Aliou donated cash and food for the visit of the governor-general, arguing that his gifts were a sign of his sympathies for the French.

Alfa Yahya's return from a second exile at this very time increased official fears that religious incitement would spread the ill will earned by the measures adopted against him. In view of his Mahdist pronouncements, the *wali* became the prime suspect of fomenting anticolonial disaffection.

The conjunction of Tcherno Aliou's religious activities and Alfa Yahya's arrival in Conakry has largely caused Tcherno Aliou to be viewed as a minor force overshadowed by Alfa Yahya's political program. Consequently, until now it has been difficult to treat Tcherno Aliou in his own right as a major religious figure with an appeal of his own. It seems justifiable, therefore, to omit from this account the much better known story of Alfa Yahya[18] and to concentrate on that of his religious counterpart.

Tcherno Aliou had been alerted by his disciples of French troop movements toward Goumba and, aided by his principal agents, he fled by the Kaba-Falaba route to neighboring Sierra Leone.[19] An accomplished rider, he would presumably have done so on horseback. He was well outside the vicinity of Goumba when French forces arrived on the morning of 30 March. When they realized he had departed, the French set up road blocks and kept a strict check on all routes into Sierra Leone, but Tcherno Aliou had successfully eluded them and arrived safely. The British authorities in Sierra Leone had meantime received requests for his extradition, with which they complied. Returned to Guinea, Tcherno Aliou was brought to trial on capital charges, together with his principal accomplices.

The nature of Tcherno Aliou's conflict with the French may be gleaned from an examination of the evidence presented at his trial, supplemented by material culled from later investigations. The trial proceedings were printed in the colonial newspaper, *L'A.O.F. Echo de la Côte Occidentale d'Afrique,* and the first issue devoted to them dealt with Tcherno Aliou's cross-examination. This material, supplemented by the testimony of other witnesses, constitutes the most detailed picture we possess of Tcherno Aliou's intentions. In the following excerpt he is being questioned by the prosecutor-general:

> "Did you not incite the Foulahs to revolt against the French?"
> "Never. I wanted to parley."
> "Tell everyone precisely what you wanted to propose."
> "I have never given orders for anyone to take up arms against the French. In the 20 years that I have lived in Goumba I have always remained a loyal friend of the French. I have assiduously paid my taxes, and my relations with the commandant of the district of Kindia have remained cordial.
>
> I have not given weapons or arms to my disciples to make war against the French. Whilst I could, I rendered all services demanded of me. On the circumstances being investigated, I knew nothing of past events, because I was not present. If anyone was killed it was after my departure and I gave no orders to that end. I left with some of my disciples because I had fears for what might happen and for my safety. I was a friend of the French. When I was brought news that the French were approaching from all sides, coming to me with armed soldiers and without any warning, as was the normal practice, I was afraid and consequently went into flight. I was informed by fugitives from Goumba that after they had passed the village of Kolentê military operations had commenced. My youngest son, Alimou, came to join me then."[20]

The prosecutor-general, regarding much of this testimony as evasive, produced an exhibit in the form of a report by M. Mariani, then in charge of the Muslim affairs office. In a passage from that report, written in 1909, the court was told how a close disciple of Tcherno Aliou had written, *sous dictée,* "If the French leave me alone in peace, I shall not make war; but I shall defend myself if they attack."[21] Even on the best reading, this evidence is no more than hearsay, though the prosecution's intention was to use it to prove a material connection.

The prosecution witnesses proceeded to provide details of the troubles of 30 March. Their accounts can be divided into two parts. In the first part eight French officers testified to the movement of French forces in Kindia and Goumba, including the invasion of Goumba and its well-known consequences, and to the savage retaliation, with official estimates setting the number of dead villagers at 400, with 240 arrested.[22] Much of this material is marginal to our purposes.

The second part consists of evidence given by eleven principal witnesses, all of them local men. This is of greater interest to us, because many of them were close associates of Tcherno Aliou and knew him well before the incident. Though not all of their testimony can be relied on uncritically, for there are obvious inconsistencies, it is from these sources that we should build on the picture that emerges from the *walí's* own testimony. These witnesses came under cross-examination, in the course of which the *walí* occasionally intervened. It was in one such instance that he established his role on the occasion of the governor-general's visit. Contrary to the allegation that he bore a grudge against the administration, the *walí* testified that on the occasion he personally donated 1,500 francs, a horse, three cows, three bulls, nine sheep, and three hundred chickens, all dispatched to M. Sazias, the commandant of Kindia, nine months before the governor-general arrived. The presents were not, the *walí* confirmed under interrogation, a tax of any kind.[23] It is obvious from this largesse that the *walí* commanded enormous resources and that his reputation was considerable enough for the French to wish to use it in a public display of support for the governor-general.

Another witness testified that the inhabitants of Goumba, when threatened with military action to force the *walí* to surrender himself, spoke of their readiness to die, having prepared themselves for this extreme stand and taken a religious resolution on it. They had declared: "We were dead already since yesterday. God is the one who looks after us. We have sacrificed our lives." (Nous sommes morts déjà depuis hier. Allah nous attend. Nous avons fait le sacrifice de notre vie.)[24]

This is hardly a statement of importance, but in the fraught atmosphere of an aggressive colonial power under local fire and of a capital trial, it was elaborated with journalistic relish. The *Echo,* for instance, construed it as an open challenge to the authority of the French. The defense counsel was at times constrained to observe that the court was in danger of assuming a verdict and proceeding to prove it with cooperative witnesses. The evidence that was accumulating established beyond any shadow of a doubt that the court was faced with a redoubtable religious figure. But to prove from this evidence that the sage of Missidi had committed a capital crime would form a hazardous project for the law. Consequently, the French legal authorities resorted to straining the arguments and finding legal shortcuts. The cross-examination of prosecution witnesses was threatening to ex-

pose them to the risk of perjury. Consequently the judge intervened to halt inter-
rogations by the defense.

Another prosecution witness declared how Tcherno Aliou had gathered his disciples and told them to prepare now for the consummation. The supreme hour of
the *mahdí* had come. "The moment has arrived," he announced. "I am going to
burn down all the villages up to the sea and will chase away all the whites."[25] According to this witness the *walí* personally owned one hundred guns, not to mention those possessed by his disciples. He also held a store of powder and bullets. In
addition, blacksmiths had been placed on a war footing and were manufacturing
bullets for this purpose.[26]

Other witnesses added further details regarding the organized network of support set in place by the *walí* with the specific intention of preparing for action
against the French. The villages of Orédioli and Dalaba, for example, situated west
of Timbo and on the southern slopes of the Ditinn plateau, enlisted actively in his
cause and sent volunteers to Goumba. Tcherno Kana, chief of Dalaba, was a sympathizer and actively corresponded with the *walí*. When news of the events of 30
March reached the village of Dalaba on the evening of the same day, there was
public rejoicing and a display of cavalry as a victorious gesture. Although this account was supposed to implicate Tcherno Kana as an accessory to the crime, it
need not prove more than a certain sympathy for the saintly aura of the *walí*.
Tcherno Aliou himself, visibly agitated by what he considered a deliberate fabri-
cation by the witness, challenged him by aggressively turning toward him, at
which point the presiding judge intervened on behalf of the witness. A similar
confrontation occurred with another prosecution witness whom Tcherno Aliou
proceeded to deflate by an implicit charge of perjury, crying out in disbelief, *Alláh
akbaru,* "God is most great." In the context of the *walí's barakah,* the cry was a
curse. The witness collapsed and was excused by the presiding judge.

The connection of Tcherno Kana with the *walí* continued to hold the attention
of the court and was once again brought into evidence. According to one account
Tcherno Kana purchased arms and gunpowder for the *walí,* an arrangement that
had been going on for a year before the March incident. If there is any truth to
this claim, it would suggest either a remarkably high level of organization on the
part of the *walí* and his followers, so that the French authorities did not find them
out, or a singular lack of vigilance by those same authorities, unless, of course, the
rural setting impeded the gathering of reliable intelligence on the plans of the
militants. In any case rural Guinea, as has already been observed, was seething
with unrest long before the formal treaty of 1897[27] completed the process of
French penetration of the area. The detailed surveillance needed in order to keep
abreast of developments in the region would be beyond the resources of a new
power. The misadventure at Goumba showed the French had miscalculated popular feeling, demonstrating in native eyes a less accomplished and a less flattering
image of French power.

Nevertheless, such failure to comprehend local realities would not hinder them.
In summing up the proceedings of the trial, the presiding judge gathered the

often shaky submissions of the prosecution and constructed an emotionally charged case against the *walí*, giving sensational details of the mutilation of the French victims, suggesting, he contended, a blind, fanatical, and absolute devotion to the commands of the *walí*.[28] The reports detailing the *walí's* complicity also revealed that the Lebel guns of the French officers killed at Goumba were later recovered from the disciples of the *walí* following his extradition from Sierra Leone, proof according to the court of premeditated guilt.

The judge pressed the view that Tcherno Aliou was driven by excessive religious and political ambitions that led him to exploit the feelings and sensibilities of people with explicit reference to their grievances on slavery. According to evidence presented in court the *walí* promised people that they would be able to recover their slaves.

Slavery was a festering issue in Futa Jallon, the linchpin of the economic system undergirding the old order. It encapsulated, on the one hand, the power and authority of the ruling elite and, on the other hand, their acute dilemma as one by one the props collapsed under the system. First, the French asserted control of the coastal markets for which slaves were bound. Then, after the establishment of military posts at the mouths of the riverain system, they assumed direct authority for river communication. Finally, with the gathering speed of the railway then under construction, the French pushed inland to subdue hinterland rulers, divest them of their traditional sources of wealth, of which slaves were a significant part, and fill the political space with an aggressive version of their colonial code. It would be surprising if there were no indigenous reaction, or a concomitant French exaggeration of it.

Slavery as a domestic institution was much more resilient, however, although in this sphere, too, the French brought direct pressure to bear. For example, they promulgated a decree in 1903 that banned slavery in all French West Africa. The measure was tightened up in 1905 by a law forbidding the constraint on any person's liberty as well as the sale or movement of slaves.[29] As I have had occasion to observe elsewhere,[30] these moves had a dramatic effect on rural Futa Jallon, for they helped to accentuate the dilemma of the traditional elite by confronting them with oppressed social elements and their rising sense of grievance. The dependence of the old order on slaves as an economic commodity is by now indubitable. However, what is less clear and even surprising is the suggestion that the *walí*, as the representative of a more egalitarian and radical puritan dispensation, was content to allow repossession of slaves to be invoked as the shibboleth of a populist cause. If it is true that he was thus identified with that cause, it would show the extent to which slavery was a deep-rooted fact in society and the peremptory, stronghanded way the French dealt with the issue. Indeed, as late as 1973 a study of slavery's continuing influence in society was undertaken, proof that it had survived much of the attempt to stamp it out.[31]

The specific case in the mind of the judge, however, concerned the recent military reprisals following the Goumba troubles when the French forcibly freed 1,500 slaves. The judge quoted a witness as saying that the *walí* had urged defiance of the French. The witness quoted the *walí* as follows: "Since we have not been heard on the question of slavery which had made us rich, we must chase off the French. If we die in the process, it is heaven, the Paradise of Muhammad, which we shall gain."[32]

The *walí's* chief defense witness was Diou Bayourou, who, with Tcherno Aliou, was sentenced to death. Bayourou was present at the residence of the *walí* when the French forces arrived on 30 March. In his account he gave the sparest details of Tcherno Aliou's religious program, although he probably possessed some of the most intimate knowledge on the question. Ouri Bailo, a leading disciple of the *walí*, was another defense witness. Like Bayourou, he was at Goumba on the day of the attack, but was not, according to the evidence, carrying arms. He is alleged to have had under him 666 sympathizers actively enrolled in the cause of the *walí* and awaiting orders to march into battle. The number has apocalyptic under-tones, and it is hard to know whether it was conditioned by millenarian expecta-tions in the circle of the *walí's* followers or whether it was only a courtroom drama.

In the intimidating atmosphere of a capital trial and the aftermath of French military reprisals it is perhaps not surprising that details of the Mahdist program of Tcherno Aliou did not emerge as fully as they might have. But the references to his religious and political allies, the followers, sympathizers, and leading disciples, would all suggest the scale of his appeal and justify, though not excuse, French fears of him. Yet, at over 80, Tcherno Aliou clearly commanded little military might. When the French decided to mount military reprisals, for example, they met with little resistance. Consequently the threat of the man must be formulated in terms of the prevailing climate of colonial intimidation, which military action merely aggravated. This might be one reason why we have allusions in the sources to rumors and innuendoes that Fulbé believed only the *walí* possessed the requi-site *barakah* as the antidote to the outrage of alien infidel rule.

French officials were keenly aware of the psychological nature of their struggle with Tcherno Aliou. In a telegram of 3 April 1912, the French announced that he had died in prison at Fotoba following a short illness. His death from natural causes, they argued, had robbed them of an important psycho-moral advantage and left them on the defensive vis-à-vis the partisans. Official communications spoke with extreme apprehension for what might follow the news of the *walí's* death. A state of alert was declared in hinterland Guinea. One source reasoned as follows:

> Without a doubt it is regrettable that the *walí* of Goumba did not receive the chastise-ment for his abominable outrage, a chastisement which would have produced on the Foulahs an enduring and resounding impression. It is equally without doubt that the influential marabouts would use the death to pretend . . . that God would not allow His servant to have himself decapitated . . . it is the Muslim mentality to be per-suaded by a show of force. In this matter the French were the more powerful side, and that was sufficient even for the most fervent of his disciples to condemn the *walí*.

These disciples do not believe henceforth either in the temporal power of Alfa Yahya or in the spiritual authority of the *walí*. From this moment they regard these two vain figures as responsible for their misery.[33]

Such official accounts are a trace too sanguine about the resolution of internal political conflicts. The reality was often far different. Indeed a few days before the death of the *walí*, M. Sazias, the commandant of Kindia, had to be hurriedly removed and sent back to France on account of rumors, rife at the time, that an assassination plot was being hatched against him for his having treacherously betrayed the *walí*, his one-time friend and ally. The *walí's* disciples consequently bore the French, and him in particular, an incorrigible grudge. Fear of further unrest led the French authorities to adopt precautionary measures. A detailed inventory was commissioned on the strength of rural Islam. Qur'án schools were surveyed, including pupil enrollment and the teachers running the schools, and the educational books used were scrutinized.[34] The chief French instrument of surveillance was the dossier filled with minutiae of religious and political personnel. Islam had invented, or else perfected, the rubric of *'ilm al-rijál*, "the science of the knowledge of men," as part of the critical apparatus for distinguishing between the spurious and the genuine in traditions about the Prophet. For their part, the French adopted the ploy of their otherwise underappreciated Muslim rivals and deployed their version of *'ilm al-rijál* to malign those leaders most likely to claim the mantle of *barakah* and to separate trusted allies from feared foes. *Barakah* was thus attacked by discrediting the leaders most likely to claim its mantle.

Here, for example, is a circular issued by the French governor-general to colonial officials with the request to keep vigilance on Qur'án schools and the clerics leading them:

It is important to be informed exactly on the number of schools. (These schools disseminate religious doctrines and the political suggestions issued unknown to us by the more or less secret agents of the big religious orders.) It is also important to make enquiries about the very personality of the marabouts who teach in the schools so that we know something of their origins, degree of learning, their means of instruction, their local influence and of any contact they may have kept with their former teachers. . . . From another point of view the administration wishes to know what subjects are being taught, what books are used and what categories of pupils the schools are designed for (children, adolescents, adults). And when a French school exists in the locality, or in a neighbouring one, it is necessary to find out whether the pupils of the Coranic schools come to complement their religious education or, if they do not attend the European school, to discover the reason for their refusal to attend.[35]

Such information, he ordered, should be compiled in "a personal file, if possible with a photograph attached."[36] Thus was born the dialectics of colonial power.

At this stage the French reasoned that Islam had proved an unreliable ally and that it was time to reverse their position and secure the traditional non-Muslim rulers in a strategy of encirclement of Muslim power. One report depicted the religious masters thus: "These Karamokhos are the greatest enemies of the chiefs because they are endeavoring to supplant them; they are dangerous for everyone concerned because, in giving bad counsel to the natives, they risk bringing upon the country as a whole a worse calamity."[37]

An unsettling fact came to light shortly after the death of the *walí:* that his religious movement had successfully penetrated the French administrative establishment. The story concerned one individual, Tcherno Attigou, who was employed by the French as a secretary of the Native Tribunal at Kindia. It emerged that Attigou was a secret but devoted follower of the *walí* and that in his position as trusted servant of the French he was able to render invaluable assistance to his spiritual mentor. He gathered important intelligence material at Kindia, which he duly transmitted to Goumba. The official conjecture is that it was from this source that the *walí* received foreknowledge of his impending arrest and was thus able to escape.[38]

Other facts, no less disquieting than the preceding, were being methodically unearthed. A certain administrative enthusiasm may have led the French to inflate the case against Tcherno Aliou, with an unrealistic notion of his stature as a conspirator. But the network of support they were uncovering suggests the *walí* had a good part of the countryside in his pocket. In this network, contrary to the preferred official line, the chiefs played an important part. The entire plateau of Ditinn, for example, was considered the *walí's* territory. His principal agents there were Tcherno Ywryno (Wurno), Sayagou, Alseini, Sarafou, and Amadou Oury Diallo. They ranged over central Futa Jallon disseminating his doctrines. Amadou Oury Diallo was chief of an important plateau village and acted as a willing foil for Alseini and Sarafou, who were religious clerics. In this connection, Tcherno Kana, chief of Dalaba, would appear to fit into a pattern of rural support bearing the imprint of the *walí's* stern doctrines.[39] All of these people were arraigned at the *walí's* trial, and all were found guilty of conspiracy. Tcherno Kana, Attiqou, and Tcherno Wurno were sentenced to internment for ten years for their part in the troubles of 30 March; Alseini, Sarafou, and Sayagou each received five years; and Amadou Oury Diallo received three.

The Rural Factor in Religious Militancy: The Shádhiliyya and the Hubbubé

The village basis of much of the emerging radical puritan order in Islam is well attested. With the decline of the power of Fugumba following the treaty in 1897, the new religious elite migrated to the villages, assured there of flocks of disciples among disaffected peasants and aggrieved former slaves who had repudiated their masters, many of them with French help.

The French were vaguely aware of the deeper connection between religious militancy and the rural setting, but in expounding the theme they again took a complacent view. They emphasized the calming effect of the farming cycle, observing that a period of apathy ensued during which the surge of energetic enterprise receded. The lieutenant-governor of Guinea wrote in this connection: "I should add that at the present time the rainy season has already commenced in Fouta, the tax has been fully paid and that the torpor into which the natives sink during the wet season will guarantee us against any incident, however minor, for a period of five months."[40]

Such official views, however, miss the significance of villages as incubators of religious radicalism. Paul Marty has noted how rural centers appear to be congenial to the development of heightened religious consciousness.[41] Rural enclavement accentuates the habit of withdrawal and retreat and allows religious masters to develop and practice rules of normative practice.[42] Small satellite communities spring up, having as their gravitational center holy men who hand down uncompromising rulings on religious observance.

The Shádhiliyya came to constitute a new magnetic field of influence in this setting. The important political district of Labé had been converted to the Shádhilí way by 'Alí al-Súfí, whom Marty calls "the apostle of Shádhilism in Futa."[43] His disciple, Tcherno Isma'íla, founded a center in Labé that, though it remained a pacific establishment devoted to other-worldly pursuits,[44] retained a strong political reputation.

The religious center of Ndama, also in the rural district of Labé, was a particularly successful foyer for the diffusion of Shádhilí teachings. The center was founded by another charismatic religious scholar, Tcherno Jaw (d. 1865), who belonged to the family of the Kalidouyabé, a chiefly lineage ensconced in the district of Koumbia. Tcherno Jaw's father, Tcherno Ciré, had been a warlord in the service of the Fulbé *mawubé* (political elite) of Labé at Badiar and Pakési. He came originally from Koggui, in the province of Missidi Hindé ('Lower Missidi'), also in Labé district.

Tcherno Jaw succeeded his father as chief and moved his capital to Ndama, which gave its name to the province as a whole. Ndama grew into a pilgrimage center, particularly of the ecstatic mystical rites of *diaroré,* and as its reputation increased, it became a center of attraction for the Hubbubé (on both, see the following section). Unable at this time to offer a substantial political prize for the devotion and zeal of his disciples, the marabout of Ndama, also accorded the title *walí,* gave them instead the rusk of pagan populations in Tenda, Coniagui, and Bassari on which to cut their teeth. In sorties and more sustained military encounters the Muslim militants made suitable examples of their neighbors. By the time he died in 1865, Tcherno Jaw had succeeded in using his religious influence to gain ascendancy in the political counsels of Koumbia.

He was succeeded by his son, Tcherno Abdul Goudousi (Ar. Gudsi), who tried to follow in his father's footsteps by pressing the war against pagan populations. But he exceeded himself in one such military operation at Kankéléfa in Kabou, where he was killed around 1875.[45]

Tcherno Abdul Goudousi was succeeded by his brother, Tcherno Ibrahima, who came to eclipse him in fame and fortune. Like his father, Tcherno Ibrahima was accorded the title "the *walí* of Ndama," a master of the sword and the inkpot.

The French, aware of his influence and prestige, wooed him with treaties of amity not only in Futa Jallon, but in Casamance as well.[46] His differences with Alfa Yahya, at that stage still a political ally of the French, led him to oppose the latter's attempt to extend his reach into the *walí's* territory. The French, though committed to the pact with Alfa Yahya, were prepared to vary that through tactful diplomacy. The administrator, M. Noirot, was sent on a mission of conciliation in May 1899, but found Tcherno Ibrahima in no such mood. The small French escort was forced to beat a hasty retreat after they came under severe attack. The French would abandon tact for toughness, and eventually, in May 1901, they took action: Tcherno Ibrahima, two of his sons (Modi Jaw and Modi Alimou) and his cousin (Modi Sori Himaya) were placed under arrest. They were taken to Conakry and held in remand. Eventually they were condemned to serve a term of imprisonment and exile to Gabon. However, the sentence was imposed in 1902, the year of Tcherno Ibrahima's death. Thus he, like Tcherno Aliou much later, died of natural causes before he could begin to serve his sentence.

Modi Jaw, also known as Tcherno Jaw, was the eldest son of Tcherno Ibrahima. After his return from Gabon, he resigned himself to a more pacific religious style and emigrated to Sedhiou, Casamance, where he established a religious center. He later moved to Boulam in the then Portuguese Guinea.[47]

Other sons of Tcherno Ibrahima continued in the same tradition, specializing in the Shádhilí practice and drawing in village congregations from the surrounding countryside. The streak of militancy now strongly emerging in rural Islam was reinforced by much of their activities. Even where individuals might not take part directly in militant activity, the tradition of revivalism—which gained currency in the string of *missidi*, or village congregations—sustained a critical awareness among devotees. Sori Bobo, a son of Tcherno Ibrahima, born about 1885, inherited the Shádhilí commission from his father. He worked actively in both Ndama and Kabou, where he presided over a flourishing tradition of Islamic learning and instruction. Two other sons, Amadou and Modi Alimou, also practiced later at Ndama and Kabou.[48]

A fifth son of Tcherno Ibrahima, Modi Yaya, was installed at Tabadian in the province of Damantan in Niani-Ouli. The sixth son, Modi Labbo, started out in Casamance before moving for a time to Guinea-Bisao (Kabou). He then returned to the village of Boussoura (Basra), where he carried on his professional activities as a cleric of Ndama, directing an important Qur'án school there. In his hands the Shádhiliyya strengthened the power of the religious network that knit together outlying centers.[49]

The more I have reflected on the matter of the religious network, the more convinced I have become of its central importance in the revitalization of the cluster of village congregations in Muslim Africa. The example of the Jakhanké is now much better known,[50] and in their case too the rural setting was indispensable to their centuries-old vocation. The network facilitates the transmission of resources, ideas, and personnel. It develops a keen sense of solidarity and thus helps to foster the idea of an experimental community among those who feel untainted by the corruption of the larger society. A moral bond galvanizes people in a new experience of common loyalty and obligation. The very unrepresentativeness of the network enhances both the value of membership and the feeling of moral separation—and superiority. Thus the reforming, or revolutionary, potential of the network is out of all proportion to its size. In the matter at hand, it is obvious that Ndama inspired the emergence of a strong network of village congregations in Futa Jallon and beyond, congregations that became relay points for the religious practice of the original center at Ndama. The dependent character of the congregations brought them into interaction with each other and with those outside. A richly endowed religious center, not needing to draw on resources beyond its borders, is hardly compatible with the dynamism characteristic of the *missidi* and its residents. Corporate endowment is scarcely conceivable outside the urban area, whereas the *missidi*, supported by the widow's mite, is preeminently a village structure.

The paths of Tcherno Aliou and Tcherno Ibrahima indirectly crossed at a certain point in their careers. Tcherno Diakaria, a student and disciple of Tcherno Ibrahima, was eventually drawn into the circle of Tcherno Aliou's movement. Born in about 1850, Tcherno Diakaria created a Shádhilí center in Binani in deliberate imitation of the monastic-style establishment at Ndama. Regarded as extremely withdrawn and self-possessed, he remained in active contact with the *walí* of Goumba. His significance lies in another direction. The habit of monastic withdrawal is obviously not at variance with religious militancy, and the *missidi*, under the Shádhilí *'ulamá*, such as Tcherno Aliou and Tcherno Diakaria, played a critical role in fomenting ideas of religious radicalism. Historians, thrown off the scent by the unassertive profile of rural retreat and residence, have consequently misappropriated the *missidi* in their explanatory scheme.

Nothing embodies the spirit and outlook of the *missidi* as eloquently as the *diaroré*, which at the same time expounds one aspect of the urban-rural theme. The *diaroré* was an ecstatic religious discipline established by Shádhilí *'ulamá* as an instrument of control. Marty observes how the *diaroré* prayer rites became a technical discipline in the hands of those of the Fulbé *tcherno* class who were members of the Shádhiliyya, going much beyond the simple *salát 'alá al-nabí*. It came to assume the marks of rites of separation, if we may use the categories of liminal theory discussed elsewhere.[51] It is obvious that the *diaroré* rites would appeal to disaffected peasants and manumitted slaves as marginal groups. The long arduous road to complete and final social integration would be foreshortened or even preempted, and a marginal people could acquire the distinction of a religious elite. The *diaroré* rites emphasized the transformation of individual consciousness through egalitarian participation in a common experience where social distinctions, class differences, and economic status ceased to exist, or to matter. But the *diaroré* not only created an egalitarian spiritual fellowship, it also heightened the awareness of initiates of the wider fellowship represented by other *missidi*, and at an advanced stage it organized the *missidi* into an articulated network of prayer and spiritual devotion. The historical experience of the marginality of slaves and a disinherited peasantry was replaced, through the *diaroré*, by the principle of universal adoption. The old identity, which had carried the stigma of oppression and inferiority, was exchanged for the bold assurance of the *missidi*.

The *diaroré* itself consisted of the loud incantation of a *dhikr* formula, uninterruptedly recited for several hours to help induce a state of spiritual intoxication. Marty gives one specific account: "A Muslim cleric of Tougué observes the *diaroré* all night. He skips going to bed and instead pronounces the *dhikr* a thousand times. From Thursday night to Friday he recites the *dhikr* ten thousand times, teaching it to his novices. However, although he starts out with that intention he may in fact suffer a fainting spell or lapse into convulsions by daybreak on Friday."[52] Of the organizational power of the *diaroré* Marty speaks with the conviction of an eyewitness as follows: "The *diaroré* enjoy an extraordinary vogue. People assemble on Thursday evening at the central mosque of the Missidi, coming from 20 to 30 kilometers away. There are also Tijánís who perform similar *diaroré* rites."[53]

The founding of the *diaroré* tradition is traced to the aforementioned Shádhilí scholar, 'Alí al-Súfí. But it was Tcherno Isma'íla, a Malinké scholar, who propagated the practice and established it on a popular basis c. 1850. However, it went through a brief slump until 1885, when Tcherno Isma'íla revived it, restoring it to its former status. Tcherno Mamadou Sharíf became head of the Diawia (from the Arabic *záwiya*) village congregation. His authority having expanded, he was able to regain possession of all the territory that had previously belonged to the Shádhiliyya and thus could reinstitute the observance of the *diaroré* rites on an organized basis. All Labé country was engulfed by the rites. From there the flame of devotion spread to Ndama, then under Tcherno Ibrahima, and then to Goumba, where Tcherno Aliou fanned it among his disciples.[54] The network was thus galvanized.

Confronted with the organizational strength of the *diaroré*, the French authorities reversed their earlier policy of toleration and decided to suppress the rites, leaving only the mother congregation at Diawia.[55] Even there, Tcherno Mamadou Sharíf came under strict surveillance, and he was reduced to pleading for greater recognition and subsisting on concessions grudgingly extracted. The whole point of the *diaroré* as a spiritual haven was thus undermined, and the great religious masters, accorded the title *walí*, reverted to the methods of the *sirruyanké* or the predatory ways of the old Almamate. As Marty observed, much of the efforts of the new religious masters proceeded under a cloak of piety; all was for personal gain.[56] The Hubbu movement, which had overlapped considerably with the revived fortunes of the Shádhiliyya, had met a harsh fate by this time, but its history has a necessary connection to the region's endemic turbulence.

The Hubbu Movement

Deriving its name from an Arabic phrase concerning the primacy of the Prophet for religious life and practice, the Hubbu movement was led by the charismatic

Fula scholar, Mamadou Juhe, and his son, Abal. Its followers included persons of free caste and a large number of ex-slaves who had rebelled against their masters, converted to Islam, and joined in denouncing the form of religion professed by the old aristocracy of Karamokho Alfa's heritage. Mamadou Juhe and Abal represented a new class of Muslims distinguished by learning but untainted by the failure of the older *'ulamá*. The Hubbubé raised the standard of an uncompromising Islam and rallied in a campaign of military confrontation. Many who joined the movement, and certainly those who led it, were fired by religious ideals: on the one hand, scandalized by the opportunism of their co-religionists and on the other, stimulated into action by the appeals of the disenchanted. Beyond these religious aspects, the Hubbubé comprised social elements whose grievances were more immediately economic, although it would be facile to construe religion here as merely a functional factor. We have the following description of the social composition of the Hubbubé: "The Hubbu movement mobilized and attracted to the periphery of Futa Jallon the oppressed, the jungle Fulbé, that is, Fulbé of inferior status and extraction who were liable to taxation and to forced labor without mitigation, descendants of pastoral Fulbé recently converted to Islam, certain unassimilated Jallonke, and thousands of slaves concentrated in the *rimá'ibé* (slave camps)."[57]

Dr. Edward Blyden, (1832–1912), the black patriot who made the study of African Muslims a subject of special interest, visited Futa Jallon in 1872 where he came upon the Hubbu movement. He recognized the economic ferment in the movement, but saw that it was with the ideological appeal of Islam. Thus, though economic issues were equally salient, religion provided the Hubbubé with an explicit identity and a galvanizing ideology:

> The Hoobos are renegade Fulbé in revolt against the king of Timbo. Twenty years ago, on account of the exactions imposed by the Almamy Umaru, they rose in revolt and with their families removed themselves to come and settle the grazing lands between Futa Jallon and Solima country. They are called Hoobos or Hubus because following their departure from their homes they were chanting in chorus a verse from the Coran in which the word Hubu appeared twice. It says this: 'Nihibu (Nuhibbu) Rusul (Rasúl) Alláh Huban (Hubban) Wahídan,' which means those who love the Envoy of God (without compromise).[58]

Though the verse as quoted does not occur in the Qur'án *in stricto senso*, the notion of uncompromising adherence to the divine command does appear in one verse (ii:160). In any event, Blyden's account makes clear that both economic and religious factors significantly molded the character of the Hubbu revolt. It also indicates that the Almamate was faced with an ever deepening economic crisis, of which the root cause was unquestionably the issue of slaves. The contraction of sources of slavery and the rapid disappearance of traditional trading outlets brought the local *mawubé* face to face with an outraged section of the citizenry. Islam constituted the only accessible ideology to this disaffected and overburdened class of people, and it was accordingly adopted by first stripping it of compromising associations and stiffening it with a stern call to reform. Against the suffering being endured at the hands of the Timbo rulers, the Hubbu leaders defiantly raised the exclusive demands of religion, and by that standard the existing aristocracy was censured as unfit to rule and command. It was this religious mood that *al-Hájj* 'Umar al-Fútí (d. 1864) was to exploit to great effect in the Tijániyya movement. Thus, if people rebelled because of intolerable social and economic conditions, they were no less agitated by the offenses against the religious prescriptions. Religious commitment became the motive force by which social and economic grievances were expressed and canalized.

In the end Juhe's son, Abal, led a community of discontents to the village of Boketo in the rural country southeast of Timbo. There the Hubbubé, repudiating the authority of the Almamate, set up a religious republic, militant if not triumphant. In it slavery was abolished and a call issued to former slaves to repudiate their masters and emigrate to Boketo, where the egalitarian principles being invoked would eliminate their servile status and thus lead to the moral preeminence of that agrarian community. In this way Boketo would conform to the liminal description of Victor Turner,[59] particularly to the evaluation of that material offered by Humphrey Fisher.[60] Yet Boketo had a fatal defect, for in isolation from the numerous Shádhilí *missidi* where the *diaroré* rites kept alive a sense of network support, it became an extremely marginal community. As such it failed to compensate for its relatively small size by being linked with the *missidi* network and benefiting from its characteristic system of mutual aid. Instead it attempted to redress political and economic grievances and in the process excited the fury of local rulers without gaining the support of rank and file religious groups. The Hubbubé began to prey on trade caravans and to live by loot and plunder. Dr. Blyden recounts the manner of their eventual demise thus: "The Hooboos, those renegade Foulahs, who for thirty years have been a terror to caravans passing through the districts which they infested, have been scattered by the military energy of Samudu, a Mandingo chieftain from the Konia country, due east of Liberia. Abal, the chief of the Hooboos, has been captured and banished to a distant region."[61]

Without the advantage of the network system, the Hubbubé became vulnerable refugees, weakened by the absence of popular support and by logistic dispersal and pursued by the forces of the land. Decaying from within, they were eventually defeated on the path of escape by Samori Turé.

Although the Shádhiliyya escaped this dramatic fate, in time its power faded as well, in its case, at the hands of the French who outlawed the *diaroré* rites and isolated Diawia. Thus was destroyed the network character of the Shádhiliyya. To all intents and purposes the order was emasculated as a rural force and with it any idea of rural Islam as incubator of the radical tradition in religion. At this stage a historic shift occurred: The decolonizing movement of the mid-twentieth century became the successor to this radical tradition, and that movement was an urban phenomenon, in part because of the disproportionate concentration of imperial resources there and in part because the rural profile of militancy had been over-taken and tamed, thanks to the railroad, harbinger of the new world order.

The demise of the Hubbubé precipitated wide-ranging repercussions in rural Islam. Tcherno Aliou, for example, sought new support among the Susu popula-tion on the peripheries of Futa Jallon. After the suppression of the Hubbubé in the 1880s, the Shádhilí *'ulamá* and their *missidi* were left as the last resort for the disenchanted. In the final analysis the Hubbu fate would be reserved for the *mis-sidi* network, too. But not until 1912 did Shádhilism face that reckoning, and Tcherno Aliou was the last flare before the final clamp-down. We need not, there-fore, take at face value the Mahdist claims imputed to him in order to appreciate his significance as a representative symbol of his age, both in its past and poten-tial. The mood of the times was set on edge from the inciting nature of the claims and counterclaims of local clerics and from French colonial provocativeness, pro-ducing rising expectations for a happy, if illusory, consummation. The lofty and exaggerated claims associated with the *walí* reflect, if not the whole truth, then at least the extraordinary nature of the crisis in which indigenous structures and in-stitutions were engulfed.

Environment and Religious Militancy: A Postscript

I have stressed the rural dimension as a congenial environment for cultivating re-ligious militancy. The wider methodological implications of this inclination for areas outside Africa need not concern us here. However, something should be said about the general question of Islamic militancy in terms of the urban-rural con-figuration. Several comments are offered by Islamic writers on the subject. Some of the most systematic remarks are those of Ibn Khaldún (1332–1406).

In his *al-Muqaddimah*, Ibn Khaldún contends that urban conditions are injuri-ous to the cultivation of courage and the moral life. He stresses the blunting effect of the urban environment on the critical powers of religion. According to him, re-ligion is a noble calling whose ends are opposed to those of commerce and urban living. The person who takes up religion would stand in critical judgment over the one committed to commercial and urban values:

> Because the things [religious officials] have to offer are so noble, they feel superior to the people and are proud of themselves. Therefore, they are not obsequious to per-sons of rank, in order to obtain something to improve their sustenance. In fact, they would not have time for that. They are occupied with those noble things they have to offer and which tax both the mind and the body. Indeed the noble character of the things they have to offer does not permit them to prostitute themselves openly. They would not do such a thing. As a consequence, they do not, as a rule, become very wealthy.[62]

As opposed to the single-minded and elevated nature of the religious vocation, Ibn Khaldún points to the slippery ways of commerce: "We have already stated that traders must buy and sell and seek profits. This necessitates flattery, and evasiveness, litigation and disputation, all of which are characteristic of this profession. And these qualities lead to a decrease and weakening in virtue and manliness."[63]

This occupational classification has a corresponding justification in environmental factors. Town life, Ibn Khaldún avers, is suited to the pursuit of commerce in the same way that the countryside is adapted to the special concerns of religion. With great coherence and the force of an original mind, Ibn Khaldún describes the social conditions pertaining to the urban-rural matrix and the historical consequences of events there:

> *Countrymen are morally superior to townsmen.* This is because the soul is, by its nature, prepared to receive any impressions of good or evil that may be stamped upon it. . . . Now the townsmen are so immersed in luxury, pleasure-seeking and worldliness, and so accustomed to indulge in their desires, that their souls are smeared with vice and stray far from the path of virtue. Countrymen, though also worldly-minded, are forced to confine themselves to bare necessities; they do not seek to indulge their desire for luxury and pleasures. Their habits and actions are relatively simple, hence they are less subject than townsmen to reproach on the grounds of vice and evil-doing.[64]

Thus it is, according to Ibn Khaldún's view, that we may treat virtue and the moral life as specifically religious concerns and seek their best expression in rural simplicity. We should also perceive the contrast to this rural morality in the forces of corruption and decadence engendered by life in the urban environment. In Ibn Khaldún's view, then, the "sacred" potential of religion is better developed in one set of circumstances than in another, and "secular" priorities are not necessarily conducive to religious integrity. It is, of course, a wholly different matter what Ibn Khaldún thinks might create one set of circumstances rather than another, a question I shall examine in Chapter 9. However, on the issue of fundamental moral motivation, Ibn Khaldún is convinced religion is the key, and rural or simple living conditions its most hospitable crucible.

This dichotomy is also important, in Ibn Khaldún's view, for understanding the nature of militancy, for that too is a consequence of rural, or at any rate nonurban, living conditions. He says that townspeople are in the habit of relinquishing the task of self-defense to their rulers and a professional military class. In the course of time they lapse into habitual lethargy,

> accustomed, like women and children, to look to others for protection; and with time this habit of dependence becomes a second nature. Countrymen and nomads, on the other hand, live a more isolated life, far from large towns and garrisons, undefended by walls or defenses. Hence they look for protection to themselves alone, not trusting others. Always armed and watchful . . . they are ever on the lookout for any sign of danger . . . being full of confidence in their own courage and power. For courage has become one of their deepest qualities and audacity a second nature to them, emerging whenever occasion calls.[65]

Ibn Khaldún's observations are useful in the effort to grasp the nature of the internal contradictions in Islam in Futa Jallon. Once his material is supplemented with the network character of the *missidi,* we have an explanation for the power and resilience of rural Islam before the colonial subjugation. To augment Ibn Khaldún in this way would be in keeping with his own analytic procedure, although, of course, it would expand that procedure in a fresh direction. Yet the force of his original observations remains undiminished. Environment, as he rightly noted, has played a critical role in molding the expression of religion.

The reference to nomads opens up the important issue of mobility (*safar*). Two levels of analysis may be indicated. First, Fulbé nomads (*wodabé*), Somali herdsmen, the Tuareg, the Tajakant and the Sanhája Berbers, Bedouin groups, and the warlike Mongols all had in common a migratory way of life. Their effects on settled populations and corresponding political structures have been very real, and sometimes dramatic. The traditional explanation that traces the impact of Saharan religious groups on Black Africa to the racial dialectic should now be revised to take more explicit account of the militant tendencies of nomadic groups, whether they be Saharan *awlád* or Fulbé groups. For example, 'Abdalláh dan Fodio castigates the world of traders as a source of mischief and corruption.[66] This recommendation is not to deny that there was ethnic tension in African Islamic militancy but merely to state that militancy had as one of its roots the radical, status-quo upsetting ethos of mobile populations. Second, religious specialists, adopting a residential center, have often availed themselves of the option of defiant mobility to strengthen the religious vocation. In that way, the sedentary religious life is reinvigorated with periodic journeys attracting personnel, goods, materials, and ideas that renew and revitalize the vocation. The network, in the way we have expounded it, exists to provide this option and to support those involved in it. The economically weak and dependent centers of the *missidi* were able in this way to foster a strong sense of professional solidarity, and their impact, especially through the *diaroré* rites, produced the expansion of the power and authority of the Shádhiliyya and the *awliyá*.

In religious circles the practice of retreat (*khalwa*) and the theme of *safar* share a common history and a common purpose, which is to revitalize the religious spirit and to set it in critical contrast to the alleged natural corruption of settled living. One popular religious manual, *al-'Awárif al-Ma'árif* ("The Bounties of Divine Knowledge"), composed in the thirteenth century by Shaykh Shiháb al-Dín al-Suhrawardí, a Qádirí *muqaddam* himself, brings together mobility and religious retreat in order to stress the reform capacity of spiritual discipline. The *'Awárif* assimilates travel into a spiritual exercise and subsumes it under the practice of *khalwa,* or that form that transposes *safar* into a symbolic retreat:

> The being separated from one's native land, from friends and familiar things, and the exercising of patience in calamities cause lust and nature to rest from pursuing their way; and take up from hearts the effect of hardness. In subduing lusts, the effect of *safar* is not less than the effect of *nawáfil* (supererogatory devotions), fasting and praying. On dead skins, by tanning, the effects of purity, of softness, and of delicacy of texture appear; even so, by the tanning of *safar,* and by the departure of natural

corruption and innate roughness, appear the purifying softness of devotion and change from obstinacy to faith.[67]

Two concluding notes: One is how the *hajj*, the Muslim pilgrimage, the most characteristic form of religious mobility in Islam and a most potent canonical source of *barakah*, has restored townspeople to some of the advantages that naturally devolve on those living in the countryside. Urban pilgrims are no less blessed than their rural co-religionists, and their example would thus even the balance between urban religious practice and the otherwise purist exclusiveness of rural saints. The pilgrimage regime as such imposes disciplines of self-denial, spiritual concentration, and the exposure to frontiers beyond the land of familiarity and habit, thus raising morale. Accordingly, the *hajj* reforms personal life and creates a sense of religious agency. The revered pilgrim, then, returns with a self-assumed mandate to change and rejuvenate religious practice. Yet the majority of such urban pilgrims may opt to settle back into normal accommodation, leaving the countryside as the bearer of an unbroken, cumulative reform legacy. Certainly one of the implications of Ibn Khaldún's contentions is to call us to a fresh appraisal of the significance of the urban-rural environmental configuration for religious practice. It would be consistent with this configuration to predict that the *hajj*, with its *barakah*-charged power, would affect rural sensibilities in a more militant direction than the corresponding urban situation, which leaves Ibn Khaldún's theory with enhanced significance.

The second note takes us back to Tcherno Aliou as the *walí* of Goumba and to his confrontation with the French in territory he once controlled. His public trial was intended to serve a public lesson that the old moral order had failed abysmally, not by the will of God but by the superior might of the French. In that light the French saw popular notions of *barakah* as a major obstacle in the drive to humble Tcherno Aliou, whose stature as preeminent moral broker implied illegitimacy for colonial authority. The colonial obsession with an otherwise feeble Tcherno Aliou makes sense especially for its spiritual and psychological significance. Colonialism was in search of a metaphysic of legitimacy, of imperial ascendancy as a moral construct, with the new colonial masters as officer *walís* entitled to the moral and social prerogatives of *barakah*. The treaties of capitulation imposed on local rulers were for that reason composed in the sacred Arabic, to invoke the implicit pedigree of the religious *fatwa* and to insinuate its sanction. Written authority has unassailable reputation in religious circles, so that it was politically convenient to construct the treaties by appealing to the *barakah*-charged medium of Arabic. The *madrasah* educational system that the authorities promulgated in hinterland districts was meant to overtake the Qur'án school as the dispenser of the efficacious *barakah* of the master of the world, and to resonate as such with the subject races reared in the habit. The colonial order would be morally better for being perceived as an exalted calling, as a struggle of the forces of progress and enlightenment against those of disorder, backwardness, and superstition, sentiments that find their classic expression in Muslim *jihád*, which in fact was what colonialism aspired to be. In the end, colonialism as a *mission civilisatrice* felt compelled to pursue its mandate with the passion of absolute truth and moral destiny, and that passion, fed with the doctrine that might is right, lit a fire in which any rival claim for truth had to be consumed. Consequently, by the fact of his spiritual proximity to the idiom of colonial ascendancy and by his symbolic defiance of it, Tcherno Aliou came to stand in the direct path of that fire. In pursuing him to his rural base, the French intended to demonstrate the range of their metropolitan reach but showed instead that political coercion had limited moral appeal with a Muslim population conditioned by religious habit and practice. Thus, not surprisingly, the power discourse of colonial hegemony that was constructed from unrespected local categories would, in the fashion of historical reversal, in time be subverted by them.

5

Saints, Virtue, and Society in Muslim Africa: The History of a Theme

I want in this chapter to return to the subject of saints but to do so in a thematic way. Clearly the personality of Tcherno Aliou, described in the preceding chapter, belongs equally here, but the theme merits repeating in the context of a phenomenological examination of saints and saintly virtue in Muslim Africa. Thus, beyond the historical issue of the status and fate of particular saints and saint-types there lies the important domain of saints as a religious phenomenon, and it would be useful to explore further in what ways sainthood, for example, represented the norms and values of the old world order. Saints are the eloquent epitome of their age, uniquely equipped to stand with their people as they face a new dispensation.

To begin with the Western view, in 1893, André Gide, the celebrated French writer, visited Africa, desirous of resolving certain Epicurean conflicts of the flesh while also obtaining the serenity of spirit with which virtue is prone to visit on her children. He testified, or perhaps we should say, he was anguished that: "The demands of my flesh did not know how to dispense with the consent of my spirit. . . . I saw at last that this discordant dualism might resolve itself into harmony. At once it became clear to me that this harmony should be my supreme aim. When in October '93 I embarked for Africa, it was . . . towards this golden fleece that my drive precipitated itself."[1]

Gide's carnal conflicts would strain the resources of most religions, but if any community of moral sensitivity could meet his needs, perhaps that would, indeed, be Muslim Africa, whose saints are so adept at mollifying the flesh without at the same time foregoing the spirit's consolation. In Muslim Africa, Gide's instinctive wish to transcend the conflict between flesh and spirit could be greeted as sound, even if the peculiar fierceness and introspective individualism with which he addressed it would continue to carry its indelible Western imprint. His colorful excursions into the fleshpots of Morocco were not at bottom incommensurate with the rather earthy understanding of virtue prevailing in Muslim Africa. There we do not have the arid, sterile conception of virtue with its superhuman feats of denying the flesh, and releasing thereby all the vital energy compressed in the libidinal urge, only to dissipate it without echo in a vacuum. Thus is the "secular" dissolved to release the "sacred" as spirit without form, as pleasure without concept.

Saints in Society

In Muslim Africa, by contrast, the saint is distinguished by strong social ties rather than by retreat into the contemplative life. The cultivation of virtue is in fact the cultivation of society, of the company of persons. The goal of the saintly life can be said to be the regard and devotion of the community, not the accumulation of charismatic power in the individual, as I shall attempt to show in later parts of this chapter. The saint thus comes to embody the spirit of society—its scarcity and plenitude, its torment and triumphs, its egalitarianism and privilege, its materialism and spirituality, its esteem for tradition and disposition toward innovation, and, in one example we shall consider, its tendency toward messianic agitation and its need for prudent accommodation. The saints of Muslim Africa may combine extremes and even espouse extremism, but they do so without forsaking the world.

Saintly virtue rests on this paradox of apparent spiritual extremism tied to a wisdom about what the world demands. The saint is at home in the confines of everyday routine, showing forth virtue by being unburdened by the world. If a saint gives up the material comforts of home, it may be only to seek similar conditions in unfamiliar surroundings. Thus material life is not disdained; rather, it is elevated to a higher plane. The body is not despised; rather, its gratification now earns meritorious favor as the saint's attention to the needs of the body demonstrates his virtue. The extreme of self-denial *(zuhd)* evokes its fulfillment in the social eminence *(jáh)* and worldly acclaim that success would bring.

I shall begin this chapter with a consideration of the scriptural sources concerning sainthood in Islam and move from there to a study of sequential expressions of saintliness that emerged in North and West Africa as Islam expanded across the continent. In doing so I will distinguish, as Muslims do, between "saintship" *(wiláyah)* and "sainthood" *(waláyah)*. The former concerns the organization and expression of saintly power, whereas the latter relates to the personality of the saint and the dynamics of saintly power. "Saintship" may thus be bequeathed and perpetuated in an organized fashion, whereas "sainthood" has to be acquired by individuals. "Sainthood" is personal charisma, whereas "saintship" is institutional charisma; though one may distinguish between the two, they are usually found in patterns of interplay. I shall also draw special attention to the Islamic concept of *barakah* ("favor," "grace," "virtue") and its transmutation into indigenous social categories. Needless to say, the confines of space will dictate that only a few select items can be chosen to indicate what is typical and distinctive about saintly virtue as it charts a course from the eleventh to the twentieth century in Muslim Africa and from the northern rim of the continent down its western coast.

Scriptural Foundations of Sainthood

The common Arabic word for saint is *walí*, strictly speaking a "friend" or "patron." It occurs numerous times in the Qur'án with this meaning, often with God being the "friend" or "patron."[2] The Qur'án's major stress is on God as the only *walí* worthy of trust and dependence *(tawakkul)*,[3] but a special place also is reserved for those whom God regards as his friends *(awliyá)*.[4] A further step is taken when a forensic meaning is applied to the term and human patrons are given a status in contract law such that they may act as deputies for their clients.[5]

Given this range, there is some Qur'ánic justification for the claim made by and about many of the saints of Islam that God may enter into a relationship of special intimacy with his creatures, so that they hold the status of "friendship" or "nearness in favor" to God. They are close to him: "near ones" *(al-muqarrabún)*, who will receive the superlative reward of Paradise.[6] This word is from the same root (q, r, b) as the standard terms for a relative or kin *(qurbá)*. Making up for the abolition of natural kinship in Islam,[7] the Qur'án assures believers that God himself will provide for them a next-of-kin, and the word used is the same as that for nearness.[8] Perhaps the most striking image of God's closeness to human beings occurs in the trenchant verse:

> We indeed created man, and We know
> what his soul whispers within him,
> and We are nearer to him (agrabu ilyahi) *than the*
> jugular vein.[9]

In Súfí circles and similar religious contexts, "nearness to God" has come to stand for a life marked by prayer and supererogatory acts of devotion. Consequently, the "saint" is one who leads a life of religious devotion, keeping close to God in prayer, praise, and supplication, and to the people in various acts of mediation and intercession. The "saint" becomes manifest to people after receiving the inner assurance of divine "friendship," although often the public manifestation of sainthood precedes final confirmation of the inner call.

The Holy and the Sacred

Let me give a word or two on more general notions of the holy and sacred in African traditional religions. African notions of the holy and sacred are infused by a sense of danger and avoidance. The sacred contaminates, and it renders persons vulnerable to invasion by spirit forces, a contamination that can spread from contact. The Biblical rule that those who see God shall die (Judges 13:22; Exodus 33:20) finds resonance in numerous African traditions in which elaborate rituals of decontamination and desacralization are staged to nullify the effects of the spirit's encounter with individuals. These rituals of desacralization may pose a paradox in the sense that the spirit is chased off in action that appeals to the spirit and thus draws it into our affairs at the same moment that it is being kept at arm's length. Whatever the case, in these traditions, "nearness to God" is a calamity that individuals must take care to avert; hence the use of prophylactic rituals to fend off the spirit. It becomes an extremely important matter that we know the actions that would provoke the spirit to descend into our midst, and important, too, that we recognize the effects in affliction that the spirit's intervention produces. The many examples in the Bible in which, for example, a dream or vision puzzles, or where an epidemic, personal misfortune, or strange illness threatens, are things that portend the unwelcome attention of the spirit. Thus the prophet as novice is reluctant, the seer fainthearted, and the preacher hesitant about being invited into the spirit's company and presence.

Pre-Islamic Africa exhibits all these tendencies and prevarications, and in ritual seances the oracles will employ diversionary and evasive techniques to send the spirits off the scent. The holy man, the holy woman, is feared and appropriately appeased and assuaged. In any case holiness is a potent force and must be kept on the outer margins of everyday life and concerns. The shrine is located outside the village, perhaps best in the bush, and its most efficacious rites are nocturnal, or otherwise secret. This gives religion a shadowy, contagious reputation and encourages people to devise techniques of control and manipulation to deal from a protective position with life's problems. Good and evil are not separate entities, or past and future distinct chronological spheres. Rather, good in religion consists in averting from individuals the dangerous attention of God, whereas in matters related to community life and collective solidarity the rule is reversed and the attention of the spirit is safely invoked and marked for tribal security. Evil comes when the rituals fail or are neglected and individuals exposed to the spirit's attention. Misfortune indicates past transgression, and infringement of established rules would invite future retribution.

The introduction of Islam, as explained in earlier parts of this book, challenges such religious attitudes, and in the matter of the holy and sacred, Muslims specifically contribute by bringing the entire traditional African landscape into Islam's juridical scope and ruling with the Qur'án. Such change may be gradual over a period of time, it may be subtle in terms of hidden connections with preexisting phenomena, it may be cultural with the instrumental use of Arabic phrases and sartorial garb, or it may even be structural in fixing the center of activity in the Islamic calendar and in the mosque or in officials connected with the mosque. In the end, however, where these patterns, or some of them, converge, there would occur a decisive, fundamental change. The point at which Islam first encounters local populations would be observably different from the point at which these populations come out, and that difference defines conversion. It demonstrates one dimension of the missionary role of Muslim religious agents, a role in which prevalent notions about spirit forces and the ambition for the preservation of life and whole estate of man are developed with Islam offering the answer. In this regard, since Muslim notions of the saint and sanctity are influenced by ideas of merit and reward at the hands of the elect, then ordinary people are offered through the mediation of this class of religious specialists protection from unseen spirit forces. Holy men and holy women thus have their social function defined for them as brokers of popular religion.

The Roots of Saintship in North African Islam

Contrary to the standard depiction of many Christian saints, saintly virtue in Muslim Africa was typically cultivated with a militant, or, at any rate, worldly, end in view rather than primarily for the sake of solitary retreat. From the military redoubts of Northwest Africa men emerged carrying in their hearts disdain for the non-Muslim world and in their hands the sword to overcome it. Ascetic practice *(zuhd)* developed alongside the study of law *(fiqh)*, and together they helped sharpen the instruments of armed struggle *(jihád)*. The religious recluse would typically occupy his time with the study of juridical sources, seeking in the process to strip local practice of historical and circumstantial accretions and refine it to a purer Islam. Religious leaders thus came naturally to look upon worldly means as a legitimate instrument for their end. One modern authority observes in this regard that whereas elsewhere in the Muslim world the ascetics *(zuhhád)*, who abandoned all worldly contact, were pitted against the jurists *(fuqahá)*, who were immersed in worldly affairs, in North Africa they made common cause, and many religious figures in fact combined the two functions.

> In Ifriqiya, *fuqahá* became *zuhhád* without ceasing the study of *fiqh*, or cutting off relations with the *fuqahá* who demonstrated no interest in asceticism. As *zuhhád*, however, they did not become detached from the world, and they remained in constant communication with the people. They were guardians of the common people's interests, and challenged the rulers to show regard for these considerations. They were admired by the people for their piety, devotion, and independence with respect to rulers. They were not marginal to the mainstream of Islam in Ifriqiya, but rather its core. They were the true leaders of the people.[10]

Through this synthesis of jurisprudence and asceticism the *jihád* tradition was fomented; holy personages carried it into the citadels of power. Thus in the numerous eruptions of reform and renewal the saintly ideal—that is, the exemplary force of the holy and learned figure—was the ideological trigger and the guide for action. The military application of the doctrine of struggle *(jihád)* had its religious counterpart in the purification and discipline of the flesh *(nafs)*, a combination that allowed the ascetic *(záhid)* to assume leadership of affairs. Ascetic spirituality thus combined the prestige of learning and the power of religion to lay claim to political power.

One such religious figure, 'Abd Alláh ibn Yasín (d. 1059), in 1040 launched the religious revolution in North Africa that was to lead to the establishment of the Almoravid Empire. Ibn Yasín was a commanding, ascetic figure, and the sources describe how he was rewarded with miracles as God's recognition of his saintly stature. Thus the seal of *barakah,* of efficacious virtue, came to be attached to his person, and after his death he became a source of blessings for people who came to his tomb seeking rescue from various pains and obstacles in ordinary life. The Arab chronicler, al-Bakrí, writing in 1068, recounts how a cult grew up around the tomb of Ibn Yasín. "On his tomb stands today a mausoleum, which is well-frequented, and a hospice *(rábita)* always full of people. . . . Even now a group of them (the Almoravids) would choose to lead them in prayer only a man who prayed behind 'Abd Alláh, even though a more meritorious and more pious person, who had never prayed under the guidance of 'Abd Alláh, was among them."[11]

Al-Bakrí reserves undisguised scorn for Ibn Yasín and his followers, scrutinizing the man's heritage with the unsparing eye of a rigorist. The saintly heritage *(wiláyah)* in Islam as a synthesis of *zuhd* and *fiqh,* of renunciation and the code, is held by scholars of orthodoxy *('ulamá)* to be in excess of accepted guidance, and al-Bakrí represents their position. Yet the saints *(awliyá)* have often been the real architects of the changes that the *'ulamá* idealized in doctrine, thus giving practical expression to the aims of the code. A similar irony characterizes the Almoravid conquest of Spain (Andalusia), where the ascetic ideals of desert life triumphed over the cultured tastes of urban living. The rewards of saintship—victory in God's campaigns—were eloquent vindication of the superiority of virtue, and it is a bold individual who would say which made which: the saints or the rewards.

The legatees of the Almoravids were less equal to the challenge of living in the world and against it at the same time than the Almoravids had been. These were the Almohads, whose initial leader, Ibn Tumart (d. 1130), claimed the title of Mahdí, meaning Messiah, in 1127. He sought to make a firm distinction between *fiqh* and *zuhd,* between religious Thomism and freewheeling experimentalism—a Thomism that stressed the binding authority of received tradition and an experimentalism that shifted the locus of authority to the individual and his cultivated insights, leading him to claim direct access to truth. In that cleavage he asserted his own towering authority, burdened by few scruples and buoyed by the single idea of a victorious monotheism. Even in this stern, uncompromising opponent of Ibn Yasín, then, worldly reward was understood to be the natural appurtenance of religious virtue.[12]

The Almoravid movement and its Almohad reaction, feeding on earlier forms of religious activity, combined to discharge an enduring element of devotion to jurisprudential sources *(usúl al-fiqh)* into the stream of religious life and practice, and from that source Súdání Muslims of sub-Saharan Africa imbibed copiously. By that channel *fiqh* and *zuhd* arrived in sub-Saharan Africa. Both Marty and Trimingham are correct in saying that a full-blown cult of saints as practiced in

North Africa—centered around the tombs of the holy—did not take root in Black Africa, but other kinds of saint veneration took its place. Classical Islam accommodated itself to local practice, sometimes to the extent of becoming thoroughly mixed in it, as seen in its involvement in charms, amulets, talismans, and the whole company of divinatory practice, particularly in oneirology.[13] Muslim classical sources on amulets and charms became overlaid with indigenous associations: For example, amulets, inhabited by domestic spirits, were tangible vessels of *barakah* as well as channels of orthodox charisma. However, Islamic law had an inhibiting, regulatory effect on local expression, for Máliki law, the predominant code in Muslim Africa, emphasizes exoteric *(záhirí)* authority against esoteric *(bátiní)* understanding. Yet it is fair to say that, for all their public declarations in support of legal sobriety, religious leaders were not prevented by an equally calculated prudence from yielding to the popular demand for *barakah*, that is, for the worldly uses of religion and for saints as living assurances of *barakah*.

Cenobitic Overtures in West African Islam

The Almohad Empire eventually collapsed, in Spain first (1235) and then in North Africa (1269), although Hafsid rule in Tunisia continued the Almohad line. The religio-political unity of North Africa virtually ceased after the Almohads; the only carryover was the tradition of saintship, which continued unabated. The Súfí orders, inspired by Qádirí devotional materials and by the juristic sources in *fiqh* and *tafsír* (exegesis), grew in power and influence. The Qádirí order, founded after the twelfth-century scholar and mystic 'Abd al Qádir al-Jílání, spread widely in many parts of the Muslim world, spawning a number of smaller orders that developed their own autonomous rules. One such order was the Shádilíyáh, founded after Abú'l-Hasan al-Shádhilí (1196–1258), although it was his disciple, Ibn 'Átá Alláh (c. 1250–c. 1310), who established and popularized the order in the Maghrib. It had its base in Fez, and in the eighteenth century it was taken from there to sub-Saharan Africa by a returning student.

Our knowledge of the Shádilíyáh in West Africa has hitherto been extremely fragmentary. Bits and pieces of information, picked up from a disparate spread of sources, are strung together in many accounts without a central organizing idea. The French administrator and scholar, Paul Marty, who published a number of pioneering studies from 1913 onward, drew attention to the presence of the order in French Guinea in a work published in 1921, but he was quick to belittle its religious influence while somewhat inconsistently exaggerating its political threat. The picture he paints is of an order that was haphazardly strewn through hinterland villages, alternately preying on simple folk and being exploited by unscrupulous religious masters. Marty's commitment to the position that the cult of saints, so pervasive in North African Islam, was entirely unknown in Muslim West Africa came to determine his rather impatient handling of the material. Confronted with undeniable evidence of both the organizational and devotional strength of the Shádilíyáh, Marty stumbled after a conspiratorial menace in order to avoid recognizing its genuine religious force. Scholars who have followed him have been equally misled. For example, J. Spencer Trimingham, well known for his pioneering works on African Islam and much else, picked up Marty's view and elaborated it. When he had to deal with the widespread importance of *barakah* among the Shádilíyáh, Trimingham dismissed it as thinly disguised magic and thus different, in his view, from its North African counterpart.[14] This view of the matter led to a very hazy picture of saint veneration in sub-Saharan Islam and suggested that the Súfí orders played little enduring role there.

The truth is quite otherwise. Under Súfí stimulus saintly virtue has been cultivated in a wide variety of situations in Muslim West Africa: in battle, in study, and in politics, as well as in marshaling students and disciples and in providing remedies for illness to the general public. The French scholar Vincent Monteil portrays a typical instance as follows:

> A marabout *(walí)*—or perhaps even a mystic—comes to settle in some part of town; as an eremite, his *barakah* renders him fame. He becomes indispensable to the population: he has charge of rain, of harvests, of troops, and of sickness. He intervenes in disputes. He is protector of the weak and the oppressed. He instructs children in the rudiments of the faith. He takes himself a wife from among the leading families, and becomes a *shaykh* or *muqaddam* (religious leader). The people then build him a *záwiyah* (religious center).[15]

Such patterns characterized the spread of a number of Súfí orders—the Qádiriyáh, the Tijániyáh, the Mourides, the Hamalliyah, and the Shádilíyáh. Let us take the last, a little-known order, as an example of how saintly virtue had its impact on Islam below the Sahara.[16]

The man responsible for introducing the Shádilíyáh to West Africa was ʻAlí al-Súfí, described in the sources as "the apostle of Shádhilism" in his part of Africa. He received the *wird*, the office of initiation, from a Moroccan spiritual director *(murshid)* in Fez and subsequently brought it to the plateau area of Futa Jallon in Guinea in the eighteenth century. The litanies he bequeathed to his flock emphasized attachment to Fez as his spiritual birthplace, and his disciples went on to give it a veneration second in importance only to Mecca and Medina. A disciple of ʻAlí al-Súfí, Modi Sellou (1760–1813), the political head *(alfa)* of the district of Labé in Futa Jallon, expanded Shádhilism in Labé.

Tcherno Ismaʻíla, a student of ʻAlí al-Súfí, made the order a political success. At first he concentrated on broadening and deepening the spiritual resources of the movement, creating a religious center he called Diawia *(záwiya)*. Its focal point was the *missidi*, the word for "mosque" in the Fula language. The *missidi* was then replicated in numerous adjacent communities, resulting in a network of ideologically related centers. Diawia, in Labé, became the prototype, and from there sympathizers ranged far and wide.

The central organizing principle of the Shádilíyáh *missidi* was the *diaroré* prayer ritual. Tcherno[17] ʻIsmaʼíla developed it as a complex technical exercise directed to both social and religious renewal. Through the discipline of retreat and renunciation, the *'ulamá* gave themselves up to the intoxicating fervor of the *diaroré,* sharing this ritual with a motley crowd of social outcasts, ex-slaves, and economic insolvents. Thus the *missidi* offered a spiritual haven of social relief just as the *diaroré* offered mystical elevation. Through these two, the initiate was adopted into a religious community and invested with a new status. Thus rehabilitated, he upheld the authority of the Shádhilí *'ulamá* in their contest with the older political and religious elite. This bolstered the authority of the masters of *diaroré* while conferring on the disciple a sense of chosenness.

The *diaroré* consisted of the loud incantation of a *dhikr* formula—a cycle of litany "remembering" God in gratitude and expressing his praise—that was recited for several hours without interruption to help induce a state of spiritual intoxication. The more advanced *'ulamá* spent whole nights in *diaroré* retreat and initiated novices in that setting.

Under the impact of such prayer the *missidi* became a model community—not exactly the *communitas* of Victor Turner, but still an egalitarian fellowship of religious radicalism.[18] Those who entered the camp of prayer were henceforth set apart from the masses by participation in a redeemed fellowship, a fellowship of virtue. Slaves, dispossessed peasants, refugees, and other flotsam and jetsam of society were incorporated into the ranks of the spiritual elite, their worldly stigma dissolved in the atmosphere of divine acceptance. At the head of *missidi* is the *walí,* reassuring symbol of virtue and its reward, and under his authority the devotees bind and consecrate themselves in service. The *missidi* is the vanguard of virtue, and the *walí* the unique spiritual commissar who wafts over his motley amalgam of *refuseniks* the breath of felicity.

Diawia came under a cloud following the death of Tcherno 'Isma'íla, although Shádhilism continued to expand in other areas. With the accession of Tcherno Mamadou Sharif, the youngest son of Tcherno 'Isma'íla, however, the center went through a revival. Shádhilism once again regained the initiative, and the *diaroré* rites, for a while interrupted, were reintroduced on an organized basis. All the Labé country was now engulfed by the rites, and from there the flame of devotion spread to numerous important locations in the Fula country and beyond. One leader, Tcherno Jaw (d. 1865), chief of the district of Ndama in Labé, gave the rites a strong political basis by refashioning his subjects into the butt of military operations against adjacent non-Muslim populations. These military thrusts were often called *jihád,* but they scarcely conformed to the classical specifications, in that they were not precipitated by a situation bringing danger to the Muslim community and were not preceded by formal overtures of peace. Even if this activity was not *jihád,* however, it was certainly a fusion of religious ardor with political boldness, and Tcherno Jaw, as its sponsor, achieved an elevated status through it and was accordingly ascribed the title "the *walí* of Ndama"—another worldly saint.

Tcherno Jaw's initiative was inherited by his second son, Tcherno Ibrahima, whose influence extended much beyond Futa Jallon. The French, recognizing that fact, wooed him in a gambit to exploit his influence, but in 1899 the two sides collided on a path of inevitable conflict of interest. In that sense, French involvement compounded the incendiary urge that Sháchilism had exploited so successfully in an earlier era and gave local grievances a new external focus.

The man whose career brought matters to a head was Tcherno Aliou (c. 1828–1912)—frail, lame, and partly blind, but so considerable a force in the area that he was given the title *walí* of Goumba, whose *barakah* held sway over the whole region. His retreat center at Goumba, situated on the lower escarpment of the Futa Jallon plateau, was for that reason perceived as a formidable challenge to the French, who responded to his influence by according him the treasonable status of Mahdí—"Messiah." The French soon controlled the area and captured the centers of Sháchilí influence. Sháchilism had reached a watershed in Muslim West Africa, and the saintly virtue that propelled it, for so long a force to be reckoned with in the rarefied political atmosphere of the plateau, henceforth had to seek the low ground of accommodation with the French colonial authorities.

We have already described this subject in detail in the previous chapter. What we should stress here is that the history of Sháchilism shows there were real and enduring links between West African and North African Islam and that the synthesis of law and devotion and of involvement and retreat had assumed as viable proportions in West Africa as in the North. In neither area did the *awliyá* avoid controversy. On the contrary, they often became the public focus of social and political unrest and, by their own claims, the filters and instruments of divine sanction. Since they perceived no dichotomy between the word of God and the world of politics, they had correspondingly no hesitation in taking command of events and of crowds to avenge their cause. For them saintly virtue had a robust, worldly face to it; they viewed worldly success as the proof and sanction of inner virtue. In their minds, faith and works, form and content, dogma and practice coalesced naturally.

The *walí* was a moral exemplar, the impeccable guarantor of *barakah*. The *barakah* he possessed was proof of the intrinsic worth of virtue and the merit associated with his literacy in Arabic, the sacred tongue. Although he bore the stamp of humanity and carried the marks of earthly limitation, the saint was guaranteed divine forgiveness and acceptance should he fall into sin. This guarantee endowed him with the capacity to give the assurance of *barakah* to his disciples and thus to act as an intermediary between God and human beings. In some Islamic traditions the saint provided this link not only by bestowing spiritual blessings *(barakah)* on his followers but by instructing them in matters of doctrine so that God Himself might become directly accessible to the aspirant. In Muslim Africa, however, this pedagogical role remained unimportant; instead the saint, sealed with *barakah*, assumed, or was made to assume, the anointed role of guide and savior.

Virtue and Spells

It is instructive to set this understanding of the saint alongside indigenous African conceptions. Unlike his counterpart in the indigenous culture who specializes in spells, incantations, and other forms of divinatory control, the *walí* is distinguished by *barakah* as a social force rather than as spirit power that one fears and has to avoid. *Barakah*, for this reason, can be institutionalized and organized with public following and support, centered in the *walí* and affirmed in his devotees. The organizational and social dimension of saintly power is therefore integral to the Muslim tradition: Sainthood—individual charisma—is buttressed by saintship, an historically transmitted line of succession. In traditional divination, *barakah* existed as dangerous power that could harm the uninitiated. The code regulating it emphasized avoidance and the negative results of breaches. In effect, *barakah* in traditional Africa was a magical force in the possession of certain un-usual individuals who developed a specialized art for it. In such circles the magi-cian is answerable primarily to his or her art, not to any public or popular accred-itation. Thus, if the evil eye is potent enough to accomplish its objective, then it does its work irrespective of whether or not the harm being inflicted is ethical. Magicians are vindicated by the potency of their art, not by social approbation. This tradition is quite different from the Muslim notion of *barakah,* or at least from the Islamic transformation of the notion, which implies both personal virtue (the saint is "the blessed person," *al-mubárak*) and efficacious power.

Although writers like Trimingham tend to lump magic and *barakah* together, local populations are more discriminating. They recognize that the *walí* is differ-ent from the diviner or magician, whom they call *sirruyanké* (from Arabic *sirr,* "secret or esoteric knowledge").[19] The *sirruyanké* is the unrooted individualist, without community or tradition. Some *sirruyankés* have indeed aligned their practice with Islam. One *sirruyanké* adopted the feasts of Ramadán and the *hajj* as times to dispense prophecies and prescriptions. But as such Islam is only a veneer. Such diviners claim to be able to assume the form of a monkey or other animal and to receive from Allah communications that cause them to make predictions about events not in the Muslim calendar but in the farming calendar: rain, har-vests, fat kine succeeding lean and vice versa.[20] Such predictions lend themselves easily to exploitation and extortion, and many *awliyá* have been careful to guard their reputations against such religious adventurism.[21] In a treatise on the subject, called *Masálik al-Jinan* ("The Paths to Paradise"), the Mouride leader, Ahmadou Bamba, to be considered presently, draws a distinction that puts the *walí* on the same side as the *nabí*, the prophet.

> The equivalent of the miracle of the prophet (*mujíza*) exists in the charisma (*karáma*) of the Saint (*walí*) because the latter is the heir of the former. The prophets are the proof of the existence of God and the saints are the signs that his religion is the true one. The prophets are spotless and the saints are preserved and honored. Both share in divine immunity (*'isma*), as shown by the Gnostics. Immunity is only necessary for prophets, not for the saints.[22]

Even so, we should not press the division too rigidly. In the large gray area be-tween genuine moral power and popular thaumaturgy it would need a saint of exceptional sensitivity and agility consistently to see the difference and to keep to the straight and narrow.

As we move to one particular consideration of sainthood in Muslim Africa, we shall see that only a faint line separates the refined power of *barakah* from its coarse analogues in popular religion, or at any rate in popular religion in its lower forms. If an undeveloped, popular sort of Islam moves into this shared space with popular religion, then it is a pretty sure thing that it will assimilate accordingly and reflect the crudeness of its milieu. At that level, the line between the two can become blurred to the point of nonexistence.

Sainthood and Saint Veneration: The Mourides of Senegal

The founder of the Mouride (Ar. *muríd*, "disciple") brotherhood of Senegal was Shaykh Amadou Bamba (c. 1852–1927), a man deeply influenced by the interior devotion of the Tijání order of Súfís, although his own roots lay in Qádirí soil.[23] Over the course of time, his Mouride brotherhood outpaced its counterparts in vigorously cultivating the unthinking obeisance of rank-and-file neophytes, called by the Mourides themselves *tálibés* (Ar. *tálib*). Wrapping themselves in the mantle of *barakah*, the Mouride leaders' claim over the bodies of their disciples came to be complete and total, so much so that, after a point, religious instruction, with its accompanying initiation into grades of spiritual enlightenment, was almost entirely missing in the otherwise close relationship between the postulant and his spiritual axis. Instead the *shaykh* mounted the disciples like cavalry, driving them into virgin fields of submission and physical labor on the peanut plantations of the brotherhood, a cash-crop enterprise conducted for the exclusive benefit of the *shuyúkh*. At its extreme form this submission may in fact, if not in theory, substitute for submission to God, with *barakah* investing the *shuyúkh* with a semidivine status.

The manifestation of this kind of divine *barakah* over crowds of illiterates brought the Mourides to the hostile attention of the French colonial power. Paul Marty, whose acute analysis of the Mourides remains a classic, describes the extraordinary appeal of Amadou Bamba. Describing what he saw in 1913, Marty wrote:

> The mere sight of Amadou Bamba at prayer or giving his blessing with a stream of saliva on the prostrate faithful plunges some into hysterical outbursts which everyone wants to share. They roll at the feet of the saint, they kiss his sandals and the hem of his robe, they hold out their hands to him. With compunction he lets fall a stream of saliva on the open palms, which close up, clasp together, and spasmodically rub the face and body. Then there are shudderings, fainting fits, epileptic convulsions, followed by contortions and extraordinary leaps, all this accompanied by a horrible yelling. Madness finally takes hold of everyone.[24]

The French took strong measures to curb Amadou Bamba's power. He and his followers were harassed. Having first installed themselves at the village of Mbake-Baol in the rural hinterland of Senegal, the *shaykh* and his followers moved to a new center he built at Touba, also in Senegal, in 1887. Since there was no abate-

ment in the hostility of local commandants, Amadou Bamba and his disciples removed to St. Louis, then the capital of colonial Senegal, in 1891. But proximity to
power merely served to inflame official sensibilities further, and the *shaykh* was
apprehended by French troops. He was sentenced to imprisonment and exile in
Gabon from 1895 to 1902 on charges of political subversion. But his *barakah*
guaranteed his popularity with the crowds, which in turn cast him inevitably into
a feared political figure in the eyes of the French. Furthermore, Amadou Bamba's
association with the Tijániyáh, which was regarded in colonial circles as inherently subversive, established his culpability as needing no further proof. Amadou
Bamba returned to Senegal in November 1902, but he was arrested again the following year and condemned to a fresh term of exile, this time in Mauritania, from
1903 to 1907.

Each French action against Amadou Bamba appears to have increased his
barakah and raised him in the esteem of his followers, who proceeded to ascribe
miraculous powers to him. Historians of religion will be led astray if they try to
decide whether it was a garrulous *shaykh* who led an ignorant and willing crowd
or an irrepressible crowd that molded the *shaykh.* The real picture seems a mixed
one: The stimulus of popular expectation undoubtedly intensified the impulse to
sainthood in Amadou Bamba, but the dramatic nature of his exile absence increased the loyalty of his devotees too, and a cult of saintly personality grew up to
fill the vacuum created by his absence. The tenacity of belief in *barakah* explains
why those who are believed to possess *barakah* can do no wrong, and why doing
wrong to them is perceived as a *poena vicaria.* Thus when Amadou Bamba returned in 1907, he was a greater saint than when he left.

The tenacity of *barakah* has roots in pre-Muslim society. The spontaneous and
overwhelming nature of the response to Amadou Bamba as *séringe* (Wolof for
"holy man," "saint") cannot, therefore, be explained solely on the grounds of
strong Islamic influence. Most of his followers were ignorant of even the most
basic tenets of the faith. For them Amadou Bamba cut the figure of the familiar
charismatic personality, which in the pre-Islamic era was designated *borom bayré,*
a Wolof phrase meaning "possessor of success and fame." The Muslim saint, when
he appeared, was assimilated into this traditional African paradigm as both *borom
bayré* and *borom barké,* a man of both worldly and spiritual achievement.[25]

This double level of understanding appears to have operated in Amadou
Bamba's relationship with his disciples. In his own mind he was a devout, humble
Muslim, eager to behave, think, and be esteemed in strict accordance with the orthodox code. Indeed, when first approached by an overzealous disciple who saw
in him the marks of greatness, Amadou Bamba treated him with undisguised disapproval, sending him packing with the advice that he put his mind to better and
more useful pursuits.[26] Even later in his career he forbade his disciples to render
him the obeisance that he deemed properly due to God.[27] In his rules for novices
he stressed submission to God above all else,[28] and in his prolific writings, the
theme of obedience to God is the persistent and incomparable standard alongside

which all else fades into insignificance. He spoke at length concerning his unworthiness and expressed distress at evidence of his weakness. Praying to God, he said, "I desire your help in the midst of terror and vengeance. Today my heart is overburdened with sadness. My being is too weak to bear what I face. Forgive. My misfortune is plain, and my heart is anguished."[29] These words were spoken shortly before his first exile, an exile that was to resonate with the rising chorus of popular adulation.

Whatever his inner feelings of inadequacy, Amadou Bamba had to respond to the undeniable strength of his support among the peasant populations, and he tried to form order out of the chaos around him by moving in the direction of undisputed authority. In one of his devotional manuals he listed four qualities as necessary in the disciple: (1) a sincere and unshakable love for the *shaykh,* (2) unquestioning obedience to the commands of the *shaykh,* (3) abandonment of all opposition, including inward resistance, to the *shaykh,* and (4) the giving up of any preference for the disciple's own private thoughts.[30] Elsewhere he wrote that he who does not have a *shaykh* for his training will come to grief, "for he who does not have a *shaykh* for his guide will have Satan for his *shaykh.*"[31] "Truth," he said, "consists in the love for one's *shaykh.*"[32] In another work Amadou Bamba says that the *walí* inherits the power of miracles from the Prophet to whom the *walí* is attached by a mystical chain of initiation.[33] "Saints," he wrote, "are the authentic signs of the Prophet's religion, and of his truth. . . . Saints are preserved from error and invested with honor."[34] This point of devotion to the Prophet is stressed in the numerous details on performing the *dhikr.* At its height the *dhikr* is nothing but the imitation of the Prophet, the Perfect Man (*insán al-kámil*) or the true intercessor (*shaffí', mushaffa'*).[35]

Recognizing in his disciples material requiring the iron hand of discipline rather than the persuasive pen of the scholar, Amadou Bamba elevated physical labor to the status of a religious principle. "Work," he contended, "is a part of true religion. The human body, since its creation, exists only to accomplish the work ordered by God."[36]

It would be unfair to blame Séringe Bamba entirely for the coarse bearing of his followers, for he was following where they led. Amar Sambe, a local Senegalese scholar, testified to the compelling interior impetus produced in the *shaykh* by his following when he recalled that in his youth wandering, drunken *awliyá* were a familiar sight; yet their followers remained undaunted. He writes: "When I was a child in Koranic school at Kébémer (Senegal), a marabout passed frequently in front of the school, staggering, held upright by his *tálibés.* The *séringe* always had a foot in the vineyard of the Lord. Despite this fact, his followers liked to maintain that their *shaykh* had so much *barakah* that strong liquor transformed itself into milk when it reached his stomach."[37]

Such marabouts were the early precursors of the confluence of pre-Islamic ideas on *barakah* with their Muslim analogues. Amadou Bamba was not nearly that idiosyncratic, mainly because by the time he arrived on the scene a general elevation in the practice and understanding of Islam had occurred. However, as it stands, the anecdote suggests the wide margin of credulity available to the local *walí* if he wished to avail himself of it.

The central importance of discipleship per se in Mouride practice is dramatized in the nature of its simple initiation ritual, which has supreme value for the Mouride *tálibé*. It is called in Wolof *njebbel* (Ar. *bay'ah, talqín*), meaning "personal and physical surrender," and is the crux of Mouride life and philosophy. In the *njebbel* the neophyte declares to his master, "I surrender to you my body and soul. What you forbid, I refrain from, and what you command I obey."[38] That unadorned formula binds the disciple to the *shaykh* in a relationship that is, for all practical purposes, indissoluble, though in theory the disciple can repudiate the link in an extreme crisis.[39] The neophyte is told by the *shaykh* to make unquestioning obedience his watchword. *Del deglu ndiggel,* he says: "You must hear words as commands."[40] *Barakah* thus turns into muscular piety.

An extreme branch of the Mouride movement, called the Bay Fall, take the step of personal submission to its logical conclusion. According to them the canonical obligations of Islam are superfluous. In an arresting metaphor they ask, "Why carry your bags on your head if you are riding on a train?" The train is headed for salvation, Amadou Bamba is the locomotive engine, the carriages are the Mouride *shuyúkh,* the passengers are the *tálibés,*[41] and the baggage, by implication, is the religious code. It follows that the servitude of the Mouride *tálibé* furnished the basis of Mouride power. On the Mouride farm, called *dára*, the *shuyúkh* tether their *tálibés* in accordance with their right to command ultimate obedience. In the terminology of the Bay Fall, the *tálibé* is called *tak dér*, "the laborer," after the wide leather belts used to hold their ragged clothes together as they toil unquestioningly on the fields of their masters.[42]

The Mourides are by no means unique in exploiting their followers' perception of *barakah* for the benefit of their religious superiors. On the contrary, in the most representative tradition of Islamic education the schoolmaster in African Islam looks upon his students as indentured servants secured to them by virtue of the teacher's *barakah*. Even the expectation that the student will receive religious instruction is qualified by the view that the schoolmaster has powerful *barakah* with which to control mind as well as body.[43] The Mourides are merely pressing this tradition to its logical conclusion and building the entire edifice of social control on it.

We need a broader perspective to understand the wider connections of Mouride extremism. Its counterpart in the wide spectrum of Súfí spirituality is the call to physical renunciation, an arming of the soul with the weapons of struggle and vigilance against the lures of the carnal body. This philosophy, essentially, is *zuhd,* and it was powerfully preached in the Tijániyáh brotherhood, with which the Mourides share some affinity. There the devotee was urged to beat the carnal self "with the whip of the Book, bind it with the halter of reproach and judgment, set limits upon it with conscientious rebuke and reprimand, and place the saddle of firm intention upon it with the girth of determination. Then mount it with the profession of the holy law (*shari'a*) and ride it into the fields of Truth (*al-Haqq*, a Súfí term for God)."[44]

Even for the seasoned adept the challenges of genuine spirituality demand superhuman resources, and the Mouride instinct to have recourse to saintly intercession is fed from this reality. Unaided human effort is too bedeviled by uncertainty to guarantee success. Through the servile channel of farm labor the Mouride masters have taken individual responsibility out of the hands of ignorant crowds and offered instead the duty of collective subservience and the privilege of the blessed assurance they as leaders can give. *Barakah* is in the eye of the beholder, but especially in the face of the beholden one.

The power of the *shaykh* in the Mouride tradition is in exact proportion to the adulation of the disciples. As Mouride theology affirms, the *shuyúkh* occupy the ranks of honor (Ar. *maqám*) to which their followers' faith and enthusiasm carry them. It seems, therefore, that the cultivation of saintly eminence is but a shorthand for the cultivation of society. Today, despite a number of premature jeremiads, the Mourides number well over a million, and at the Grand *Maqál*, their annual pilgrimage to Touba, up to half the total membership may attend. One could scarcely ask for a more impressive demonstration of group and religious solidarity, of tangible expression of charisma, of what has been called the "versatility" of charisma.[45]

In the case of Mourides we seem to have a stunning example of how even sober-minded *shuyúkh* may be made to follow the lead of their followers as they reap the reward of popular obeisance. Yet one should recall that the Mourides are hardly alone in fusing concepts such as *borom barké* (spiritual success) and *borom bayré* (worldly renown) to define who their masters are. These *shuyúkh* are personal embodiments of the concept of *barakah* as *bayre*, what the Manding people call *yirwa*. *Barakah* is a life force that attaches to certain persons from whom it may be acquired, or forfeited. There are recognized rules for obtaining and retaining it, as well as for losing or regaining it. Its supreme characteristic is its personal and social expression, with rules about who may give it and who receive it and how the two classes deserve each other. As such, saints are preeminent repositories of *barakah*, representing in their own persona the concentration of inherited *barakah*. They are not just eminent souls who impart their blessing (*barakah*) to a few devotees in the isolation of retreat centers; they are movers and shakers in the larger world, designated souls that give voice to the abiding wish for consolation and security. The blessings they distribute assure orthodox merit and material benefits. Hence a claim to be near to God—to be God's "friend"—tends to become plausible in proportion to its social and historical uses.

"Sainthood," then, represents the domestication of *barakah*; "saintship," the social organization of saints. The two complement each other when disciples, fortified with the *barakah* of the saint, embrace their master's teaching in the charismatic collective setting of community practice and action. It is in relationship that the true mettle of *barakah* is proved. The Mouride case is merely the extreme, provocative point of the spectrum: There the complex interaction of sainthood, saintship, and society acts to bring wildness into line with *barakah* and its many useful social functions. However, alike for the Mourides and the more mainline groups, the context of dramatic historical change offers sainthood and saintship visible structural vindication and a self-perpetuating expansive popular outlet.

Part Three

Education and Society: The Roots of Muslim Identity

Education has been a fundamental theme throughout the continuing process of change, adaptation, and conservation of the Islamic tradition in Muslim African societies, and long before the advent of the modern West, Muslim Africans have expended impressively disproportionate resources on Islamic education. They have done this as though confident that their diligence would more than compensate for their lack of proficiency. Such an attitude at once places education in these societies on a plane different from where the modern West puts it, because for these societies the irrepressible framework of all learning is religion and what religion sanctions, or can be made to sanction. The famous dictum of al-Ghazálí (1056–1111) is worth citing here: "I sought knowledge without God, but God forbade it that knowledge should be without Him" (*utlibu-l-'ilm min dúni -lláh fa abá Alláhu 'an yakúnu li-khayrihi*).

Ibn Khaldún concurs. Writing in 1377 in his *Muqaddimah*, he cites accepted custom as giving "preference to the teaching of the Qur'án. The reason is the desire for the blessing and reward (in the other world resulting from knowledge of the Qur'án) and a fear of the things that might affect children in 'the folly of youth' and harm them and keep them from acquiring knowledge."[1] Ibn Khaldún recognizes that a few authorities differ from this approach to education. One of them, for instance, urges that education begin with poetry as "the archive of the Arabs," but that view is a minority one. He continues, saying that children put on that kind of syllabus "might miss the chance to learn the Qur'án. As long as they remain at home, they are amenable to authority. When they have grown up and shaken off the yoke of authority, the tempests of young manhood often cast them upon the shores of wrongdoing. Therefore, while the children are still at home and under the yoke of authority, one seizes the opportunity to teach them the Qur'án, so that they will not remain without a knowledge of it."

Such fusing of religion and learning the modern West rejects. It does not view knowledge as accountability to the past but rather as individual entitlement. Mil-

117

ton's formula is the opposite of al-Ghazálí's, to the effect that the goal of learning is to repair the ruins wrought by our forebears and to create for ourselves the right conditions for our improvement and progress, in effect "to be like God."[2] Modern attitudes to education as "self-entitlement" are in continuity with that sentiment. In spite of modern attitudes, Muslim jurists would charge Milton with *bid‘a makrúh*, reprehensible innovation, and canonize al-Ghazálí in his place. However, Milton sometimes acted better than his rationalist effusions, for he also wrote passionately about discipline being better than liberty, speaking in that sense for the great Muslim jurists. Yet his legacy has endured for the most part in terms of an overweening confidence in the limitless human capacity to know, to do, and to be, and it has lasted throughout the great stages of the evolution of Western consciousness. An important expression of it is the view that education is the unfettered search for truth and the rolling back of the frontiers of ignorance. As Milton puts it in a famous passage, "Though all the winds of doctrine were let loose to play upon the earth, so Truth be in the field, we do injuriously by licensing and prohibiting to misdoubt her strength. Let her and Falsehood grapple; whoever knew Truth put to the worse, in a free and open encounter?" Milton is here the avatar of free intellectual inquiry, of the quest for truth as the greatest safeguard against bigotry, intolerance, repression, and conformity, and the Western tradition bears the imprint of his ideas as a high and holy calling. It is inevitable, therefore, that when the West subsequently encountered non-Western cultures it should seek to refashion them into its own archetypal image, and nowhere has this encounter been more riddled with misunderstanding, more fraught with tension than in the field of Muslim education. The West was determined to cut asunder the venerable cord of religion and learning that Allah had knit.

In the three chapters that follow, I describe and analyze Muslim education within the context of Western influence. The first is an autobiographical piece that portrays the world of the Qur'án school from within by focusing on a child's view of the institution and its leadership. It is an example of how the Qur'án school molds society through its children, how it fixes society's public character and ethical outlook, how it forges family and other social relationships and individual and collective solidarity. The Qur'án school in that setting is a radical departure from the criteria of Western style schools in several important respects: in how the Qur'án school is set up and its manner of recruitment; in the leadership of teacher and community; in its view of knowledge as rote memorization and the correct pronunciation and articulation of the word; in offering from propitious portions of the sacred text powerful medicine to improve intelligence and combat evil spirits; in its manner of recognizing and rewarding children's ability; in its complete ignoring of the mother tongue as a suitable vehicle for instruction; and in the total absence of any idea of economic employment as the goal or expectation of training. In that form, the Qur'án school, far from being a historical relic, has survived many centuries of practice and, more recently, relentless onslaught from a hostile, uncomprehending West. With it has survived its formula of uniting religion and learning and placing God at the center of education.

The second chapter expands this theme and its continuity in African states by focusing on the Arabic language itself and the ancillary position it customarily occupies in the modern education syllabus. The special character of devotion to the Arabic language in African education is connected to the divine status Muslims perceive for the language. As long as that perception continues, Arabic will perdure as a language without equal or parallel. Even non-Muslims would concede the principle of the special status of the language without understanding the full implications of such a step. All of which strengthens Muslim objections to the secular status quo and their wish to assume political power to extract the requisite concessions for themselves. This Muslim attitude to secularism may be one reason why in the highly charged atmosphere of religious political activism Muslims have tended to regard education as a touchstone.[3] Their views on religious freedom have been expressed by their stance on Muslim education, and they have organized themselves around educational issues to express their objections to the national secular state, objections that have been smoldering through much of Muslim Africa and beyond. Consequently, the Qur'án school has remained an extremely durable institution, and its spontaneous proliferation in Muslim Africa has invested it with corresponding social and political significance. For example, when Muslims have agitated for state support, they have desired to obtain a fair share of the allocation of public resources for Qur'án schools, among other things. In that sense the Qur'án school is crucial in Muslim efforts to mark out boundaries and set forth rules of identity for practice and self-understanding.

The third chapter describes Muslims in a modern West African city and their struggle to modernize the institution of learning in reaction to strong competition from Western and Christian schools. Modernism seems to have inserted an active factional ferment into the ranks of Muslims. Those Muslims who wish to make the transition into new forms of society in the new world order must at the same time address the African pluralist milieu and its constraints on a unitary code. Muslim sensibilities have their source as much in standard sources of Qur'án, Hadíth, and law as in African values and customs, with a significant influence added from Western impact. In the nature of the case, Muslims have been keen to participate in the new world order, but for a very different reason: to grasp the opportunity to repudiate, hopefully once and for all, the reigning confidence of the West that its secularism is the universal destiny for all humanity. The reality, of course, is that the West remains dominant, though in African societies that dominance is blunted by social and ethnic factors. In any case, Muslims thrive in that qualified, multifaceted cultural setting, even though they remain embedded in the ethnic factionalism of their milieu.

6

A Childhood Muslim Education: *Barakah,* Identity, and the Roots of Change

Historical Background

The Gambia, where the following story took place, was a British colony until February 1965, when it gained independence.[1] As a political entity its roots go back to the medieval empire of Mali, of which it formed the extreme western point. Records attesting to its history reach much further back, in fact as far back as 500 B.C., when Hanno the Carthaginian sailed down the West coast and made observations on the country and its culture. There is a tradition, for example, that the Greeks first saw in Senegambia the instrument, totally new to them, to which they gave the name *xylophone.* The name simply means "wooden instrument," which is what the *balafon,* the indigenous name, is in that part of West Africa. It is constructed without any metal parts, including nails and wires. The French scholar, Raymond Mauny, in his work, *Tableau Geographique,* proposes a bold, novel hypothesis of sailors from the Senegambian-Mauritanian coast crossing the Atlantic centuries before Columbus and his crew. In any case, these examples make the point that the Senegambia region is full of history, which is preserved in documentary, archaeological, and oral forms. A good deal of it is enacted in local musical traditions in which the *balafon* features prominently.

The country was named after the river that was the most navigable waterway in premodern Africa. A ship drawing fifteen feet of water could sail over one hundred and fifty miles inland. At the headwaters of the river are soils rich in gold, which made its way down the river to European trading ships. Coffee, ebony, hides, wax, ivory, and spices were also brought down the river, which thus became an essential artery of the regional economic trade. The major location from which trade was controlled was James Fort, built on an island in the estuary, twenty miles from the sea, and described in one source as "a slab of friable rock which scarcely projects above the river at high tide."

James Fort was originally built by Baltic Germans who were servants of the Duke of Courland in Latvia. The fort was constructed on an island purchased from the local chief. The fort changed hands several times before the English acquired it in 1661 and renamed it after James II. The English abandoned the fort in 1709, then returned through the Royal African Company in 1713. In 1715 a Welsh pirate captured the fort, only for the Company to reoccupy it in 1721. However, in 1725 the powder kegs in the storeroom accidentally exploded, killing eleven of the nineteen Europeans there and doing considerable damage to the buildings. Repairs restored the fort to some semblance of life, until its final destruction in 1778 by the French. Though the English succeeded in retaking it and expelling the French, the fort was allowed to languish in its dilapidated state, and henceforth it sank into the country's marine psyche as a biodegradable relic.

The river once teemed with marine life, and it is still one of the world's best bird sanctuaries, with over 450 different species. The country is famous for its beef and cattle, and there is also abundant seafood, including shellfish. The cash crop is groundnuts, farmed by the men, and the staple food is rice, which is produced by the women. The Gambia has sixteen languages and two main seasons, wet and dry. A cool spell occurs between October and March, called the Harmattan, after the northwest trade winds that sweep from the Himalayas and across the Sahara, blowing fine desert dust right up to the western rim of the Atlantic and thus feeding into the ocean currents that arch off the African continental shelf.

With a population of just over a million and few natural resources, the country has been bypassed by modern communication routes and consigned to the cosmopolitan backwaters. But historically the Gambia had been at the crossroads of attempts to open up Africa, an indispensable coordinate in geographical knowledge and exploration of the continent. The river brought the traveler virtually to the doorstep of the great trans-Saharan routes that dissected and knitted the grain and gold-producing regions of the area. Today, however, the country languishes in relative obscurity, protected from the glare of exploitative world attention and mostly free from internal upheaval. However, in July 1994, a group of junior army officers in their twenties seized power in a bloodless coup d'état, with the first reports speaking of no general disturbance, only a minor, brief traffic jam a few miles from the capital. The president and his family fled to a visiting U.S. frigate berthed in the harbor, to take sanctuary first in neighboring Senegal and eventually in London. He had ruled for over thirty years with few accomplishments to his name. After the coup there followed an abortive countercoup. Discussions have been held to return the country to democratic civilian rule, but they have so far stalled, and all local political activity has remained suppressed. Lacking the reflex of political excitement, the country seems to have returned to its customary sluggishness.

In that soporific state the Gambia has resisted attempts to yank it into the mainstream of world events, either into the primeval eddy of militant *jihád* or into the path of aggressive missionary endeavor. Its predominantly Muslim population follows the orders of the Prophet with mild disposition and gentle means, which fosters amicable relations with its pagan and minority Christian neighbors. The Christian population is formed from a nucleus of freed slaves or recaptive Africans, on which see Chapter 8 for more details, with some conversion occurring among the autochthones, those acephalous populations that Islamic orthodoxy has for the most part ignored or annexed as tributaries. Right from the heyday of colonial rule, Christians have settled into the easygoing ways of the population, offering education to the largely Muslim population without expecting or wanting converts among their pupils, as if instinctively surrendering the policy of active evangelism in return for the Muslim rejection of *jihád*. The two traditions of a pacifist Islam and an accommodating Christianity have created an ethos of religious and political moderation that has fitted in well with the country's pluralist make-up. The Gambia is probably the first and only Muslim country in the world that has observed as national holidays Christian feasts, such as Good Friday and the Feast of the Assumption of the Blessed Virgin.

Georgetown, the district headquarters of the local colonial administration at the time of this story, is the natal town of my mother. It is an island in the middle reaches of the river, about 170 miles from the mouth of the river. It had been a Portuguese slave fort until centuries later when the district commissioner made his home there, as did the chief. The government established in the town a secondary boarding school in 1927 for the sons of chiefs and instituted a stiff Islamic religious regime to persuade otherwise reluctant Muslim parents to send their children there. The Methodist mission opened a primary school, but it was maintained by the local district council. A Creole schoolmaster and his wife were in charge. It was effectively shunned by local Muslim parents until a colonial education officer, a maverick Irishman, went on a campaign to persuade town elders to support the school with assurances of government backing and exaggerated promises of riches. He would follow the women to their farms and tell them in his sanitized Mandinka that if they sent their children to school then they could retire from their drudgery with the income of their educated offspring. My mother, for one, heard the message and allowed me to enroll in the school after several years of attending the Qur'án school. Briefly, then, that is the background to the story of this chapter.

Enrollment

> The rod produces an effect which terminates in itself. A child is afraid of being whipped, and gets his task, and there's an end on't; whereas, by exciting emulation and comparisons of superiority, you lay the foundation of lasting mischief; you make brothers and sisters hate each other.
>
> —*Samuel Johnson (1709–1784)*

One day my brother suggested to my father that we might be allowed to start Qur'án school. Father was impressed by this pious request. We were still very young. He had always hoped to give us both an early start in life. So this suggestion coming from us unsolicited at such a tender age must have pleased him very much.

He did not give an outright answer but swung suspended in the hammock, his eyes shut, his legs flung over the sides of the hammock, and his head held back: He was relishing the special nature of his sons about to embark on the real business of life. He said nothing, but his silence was filled with the eloquence of gratitude to God. A few days later, over chicken curry, my father told us that he had made arrangements for us to start Qur'án school the following Wednesday. My brother, excited at the news, choked himself by swallowing too quickly. So we dragged him off and laid him near the clay jars. He had a distressed stare in his eyes. My father, unmoved, reminded us of a proverb that says that when children steal the trousers of their elders they must button them at their throats. What this proverb had to do with Qur'án school or the curry was not very obvious. But who dared to tell him that!

On the appointed day we turned up at the Qur'án school, a willing pair of lads, full of life like the firstfruits before their full seasoning. What a strange and austere place the school was! Often we had peeped through the fence to see children squatting on the ground in a circle. In the middle was the bonfire around which everyone was crouched. In the night air the children seem transformed with their pale, ash-laden faces, the wooden tablets held slanted or across their folded legs, and in trusting loud voices they shouted the sacred script prompted by tiny scrawls on their slates. To us outside, there was something, if not comical, then most certainly mysterious, forbidding, and also impressive, about these ashen-veiled children chanting in what was the totally incomprehensible language of Arabic.

Once I tiptoed to the fence, held my breath, and listened carefully just in case some light of understanding might descend on my darkness. One of the boys noticed me. He slipped out quietly, crept up beside me, and gave a loud yell. I panicked, and the entire Qur'án school broke up and chased after me. Before I had a chance to turn the corner a muscular fellow grabbed me by the neck and flung me over his shoulders. When they had finished with me I had learned my lesson about the Qur'án school. The light had descended on me with uncomfortable suddenness.

I felt uneasy when we enrolled in the Qur'án school. Friends we certainly had none, although with a certain amount of give-and-take we were soon to acquire some. Our first day at school was a curious experience. We first tried to find out if the teacher liked children. We observed him closely, expecting at any time to hear him tell some favorite children's stories. He was a lanky, middle-aged man with a dark mark in the middle of his forehead, a sign that he said his prayers regularly. He wore a thin white gown called *abayah* and a white skull cap. He constantly worked at his teeth with a piece of chewing stick, which gave him a slightly impatient and clumsy appearance. When the chewing stick was at the back of his mouth at the big grinders, for example, and he was about to say something, he twitched his eyes wildly, his cheek puffing impatiently. Then he moved his hand forward, sucked the saliva from the chewing stick, spat it out, cleared his throat, and said what he had to say. As soon as someone started to say anything in reply he went back to his teeth, repeating the process while he listened. He seldom looked you in the eye. My brother and I looked carefully at his hands to see if we could detect in them marks of kindness to children. They flicked about a lot, and we decided that such haste and energy would not suffer fools, or, for that matter, children, gladly. We concluded that we did not like him very much but that, as we were afraid of him, we had better try not to cross him. We would give him a nickname, such as Mount, because of his sinewy limbs, or Giraffe, on account of his elevated head, but perish the thought. I wonder if he knew how closely observed he was.

The Teacher

The parents imposed on the children a duty that tied them to the teacher in an authoritative sort of way. To earn *barakah*, they said the children should call him "Teacher." *Barakah* was virtue that could be attached to you or removed and assured you of blessing and success in life. The Qur'án school was a source for it, with the Teacher its sole agent. The short distance children traveled from home to the school gave no indication of the great symbolic distance they were now traveling to be for the first time under the control and direction of the *barakah* of Teacher, whom they held in respect bordering on fear. Teacher's habit of theatrically clearing his throat became in time an overhanging threat, a sign that he was about to descend on the children without mercy. No doubt their disposition to distrust him exaggerated his intentions, but experience would teach you that you took the man for granted at your peril. For his part the teacher came to regard deference to him as confirmation of his view that his students were now beholden only to his personal *barakah*, which was his to give or withhold. Indeed this point was conceded to him many times when nervous parents asked him, indeed begged him, to mend their wayward children, often with the cane and sometimes with physical labor, so that they would earn his *barakah*. It was widely assumed, or widely feared, that anyone like the Qur'án school teacher who had such an intimate knowledge of the Qur'án and of the divine language, Arabic, had a particularly powerful *barakah* at his disposal, and it was this assumption that led many parents to entrust their children to him. In the past we had watched children being formally handed over to him. Now it was our turn.

The ceremonies over our induction into the Qur'án school were quickly done, partly because the teacher was a highly practical man who had little time for preambles and partly because parents did not like public displays of any kind. Then followed the serious business that was to engage the teacher for all our childhood life, that of instructing us in the Arabic Qur'án.

Our Teacher (we could not get away from the possessive adjective) did not pretend to us that this instruction was an easy matter. The lessons started with the alphabet, which began with the *alif,* a sort of upright dagger, and with that we pierced the sacred veil of the mysteries of the divine language. The bilabials and the hard consonants presented little difficulty. Letters with similar pronunciations, however, we mixed up. For example, the *ha,* with a softer sound, was not differentiated from *ha,* with a more assertive thrust behind it. Only in writing did we distinguish between the two. Similarly, and even more unpardonable, the *'ayn* and the *ghain* suffered from our tendency to bring everything down to our own level. *Ghain* was difficult. In sound it was like another letter, the *qáf.* But since there was yet another consonant, the *káf,* we went further with simplification by watering down the *ghain* until it became an indefinite and indistinct *gkain.* With elisions we committed offenses so abominable it would be kinder not to say a word.

As soon as we were able to press ahead to the twenty-eighth and last letter, the *ya,* we were ready to begin spelling single words. Knowledge of the alphabet was a great asset. With it we plunged into the mysteries of divine revelation. The *Fátihah,* the opening chapter of the Qur'án was the first we memorized. We memorized the recurrent formula: "In the name of God . . ." which comes, with one exception, at the beginning of every *súra,* or chapter, of the Qur'án. Then the *Fátihah* proper, which opens with the words "Praise be to God, the Lord of the worlds . . ." and ends with "Guide us on the straight path . . . the path of those who go not astray. . . ." Finally we said, "Amen." Thanks to the bliss of rote learning, we thought the "Amen" was simply part of the whole piece, rather than being what it patently is, a response coming at the end of a prayer. Thus we rushed to the end of the *Fátihah* with a resounding "Amen" as a sort of great personal triumph. With it we slammed the door on ignorant humanity and felt jubilant.

But the *Fátihah* means what it says; it is simply an opening, a significant step forward, yes, but still only a beginning. By the standards of the school learning it was a very small beginning at that. We had to press ahead. New boys had a period of grace in which no bad marks were recorded against them until they had learned to settle into the school. So at the beginning they were inviolate. But, thanks to the teacher's desire for quick and practical answers, that period was very short indeed. Consequently, slamming the door on ignorant humanity with the *Fátihah* was a hasty reaction.

A few weeks later Teacher (the possessive pronoun became understood, and in its place "Teacher" stood alone, the symbol of monopoly title to *barakah*) pulled us by the ear. His voice, charged with *barakah,* trembled as he cleared his throat. He reprimanded a number of big boys and then proceeded to impose an atmosphere of defeat over the entire school. He pulled out a scruffy little piece of paper and began to call roll. A few boys were absent, and teacher jotted down their names in his black book. When he called a boy's name and there was no answer he would hum to himself as if evoking a lost tune, and with an expression of impatience on his pale face he would wet the point of his reed pen with his tongue and scrawl a few characters into his black book. Then he would clear his throat and emit a long stream of saliva, which he always managed to direct whichever way he wanted with masterly precision. After the roll call, the chief end of which had been to find out not who was present but who was absent, Teacher started to assign new tasks and redefine old ones. He operated a kind of merit system and rewarded the faithful with appropriate favors, from being in charge of the overall running of the school, with powers to punish and correct, to being relieved from carrying out some of the more strenuous school duties. Conversely, he meted out punishment on a sliding scale depending on the seriousness of the offense. To his special favorites he gave unexpected bonuses, like entrusting to them new recruits. On this particular day some of the senior boys had won his special favor and were therefore rewarded with the privilege of supervising those of us who were new to the school. Children would soon learn this privilege was more theory than fact, for Teacher still continued to exercise supreme control. Perhaps his assigning us to some of the senior boys was his way of sealing the stamp of defeat he had already riveted on the entire school.

For Teacher power and *barakah* belonged together, which was why discipline and vigilance were necessary. His task was to lead and educate, and that was what power was about. In fact, his bamboo cane was the symbol of the school. Without the cane the gathered children would be a mere herd, good for the wild but scarcely for the garden of learning. Teacher valued the cane for that reason and carried it, often across his shoulder, as a professional emblem. With it he would point to a word on the slate and tap it several times next to your right index finger, indicating that it was not being correctly pronounced. And then as punishment he would smack your finger still stuck on the offending word. You were not allowed to pull away your hand with the cane beside it, or on it, as Teacher preferred. In that position, Teacher was free to spike it.

Teacher, preeminently steadfast, believed in the practical exercise of authority, and when he theorized, which was seldom, it was to confirm it. When he delegated authority, which was also seldom, it was to announce and ratify it. He organized the school in such a way that some of his own character rubbed off on us. A constant stream of information reached him, and one must presume, from its accurate nature, that he had a reliable spy network operating in the school and perhaps even farther afield. He had a loyal circle of students and disciples whose fidelity could be taken for granted. They were responsible for translating all his wishes and desires into action. Teacher learned to relax, not so much his grasp over the school, as his mind. Then he would reward this or that faithful student and throw open more doors of opportunity for us to seek his *barakah* as a coveted prize. It would bring a smile to the faces of parents for them to know that their children looked up to Teacher as a fount of *barakah*, an insurance against moral failure. As long as that understanding was there, Teacher felt no need to justify his authority by theorizing.

Pupils

The senior boys assumed their functions as watchdogs of *barakah*. When they allotted new work they expected their subordinates to be prompt in discharging their duty and the result to be impeccable, and they therefore squeezed us hard. After all, Teacher had set them up as noncommissioned vigilantes of virtue, not because of any accomplishments of theirs but to establish a pecking order.

Among the rest of the boys certain rules on bravery and cowardice were in force. To be weak and timid was considered a bad thing, whereas to be known to be brave and strong was a noble thing. I vividly remember one incident in which this crucial distinction was made. In the early afternoons we usually went to the nearby bush to gather a few twigs and sticks, which we brought back to the school to use as fuel in the evenings when we had lessons. This task was a very important aspect of school life: Good and brave boys fetched extra loads of firewood of good burning quality. To guard against lazy boys benefiting from a lucky find, such as stumbling on a neat pile a farmer might have gathered on the boundary with another farm (farms otherwise had no fences), Teacher looked for a consistent track record. This maintained a high level of performance while keeping the pressure on laggards among the children.

Going to the bush to fetch the evening supply of fuel involved the risk that one or other of the boys would hold you to settle old scores or make humiliating demands. In the bush old loyalties were reawakened and alternative alliances formed across official Qur'án school lines. Boys broke up the old formations and formed new ones according to their age groups, their common affiliation to an initiation rite like the circumcision ritual, their common tribe or ethnic unit, the closeness of their family connections, blood-ties (brothers of the same mother hardly ever found themselves on opposite sides, although half-brothers of the same father sometimes did), or even according to their common interests in games and other forms of play. Thus, in addition to public rules of compliance, there was another set of complex rules sustained by jealousies and vigilant sensibilities. That always made going to the bush a hazardous business.

Late one afternoon, after we had collected the evening supply of fuel, we brought the bundles to a central place where we all usually gathered before making our way back to the school. While we were sitting near our bundles a sudden silence fell over the ground. The boy who broke it turned out to be the chief protagonist in a quarrel with another boy. His opponent also made a challenging stir, and before long they were asking each other aggressive questions that neither of them stopped to answer. Their language grew more belligerent, and as the stakes rose they used fierce and uncompromising words. The verbal violence escalated to such an extent that when their bodies touched it sparked the final confrontation. They exchanged clenched fists, tightened their grips on each other, flung each other about, stamped, kicked, and wrapped their long wiry legs around each other in the style of traditional wrestlers. In the dust that they raised it was hard to say who was gaining the upper hand. Some of the other boys were cheering, not so much one side against another, but the fight itself. One of the big boys was circling the fighters, clapping his hands and encouraging them. He would have been disappointed had the two contestants stopped suddenly, for he was committed to it with the intensity of a participant, with as much of his own honor at stake as that of the two pugilists. Flaunting the matador's banner seemed much more appropriate to his character than playing the role of peacemaker. From spurring on the fighters he turned to organizing us. He asked us all to sit round in a circle. After the contest was over he had us all swear an oath of secrecy.

The fight was a draw. In the event, neither of the contestants gave in and the inciter was satisfied that he had been amply rewarded for his exertions. Some of the younger boys, including my brother and I, felt very out of place among this trigger-happy band. There were a few bloodstains on the collars of the fighters, and these were quickly attended to by the inciter, who washed them off at a nearby pond, so there were no tell-tale signs. The drawn fight reinforced the high value the boys put on bravery and strength, and it delineated more sharply the division between the strong and the weak. A new alliance was forged between the two fighters, both of whom had until then represented rival factions. Teacher might have been a very knowledgeable man, but here was a whole world about which he knew little. What he did know was siphoned off from boys under direct pressure from him but who were under even heavier pressure from the other boys not to spill, or from some chance remark that alerted him. Sometimes he reacted by ignoring the incident; at other times he followed the clues with scientific thoroughness. If he failed to get to the bottom of the affair, he inflicted heavy punishment on us all, as if we were a subspecies to be extinguished at his hands.

The bush fight turned out to be one of those incidents that Teacher followed up with relentless energy. He had caught wind of it, and the parents of the boys concerned had taken up the matter with the chief. Teacher's public reputation was at stake. This risk to his reputation, plus the fact that he was in danger of appearing ignorant of a whole way of life right under his own nose, strengthened his resolve. One Friday morning, before we adjourned school to prepare for the Friday Congregation Prayer, he summoned us into his presence and demanded an explanation. He first revealed that he knew the entire story, but that he would give us a chance to tell it ourselves. If not, we would be admitting guilt in a collective way and then it was up to him to decide what should be done. A unanimous silence fell on the place, which did not please him. He picked up one small boy. Crushed between Teacher's direct pressure and the hidden but no less powerful counter-pressure of the other boys, the little lad staggered to his feet and made as if to run away. He fell down near the entrance, where Teacher had preceded him. Teacher perhaps thought this was an act of unsolicited surrender, but any illusions he might have had on that score were dispelled by the lad blubbering and bursting into tears. Teacher had him dragged away.

As a rule, when Teacher was going to cane us he halted abruptly and then rocked slightly from side to side before steadying himself. He looked the consummate professional of whom it could truly be said that he was born to the craft. Beating us was for him something of a sacramental duty: He formulated the pious intention and had it silently declared, his hands gathered as if in supplication to

God, and his teeth clenched to signify unflinching resolve in undertaking and completing the Lord's business. The tyranny of the cane must stand between the unregenerate anarchy of misbehaved children and their imperiled destiny before the Creator. Indeed, everywhere tyranny is better than anarchy, as the masters tell us. To one doctrine he consistently adhered: We were what he called God's sun-baked mud bricks, made of unregenerate mud, extremely fragile, and needing recasting and remodeling. He cracked the whip over us at the same time as he cleared his throat, giving a loud yell as if prodding a donkey, and ending the ritual by reminding us that as God's mud bricks we needed all the thrashings we could get. As long as this need was there, he was happy to oblige.

That Friday morning Teacher confirmed that we were all, without exception, God's mud bricks. These bricks were clearly uneven in quality, but some were made of sterner stuff than others. If there was any credit to be claimed for these, it was because he, Teacher, had worked hard to get them transferred from his black book to his roll of honor. Essential to that slow process was the cane, judiciously wielded and selectively applied. In the case of students of unequal talent, the cane was again unquestionably valuable. It raised morale and brought about a leveling process in which the slow were made to catch up with the not-so-slow. Teacher cracked the whip several times before anyone screamed. Presently, however, some of the little ones started screaming and yelling. Then the general confusion died down to a long and monotonous sob, with an odd voice or two rising above the rest. It was difficult to say which was more gibberish, little boys crying after being flogged or shouting their chants in an incomprehensible foreign language like Arabic. No doubt Teacher would have said that the divine language, no matter how badly chanted, had superior merits. The sobs of children were just the sound of inferior straw bricks snapping.

The flogging did not make canaries out of us, and, if anything, it stoked the fuels of resistance. This is a delicate matter. Teacher went apoplectic with any hint among us of anarchy, the riotous condition, for in his view such condition was akin to bad manners. Resistance, however, he considered more rationally: It was evidence of native fiber and could, when reclaimed and directed, be the opportunity for phased personal improvement.

The matter of the bush fight and its consequences at school had gone beyond all previous bounds. Our parents heard about it. My father, true to color, did not react immediately. It was Mother who started to get worried. She began to imagine the worst possible things that could happen among us in the bush and gave us advice about choosing friends. Mother let off steam by occasional and scattered vents of anxiety. She was like a thatched roof over a kitchen out of which smoke filtered in short, small puffs rather than the entire roof going up from suppressed force. By the time she had got round to another one of her bursts of warnings we had gone off. Towards evening we all drifted towards the school in preparation for the evening recitations.

Bonfire

Reciting the Qur'án by the light of the bonfires was the highlight of everyday life at the school, a time when everybody, including the smaller boys, came together to recite the portions of the Qur'án they had copied on to their slates earlier in the day. The abler students who had memorized their scripts often went through the evening exercise with flying colors. The slower students had a more difficult time of it, struggling with old scripts of a day or two previous. Teacher hovered menacingly over the slow students, ignoring completely their successful colleagues. Those who had little, such as intelligence, he felt, even that little should be taken away, such being the logic of the higher wisdom. The bonfires, however, were a collective indulgence. Teacher would have us believe that our fire was different from heathen fires. The heathen, he said, treat fire as an object of worship, their egos absorbed in its rage as they fret distractedly after salvation and immortality, rather than being tamed with the word from high. It is hard to tell how much Teacher was subliminally influenced by fire rituals prevalent in much of non-Muslim Africa, and if in his reaction he was deflecting attention from his own pre-Islamic roots in the culture. For example, his own non-Muslim Fulbé cousins practiced fire-eating, putting a bundle of loose, smoking straw into their mouths, then blowing and puffing to fan the flames, and removing the bundle as it blazed, with the audience bursting out with loud applause. We as children attended many of these fire rituals that were staged in defiant proximity to the Qur'án school.

At any rate, Teacher spoke derogatively of heathen fires that blazed and babbled as short-lived spectacles, the tongues of flame leaping in vain reach for the sky above only for their brief upward darts to be quenched in the trackless void. Heathen fires presume to bring God down to our level, while the Qur'án school fire pointed us to the exalted truth above. The school's fire thus retained an abiding luminous merit at its heart even after the sparks had subsided, as was appropriate to its role in assisting human beings to take custody of the word of God. The children were not allowed to stare into the fire or to be silent before it lest, being at the center, the fire should incite them to mute heathen introspection, consuming them in its brief glare and then abandoning them to the darkness beyond.

Yet we made a concession to its obvious centrality in education, which Teacher did by infusing into the nightly practice elements of ethical teaching and orthodox assurance. In that connection, he said that at the Last Day, when all the souls were assembled before the judgment throne of God, the flames of the Qur'án school would rise before God as our witnesses to plead for mercy and forgiveness. He said that on the strength of that plea God would wipe out our sins, increase our merit, and count to our benefit all the good works we had done on earth. The flames would also bear witness to the number of times we had attended the evening recitations, and God would multiply all our good works by that number.

He said even friends and relatives who were in mortal danger of hell fire would find that the approaching flames of punishment would be turned away by the merciful flames of the Qur'án school. Teacher said—and we found all this very impressive teaching—that God would never let any of His faithful creatures suffer punishment by fire when these same creatures had studied the divine revelation by the bonfires of the Qur'án school, and He would never let them toil in the heat of ultimate loss after they had toiled in the heat of the noonday sun, gathering firewood for the Qur'án school. He said that just as some of the boys were unstinting in the way they went in search of fuel for the school, so God would be unstinting in collecting good marks for us and would raise our rank in Paradise just as some of us had raised our quota of fuel for the school. The entire school gave Teacher its complete and total attention whenever he waxed strong on this theme. Any discussion about the ultimate judgment and God's providence always received the undivided attention of the school, partly because it was widely believed, and feared, that Teacher was the only man qualified to tell us anything authoritative about it, and partly because many of us had dreams about death and the judgment that puzzled us and we were pleased if somebody could explain some of our secret questions.

It was therefore important who Teacher chose as head boy for the evening recitations, often a favorite who was well versed in his scripts and generally ahead of the rest of the school. We referred to him as "fireman," but I think Teacher would have given him a less mundane title, such as night angel and companion of the commander of the word. In any case his job was to make sure that there was enough fuel to keep up a constant blaze to enable us to recite our scripts reasonably well. Sometimes the fireman would forget to bring more firewood. Having mastered his own script he forgot that the rest of us still needed illumination. Teacher might be somewhere in his house or have his back turned to us, but he would notice immediately we were not reciting our scripts properly. He would give one of his characteristic signals, like clearing his throat or flapping his baggy trousers with the cane, any of which was enough to send us scurrying to our slates. The fireman would hasten to place a handful of sticks onto the fire. As these burned he would grab a few heavier pieces of wood and toss them in as well. He was overreacting, attempting to dispel any suggestion of tardiness, though he would be equally unwise to spend all the fuel in one blind moment of enthusiasm. It would be quite a time before the fire needed restoking.

School

The Qur'án school was something like a moveable feast, taking up residence wherever there was need and demand, though, of course, it followed certain rules of collective decisionmaking to establish it. Our particular school was "called" by a leading head of family whose many wives and other women relatives had produced, and were producing, large numbers of children to justify establishing a school. Such a school could be supported from the labor the children would provide on the farms. The men folk would produce the millet and sorghum, and the women folk rice and vegetables, with well-wishers contributing cash and other gifts in kind. To have many children was considered a blessing, but to have them learn the Qur'án was even more blessed, for the special *barakah* of it would rub off on the entire community. Children made Qur'án schools, but far truer is that Qur'án schools made children, and made them into the image of God's word. You might know a Muslim community by its many mosques, but you could not make a Muslim community except by Qur'án schools. The brighter the bonfires of learning, the sturdier the rod that marshals the children, we could hear Teacher say, the greater the community's aggregate *barakah*, as if the Prophet had said, "by the fire and the rod you shall receive *barakah*."

A word is necessary about the stages of learning through which Teacher himself went. As a Fula, Teacher had had the education Muslim Fulbé gave their children. There are four main stages in that system: *jangugol*, reading; *windugol*, writing; *firugol*, vernacular exegesis; *fennu* (Ar. *funún*), higher studies. Reading is a laborious process consisting of singling out and chanting the separate words of the *Fátihah*, then picking through the first rubric division of the Qur'án (*hizb*, pl. *azháb*) (*súrahs* 94 to 104 in reverse order), then returning to the *Fátihah* for pronunciation and covering the same rubric division. Then follows a third going over when the *Fátihah* is studied for proper reading and enunciation, what the Fulbé call *rindingol* or *fineditugol*. By this stage *windugol*, writing, has commenced and is pursued concurrently.

What is special in this system is the use of the Fula language in oral exposition and rhetorical training; it allowed the language in time to be fixed with the transcribed conventions and conceits of literary Arabic as the masters employed it in theological argumentation, rhetorical demonstration, oral ornamentation, and didactic guidance. In effect Fula was transformed into a tool of scholastic practice, a half-way house between the penalty of primitive stigma and the merits of revealed truth. The religious use of the language excited Fulbé ethnic consciousness, with religion often providing the channels that guided political expression and shaped social identity. Even non-Muslim Fulbé found they needed the linguistic materials developed in religious work, leaving these ethnic Fulbé always one step short of conversion to Islam. In one historical example, it needed only the presence of a Christian medical mission among non-Muslim Fulbé to bring about indirectly the conversion of the whole community to Islam. Muslim Fula and Mandinka clerics came periodically to the clinic for medical attention, and while undergoing treatment they stayed for weeks at a time with their non-Muslim Fulbé compatriots, propagating Islam. By the time they finished treatment, they had converted the entire village to Islam, thanks to the Christian missionaries who opened a path for them![2] However, two centuries of active Islamic preparation had sowed the seeds for this otherwise sudden flowering, and Teacher was the seasoned fruit of that long and deep preparation.

To return to the Qur'án school now placed under his absolute authority, on certain occasions it and the general town community joined together in the religious performances. One such occasion was the all-night chanting on Islamic feast days. Teacher, as far as I remember, did not attend these occasions but he let his students go. It was the other Muslim community leaders who took charge, usually by volunteering to give their time and services. The Qur'án school had its own sessions of all-night religious vigils, but they were not very popular, largely because they were no change from the normal routine of Qur'án school life, whereas vigils in the community took place outside the school and without the presence of Teacher. Later on some local Tijání[3] leaders became closely identified with organizing all-night vigils, which virtually completed Teacher's exclusion because he was a staunch Qádirí[4] and would not be seen consorting openly with his Tijání archrivals. In Teacher's view the Tijání clerics were the Cherubim who looked to their hearts for loving God, and the Qádirí clerics were the Seraphim who attended to their heads for knowing God's ways. As a consequence, the Tijání people flirted with demagoguery, whereas the Qádirí people sought after virtue in knowledge and understanding. These fine doctrinal points were sharpened by the unstated though no less real subject of ethnic sensibilities. Teacher was a Fula, originally from Futa Jallon in Guinea, whereas the men who led the Tijání vigils were Wolof from neighboring Senegal. The two people rarely socialized together. The Wolof Tijánís were too populist for Teacher, who as an affiliate of the stringent Qádiriyáh confraternity had too high-minded a view of the word of God to trust the crowds with it. Crowds lack for regulation not speculation, confinement not exposure. For that reason the Tijánís were a public hazard and a religious nuisance, though to answer them would play into their hands.

His scruples notwithstanding, the vigils continued, organized by compound heads. A large open courtyard at the town center was the setting. A canvas tent was erected on bamboo poles and rhun palms. The community leaders sat in an inner ring, and around them sat other community elders, counselors, advanced Qur'án students, and so on to the periphery, where the women sat. A small wooden table was placed in the middle, and on it were offerings of kola nuts, candles, and other things. A small kerosene lamp burned with a dense glow. The Muslim leaders who organized the vigil sat round the table, dressed in thin white robes and wearing white skull caps. In front of them were copies of the Qur'án and a few religious texts, such as eulogies on the Prophet (*Madíh*) and accounts of his life and the lives of his Companions (*Síra*). The chanting was interrupted by brief homilies and selected recitations from well-known religious works. Sometimes prose passages, after being read out in the original Arabic, were translated into the vernacular, but verse was not translated for fear, I think, of losing the poetic effect.

The chanting was frequently interrupted by refreshments. Just like the other aspects of the vigil, the interruptions were informal. We did not serve any refreshments if people were chanting or listening to a recitation. Many of the chants were not written down but recited from memory. A man would begin with a short familiar chorus, and after it had been well received he would follow it with a long impressive solo performance. Then the company would recite in unison. After this would come refreshments, and here some of us lads became useful. The candles and the kola nuts were beyond reach, but we were given charge of distributing biscuits, bringing in buckets of tea, and passing round the tin mugs. We distributed the tea from tall metal jugs. After people had refreshments they resumed the religious exercises, while we collected the mugs to wash them up. Refreshing the saints required the performance of less elevated chores!

History came alive during the vigils. Scenes representing Muslim armies engaged in battle were recalled. Many chants celebrated the bravery of Muslim generals and the miraculous victories of hard-pressed Muslim armies. Moving scenes involving the conversion of hitherto implacable enemies of the faith, such as certain Quraysh leaders, were evoked, and the growing strength of Islam in its early days was vividly brought out. The vigils ended with the Prophet ascending and appearing before God (the *mi'ráj*), confessing his unworthiness but pleading on behalf of his followers. God granted his intercession, and so Muslims throughout the world were bound together in a community of mutual intercession. Such was the extent of the freedom even Tijání adepts would allow to religious credulity. Although in the vigil a *muríd* devotee might appeal to a personal saint, the crowd was never publicly invited to seek saintly intercession, or even to invoke the permanent patronage of the founder, Shaykh Ahmad al-Tijání himself, notions alien to the form of rigorist Málikí Islam the community had received. A vivid example was the rigorist teaching that following the fortieth day after death, the soul of the deceased lapsed permanently, having no further contact with the living. The Tijání masters would have liked to ameliorate such teachings and to introduce ideas that were in provocative contrast to Teacher's attitude of stringent adherence to the unembellished facts of law and injunction.

At the dawn prayer, the vigil broke up and the Cherubim took flight. The dawn prayer, a ritual obligation, took precedence over the intercessory exercises of the vigil. We had offered to God the free and voluntary submission of our hearts; now we were to perform obligatory prayer as commanded from on high, with the Seraphim at hand to watch over us. The mystic disposition to seek "God's face" must yield to the appropriate humility of prostrating before the exalted law.

Teacher, nosy proxy of the archangel himself but coming down to earth through the effective spy network he had planted among us, was up-to-date on all the happenings at the vigil. No saints would be allowed to stand between him and his spoils. He knew, for example, which of the students performed well and which of them fell asleep during the night. He regarded falling asleep during religious exercise as proof of idleness, which he felt duty-bound to rectify. Offenses during vigils did not immediately lead to corporal punishment but merely to being tagged with the stigma of an offender released on the promise of good behavior. The next offense, however slight, brought the cane.

Discipline

Not long after a vigil I had occasion to fall into Teacher's grip. I had been reported to him as one of those who had fallen asleep on a mat near the tea buckets. Teacher knew that I had been up-to-date on my lessons and that he seldom had cause to rebuke me about my lessons. In spite of that he took a serious view of the matter. A little later I fell foul of him again. He called me one morning and asked whether I had finished reciting the portion of the Qur'án he had copied out on my slate the previous day. I said I had memorized it, and when he asked me to recite in front of him I did so, whereupon he directed me to wash off the old material so that my slate was clean and ready for the new material. During midday recitations he asked if I had washed my slate. When I answered, "Yes," he asked me to bring it to him. I brought the wooden slate to him, but the Arabic characters were still faintly visible on it. That was not really my fault because the ink we used for writing was crudely made by us under Teacher's own supervision, and we did so by rubbing the surface of metal cooking pots. Sometimes not enough soot had collected on the pots, and no amount of scraping would coax any more of the precious substance. The scraping, in fact, was bad for the ink, causing it to dry and to stain the wood. This was what happened in my case. I had scrubbed the stubborn surface with all my strength but after it dried the characters were still clearly visible. Teacher was furious. As he turned the slate over and over I noticed his thin bony hands flicking and a growing impatience rising in his voice. It was only a matter of time before he reached for his cane and with it he tap-tapped the slate, a sign that I was to keep my right index finger where the offense was, his way of rubbing it in. However, my hand recoiled by reflex. When I steadied it enough to point to the state I was making circles in a futile bid not to be smacked. Teacher, fed up with my dodges, abandoned the chase and settled on capture.

Teacher's face tightened and furrowed; then his throat vibrated menacingly as he cleared it. He raised his cane, placing it first behind his neck across his shoulder and then bringing it down to rest where he was seated on the prayer rug. He then picked it up, and, as his fingers closed round the cane, his face loosened and his wrist relaxed. He was muttering to himself, his tone one part declaratory and the other doxology. He loved his craft, and now he would thank God for it.

He pulled both my ears and I crawled on the ground towards him. I stooped as low as I could without touching the ground, and then I felt his hand fly past my head as he tried to hit it. I think I cursed him secretly. There was a legend at school that Teacher's left hand delivered the most deadly slaps across the face. So when any of us went to him expecting to be punished we moved as close to the left hand as possible, trying thus to reduce the effectiveness of his left-hand swipes and leaving him with the weaker right hand. I remembered this ploy, and when he pulled me by my ears I dragged myself to his left side as close as possible. But I was at a disadvantage. With my two ears firmly in his hand he could balance me on either side of him as he pleased. He swayed me to the right at arm's length, and when I tried to recover my balance, he closed in with a powerful left-hand swipe. Then he grabbed me by the ears again, pinched me tightly, and shook me firmly as if to test his grasp on the substance of power.

This side of Teacher was not easily understood by parents and guardians, but it was one that we had no difficulty in appreciating. As far as he was concerned he approached this aspect of his job with as much care and thought as he did the religious and educational aspects. By constantly referring to us as God's mud bricks he took the divine law into his own hands. One could not say he actually enjoyed beating his students. But he always stood for strict discipline and saw even the ritual prayers as God's way of containing us, of reducing us to postures of submissive obedience, as close as we could be on this side of the grave to the dust of our origin. The mud bricks idea attained the same purpose. His cane rested beside him as by divine order. His hands were as much adapted to wielding the cane as his great prominent forehead was to touching the floor during the prayer prostrations. A devout servant of God, Teacher regarded himself as responsible, before God, for the minds and bodies of his pupils, and he expected to receive his reward from God in accordance with the diligence with which he performed his duty.

Learning: Medicine and Individual Effort

A common practice at the school was to collect the water with which we had washed our slates if the relevant portions were from highly auspicious parts of the Qur'án. We collected this water in small bottles and took them home for use as medicine. We had to obtain Teacher's permission for that, but he was never known to object. In fact, it was he who told us which sections of the Qur'án were useful in that way. We could not recall a time, however, when he taught us that the holy water could help us acquire quick minds, and yet it was precisely this hope that sent many parents in search of the right Qur'án medicine, at great expense and trouble, which they made their children drink, alas, often in vain.

Although the number of parents who resorted to this mind-quickening device was large, that did not mean that there were not bright boys at the school. Teacher could in fact boast of a fair number, and occasionally he had a chance to receive public honors for the many bright boys he had helped to set on the right course. One such occasion presented itself. A number of his pupils had finished reciting up to the thirty-sixth *súra* of the Qur'án, *Ya Sín*. This was considered to be an advanced stage of proficiency and was traditionally celebrated by the community on the school premises and occasionally at the mosque on a Friday. Given the peculiar numbering of the *súras* of the Qur'án, so that it reads back to front, with the higher *súras* occurring earlier, *Ya Sín* in fact was the second stage in Qur'án recitation. The first was the sixty-seventh *súra: al-Mulk*, "the kingdom." That particular chapter opens with a general prayer: "Blessed be He in whose hand is the kingdom, He is powerful over everything, who created death and life. . . . Thou seest not in the creation of the All-merciful any imperfection. . . . And we adorned the lower heaven with lamps." It was considered a meritorious act to make some kind of voluntary offering after reaching that *súra,* but in importance it ranked below *Ya Sín,* which starts by venerating the Qur'án.

Examination

On the occasion when Teacher was to present his successful students before the community a few preliminaries started the proceedings. It was a Friday, and people were returning from the congregation prayer. A number of distinguished visitors had also come to town. The mothers of the boys had cooked big meals to feed the crowd. The local *imám* and his followers were among the visitors. However, the Qur'án school was out of bounds for certain visitors, such as the chief and colonial officials. Even the *imám* did not come there as a rule. The wife of Teacher was not expected to do any cooking, but she supervised the seating arrangements in the forecourt. The candidates themselves were specially prepared for the exercise. Their heads were shaved and they wore clean gowns. They were expected to perform ablution, in other words, ritual cleansing, before attending the ceremonies. The parents brought a small offering of kola nuts, which was formally introduced to the gathering and then laid aside to be distributed after the introductory prayers. Important dignitaries and visitors were specially welcomed, and other proceedings of protocol duly completed before coming to the highlight of the occasion. Prayers were an important part of the proceedings and were led by the *imám,* who began usually by making everyone join in reciting the *Fátihah,* and ended by thanking Teacher for his leadership of the school. Then Teacher would introduce the pupils and announce the portions of the Qur'án each would recite in turn.

By the time we reached that stage the students had had sufficient time to pull themselves together and to get used to the rather august atmosphere of the meeting. Teacher, the *imám,* and distinguished guests and visitors sat near Teacher's house, directly opposite the gate of the compound. Facing them were the students, who were in turn surrounded by former students and other Muslim dignitaries, friends, and relatives. The women waited in a nearby house and appeared when it was their turn to distribute the food and the other refreshments.

Then came the climax of the ceremony. The students began with the formal opening, announced the *súra* and verses from which their selections were taken, and then commenced the long, arduous task of recitation. Teacher was supposed to prompt them if their confidence wobbled, but he preferred instead professional detachment, like a giraffe with an elevated head overseeing a fish market. Teacher had never seen his task as that of helper of the disadvantaged, as a one-man affirmative action brigade, for that would put him on the same side as the students. After all, as priest of the word, he was selectman of heaven rather than an equal opportunity agent. He would not compromise his standing by being seen on the side of half-baked children floundering through God's word. Fortunately in this case there was no need to suffer principle. One by one they recited their pieces with confidence, to the great satisfaction of the people present. That was Teacher's supreme moment of triumph, which had enabled him gracefully to endure the long and complicated preamble. The verdict of the examiners was still to come, but there was no doubt the students had fully justified Teacher's faith and high hopes. The main part of the business thus completed, the assembly started to disperse. People shook hands, offered short extempore prayers, and departed. There was no public congratulation of the students, or rather such congratulation took other forms. People came to them and prayed for them, but beyond that ignored the children completely. I have often wondered if, because the adults wanted on such occasions to have the Qur'án hold center stage, they made such a point of ignoring the children beyond mere form lest children have the wrong idea that they held center stage. So here were the children, their egos enticed and then ignored by public clamor, left to seek remedy in boasting, posturing, and other forms of macho behavior, behavior by which they look to themselves for remedy of the slight they suffered at the hands of all-powerful adults.

While the dignitaries were dispersing most of us stayed behind because it was time for refreshments. The elders had shared out the kola nuts among themselves, and now it was our turn for a share of the good things. Just as I was getting up from where I was squatting an elderly man walked up to me and stroked my shaved head with his rough hands. "My son," he said, "I shall look forward to the day when you also will be inducted into the holy order of Qur'án scholars. I pray for the hastening of that day." His rough thick hands brushed down the side of my head, touching the right ear Teacher had pinched so severely. I ducked quickly, and uttered a faint "Amen," perhaps more to celebrate my escape than in answer to the prayer of my elderly visitor. Then I turned my mind quickly to the meals that were being served in a neighboring compound.

That evening, at the Qur'án school, Teacher announced that the examiners had returned a unanimous verdict in favor of the students, and that having attained such high standards it was now up to the boys to decide whether they wanted to continue at the school as full- or part-timers or go elsewhere for further education. Some of us indicated we were opting for a Western-type education, and this did not please Teacher at all. He advised us to continue at the school on a part-time basis while attending the other type of school, which he could not bring himself to name directly. We would earn *barakah* only as his pupils, which we could not forego.

The competition he faced from Western-style schools hardened Teacher. The Western school, he contended, created a drop-out culture, and although it boasted of its principled abjuring of the cane, nevertheless by inciting in children attitudes of superiority and inferiority, and withal a festering insecurity, it resorted to a weapon far more callous.

The Western school was, therefore, a moral breach, Teacher charged, an extension of infidel alien penetration into African soil. He predicted that children would be torn from their roots, and young men and women detached from the stem of tribal solidarity, all of them transplanted into a culture of competitive individualism that had not a shred of compassion and offered the illusory promise of economic advancement. A few such people, he warned, would make it, but the great majority, drop-outs all, would reap only personal disenchantment and loss of identity. Brothers and sisters would be turned against each other, driven apart by competition. Whether they passed or failed in their exams, the children would have lost all sense of family and community solidarity. Consequently, the society needed all the ammunition it could muster to avert such a calamity, and so Teacher's own example of wielding the cane should find collective resolve in community resistance. But Teacher was dreaming, for, even if he had moral right on his side, he knew an irresistible force had entered the land, heralding a permanent, aggressive new world order. The hegemony of the infidel West would seek to make public example of the very tradition Teacher was raised to foster. As it was, some of us (God forbid!) would bend and be lost to it.

Teacher's dramatic personality, to which orthodox stringency gave a sharp edge, was bolstered by the specter of the infidel West. Religion polarized his thought, causing him to divide the world neatly between truth and error, between lawful and forbidden, purity and pollution. For him, education not founded on religion was in principle unsound, and a state education that made religion suit all tastes rendered religion worthless. The end of education should be, he stressed, *Sapiens atque eloquens pietas* (piety endowed with the power of thought and expression), as the Puritans would put it. This theocentric view of education, Teacher felt, would not be spared by a Western humanism in which human experience is given primacy over revealed truth, and where the connection between education and religion is severed for good, driven by the specious argument of education as a neutral channel for ideas. This neutral humanism would make our ultimate end the dissolution and dissipation of all life into the universe, whereas religion sees death not as the end but as the harbinger of a fuller, more complete existence. Secular humanism promises freedom in education but in fact sets up a structure of opposition to God. Education for freedom is the banner cry of the West, yet freedom without purpose is human delusion. So the West masks the delusion by emphasizing the building of national character and civic virtue as the goal of education. The delusion thus remains because nations, especially proud ones, are a nuisance among themselves and to their people unless they, too, live under God's law. (Teacher had escaped the draft in World War II but had come close enough to sense how nations boasted vainly in the sword.) Society must not be satisfied with the view that giving its children the tools of literacy and professional skills will ensure prosperity and virtue, for without ethical character, without integrity and spirit, in fact without *barakah*, no system of education, however efficient, can inculcate habits of virtue and love for truth. On the contrary, efficiency may produce ruthlessness. The child is not just a hollow vessel that the school packs with information and facts; rather, the child bears the divine imprint, a living spiritual entity whose security and welfare should come before any neutrality ideology. The child must be formed, not just tutored, directed, not just informed, inspired, not just instructed, motivated, not just rewarded, affirmed, not just evaluated, and commissioned, not just congratulated. The child is not an animal. It must know God, the master of the world, and is, thereby, fit for knowledge. That, in a nutshell, was the whole case for education and the cause that fitted (and fired) Teacher's Puritan temper.

Since God created all children as equal before Him, He also made their egalitarian formative education a high and holy calling. Education is moral growth, and though its effects are practical and national, its enduring fruits are spiritual and symbolic. The Western school system, by contrast, is based on class, rank, status, race, money, and power, which necessarily divide us. It makes secular education an individualistic enterprise and repudiates the values of cooperation, community, and commitment, the "three Cs" of moral education. It is a denial of God's sovereign justice. By taking over the education of African children, Teacher would intone remorsefully, Western colonial powers, the English, the French, and the Portuguese to be precise, had imposed captivity without visible chains. In the sparsely clad children of Africa, the Western colonial powers saw defects that well-tailored school uniforms would hide. The whites think: Bring his children to a sense of sexual embarrassment, and the pygmy father will throw away his ancient tribal heirloom and welcome his modern Western savior. After all, what is straw beside the torch of knowledge?

Western education sets its face against community and conformity, but is dishonest, for such education standardizes children by the very standard of individualism, and suppresses their individuality by the rule of battery-run individual tests, which are objective only in a subversive sense. Separated from kith and kin, children become conventional, their tribal kit and caboodle replaced by the school uniform and their leisure organized by gym rules. In response, Muslim Africans must resist by passive defiance first, and then with the curse in their daily devotions. If the West opposes God, Teacher would say with his cane-bearing hand trembling in pained defiance, then the people of God should make the West an anathema, a ransom to divine displeasure. Compromise, which had no honor with him, had on this subject abandoned him entirely, and he would retire, still ill at ease, from battle with the invisible and imperturbable enemy. However, assured of the adulation of his students, whom he would rouse to strong chanting of the Qur'án, his hackles began discernibly to subside.

Conformity

Teacher had indicated with his own attitude that times had changed and that we would have to adapt to succeed. Precisely how or when, we did not know, except that we could see our elders juggling their options and biding their time. Even in the confined world of children old patterns were beginning to shift in the final years of the Qur'án school. Numerous bush fights had produced a rapid turnover in friendships and alliances, and tension increased among the boys. That hardened the mood and drove us to seek relief from duties our elders had imposed on us. Teacher's authority we accepted implicitly, but we wondered whether its source in divine injunction was entirely to our benefit. So we asked why the ritual prayers could not be skipped, why it was necessary to observe the obligatory fast of Ramadán[5] in all its tiny details, why in Islamic law duties were classified as required, recommended, indifferent, reprehensible, or forbidden. Why not just recommended and indifferent? That would take the coercive and the punitive out of religion. The boys who pressed such questions came to be looked upon as rebels, causing the rest of us to side with Teacher as champion of orthodoxy.

In many ways our particular Qur'án school was a mild regime compared to other schools. In school we might talk lightly of conformity, but other schools had a far harsher regime, indeed something of a boot-camp culture of confinement and draconian measures of labor and submission. It is a widespread practice in all Muslim Africa, and for further references the reader is referred to Chapter 3, in which the role of the Qur'án school is examined.

In time many of us began to develop definite feelings about the Qur'án school, although we never questioned openly some of the fundamental principles on which it was based. Teacher, as the driving force of the school, made that kind of opposition impossible to contemplate. We accepted the rule of *bila kayf*, meaning "without asking how." Teacher might give it a more instrumental interpretation, such as, the more grounded we are in Scripture the more stored we would be for the future. Thus we accepted the teaching that God gave us minds to train and develop in divine service so that at the end of our appointed earthly course we could render an intelligible account of our stewardship to the Creator. That was one of Teacher's basic teachings. He said God had no use for illiterate minds. The Qur'án school was the obvious place where we could learn to be literate in Arabic. We also venerated the teaching that the flames of the bonfires of the Qur'án school would rise to defend us on Judgment Day, bearing witness to our diligence and perseverance *fí sabíl illáh* (in the way of Allah). God's mud bricks, as Teacher was accustomed to regarding us, needed expert handling if they were to occupy their rightful place in the ranks of Heaven. Off limits to political officials like the chief and the district commissioner, the Qur'án school was our province of virtue. Pious people, visiting religious notables, and important community dignitaries came there on visits. We had the benefit of seeing some of these men at close quarters and learning about the wider Muslim world. The accounts of travelers to the school filled us with great curiosity and longing. Moreover, for those of the students who were destined to play important roles in the larger Muslim community outside, to have had the school in their academic pedigree was an advantage. That advantage in the community, plus the attractiveness of travel to other Muslim lands, made the school an essential and necessary part of our early education and training. The mood of questioning, however intense, did not change our basic attitudes towards Teacher and the school.

One day, at meal time, my brother asked my father if he thought it would have been more pleasant, and less risky, if God had allowed us never to have left heaven, rather than plunging us willy-nilly into the world and all its hazards. Why put us to a test few could pass? He asked this question after a night of heavy rains accompanied by thunder and lightning, and since he was frightened by these he thought it was not equitable for God to be sheltered in Heaven, leaving us to face life's trials here. My father coughed advisedly and asked my brother to put his mind to other things. But the bait my brother held out was too tempting to be ignored. I too began plying my father with questions. Why was it, I asked, that although God was merciful and kind He still would like to roast people in hell-fire? Why did He create all of us and then place some with the good and some with the bad when He could have saved Himself the trouble by making us all bad or good, or not making us at all, which would be better? And anyway why must people like Teacher be automatically destined for Paradise when the rest of us had a fifty-fifty chance? And why . . . ? I was not quite finished but I did not have time to put in another question. My father fixed his cold and deliberate eyes on me and I froze. "God," he said, "is not a subject for idle speculation." It did not help me, though, to be told I was too young to question the Creator's ways when I was old enough to bear the burden of learning His word, but that unsatisfactory situation would take several years to produce an effect. In the meantime my father resorted to the evasiveness so natural to parental authority by explaining that when he was a child and going to Qur'án school he was taught that all children were born as believing Muslims, although many children grew up without the chance to develop that God-given side of them because of wrong parentage and environment. Nevertheless when a child died it automatically went to Paradise as an angel. This reassurance, needless to say, however motivated by generosity, did nothing to absolve us from present responsibility, but my father was in no mood to be challenged. So we tried, I am sure unsuccessfully, to imagine Paradise as a place for children who died a premature death. The problem was that our language has no word for heaven or Paradise, so the myth of infant immortality had little hold on our imagination.

But my father, roused to duty, would not be deterred. He explained that as children he and his friends fulfilled their duties at their school because it ensured their security in the unseen world. He said they obeyed their Teacher to attract *barakah* to themselves, for such *barakah* would be an undiminishing asset that they could pass on to their families. He said it was such *barakah* that helped otherwise vulnerable little children to fend off the unsolicited attention of the evil one and to be destined for noble ends. Then he referred to the example of the Prophet. He said when the Prophet was a baby and his mother wanted another family to rear him everybody refused to take care of him. Eventually a kind but poor peasant woman took him into her home. The woman had lived a life of prayer and that was why, aware of the great *barakah* prayer achieved, she took in a tiny baby in the belief that she would be blessed by the God who created it, little aware that she would be suckling the Prince of Creation and the Apostle of God. That short preliminary about the Prophet was by way of introduction. Then he went on to tell us that once upon a time a poor family, desirous of receiving the divine *barakah*, made a modest food offering to which they invited children from the neighborhood. The children who came were from many different backgrounds: Fulbé, Bambara, Wolof, Mandinka, Serakhullé, Diola, Berber, pagan, and Muslim, neighbors and strangers, the high and the low. After the children consumed all the food—a meal and milk offering—they washed their hands in the big calabash bowl from which they had just eaten and made the customary call for *barakah* on the household. The woman of the house then collected the water in the calabash, and, making her secret wishes over the water, she poured it over the entrance of the compound. The water was supposed to run in trickles across the gate as a symbol of protection, the idea being that the *barakah*-charged prayers of the children would seal the home against malevolent forces.

After the woman had carried out that part of the ritual she turned to go inside her house. At that point she discovered that two of the boys had remained behind, and, puzzled why they had not gone with the rest, she asked them what they wanted. The lads said they thought there might be some household chores that she wanted done and that they would be glad to help. They even offered to fetch her supply of domestic fuel from the surrounding bush. When the woman asked them why they should be doing that they replied that they had missed Qur'án school and wanted to do substitutionary deeds of merit to earn *barakah*. The woman later discovered that these boys were the sons of an important local chief. My father then looked straight at us but did not say a word. There was no need to. We took the point. He had made the point with the usual periphrasis about the Qur'án school as the repository of *barakah*, and for this reason he wished us to obey Teacher unquestioningly and call him *Teacher*. In the name of *barakah*, what my father's pagan Manding forebears knew as *yirwa*, children came to be God's mud bricks, to be chiseled and laid down four square, vessels for the streams of *barakah* set to pour from Teacher's favorable disposition.

It is difficult to exaggerate the role *barakah*, the indigenous *yirwa*, played in our upbringing and early education, an idea with deep roots in pre-Muslim Africa. Both individuals and communities could receive *barakah* or lose it; they could regain it and retain it. Whatever the case, *barakah* demands trust in its efficacy rather than emotional attachment. It is more like a living trust and doing than it is a psychological mood or feeling. *Barakah* bespeaks a world of social interaction, of the goings and comings of people, of their relationships and human interests. If you receive enough of it, you will obtain immunity against misfortune. Those who have *barakah* should expend it, and the more they expend it, the more it increases. If you hoard *barakah*, you will lose it, because it spoils from inactivity or miserliness. *Barakah* loves a generous spirit, and it will conspire with one to create another. It is not possessive or boastful. It does not seek its own but prefers others. It does not reproach except to correct. It will relent if offended. It is just but not vengeful. It does not hurt or think ill of others. It is not loose or wild but is gentle and mild-mannered. It is not evasive, impulsive, intrusive, or indulgent. It loves the truth but is not sectarian or self-righteous. It is positive and compassionate but not sentimental or soft. It does not wag its tongue at others, but craves the best for all. It is loyal without being exclusive. It shelters under patience and forbearance, and flourishes from public acclaim, but is not ostentatious. It does not compromise though it shuns rancor and spite. It cannot be purchased, though it loves a cheerful and generous giver. It does not covet and is not envious. Everyone who seeks it will find it: all it requires is a sincere spirit. It does not wilt or cloy from familiarity. It encourages but does not flatter. Like *yirwa*, *barakah* produces company though it transcends it; it rejects no one; and it forgives and embraces all. The hope of *barakah* springs eternal, and its rewards are a joy forever.

Children seek *barakah* from their parents and teachers, and a mother's *barakah* is as important as a father's. *Barakah*, when dispensed as virtue, follows strict rules of observance: Husbands give *barakah* to their wives, teachers to pupils, saints to supplicants, paupers to the well-off, pilgrims to others, the old to the young, the blind to the sighted, but the best and choicest *barakah* is that of the Prophet who also bears the honorific, *al-Mubárak*, "the blessed one." In virtually all these cases *barakah* never works in reverse: children do not give *barakah* to their parents, pupils to their teachers, supplicants to saints, wives to their husbands, the well-off to paupers, non-pilgrims to pilgrims, the young to the old, the sighted to the blind, or, what would be the ultimate scandal, believers to the Prophet, unless, that is, *barakah* as offering thanks. Also *barakah* as virtue can be temporarily nullified by a breach of the rules of respect, deference, and honor. Though you may earn *barakah*, you cannot give it to yourself. Such belief in *barakah* emphasizes the social reality of persons and their relationships with one another. Muslim doctrine reinforces this understanding of *barakah* by confronting the believer with a moral *barakah* vested in ethical duty, of becoming an authentic person from one's actions rather than from anyone else's, be they relatives or friends. People are thus brought into active relationship with each other as believers, that is to say, as persons beholden to a common code of conduct. The Qur'án, as code and oracle, expresses it thus: "Neither your blood-kindred nor your children/shall profit you upon the Day of Resurrection" (60:3), or, elsewhere: "And no burdened soul can bear another's burden, and if one heavy laden cried for (help with) his load, naught of it will be lifted even though he (unto whom he crieth) be of kin. . . . He who groweth (in goodness), groweth only for himself, (he cannot by his merit redeem others)" (35:18, Pickthall). The duties of faith create a unified ethical outlook, so that breaches can be remedied and achievements rewarded. Religion thus prescribes and proscribes for persons as individuals, rather than becoming merely a function of ethnic or racial interest.

Education in its own sphere appeals to an identical principle of making the child's competence a matter of observing a personal code, the same code that guides the community in its relations with the school. In that respect, Islam sows the seeds of personal ethical duty, so that one's ultimate moral destiny rests not on lineage rank and tribal affinity but on active merit (22:14; 36:54). Religious doctrine thus recognizes achieved results fixed in effort and enterprise, not acquired traits rooted in blood and soil.

Such ideas on ethical accountability could, with the right stimulus, inspire faith in personal freedom and ignite the impulse to explore and experiment, and that need not abandon the pattern of the three Cs of moral education. However, with the rapid pace of change induced by Western contact well underway, children were destined to grow up in a world far less stable and self-assured than that of their elders. The sanctions of tradition derived their force from communal solidarity based on kin and clan loyalty and established within fixed or sedentary territorial limits. Now, however, a new world order had arrived, requiring fresh symbols shaped by choice and personal freedom. With it, religion as authoritative transmission would not be exempt, for children would grow up having learned to question authority, absorbed in self-discovery and rejecting the old ways. It would create a form of commitment centered on self-knowledge rather than on received tradition.

Some of us, though, were too loyal not to look for assurance from the old teachings and sanctions. Thus we took encouragement from the fact that the word of God, which had the rod on it and from which we obtained divine *barakah*, would ensure our well-being against the enemy. That was why we washed our slates and consumed the holy water, and that was also why we sought Teacher's approval and commendation. God's word contained *barakah* that was for our worldly benefit. *Barakah* as an ineffable resource comes to us mediated by numerous channels of principle and circumstance. Yet how could we be sure that *barakah* would follow us into change and defiance? *Barakah* has as its opposite *danka*, which is ill omen, sometimes incurred by the curse but more often from the ill will of those unjustly wronged, and it haunts and tracks down its subject. Between them *barakah* and *danka* conditioned the moral universe of children, carefully marking out those who might be recognized agents. It was impossible to break completely free of the force of *barakah* and *danka*, and that was why even those of us who enrolled in Western schools carried in our soul a double or bifurcated loyalty. There was the awful possibility that *danka* would fill the void that the Western school in its unfamiliarity with the world of *barakah* allowed to exist in our souls. If you exclude *barakah* from the new type of education and things go wrong, then you have little remedy except self-blame, and that kind of reproachful individualism leaves you a victim of the system. Thus you cannot throw children from the old system into the new without producing an identity crisis. That was why generations of children in traditional society arrived in the new world of Western secularism with a sense of dissonance and alienation. In our particular case, change was in the offing, and we were destined for an extraordinary adventure far beyond the confines of our small obscure school and its juvenile, motley convoy. What happened to us in Western schools of assimilation as well as rejection, of *barakah* and *danka*, left our families with painful ambivalence towards Western schools. Many such traditional families continued to keep a wary distance from these schools, whatever the promises or incentives.

7

The Arabic Language in African Education

In this chapter we shall describe the Qur'án school as an educational and social institution and examine why it has survived attempts to reform or replace it and prospered in spite of the odds. The utility value of the language is not able to account for the strong sentiment that Arabic excites in Muslim society. Many Muslims have done better materially with Western languages than with Arabic, and yet such persons have maintained deep loyalty to the language. What complicates our analysis and interpretation of the data is the unwillingness of Muslim Africans to separate Arabic from the Islamic religion. Proficiency in the language is deemed insufficient without deference to Muslim Scriptural authority, a position that puts non-Muslim Arabs, for example, in an untenable situation. Muslims accord an incomparable status to the Qur'án, and the Arabic Qur'án as revealed truth is nontranslatable; together these two aspects of religious commitment lead to linguistic exclusion. Even those who accept a limited role for Arabic in the modern economy find themselves on the defensive when arguments are presented to promote Arabic teaching on the grounds of popular demand and equity. Yet governments are scarcely able or willing to invest in Arabic when its market utility is at best questionable, though they cannot ignore it when faced with demands from a religiously sensitive population.

Another important issue is educational access for women, for the traditional Qur'án school is a closed world for the majority of women. In the best documented cases in north Nigeria, for instance, only 20 percent of the pupils are girls, with the numbers trailing off after the primary stages of instruction, although a similar figure is given for girls in Western-style schools. Nevertheless, it appears that even resistance to Western-style schools in Muslim Africa is conditioned by attitudes formed with respect to Qur'án schools. Obviously Qur'án schools remain far too important an institution in society to be ruled out of order by fiat, and their existence solves as many problems as it creates. Such are the questions we should briefly examine here.

Resilience of Tradition

Lord Lugard, the British colonial administrator, reported that when he took over responsibility in 1903 for the affairs of north Nigeria there were 25,000 elementary Qur'án schools[1] with an enrollment of about 250,000.[2] In 1961, a year after independence, the government estimated that there were 27,600 Qur'án schools with an enrollment of 423,000, of which 85,000 were girls. At the same period there were 2,490 primary schools on the Western model with 320,000 students, with 86,000 female students.[3] The female figures dropped dramatically in secondary school. In fact the decline was steep enough to be almost unmeasurable, so that we would be justified to characterize it as virtual neglect. There has been some progress since, but for the majority of women things have been at a standstill.

These statistics suggest that attitudes on the matter run deep, with Qur'án schools both agents and manifestations of the problem. It indicates, too, that traditional Muslim education occupies an ineradicable place in north Nigerian Muslim society. However, the colonial authorities took special steps to avoid any involvement in it, including radically reforming the system, for fear of contravening their own policy of noninterference in domestic matters, including religion. Three quarters of a century later the Qur'án school still continues to flourish, not only in north Nigeria but also in many other parts of Muslim Africa. In western Nigeria, for example, a study estimated that over half a million pupils attended such schools.[4] A quantitative survey of this type of school in all of West Africa would be a frightful task, but if it could be done it would certainly reveal a picture of phenomenal numbers of schools and pupils. The purpose of this chapter, however, is less ambitious and very different. It is concerned chiefly with the practical problems of fitting such traditional Islamic schools into the curriculum of modern, secular schools and giving them a realistic role in providing their students with a choice of careers. There is a slightly more theoretical question of what problems an alternative educational system, such as the Qur'án school, presents for ministries of education and governments, which is of evident interest to us.

Another aspect and one that has occupied the attention of many scholars is the Qur'án school curriculum and the importance of Arabic as a literate medium in African societies, including its value in gaining access to historical texts. However, this side of the matter is beyond the scope of this chapter. Furthermore, the important social functions of a Qur'án school, touched on in earlier sections of the book, will not be repeated here except insofar as they help us to understand the impingement of secular forces on indigenous institutions and ideas. Our focus here will instead be on the practical uses to which traditional Islamic education in Africa could be put and how Muslim groups, educational administrators, universities, and scholars have tried to tackle this question.

Colonial Factor

The colonial factor was clearly of some significance in the forming of Muslim attitudes to secular education, but it is difficult to explain the entire phenomenon by that alone. Lord Lugard, for example, laid it down as a solemn undertaking that the British colonial administration would not allow Christian missions to operate schools in the north of Nigeria, a principle that was scrupulously adhered to by his successors. In addition, native authorities were given control of most of the government schools in the north and freedom to introduce Arabic and Islamics into the curriculum, which they did.[5] Alhaji Dr. Abubakr Imam wrote in 1948 that education in the north was backward and not academic enough, even at the flagship Katsina College, until at least 1932. Katsina College was founded in 1922 in a remote, hard-to-reach corner of north Nigeria, and Sir Hugh Clifford, the governor of Nigeria who opened it, saw it as an instrument to lead the northern Nigerian Muslim elite without undue distraction into the modern age with their religious values protected, but with a little cricket thrown in. To the graduates of the college would fall, he said, the duty to teach "not only the lessons learned from books which they will here acquire, but the way that good Muhammadans should live, the good manners, good behaviour and the courteous deportment without which mere booklearning is of little worth."[6] The early colonial policy was to seal the College against any Christian ideas. Alhaji Sir Ahmadu Bellow, the premier of northern Nigeria, who was a student of the college, undertaking at first by foot the 170-mile journey there from Sokoto, for one took to the College's anodyne secular regime: his favorite subjects were history and arithmetic.

Katsina College occupied a special place in the colonial scheme of things. As a matter of policy its students were all Muslims. As the Sardauna himself testified, "There were no people from non-Muslim areas among us. I see now that this was perhaps a fault; it might have been better to have had more varieties of men in the College. Anyhow, a similar College should have been established for non-Muslims, but that was not part of Sir Hugh Clifford's plan. He had in mind the special colleges for princes, I think, which they had in India."[7]

The College fostered Muslim elite aspirations and forged interregional links and sympathies among future leaders. Aspiring Muslim scholars flocked to Katsina from Nigeria and other parts of West Africa, to sit at the feet of religious masters and rub shoulders with their peers, upheld in their belief that government was their natural ally. It is perhaps misleading to speak of a curriculum for the College in the sense of formal, successive stages of learning, and certainly age had little say in how classes might be set up. The main point was that government should shoulder the responsibility for preparing the future Muslim emirs to run the affairs of their people in accordance with ancient sanction, though such a course might cost them a strong start in modernization. Yet the triumph of British policy in this regard may be seen in the extent to which the neglected non-

Muslims, *les autochthones*, lost any institutional visibility even in a postcolonial Africa.

With religious safeguards in place, academic standards improved with time. For example, in 1942 a modicum of academic standards was introduced at Kaduna.[8] As to whether such a policy of protectionism for the Muslim community afforded them an equal opportunity in jobs and careers is a different question. In fact Sir Abubakr Tafawa Balewa, later to become the first prime minister of Nigeria, urged in 1948 in a speech during a Legislative Council debate that the British contradict their own declared policy and intervene to reform women's education in the north.[9] Sir Abubakr was joined by a number of other northern leaders who felt the Muslim community would be ill served by the colonial version of the policy of separate development—in fact Sir Abubakr was their spokesman in this and other matters. Nevertheless, Muslim demands for a separate provision of educational institutions were heeded and fostered by a number of different colonial governments. In the case of north Nigeria, Lord Lugard and his successors were anxious to operate through the traditional Islamic political and religious elites, from whose ranks were recruited an entire cadre of bureaucratic officials and functionaries.[10] The official position was based on the view that "the placing at the disposal of the Emirs of the resources of an ordered State inevitably strengthened and developed all Moslem institutions in Northern Nigeria,"[11] even if this policy meant providing constitutional backing for what were described as "Fulani theocratic institutions and civil and criminal law." A similar policy was adopted for British Cameroun, Sierra Leone, the Gambia, and Zanzibar, among others. In that sense, the policy of political development for Muslim Africa placed the power and prestige of the state at the service of religion, although there was no comparable legacy in Christian Africa. If Muslim Africans feel at a disadvantage educationally vis-à-vis their Christian counterparts, they overlook the commanding advantage they enjoy politically, an advantage that can be used to remedy the defects of educational backwardness.

Reform

In Freetown colony in Sierra Leone a different kind of responsiveness to Muslims was evident from a very early time, when, through the pioneering efforts of Dr. Edward Blyden, a *madrasah* system of Islamic education was launched with government support. In 1900 three such schools were in operation with a total enrollment of 427 pupils, and by 1909 the number had increased to 500. Blyden himself was appointed the first director of Muslim education in 1901, and almost immediately he created a committee of Muhammadan education.[12] Four years later the government opened a secondary school in Bo with courses in Islam and Arabic. However, the *madrasah* scheme was in Muslim eyes tainted with the original sin of infidel sponsorship, as Fisher pointed out, and it collapsed.[13] Similar ventures were tried with some success in the Gambia colony with the establishment of the Muhammadan school in Bathurst and Armitage School in George-town. It is not our purpose to pursue this historical line much further except to add that in 1927 the British attempted a unified *madrasah* system for all their colonies in West Africa called the Amalgamated Scheme, but it too had a fitful start in Freetown and fared even worse in Lagos.[14]

Part of the reason for such a poor record was standardization, which whittled away the number of poor quality teachers without at the same time being able to find the necessary replacements. However, in the scheme worked out by Dr. Bly-den, the old style Qur'án school methods were adopted alongside a modern syllabus: rote learning, memory work, ungraded classes, and the lack of a fixed daily timetable on top of graded, scheduled courses in English and arithmetic.

How did the juxtaposition of the traditional Qur'án school and modern educational methods function? It is hardly surprising that two diametrically opposed conceptions of education should lead to a stalemate, with the Qur'án school advocates spurning the temporal rewards of secular training. Education is a live issue in Muslim communities, and it rapidly takes on the guise of political opportunity in cases where Muslims are a cultural or numerical minority. In late 1973, for example, the Belgian Parliament, under pressure from Muslims, voted to accept Islam as one of the official religions in Belgian schools. There are an estimated 120,000 Muslims in Belgium, with 20,000 children of school-going age. However, the issue of Islamic education in Belgium became political as well.[15]

In many parts of Muslim Africa Islamic education was until recently fully integrated into the social and economic life of the people. The children acquired a rudimentary knowledge of the Qur'án within a highly authoritarian, dogmatic framework. They relied almost entirely on their memory to excel in work and looked up to the teacher as their superior in every way.[16] They developed a mystical attitude to Arabic, the liturgical and divine language of Islam, mainly through the emphasis on Qur'ánic Arabic. At appropriate points in Qur'án recital, the child was initiated into a slightly higher rank at a public ceremony. Such ceremonies reinforced the popular esteem of Arabic as a mystical language, while consolidating the power and prestige of the agents and instruments of Islamic education. Historical sources are rich with descriptions of the Qur'án school, including the often highly ornate passing-out ceremony.[17]

Religion

The Qur'án school soon acquired a sacerdotal function, with pagan parents sending their children there out of admiration for it. Gradually the Qur'án school developed into a complex social institution: a public ornament, the concentrated center of mystical power (*barakah*), the stronghold of a small literate caste in a nonliterate environment, a correction center for wayward children, the focal point of learning, a missionary center, and above all the custodian and dispenser of Arabic. Within the Qur'án school, or sometimes alongside it, there was an *'ilm* school specializing in the higher Islamic sciences, such as textual exegesis (*tafsír*), the Traditions (*ahadíth*), jurisprudence (*fiqh*), law (*sharí'ah*), biography (*sírah*), philology (*lughah*), grammar (*nahw*), and occasionally, mystical philosophy (*tasawwuf*) and the science of magic squares (*'ilm al-awfáq*). This curriculum is obviously a large dose and can take twenty or more years to complete. However, within the constraints of Qur'án school education, much of this material was committed to memory, a prodigious enterprise by any standard, and held within the bounds of received dogma (*taqlíd*). The aim and purpose of education, whatever the level, continued to be the synthetic transmission of received tradition.

Two things are clear from this type of education. First, it had a ready attraction for many African communities that were deeply influenced by the attitude of reverence for the knowledge and wisdom of the elders and ancestors and where meaning and purpose were closely related to the quality of collective participation. Qur'án schooling was treated as a rite of passage, though girls received very little of it. Exceptional people, such as the members of a small literate caste of Islamic educationalists, and unusual signs, such as the characters of the Arabic alphabet, were accorded mystical importance. Second, whereas the non-Muslim African populations quickly adapted to another system of education with a completely different approach and philosophy, Muslim Africa was to some extent inured against change of that order. The difficulty of juxtaposing the Qur'án school and secular education had been demonstrated in more than one instance, and the problem is no less acute under postcolonial governments. Hence the continuing dilemma of modern educational planners who feel unable to establish and maintain modern schools in traditional Muslim areas where the Qur'án school occupies a strong position. Although educational authorities might hope to dent traditional Muslim resistance by siting pilot schools in strategic locations, often traditional Muslim attitudes to learning survived into such schools where they were not ignored. Thus, the head of a state secondary school in a strong Muslim part of the country observed that in spite of the school's favorable location many and certainly the best pupils came from outside the area, for local Muslim parents would not send their children. Muslim resistance was more than a matter of siting.

It is curious that parents who would be willing to send their children to Qur'án school, often at great cost and trouble, and sometimes out of simple admiration, should seem correspondingly reluctant to enroll them in Western-style educational institutions for the identical purpose. The fear of conversion to Christianity, which has been the conventional reason for resistance, is surely by now anachronistic, and even when under colonialism conversion might be said to be aided and abetted by officialdom that theory cannot be supported by actual cases. If knowledge and religion entered Africa in the welcome guise of Arabic and Islam, it is hard to see why the same prestigious pair should be resisted in the shape of modern schools and the Bible. Indeed, a good deal of the evidence suggests Muslim Africans welcomed education in Christian mission schools as eagerly as they did in, say, Ahmadiyáh schools. Out of 343 children in a Methodist mission school in a town in Sierra Leone, fully 211, or just over 61 percent, were Muslim, and 131 Christian.[18] In the Gambia a comparable situation was obtained where the Methodist mission school of 140 pupils had a Muslim enrollment of 87 and only 29 Methodists. In one year, the Scripture prize for the London/Cambridge School Certificate exam was won by a Muslim boy,[19] and he remained a practicing Muslim. Based on this kind of evidence we could say that something other than the fear or reality of Christian indoctrination must explain subsequent Muslim resistance to modern schools. That explanation may have more to do with the level of religious politicization in society than with the intrinsic perfidy of modern schools.

Scale

In the course of trying to determine the precise role of Qur'án schools in Muslim communities, several important factors have emerged that are of crucial importance to government educational authorities. One fact has already been alluded to, namely, the large numbers of Qur'án schools. One reason for this is lack of a central organizing body or institution that can carefully plan schools where they are needed. A second reason is that Qur'án school proprietors are at times mere operators trying to cash in on an apparently lucrative business backed by buoyant demand. The same motive of easy gain leads some people with highly dubious credentials to pose as experts in obscure areas. Both these facts were observed by Mr. A. R. Dehaini in a survey conducted in the western state of Nigeria.[20] This prompted a Muslim scholar to remark: "Many of the proprietors of these schools who have started almost penniless have grown quite rich, with sizable balance in their bank accounts, landed properties and chauffeur-driven cars."[21] In a report drawn up by Selim Hakim it is pointed out that the Qur'án school is a quick means to wealth and prestige.[22] Another fact that emerges from field surveys is the unsuitability of much of the Arabic material. For example, Dehaini found that many Qur'án school proprietors obtained on request numerous copies of political propaganda literature from non-Arab countries and sold these as prescribed school texts at inflated prices.[23] In one such primary school the class was studying a manual on the atomic bomb.[24] All this evidence suggests that the great popularity of Qur'án schools enables them to survive such scandals and liberties, and is proof, too, that the system could survive whatever interference might be implied in attempting to bring to it the benefit of the three r's of reform, regulation, and rationalization.

Lack of systematic planning of Qur'án schools is coupled with a haphazard school curriculum. It is often not possible to take the pupil through a graduated course either because the series of books on a given subject is incomplete or is organized by unsuitable criteria. Similarly, pupils are not graded by any consistent yardstick, such as age or ability. A further complication is the often unnecessary duplication of material, involving repetitiveness, imitation, and conformity. Most field studies stress this phenomenon of overconcentration and of multiplicity of material and techniques.

As we shall see in the next chapter, in Freetown all the main ethno-linguistic groups ("tribe" is used for these groups in Freetown without self-consciousness) have their own separate adult evening schools. Of fifteen such schools only two are designated as "All Tribes," and two others are described as mixed.[25] The Temne, Susu, and Limba each have two evening schools. The Loko, Aku, and Fula each have a school, with the Fula forming important minorities in two other schools, the *Taqwa* and the *Faláh*.[26] All these schools are identical in organization (i.e., voluntary effort), in their methods (i.e., studying the letters of the Arabic alphabet and rote learning of the Qur'án), as well as in their purpose (i.e., the transmitting of a dogmatic code through the mystical medium of Arabic). They depend on enthusiasts to carry the main burden of teaching and organizing, people who would certainly be unsuitable by any government standard of supervision and control.

Voluntary Effort

Another fact that emerges is the dominant role of voluntary contribution and effort. There are many disadvantages in this way of establishing and funding Arabic schools: It is first of all unpredictable and liable to abrupt change; it is difficult to regulate the flow of funds to ensure balanced development. The system is also open to gross abuse. Two examples, both from Freetown, may suffice. The Muslims at one point were able to raise by voluntary contribution the sum of £1,500 sterling towards a school project. However, the money disappeared before it reached the designated project and could not be accounted for, leading to mutual recriminations among the Muslims.[27] Perhaps the most spectacular case of misappropriation of funds raised from voluntary sources was one involving a curious Englishman who adopted Islam, changed his name and led a successful fundraising campaign. Soon afterwards he ran into trouble with the law in the course of which his embezzlement of the funds was publicly discovered.[28]

Are these examples only the tip of the iceberg? One can never know for certain, but it seems almost inevitable that without central, organized direction and with the field wide open to nonprofessional adventurers, abuses should be widespread. With the increased involvement of Middle Eastern oil wealth in many of these schemes the scale of irregular practices is correspondingly increased. For some of the major Arab donor countries, it would make sense to try to establish systems of accountability even if that involves creating structures that answer to the donors, even though that would, at least in theory, infringe the principle of local self-responsibility.

Attempts have been made, and are still being made, to remedy some of the more flagrant malpractices of proprietary Qur'án schools by introducing an orderly curriculum under adequately trained teachers. In some cases Christian schools or Christian-founded institutions have collaborated in these schemes.[29] In other cases Muslims themselves have used the familiar channels of voluntary contribution, private initiative, and local demand and resources to establish Arabic teaching on a sound basis. One of the most famous is the Ansár ud-Dín Society in Nigeria, with headquarters in Agege, near Lagos.[30] Another is the Sierra Leone Muslim Brotherhood (*Ukhúwah al-Islámiyah*), which has built numerous schools in many parts of the country. Founded initially under Ahmadiyáh stimulus, and perhaps also under Ahmadiyáh direction, it was at the time an independent organization with a total enrollment of well over 1,800 pupils in its schools, of which some 1,230 were registered in Freetown alone (figures for 1975).[31]

Such efforts, however, still leave the question of proper government supervision unresolved. The question comes up when governments are approached for accreditation and appropriate funding. Ministries of education have in response required certain standards to be met: suitable and adequate premises, materials, recognized syllabi, and, most thorny of all questions, properly qualified teachers, and in the right ratio. Not many Islamic schools, except the Ahmadiyáh schools, satisfy such stringent standards sufficiently for them to go on to the Government Assisted List. A formula has yet to be devised that combines teaching qualifications with sufficient commitment to the dogma of Islam.

Language Pedagogy

Departments of Arabic studies in universities as well as individual scholars have tried to meet some of the more pressing needs of reorganizing Islamic schools. The basic assumption is that with a literate language like Arabic it should be possible to plan a course of study that could be fitted into the syllabi of primary and secondary schools. One of the earliest books designed with such a purpose in mind was Mervyn Hiskett's work, *The Teaching of Arabic: A Handbook of Method for Primary and Secondary Schools,* London, 1963. This work recommends that the direct method be employed in the teaching of Arabic, although the vernacular remains the predominant medium of instruction.[32] The importance of Arabic is not stressed at the primary level, and interested pupils can pursue it in greater detail at the secondary level. A number of reports sponsored by universities have in the main adopted this strategy of teaching Arabic. Selim Hakim drew up a report on the use of Arabic in schools and colleges in Nigeria.[33] Musa Abdul also covered much the same ground in another report.[34] In July of 1965, a seminar on the teaching of Arabic in Nigeria was held at the University of Ibadan, resulting in a report[35] that was also translated into Arabic.[36] In 1966 Longmans Publishers issued a Teacher's Arabic Handbook for the first reader.[37] In a slightly different tradition, the Sudan Publications Bureau produced Arabic textbooks on religious knowledge for use in primary schools.[38]

However, the question of adopting Arabic into the modern school curriculum is larger than the technical matter of the adequate supply of properly trained teachers. The dearth of Arabic materials can easily be remedied and so also can the scarcity of qualified teachers. Such facts notwithstanding, the issue has continued to rankle with Muslims. Not too long ago the Department of Education of an African country decided to recruit a native speaker of Arabic to teach the language in one of its schools. It was a successful experiment, and for that reason the government decided to transfer his services to a bigger government school. However, when it was discovered that he was an Arab Christian he was retired peremptorily and sent home.[39] In another instance, local Muslims received some educational Arabic material from Israel, which was refused for that reason, with pressure coming from local Arab embassy officials.[40] A professor of Arabic in a modern African university has written critically of Arabic literature coming from non-Arab countries.[41] Part of the reason for his misgiving is that a lot of unsuitable material finds its way into schools, where it is retailed at a profit. But another part lies in the fundamental belief that Arabic needs to be protected from non-Arab hands and that its religio-cultural values are an inseparable part of it.

Perhaps the case of Kole Omotoso, the Nigerian writer, sums up the issue. He decided to specialize in Arabic language and literature for his Bachelor of Arts degree and for his doctorate. When he returned in 1972 to teach in the Department of Arabic and Islamic Studies in the University of Ibadan, Muslims objected to his presence in the department on the grounds that he was not a Muslim. A national campaign was mounted to seek his ouster. The national association of teachers of Arabic and Islamic studies petitioned the Minister of Education to remove Dr. Omotoso, saying a non-Muslim had no business teaching Arabic. The matter was eventually resolved when Dr. Omotoso moved to Ife to head the Department of Dramatic Arts, a move that ended his academic career in Arabic. He subsequently emigrated to South Africa, where he has taught in the English department in the University of Western Cape.[42]

Thus the discussion of teaching Arabic language in schools and colleges has tended to be conducted along the lines of religious dogmatism and missionary interest. Although numerous calls have been made about freeing Arabic from its traditional religious and political contexts, they have largely gone unheeded, if not mistrusted. Numerous local Muslim groups now at long last have the financial wherewithal, thanks to generous support from international Islamic organizations, to demand a religious test for Arabic. And since the prestige of the United Nations lies behind many of these international Islamic religious bodies, it gives religious dogmatism cumulative respectability.

Economics

This raises an acute question for the educational planner. If the teaching of Arabic is to be decided solely on the criteria of relevance and utility, it is difficult to justify including it in the school curriculum. In the first, the argument for prescribing Arabic for children in state schools for whom it is not their first language would be hard to make on that ground. In the second place, there would be the pressing question about how precisely Arabic equips the child for a career in the civil service and other branches of government and industry. Beyond those facts, if Arabic were to be adopted in schools, should its teaching follow the lines laid down for African linguistics, without the use of doctrinal standards?

Some Muslim leaders have called for a special scheme whereby certain careers would be reserved for students who matriculated in Arabic.[43] Others believe that with greater organization and clearer objectives they would be able to move governments to grant Muslim demands. Still others look to outside help in the manner of Christian schools.[44] In some cases the school timetable has been adjusted to include sessions of Arabic teaching. But the question is still with us: To what profitable industry can Arabic be put?

The issue was highlighted by the case of a Muslim leader who spent six years studying Arabic in Cairo in the 1940s. Upon his graduation he returned home to a salary roughly equivalent to that of a primary school teacher.[45] The present writer is acquainted with the story of a man who acquired fluency in classical Arabic, at great expense and trouble, and could only find work as a lorry driver. In recent years Libya has entered the picture aggressively, offering scholarships and entry visas to students whose qualification appears synonymous with desperation born of chronic unemployment and home-bred boredom. Given the scale of youth disaffection in modern Africa, such incentives to study "abroad" in Libya, or, for that matter, in the Sudan, can imply a major uncontrolled demographic movement with deep ideological consequences. In spite of its obvious implications, very little thought or planning on either side seems to have gone into what to do afterwards with this rescued generation. The ability of modern African economies to absorb even the best qualified Arabists is strictly limited, and with the increasing realization of the need to train for gainful employment in a highly competitive labor market, Arabic is by no means on the priority list of education ministries, though the oil boom in Arab countries may have modified this status slightly. A situation may soon be reached in which, with the stimulus of Arab oil wealth, Arabic will have exhausted its capacity to grow within a remunerative setting and the choice will become plain more quickly. The reluctance of Muslims to be content with an optional, voluntary status for Arabic will have to be resolved in the long run along the paths of Muslim resistance and reaction, for with Muslim conservatives retreating into a religious and cultural enclave, the agents and beneficiaries of modern education will remain the determining factors in the situation.

Nevertheless, we should not overlook the potential capacity of Qur'án schools to adapt and adjust to new circumstances. The very resilience of the institution proves a certain intrinsic flexibility that is capable of expressing itself in curricular adaptation and innovation. Qur'án schools might, for instance, establish a syllabus that includes modern subjects like English, French, mathematics, geography, and so on, and includes modern Arabic on that basis, and they might even fit into the demands of the regular school day by opening after hours. Some of this is already happening. Yet the central question will not go away: How much can the time-resistant Qur'án school tack and veer in the crosscurrents of increasing secularization? If the Qur'án school duplicates the primary school it is, from the point of view of state education, superfluous; if it does something radically different, such as offering religious Arabic, it is irrelevant. In either case, it would not be entitled to state resources lest primary education in the public sector be starved of scarce resources, including trained teachers.

In spite of those problems, the Qur'án school, because it offers in the Holy Book knowledge that is timeless and universal, represents consolation and security in a society in the throes of institutional breakdown, widespread disenchantment, and public corruption, ethnic antagonism, administrative inefficiency, absence of law and order, with the added woes of epidemics and natural disasters. The status quo now consists of a state whose resources are in these circumstances unpredictable in availability or in distribution. In some countries the government has not been able to pay teachers, or pay them regularly and adequately, and has been unable to honor pension contracts, leaving retired teachers of a quarter century or more of service dependent on their own wits and devices. Such teachers form a new breed of social drop-outs, and together with school drop-outs, they prove the failure or inadequacy of the state in managing education. It does nothing to weaken the credibility of Qur'án schools, whatever the limitations of rote learning and its propaganda value in the modern economy. At least the Qur'án school, even in its allegedly obscurantist way, affirms the a priori value of children rather than staking its reputation on the largely illusory guarantee of productive employment as the outcome of education. Parents would still find in the Qur'án school an institution that boasts of preventing their children from being cast on the shores of self-rejection from the undertow of low self-esteem and from the cruel winds of public cynicism and anomie. In spite of the odds, the Qur'án school in popular perception amounts to more than the sum of its formal educational functions: It is a symbol of stability, assurance, and access for Muslim parents whatever their economic or personal circumstances.

However, we should still press on the matter of the necessity of Arabic in the school curriculum. In Muslim Africa Arabic occupies the same problematic position as the nonliterate African languages, with the important difference that the latter are the mother tongue languages of Africans. In the final analysis, internal political, administrative, structural, and economic factors will decide which languages are taught in government schools and similar educational institutions. Arabic suffers from a double disability in that it is not the language of business or administration in the vast majority of Muslim African societies (the Sudan being a notable exception), and, although it is spoken or studied by important groups in Africa, it is not the first language of the majority of Muslim Africans. Continued interest in its required use in Muslim Africa is justified by reasons other than education and economics.

The African Language Factor

In conclusion, we may consider how the role of Arabic is likely to be diminished further, or at any rate seriously rivaled, by the competing interest in the use of African indigenous languages in education. In a robust policy statement, for example, the Nigerian political leader and one-time Minister of Education, Babatunde Fafunwa, enunciated a national policy to introduce mother tongues in primary education. Although a Muslim, Mr. Fafunwa insisted that the mother tongue is the child's greatest educational asset, ignored to the child's lasting detriment. The child must develop, he affirmed, with a grounding in its mother tongue. To those critics who insist that Africa's and Nigeria's staggering language count, not to say anything of the worldwide pressures for literacy (and numeracy) in Western languages, weakens the case for mother tongue education, Mr. Fafunwa replies that the demands for authenticity outweigh the difficulties.[46] No reason is sacred enough, no learning too precious, to override mother tongue necessity, because however valuable Western languages may be, they cannot "replace the deepest springs within the soul, fed by blood, tradition and climate, and crystallized in a mother tongue," as was well expressed elsewhere.[47] The same sentiment moved Thomas Carlyle to write: "Of this one thing, however, be certain: wouldst thou plant for Eternity, then plant into the deep infinite faculties of man, his Fantasy and Heart! wouldst thou plant for Year and Day, then plant into his shallow superficial faculties, his self-love and arithmetical understanding, what will grow there."

These considerations, however, have not entirely won the day. For example, in a survey and assessment of the role of Arabic in Africa, M. H. Bakalla of the King Saud University in Saudi Arabia, reflects on the potential importance of Arabic in an Africa destined to play a major role in global affairs. By implication, Arabic is to the same degree destined to play a corresponding significant role. He rightly points out that Arabic is one of the most significant languages in Africa. The geographical space occupied by speakers of Arabic in Africa, the number of people who speak and use it, the importance of the kind of African scholarship conducted in the language, the political significance of Arab and Arabic-based African communities, the bewildering diversity of indigenous tongues (a diversity that defies unity and common understanding), and the uniform pressure that historically has been exerted by Arabic on a large number of African languages, all these factors favor the retention and development of Arabic, "the language of communication and culture for more than one third of Africa. It has a role to play in Africa beyond the Sahara, and the Arabs are gradually realizing the importance of Africa which is bound to be the continent of the future. In order for Arabic to make its impact felt in this part of the world, the Arabs must work very hard in order to realize this goal. There are great opportunities now for Arabs to help Africa and to meet its needs not only economically, commercially and medically, but also culturally and educationally."[48]

Lord Lugard, with whom we began, may for the final time be brought into the discussion, for he clearly saw the importance of Arabic in the lives and affairs of Muslim Nigerians. Consequently, he made a determined effort to preserve the Islamic heritage in Nigeria, though he was equally resolved on the scientific development of African languages in the firm belief that it was crucial for children to be educated in their mother tongues. When national governments are still far from committed to what looks like the incontestable relevance of primary languages in modern education, they would be even less convinced of the value of Arabic in that context. We need to remember, as Bakalla has reminded us, that for most statistical purposes, those who read only Arabic are unjustifiably considered illiterate in Africa, so minor is the role it plays in the modern economy. In such a case, Arabic rapidly slides from the scale of national educational priorities. Its necessary and indispensable use in religious pedagogy has traditionally rescued it from languishing from public neglect.[49]

The whole subject may, in conclusion, be placed within a wider frame of Muslim consciousness. According to a Nigerian Muslim writer, one cause for Muslim resistance to modern education is "the orthodox Muslim believes that the golden age of the world was the age of the Prophet and the further away the world moves from that age the 'worse' it becomes. Moreover, the Muslim felt (wrongly) that Islam did not permit the technological advancements which were taking place in the Western world."[50] But the Western world has spawned all over the Muslim world the national secular state, which requires the use of rational planning to bring order into traditional institutions, including education. However, when the state is itself the object of stringent criticism for well-justified reasons in themselves and for others related to the case for Arabic in secular education, then it creates greater perplexity about how most effectively to proceed beyond an unsatisfactory status quo.

8

Action and Reaction Among Freetown Muslims: Factionalism, Pluralism, and Muslim Agency

Historical Antecedents

Freetown was founded in 1787 in Sierra Leone as a philanthropic settlement for black settlers from England. There was widespread public support for the scheme, with people hoping that the philanthropic effort would combine with the rewards of lawful industry to bring about the end of the slave trade. The first batch of settlers who arrived established themselves at the Province of Freedom, a name they hoped would be a harbinger of things to come. But the settlement wilted from the heat and afflictions of tropical Africa. Not for nothing was Freetown baptized the "white man's grave." Ultimate failure was averted with the arrival in March 1792 of a contingent of about 1,200 African Americans who had served in the Revolutionary Wars on the British side and who were subsequently demobilized and repatriated to Nova Scotia in British Canada. Hence their name "Nova Scotians." The cost of the expedition, borne entirely by Parliament, was £9,600. The Nova Scotians formed the basis of Freetown as a permanent settlement, and their success helped to make possible the passage of the Slave Trade Abolition Act in 1807. The British naval squadron set up a patrol on the high seas to confiscate slave cargoes that were being shipped in contravention of the act, with the impounded slaves brought to Freetown and there set free. The Africans taken from the slave ships came from all over the continent, including from significant Muslim groups, all now concentrated on one small point at Freetown and requiring the organized supervision of government, mission, and society. This second wave of impounded slaves was called recaptured Africans, or recaptives, and they formed the most significant bridge between the Nova Scotians and the rest of the African continent. By 1811 some 6,000 recaptives had been settled in Freetown, with higher numbers in following years.[1] The recaptive population outstripped that of the Nova Scotians and transformed Freetown from an overseas-controlled experiment to a full-fledged African city, different, perhaps, in the extent of Western cooperation with Africans in the century before classical imperialism, but otherwise typical of the teeming diversity and openness of social encounter. Even Queen Victoria was impressed with the sort of place Freetown grew up to be and followed as benefactor, godmother, and monarch the careers of its people.

As a Christian settlement Freetown was the first successful mass movement in African Christianity: African in kinship, membership, leadership, customs, and values, and Christian in fellowship, partnership, commitment, vocation, and worship. The same diversity that vitally distinguished the settlement also marked the work of Christian missions, with the Church Missionary Society, for example, recruiting Germans, Swiss, and others to join Scots, Welsh, Irish, and Englishmen across the denominational lines in pastoral, educational, civil, and administrative work in Freetown and beyond, with Africans providing crucial leadership.

It may be argued that what gave Freetown its special character was the juxtaposition of diverse social groups from the length and breadth of the continent, and although Christianity thrived in this setting, the religion bore the fractured if lively imprint of its context. Many of the recaptive churches, especially the Methodists, broke up into numerous competing factions centered on leading personalities, fueled by ethnic ambitions or abetted by missionary incitement. Thus religious contentiousness received something of an inflammatory boost from the open competitive environment of the search for ethnic roots and reassurance. The missionary linguist, Sigismund Kölle, was able to document evidence for over two hundred African languages among the inhabitants of Freetown. His *Polyglotta Africana* (1854) was among the first scientific comparative linguistic works of its kind, and we may with justice regard it as a radical departure from the abstract Enlightenment approach to linguistic and cultural study. Although it is a different kind of work altogether, it ranks with other eighteenth- or nineteenth-century works on non-Western culture, such as Livingstone's classic researches and discoveries or Bleek's *Comparative Grammar of South African Languages* (1865), in originality of thought and concept, and exceeds such works in terms of scale and rigor, of concreteness of detail and boldness of vision, with its implicit acceptance of non-Western cultures as worthy of study, sympathy, and engagement. As Kölle put it, the African's language is proof of the people's humanity and intelligence and of their intrinsic right to claim fraternity with Europeans. In any case, Kölle's work proved Freetown was host to an extraordinary admixture of ethnic and linguistic pluralism, too diverse to be comprehended within one harmonious ideal, but too small a representative of the whole to survive in strict isolation. This inconclusiveness inserted an active ferment into Freetown social and religious life.

Significant Muslim groups entered the settlement from two main sources; one route was from the interior, especially from Muslim strongholds in Futa Jallon and beyond, and the other from the sea, which brought African recaptives. The two communities were by no means indistinct, for recaptive Muslims had a prominent Yoruba or Hausa identity and Futa Jallon Muslims were mostly from the Fulbé ethnic group, or else were Fula speaking, who came to Freetown mainly to trade. Several of the British colonial governors of Sierra Leone, inspired by the example of Dr. Edward Blyden, followed a pro-Muslim policy, including Sir Matthew Nathan and Sir Samuel Rowe. Indeed, Sir Samuel Rowe was widely known as a friend and sympathizer of Muslims, encouraging an ill and destitute *sharíf*, descendant of the Prophet Muhammad, from Fez, Morocco, to turn up on Rowe's doorstep and appeal to his Samaritanly mercy. The *sharíf* received medical attention, was fitted with a prosthesis for his amputated leg, and sent on his way. At an *'íd al-fitr* celebration marking the end of the Ramadán fast, the governor entertained over seven hundred Muslim guests in 1879, and, in deference to Islamic teaching, served only non-alcoholic beverages. A Muslim instructor in Arabic, named Harún al-Rashíd, was employed for a time at the missionary institution of Fourah Bay College, and another local Muslim, Muhammad Sanusi, was appointed government Arabic Writer. In such ways did official government and missionary policy combine to encourage positive relations with Muslims. The Fula Muslims themselves maintained a highly efficient landlord system that gave rise to the "Big Man" of local politics, and government gladly cooperated with these community heads.

The special context of Christians and Muslims sharing the resources of the state, with neither side feeling the right or urge to exclusive entitlement, has discouraged theocratic agitation while encouraging religious involvement in the public arena. In the matter with which we are concerned in this chapter, such encouragement has tended to leave Muslims deeply splintered and factionalized without that in any way bringing about religious decline. One reason for such religious resilience may be that for Christian and Muslim alike religious identity has not carried political consequence, and although Freetown was conceived as a Christian experiment it was not operated to reproduce in Africa a new Christendom, a refurbished fideist amalgam of territoriality, rulership, and religion. The colonial administration at the time pursued a sanguine Muslim policy motivated by the conviction that Muslims were important potential allies whose usefulness was as yet underutilized. At the other end of the spectrum, mischievous and corrupt African political leaders in their time sought in vain to profit from religious manipulation, so that in both their case and in that of the colonial administrators Islam counted for something. With relative equanimity, we may thus contemplate the spectacle of a fractious Islam in Freetown without contemplating also its political dissolution. A deep Muslim loyalty, often with official backing, still sustained people even in their divisions. These considerations are important in shaping attitudes among Muslims. The settlement had impressive open public dealings with Muslims, and Muslims in turn had few inhibitions in staking a public claim in matters affecting national life. For Muslims and Christians alike, Freetown was congenial to religion as sacred and secular.

Freetown Muslims

Consequently, when we enter upon Islam in Freetown it feels like picking our way through a minefield. The record of acute rivalry and internecine struggle makes it a special case in West African Islam. The divisive factors have remarkable longevity, and an unwary student of the scene can, by probing almost anywhere at random, bring to the surface old quarrels and disputes that have in their present day equally truculent versions. Part of the explanation for the fragmentation of Muslim communal life is the strong currents of local drive and energy that, because they are often uncoordinated and not precisely focused, run at cross purposes and produce tension instead of leading to communal harmony. An important factor behind communal factionalism is undoubtedly the tribal or ethnic issue, though that is not the only reason. The divisions are deeply complex and alignments have shifted markedly across groups and within them, to such an extent that almost every major issue has acquired the character of a separate and all-sufficient cause in itself: the *hajj*; election of community heads, or, more officially, tribal headmen; upkeep of the Muslim cemetery; the religious calendar, particularly at Ramadán; hospitality to important Muslim dignitaries; and that fertile field of conflict, mosque-building, are some examples. Education, our chief concern here, is one such matter, and, like the other subjects of Freetown Islam, it has acted like a multiple time fuse, primed to go off every time the subject has come up, and each time widening the rift between the factions.

Community and Dissent

The Muslim community, in other words, the informal conglomeration of community interests, at a very early date was concerned with Western (hereafter, modern) education, and the colonial administration from the 1870s onward tried to bring Muslims the benefits of modern education through state sponsorship. The sentiment guiding official attitude was later formalized as a policy principle in the following words: "The Mohammedan question is regarded by the Government as one of the most important in the future of West and Central Africa. If Islam is properly understood, if its youth inoculated with British civilization and British ideas are utilized by British administrators and merchants, it will give to England a wider and more permanent influence upon the millions of the Soudan than can possibly be wielded by any other agency."[2] Various schemes were launched in pursuit of this principle, schemes that at first looked promising, but which invariably failed from Muslim infighting and intra-ethnicity, which flared up to engulf the very projects set up to combat them. It is significant, though a digression here, to see the extent to which Muslims utilized certain government institutions, such as the law courts, to resolve disputes, even though the litigation process might actually exacerbate tension and harden attitudes, whereas other institutions, like government schools and similar subsidized facilities, were not taken advantage of to the same degree. The number of lawsuits and legal appeals and petitions that Muslims have brought against each other testifies to endemic tension. Colonial administrators tried once to adjudicate and resolve some of the disputes, without much success. It would be misleading to suggest the Muslim community was a dysfunctional society, for some of the disputes have led to the progress and extension of Muslim life in other parts. Yet this progress must be understood in the context of unceasing tension and turmoil, often without regard to the Muslim status of the protagonists. We require familiarity with the sort of historical background sketched above to appreciate present attitudes to modern education in Freetown. Fortunately, much of this background information is available in standard accounts.

Because the Muslim settlement in the Freetown colony took place at about the same time as the Christian settlement and was in fact stimulated by it, the city was host to a special form of interreligious tolerance that was hospitable to diverse religious groups, whatever their linguistic or cultural background, including Muslims. We have seen that the original Muslim colony had as its nucleus liberated Africans who had been Muslim, or had converted to Islam. It is customary to call these original Muslim settlers Aku, a term inadequately taken to mean Yoruba Muslims.[3] The earliest Muslim settlements were in the three villages just outside Freetown: Aberdeen, Hastings, and Waterloo, but after about 1833 a large number of these groups migrated to Fourah Bay and Fula Town in the east end of Freetown.[4] From that point forward the border line between so-called Yoruba Muslims and the "natives" began to look tenuous. Mandinka, Fulani, Susu, Temne, and some other "native" Muslims lived alongside the Aku, who themselves included Creole converts, in distinct pockets around the east end of the Freetown peninsula.

The colonial administration, convinced of the need to pursue a policy of ethnic separation to preserve social balance in Freetown, acted between 1833 and the 1860s to prevent the Creole Christian community from being swamped by waves of local immigration, and since most migrants from the hinterland included important Muslim groups, this separation turned out to be the government's Muslim policy. However, the colonial authorities abandoned this policy as abruptly as they had embarked on it, a change due largely to the efforts of Dr. Edward Wilmot Blyden, who, between 1870 and 1905, succeeded in obtaining both government and mission support for modern schools among Muslims. But the fragmentation of Muslim community life, which had not been helped by the earlier official policy, exerted a negative effect on much of Blyden's initiatives, though impressive tangible results accrued from his work.[5] The Muslims in Fourah Bay, for example, split into rival factions: the Haruniyah party led by the *Jama'ah,* and the Suleimaniyah party led by the Tamba[6] men.[7] Although other issues lay at the center of such divisions, the educational factor was the immediate cause of the breach.

Temne Islam was similarly affected by endemic rivalries in which the educational factor aggravated the forces of antagonism. A Temne educated at al-Azhar in Cairo founded the Almamiyah Society in an effort to contain the growing power of the Ambas Geda, led by S. B. Kamara, the colorful Temne tribal leader, better known as Kande Bureh. The Ambas Geda was a secret ritual dance society dedicated to the preservation of Temne traditional values in an urban milieu.[8] The struggle between the Almamiyah Society and the Ambas Geda was not a conflict between secularism and Islam, as has been suggested,[9] but simply a straight contest between styles of educated leadership. Another Temne leader, Shaykh Jibril Sisay, also educated at al-Azhar, found himself at the center of Temne factionalism. After he established a modern school and appeared as the champion of educational advancement, the old elite in the Temne community decided to act in concert against one they regarded as an upstart. Shaykh Jibril was accused of misallocating funds donated for the school, and the issue became laden with political meaning. He was eventually tried and incarcerated at the Central Prisons for two years before the political scales were reversed and he was discharged. He was given a martyr's reward and sent to Cairo as Sierra Leone's ambassador, which post he held until recently.[10] The Temne community lost the school he founded and have not been able to replace it or found similar schools.

Muslim Congress

In the early 1900s the colonial officials encouraged the setting up of a school, identified at that stage with the Mandinka community. In 1905 the name of the school was changed from Mandinka School to Madrasa Islamiyah with the intention of encouraging other ethnic groups to send their children there. But the wider participation that the government hoped for never materialized and the school passed under a cloud, though it revived later under a different impetus.[11] Muslims also opened schools on their own initiative, and here again, as in the other situation, all such efforts were led by people who had to run the gauntlet of intense factionalism. In the 1920s and 1930s Muslim efforts to create schools for their children were intensified, and out of this desire for educational improvement were born the two main rival groups in modern Freetown Islam: the Muslim Congress and the Muslim Association. Within these two main factions were other competing alignments, so that no one set of factors or explanations can account for the complexities of Muslim attitudes.

In 1922 Hadir-ud-Deen, as Secretary of the Muhammadan Education Board, proposed organizing Muslims into a unified body. Divisiveness was to be confronted directly. The result, a few years later, was the Muslim Congress, registered as a friendly society in 1932.[12] A Lebanese Muslim was instrumental in setting it up after correspondence with Jerusalem. The leading lights were Aku Muslims, though other ethnic groups were also active; for example, Almamy Darame, the Mandinka headman, was among the original members.

The Muslim Congress filled two needs: It represented an independent Muslim initiative and it also provided a counterweight to the predominantly Christian influence in modern education.[13] The first object was, however, qualified by the fact that Congress received generous support from the Lebanese trading community.[14] Congress arranged for three local Muslims to proceed to al-Azhar for higher Islamic studies: Shaykh Jibril Sisay, already mentioned, who had been a student in the Gambia; Nazir Sahid; and Abdul Karím Ghazálí. The local Muslim newspaper, which carried news of the scholarships, ended with a moral piece: "He who pursueth learning, walketh in the way of Allah."[15]

However, Congress again was wracked by divisions within the Muslim community. A breakaway elitist group, the Muslim Association, was formed in April 1942, with emphasis on primary and middle school for Arabic and Islam.[16] Its founder-president was Ahmed Alhadi, Master of the Rolls, Registrar, and Administrator of Intestate Property, "who developed a remarkable gift for legalistic formulation."[17] The association built a school at the foot of Mount Aureol, support for which was raised entirely from voluntary contributions.[18] Its first headmaster was a prominent Freetown political figure, Lamina Sankoh, formerly the Rev. E. N. Jones, an ordained Christian who eventually gave up the cloth.[19] At about the same time a new Muslim newspaper, the *Ramadan Vision,* was launched under the editorship of its proprietor, Abbas Camba, and this publication joined vigorously in the campaign for modern education among Muslims. Initially on the side of the Muslim Association, it advocated the strengthening of modern schools among Muslims and castigated Congress for its niggardly performance in this area. Within a short time of its founding, the Association was overseeing four schools in Freetown and one each in Aberdeen and Goderich.[20] Congress, however, continued to be active and was in fact long to outlive its bitter rival. It held a successful fundraising campaign at the Islamiyah School room on Sunday, 22 August 1943, where a large sum, including a single £200 sterling gift, was raised.[21] And like the Association, the Muslim Congress was patronized by the Lebanese community and the government, which was keen to encourage educational projects among Muslims.

Christian Example

What united both the Association and Congress was their paramount desire to emulate Christian performance in modern education, for the overwhelming strength of Christian schools demonstrated where real power and influence lay. In this and other ways the Christian example was the direct, even if sometimes hidden, stimulus for Muslim efforts. But the Christian example, in spite of its obvious character, excited the spirit of factionalism among Muslims. The Association, fed by the *Ramadan Vision* with doses of sectarian indiscretion, openly derided the poor educational standing of Congress rank and file, and Ahmed Alhadi, A. F. Rahman, and (later al-Hajj) Muhammad Mahdi, stood out on the side of the Association as the "eager young men" of a new enlightened generation of Muslims.[22] These men were also prominent in championing a parallel educational development in the Muslim community to that which was taking place in the Christian one. It was ironic and perhaps inevitable that the Association as a Muslim organization should seek its justification in acceptance by the Christian community. An anonymous pamphlet, for example, widely attributed to Ahmed Alhadi, called attention to the contribution the church had made to the development of Sierra Leone and emphasized that although Islam had called people to similar ventures of social improvement and nation-building, the actual contribution of Muslims in this field was paltry.[23] His own example of what Muslims could do did not rise above popular sermonizing.[24]

The *Ramadan Vision* echoed such sentiments of emulating Christian example and declared, somewhat overenthusiastically: "Sierra Leone is witnessing the dawn of a new era in their awakening of higher education amongst Muslims."[25] The credit for this progress was attributed to the "spread of progressive ideas" among Muslims who had acquired the ambition to achieve equality "with prominent members of our much favored brethren the Christians."[26] Another sign of the leavening influence of Christian example was the question of higher education for Muslim girls, although in the venerable Muslim tradition, the sanction and justification for this change was found in the Qur'án.[27]

The *Ramadan Vision* became carried away by its own enthusiasm. Its editor launched a colorful diversion and founded and became chief organizing secretary of the Fujalto Muslim Orchestra, intended to increase the pace of educational reform among Muslims.[28] The orchestra openly sought and received Christian assistance and blessing. Its musical director was Mr. C. W. Mann, a Christian organist at the prestigious Holy Trinity Church, Freetown.[29] The second performance of the orchestra was at Holy Trinity School during the *mawlid* celebrations.[30] Musical programs included familiar *madih* praise songs on the Prophet as well as some Christian music.[31] What seemed an enterprising if slightly unusual innovation in Freetown Muslim educational and social life ceased when the orchestra was disbanded following the withdrawal of its founder from active life.[32]

In the run up to independence (1961), education continued to play a critical role in the life of Freetown Muslims—and with no abatement of the factional spirit, leaving aside the activities of the Ahmadiyah Missionary Movement in Sierra Leone, which will be considered separately. The prelude to independence found the Muslims increasingly out of step with their Christian counterparts. Not for the first time, some Muslim representatives at a public meeting pointed out the inadequacy of traditional Muslim education and recognized that political independence would reveal even more the inappropriateness of an al-Azhar type of training.[33]

Muslim Brotherhood

In the Orthodox Muslim community—perhaps more on the fringes of it ideologically because of proven Ahmadiyah influence—one of the most ambitious educational enterprises was the educational work of the Muslim Brotherhood, al-Ukhúwah al-Islámiyah, founded in Magburaka by al-Hajj Sori Ibrahim Kanu.[34] The Ukhúwah should be strictly distinguished from the politically militant Ikhwán al-Muslimín, the radical Egyptian movement founded by the fundamentalist Hasan al-Banná (1906–1949).[35] The Ukhúwah was founded in 1958, reputedly under the aegis of the Ahmadiyah,[36] and soon after its creation it built its first primary school in Magburaka. By the time of the death of its founder in 1972 the Brotherhood had increased the number of primary schools to thirty-eight, of which only one was in Freetown, and three secondary schools, one each in Freetown, Sefadu, and Magburaka.[37] Most of its educational strength continued to be concentrated at Magburaka, although its secondary school in Freetown was flourishing with a record number of pupils in attendance at both the primary and secondary levels.[38] In Magburaka it also ran—and continues to run—an Islamic Institute, which, unlike the primary and secondary schools, was staffed mainly by Egyptian teachers paid from Cairo.[39]

The Brotherhood Secondary School in Freetown was founded in 1969.[40] The curriculum included modern secular subjects alongside Islamic subjects. It was coeducational, and the audit report for 1970–71 revealed it had 354 boys and 81 girls, though a slightly smaller number is given in the books of the school.[41] By 1975 its enrollment had more than doubled—with the attendant strains on space, facilities, and staff. Another school with a strong coeducational and secular emphasis was the Wanjama Muslim Academy, which tried to produce candidates for agricultural training at Njala.[42] However, the school hardly got off the drawing board before it was closed.

Factionalism

All this educational activity took place against a backdrop of intense factional rivalry. At a Muslim meeting where the Supreme Islamic Council of Sierra Leone was created, the Muslim Congress came in for harsh criticism. It was taunted for its lethargy in modern education. It was pointed out at the meeting that there were eighty-four primary schools in the Western Area, i.e., the Freetown peninsula, of which thirty-three were Christian schools and only one, a secondary school, could be credited to Congress, a meager effort in its forty-two-year history. "Other than studying the phases of the moon and nominating *imáms* to officiate at congregational prayers, the Congress body—composed of Old Heads—," it was suggested, achieved very little by way of modern schools.[43] The "eager young men" of the day carried this reproach to its logical conclusion by accusing Congress of being responsible for the relative backwardness of the Muslim community and for allowing the Christian community to dominate schools in Freetown and elsewhere. These sentiments lurked behind the anxiety of, say, the Sierra Leone Muslim Brotherhood (SLMB), Ukhúwah al-Islamiyah, which wanted to dissociate itself from Congress. In a letter to the Sierra Leone Broadcasting Service, the secretary general of the Brotherhood expressed this position in forceful terms. The organizational model was here again the Christian example, with which the main part of the letter opened.

> For your information, the forming of the United Christian Council was only to unite all Christian religious bodies and not with the idea of interpreting the individual educational policy and activities. Therefore the Sierra Leone Muslim Brotherhood does not and will not be prepared to pledge its responsibility to any Muslim organization in Sierra Leone. But it gives the full (sic) respect to the oldest Muslim organization in this country, which is the S/L Muslim Congress when it comes to religious activities such as celebrations. But in the educational line, the SLMB does not and will never be prepared to surrender its rights to any other Muslim organization in this country, and as such, it will not be in our interest for any other Muslim organization to represent the SLMB in all Government affairs and it owes obligation to no other body as far as educational matters are concerned.[44]

The Muslim educational vanguard was being led by men who were also keen to shake Islam out of its torpor. Both the men educated at al-Azhar and those educated nearer home had found themselves joining forces against the conservative elite of traditional Islam. This anticonservative coalition, mobilizing behind modern education, wished to assert Islam's claim to the modern world rather than forcing it into the split between sacred and secular. It is this split that the old guard would perpetuate with their obscurantist village Islam, which has no relevance to national life. In a play by Abdul Karim Ghazali, village religion and its traditional stalwarts are pointedly caricatured when the pagan priest and Muslim cleric are joined in their disdain for modern education, represented by the clerk (Clark), who, true to character, butts into their conversation. The reaction to the clerk shows village Islam and paganism to be tied to a fading world. Here is the dialogue in the Krio language:

> (De Clark cam mix pan de tok.)
> **Clark**: M'hm mh, Pa nor mek dis man ton you lek how in day'o.
> **Alpha**: Me pekin, go sidom saful nar inlgish book you sabi; you no sabi but god. Lef we leh we tok; way tin you day do sef not to trainin. Wen too big people day tok, you nor for put mot day.
> **Merehsinman**: Nar true word you tok so; dis book way den lan nor mek dem get trainin.

Translation:[45]

> (The clerk came to interfere in their conversation.)
> **Clerk**: M'hm, mh, Old Man, don't let this man make you into what he already is.
> **Muslim Cleric**: My son, go and sit down to the English book you know how to handle. As for God you know nothing about Him. Leave the two of us to continue our conversation. In fact what you have just done is bad manners. When two elders are engaged in conversation you should not interrupt them.

Pagan priest: That's absolutely right what you said then. This modern education of theirs leaves them wanting in manners.

It is said that when this play was performed before a local audience in Freetown, the Muslims, perhaps not seeing the point, objected that this was a play about paganism, not Islam.[46]

There was a rapid turnover in Muslim welfare associations, particularly those concerned with modern education. The Muslim Association, so strongly hailed by people like Proudfoot for a promising future,[47] had long ceased to exist. Its challenge to the Muslim Congress was never a serious one in organizational terms, though its brilliant leadership under Ahmed Alhadi gave it a precocious strength. Too closely identified with the Creole Christian community, the Association proposed to fulfill a need for which it did not possess the experience and contacts of its Creole counterparts nor the support and understanding of the majority of the Freetown Muslim community. Squeezed between the two it moldered away and was in fact a spent force long before the death of Ahmed Alhadi in 1958. Fula Town Muslims also had an organization for running the Omaria School, opened with entertainment by the Fujalto Orchestra on 1 September 1958. More from lack of support than from factional rivalry, the school was taken over by the municipal authorities. Abdul Karim Ghazali, very much the target of the Muslim anti-Israeli lobby because of his alleged contacts with Israel, taught at the school.

Foreign Support

Foreign support for Muslim efforts in modern education raises several different issues. The dearth of teachers in Arabic and Islam could be corrected by a supply of appropriately trained teachers from Egypt and elsewhere, as the case of the Muslim Brotherhood suggested. But if the aim is to train people who could fill jobs in the civil service and technical fields like agriculture, forestry, engineering, and similar specialized areas, then should a Muslim school apply rigid religious criteria in its selection of materials, aid, pupils, and staff? It is a pressing dilemma: If a school adheres strictly to traditional Islamic religious formulae its capacity to make a meaningful contribution in secular fields would be correspondingly curtailed. On the other hand, if it is not necessary to insist on a separate Muslim identity then it seems superfluous to have separate Muslim schools. Existing secular and government-aided schools and institutions are better placed than any fledgling Muslim school, with a few minor exceptions. It does not seem possible to resolve this problem, which presupposes that the much wider issue of secularization and its significance for traditional religious structures has been confronted adequately. Both the older and the more recent Muslim organizations were characterized by their "Islamism," in other words, an ideological commitment to Islam, with the difference that the more recent bodies stress the Pan-Islamic aspect. This emphasis has profound implications for modern education.

Modern Muslim schools receiving help from Arab countries are under constraint to submit to Arab political demands. Abdul Karim Ghazali's delicate position testifies to the reality of this problem. Another was the gift of books on Arabic and Islam from Israel, which touched off a flurry of activity in Congress circles, culminating in a general meeting of the Board of Imams on 6 August 1968. A petition was suitably drafted and sent to the Minister of Education, the press, and other bodies.[48] It rejected the offer in disproportionate and highly charged language.

The Ahmadiyah contribution to modern education among Freetown and other Sierra Leone Muslims was unsurpassed in the history of Muslim contact with Western educational institutions. Originally stigmatized by the Muslim Association, who in the main spurned them,[49] the Ahmadí missionaries were cautiously received by Congress, and they started work in Rokupr and Bo.[50] Their first school in Freetown was opened in January 1959 and, like the others, it went onto the Government Assisted List.[51] The first secondary school was opened in 1964, and it has remained the only Ahmadiyah school there.[52] An offset press began producing educational materials for use in schools, including a course in Qur'ánic Arabic for beginners.[53] The introduction of Arabic teaching in schools was important for attracting children from the wider Muslim community. Previously the Ahmadis did not lay much emphasis on knowledge of Arabic, preferring instead translated work, which caused loss of support from traditional-minded Muslims. With the new policy of teaching Arabic they should appeal to more and more Muslims, provided other considerations like politics, both local and international, does not interfere. Local political pressure could mount because of Ahmadí insistence on avoiding direct involvement in popular political demonstrations. International political pressure was beginning to be felt in the 1970s with official Saudi Arabian and Pakistani opposition to Ahmadiyah Islam, regarded by both countries as heretical. Sierra Leonean Ahmadís faced an uphill task. Being a modernizing organization among local Muslims is hard enough, but to add an avoidance of politics in a country that thrives on political maneuverings while also facing the counterweight of Saudi Arabian and Pakistani sanctions is to raise a fundamental question about its survival in its present form. With the ban by Saudi Arabia on Ahmadí pilgrims, the number of Ahmadí Muslims who remain unaware of the cleavage between Ahmadiyah Islam and Sunni Islam is decreasing. With financial support by orthodox Muslim countries like Saudi Arabia, Libya, and Egypt the scales could be turned against local Ahmadís. The political implications of Pan-Islamism might force the government to bring Muslim activities and organizations under strict control, with all that means for Ahmadiyah political neutralism. The time seems not far off when Ahmadís will no longer be able to straddle the divisions in Sierra Leone Islam, or even to profit by them.

Developments in other spheres of Islamic activity have emphasized the divisions among Sierra Leonean Muslims. By far the most important single external factor has been the involvement of oil-rich (and oil-enriched) states of the Middle East. But the dominance of Egypt before and after the boom in oil wealth has remained unchallenged. In 1961 Egypt began an educational mission to Sierra Leone. At one stage it had about thirty Egyptian teachers, paid from Cairo, teaching in the country. There were, according to officials at the Egyptians Cultural Center in Freetown, 252 Sierra Leonean students in Cairo, most of them studying technical and similar subjects, although a number were at places like al-Azhar.[54] An estimated 15 Sierra Leonean students were in Saudi Arabia, and a smaller number in Libya. Morocco established an educational scholarship scheme in Rabat in the 1960s for Sierra Leoneans, but it was discontinued following student discontent with social amenities provided at the center.[55] Another kind of contact is the one in which national Muslims are supported directly from the Middle East either as full-time missionaries or as grant-aided workers. Among the former was Shaykh Sallah Janneh, a graduate of the Islamic University of Medina and appointed missionary by Saudi Arabia to Sierra Leone.[56] Another was al-Hájj Abdul Rahmán Kamara, supported by Saudi Arabia and once posted to Port Loko, a strong Muslim area.[57] The *imám* of the Huasa mosque, Malam Muhammad Bello, was also supported from Libya to help with some Islamic teaching.[58]

Support for individual Muslims has been undertaken alongside support for local Islamic projects. Apart from the Ahmadiyah Movement, the Muslim Brotherhood, as already pointed out, was the organization most seriously committed to modern education. Five Egyptian teachers worked at its school in Magburaka, plus two nationals. Enrollment in its schools in Freetown was well over the 1,800 mark.[59] Although suffering from bad organization and the legacy of the dominant personal leadership of al-Hájj Sori Ibrahim Kanu, support for the Brotherhood had not diminished in the mid-1970s. If it fails it would be for reasons other than support or finance.

Organizational Impetus

Another organization prompted into prominence by political independence was the Muslim Cultural Society, though this particular organization took some time emerging, being founded only in 1973. In a public statement the organization wrote: "It was only after the independence of Sierra Leone and due to the broadminded and democratic policy of Government that Muslims attained their lost rights. . . . We are proud to say that our Government under the able and dynamic guidance of our beloved President Dr. Siaka Stevens has always given assistance and patronage to Muslims, so that they can fulfill their religious obligations."[60]

In spite of its self-confident claims, the Cultural Society was a newcomer to the hurly-burly of religious politics in Freetown. It had three primary schools with a pupil enrollment of 380.[61] It had the makings of a library of Islamic books at its center for cultural activities.[62] Here it was only duplicating the fairly good library facilities of the Egyptian Cultural Center on Pulteney Street in Freetown, although in the latter case poor shelving made for difficulty in finding books. The Cultural Society also organized classes in Qur'án reading at their center.[63]

The Kankele (sometimes also Kankaylay) Muslim Society has a history similar to the Muslim Cultural Center. The word "Kankele" is derived from the Mandinka, *"kang kili,"* meaning "one voice," unity, solidarity, thus illustrating the Mandinka origins of the Society. It was founded by al-Hájj I. B. Turay, one-time Propaganda Secretary of the Muslim Congress. He is the father-in-law of Shaykh Sallah Janneh. On 3 November 1974, the foundation stone was laid for a center that, it was hoped, would house after completion some 2,200 students, all girls. On this day the Kankele organizers collected £4,531 sterling in donations from individuals and branch offices. It was estimated that the center itself would cost £150,000 sterling to build.[64]

The Kankele Society, in one aspect of its activities, brought two themes of this chapter together into sharp focus, namely, the matter of Christian example and stimulus and, secondly, of outside foreign support. In a letter addressed to then President Anwar Sadat of Egypt (d. 1981), al-Hájj Turay drew attention to the urgent importance of education for Muslim girls and women, because of the comparative Christian excellence in this area. He was anxious that in time Muslim women should compare favorably with their Christian counterparts. Because of the confidential nature of this letter I cannot quote any part of it here, but it is worth noting that at the time there were only six female students in Cairo, three of whom were the Razzaq sisters from Hastings, near Freetown.[65] The letter was accompanied by an architect's plan of the proposed building. No precise figure was quoted in the letter concerning the cost of the building and the appeal for funds was couched in general terms. There was a good chance of the Egyptian authorities responding, but there could be difficulties, one internal and the other external. The Kankele had appealed in the same terms to Saudi Arabia for funds without acknowledging this in the letter to Cairo. It was unlikely that these and similar possible sources of funds would be unaware of each other over this matter, which could inhibit outside support. The internal difficulty could arise out of increasing government involvement in local Muslim organizations to try to bring them under check. Muslim organizations appealing over the head of their government to foreign governments could quickly assume, or be alleged to assume, a political character.

Competition

Competition for support from the Middle East was rife among Freetown Muslims, which had driven the factions apart, paralyzing national umbrella organizations like the Supreme Islamic Council and causing a flare-up of individual associations led by younger men. This was another of the divisions in Freetown Islam: Younger men with some modern education were impatient with the old elite. What fed this smoldering discontent with the old was the prospect, among other things, of wresting power and control from traditional centers of power by appearing as successful men in the modern world with the ability to utilize interna-

TABLE 8.1   Principal Tribes in Freetown: 1891–1953

	1891	1901	1911	1921	1931	1947	1953
Creoles	17,815	16,505	16,716	15,791	20,970	17,331	17,000
Temne	2,897	4,494	5,007	8,358	11,405	...	19,000
Mende	1,015	2,291	2,557	4,094	3,828	...	11,000
Limba	693	1,423	1,611	2,941	4,960	...	9,000
Kru	1,234	1,903	1,551	4,744	4,460	...	7,000
Loko	115	198	382	775	1,633	...	4,000
Mandinka	1,256	1,037	1,021	1,461	1,352	...	4,000
Fula	244	270	289	499	1,119	...	4,000
Susu	1,434	1,417	1,311	1,346	1,450	...	12,500
Others	3,330	4,925	3,645	4,133	4,181	...	7,500
Total	30,033	34,463	34,090	44,142	55,358	64,576	85,000

±5,000

tional channels of contact. The traditional elite were keeping their powder dry against the day when the present proliferation of young talents would be a spent force and familiar patterns of the old elite reasserted themselves. At the time, the two sides were content to leave matters as they were.

By carrying over competitive factionalism into international politics in dealings with Arab governments, Freetown Muslims introduced political calculations into their activities. This politicization caused the government to step in decisively. The government instituted controls over Muslim pilgrimage. The Supreme Islamic Council was brought under close government supervision. The organizational power of Muslim groups, which enabled them to campaign on a national basis to recruit new members and collect funds, was anxiously watched by the government. Perhaps it was to allay such government surveillance that local Muslim organizations decided, after a particularly successful fundraising campaign, to hand over to the government the proceeds, amounting to £22,000 sterling. The government reacted by raising airfares for the pilgrimage organization.[66] In June 1975, a delegation of the National Executive of the Sierra Leone Muslim Pilgrimage Movement, led by Hajji Dankay Kabia, went to see the president to try to regain control of pilgrimage affairs.[67] The Saudi Arabian ban on Ahmadí pilgrims further complicated relations with the Sierra Leone government. Visits by Arab government officials were another potential area of conflict, for Muslim organizations would want to capitalize on such visits for their own sectional interests.

In the final analysis, however, what was of material significance for the configuration of religious life in Freetown was not external foreign involvement, which merely influences existing local factors, but the internal balance of forces. The most important element in this respect was the ethnic/linguistic factor, as alluded to already in Chapter 7, where we noted that all the main ethno-linguistic groups had their own adult evening schools, and that only two schools were designated as "All Tribes," and two others were described as mixed.[68] The preponderance of such sectional interests in Sierra Leone Islam means that local Muslims were a long way from organic unity. Muslims in fact seemed prepared to take sectionalism for granted and were concentrating their energies on ensuring a flow of funds from outside. It was difficult to foresee a time when Arab support could be important enough to be used as a lever to force Muslims to unite. Fragmentation seems inseparable from the vitality of Freetown Muslim life.

Urban-Rural Islam

A final theme is the continuing dichotomy between the Islam of Freetown and other urban centers and the Islam of the village, a dichotomy that is rapidly diverging through the impact of modern education on the younger generation of Muslims. In colonial times, rural Islamic interests maintained a stronghold on Muslims in Freetown through the institutionalization of traditional structures of authority. The system of "Tribal headmen" and the ancillary organizations spun off it, by which the colonial bureaucracy structured its relations with the various communities, embodied and perpetuated the power of "village" patronage politics. But such structures are archaic in an independent Sierra Leone, and national politics have destroyed the built-in mechanism of protection for entrenched interests. As Banton observed,

> In this way a tribal system, which in the country encompasses the whole social life of each member, in the town forms a secondary system in relation to the larger urban society. In such a situation there is the likelihood that the tribal system may dissolve. Nor, in the long run, can it hold at bay the disintegrative forces unless also its institutions are adapted to the demands of its new environment.
>
> Thus, if a tribal social system is to survive transplantation into a new, urban, environment, it will have to be adapted to that environment without sacrificing its tribal identity. The two requirements, of adaptation and integration, are inter-related.[69]

Hence the proliferation of numerous little groups organized by men who have been powerless in the old power structure and who are aware of the advantages that modern education gives them. They were swiftly challenging the authority of the custodians of "village" values by throwing down the gauntlet on issues like modern schools, girls' and women's education, modern techniques of religious propaganda, adult literacy classes, and modern social amenities. Clearly they had an advantage over the older men.

There was also at the time of this study a marked change in the attitude of the younger men, for example, towards the Arabic language. The Hausa *imám* was trying just as hard as the graduate of the Islamic University of Medina to work in English. All the organizations led by these men published primarily in English.[70] The religious life was explained and studied through the medium of English. There was critical objection to the use of amulets and traditional methods of healing and other forms of therapy. These educated young men showed little respect for their so-called crystal-gazing elders and some justified apprehension that village Islam would set Muslims back by locking them into the sacred-secular split. Consequently, they pressed for the use of modern tools in the understanding and propagation of Islam. In one meeting of the Muslim Congress, the younger men argued in favor of countering hostile Christian propaganda against Islam with an intelligent, systematic exposition of Islamic teachings. The senior elders present felt called upon to defend their own position here, for they sensed their own credentials were being questioned and that, furthermore, they were being publicly relegated to the sidelines. Their strong reaction confirmed that matters were about to move beyond their control. It was clear that the meeting was wielding a many-sided weapon that could be used against their Christian opponents at the risk of exposing a deeper cleavage in their own ranks between religious isolationists and young activists. Thus in meetings where old and young were present the discussions could be edgy, or else vitriolic, and, in moments of supreme self-restraint, sullen. A casual glance at the official records of the organizations reveals this same atmosphere of mistrust or lack of confidence, with skirmishes over minor details and without apparent cause.[71]

If local Muslim reformers accept the normative Western tradition of separating the sacred and secular, they would take Islam, or how they view Islam, out of the public sphere and leave it in the hands of village obscurantists. Such a position would sap the reform impulse and would, consequently, be unacceptable. By the same token, if the reformers affirm Islam as part and parcel of national affairs, then they must, on its behalf, adopt modern tools shaped by a normative Western secularism that they have on principle repudiated. Thus, whether the protagonists accept or reject the doctrine of separation, it seems impossible for them to proceed with any effect without adjusting to its central logic. This issue implies a fundamental revamping of religion as a state idea, and, if the modernizers have their way, a replacement of it with voluntarism.

Part Four

Muslims and the Secular National State in Africa: Politics and the Religious Potential

Colonization by European powers has hustled Africa into the modern world system and there abandoned it to the double jeopardy of renouncing ancient custom and embracing the little-understood doctrine of the primacy of the secular state. Following political independence, African countries inherited from their European masters the secular state apparatus with the demand to operate it to deal with local, national, regional, and international priorities. The national state was thus set up to respond to issues created beyond its capacity and often contrary to its structure: first, to the issues of Western-imposed economic reforms whose beneficiary was the West itself, and, second, to internal ethnic, linguistic, and religious pluralism. For one, the demands of market reforms changed the state into a contract power, an economic broker that imposed an export premium on primary products by the contradictory strategy of low unit prices for domestic enterprise. Thus were the peasants and workers of local productive enterprise reduced to the "wretched of the earth," scapegoats for a national state bedeviled by historical contradictions. For another, ethnicity sowed disaffection with the balkanized postcolonial state and encouraged irredentist feelings.

The secular state as an imported structure could not comprehend why it did not receive the absolute and unquestioning loyalty of its citizens. Forced to reflect on this credibility crisis, the state tried to rescue its authority with an appeal to general, comprehensive norms, such as political absolutism, and how only the instruments fashioned by the political sovereign must command unquestioned loyalty. The unitary state idea was thus promulgated to legitimize transforming the political society into the ethical community, the civil into the official, and national leaders into messianic champions. The will of the state hardened into an absolute, comprehensive norm, with ultimate human destiny its hostage.

Without the benefit of the long evolution of the Western secular state tradition and the fruitful role of religion in preparing the soil and demarcating the boundaries, the new societies of Africa were exposed to the distortions and excesses of secular dogmatism. Had the authority of the sovereign national state been staked only on the ethic of economic success, then economic failure would have called into question merely its instrumental effectiveness. However, the national state identified its right to govern with the obligations of the moral community, specifically with ethnicity as moral template, transposing faith and trust in an ultimate moral order into unqualified loyalty and submission of its citizens. Commanding the resources and having the force to compel and intimidate, the secular ideological state expanded by using ethnicity and race as shibboleths. The state thus became a target for dissent and for the kind of debilitating skepticism that radical religious thought has typically encouraged. That religious dissent is the subject of this section.

To look at the issue at its source, the rise of the Western secular state may be described in three stages. In the first, Christians who came to faith in the catacombs of the Roman Empire saw that church and state were different and separate realms of life, as implied in Christ's teaching about distinguishing between Caesar and God. In the view of Christians, revealed truth may dispense with the instruments of political power as believers wait to give account to God in the afterlife. Later, however, the tables were turned and Christianity was legitimized and co-opted by the state. Christians themselves took up the instruments of state power to inflict suffering on fellow Christians with whom they disagreed. In this second stage the theoretical distinction of the first stage, once conceived as tenable for doctrinal and eschatological reasons, was now considered necessary for worldly reasons in order to separate warring religious factions from each other. In this stage religion was detached from state authority and from territorial expression, and the two pursued independent paths. Citizenship no longer carried religious import, and vice versa. Indeed, rulership, territoriality, and faith were broken loose from one another and allowed to go their separate ways, although, in fact, this did not happen, or did not happen cleanly, because each component retained too strong a memory of the earlier unity to be satisfied with its divided portion of it. A third stage followed in which state authority aspired to the status of a metaphysical absolute, in which the will of the nation state became omnipotent and definitive of the truth about human beings. The church responded by accepting the role of cultural underwriter and retailing religious allegiance on behalf of the national state. The church took this limited role particularly in the nation state's bellicose phase when it became a unitary Leviathan infusing from the absolute, undiluted loyalty of its citizens and thus flooding out the claims of religion except where useful. The West discharged precisely this legacy to Africa after national independence, and Muslim Africans could not avoid encountering it.

As committed Muslims see it, the state as it has operated in Africa or elsewhere is hard to ignore: Its predominance brings it four square into Islam's comprehensive sphere, thus causing Muslims to bristle at the autonomy the modern West claims for state jurisdiction. Such a claim turns the state into an explicit rival religion bolstered by an impregnable system of rewards and inducements, as well as sanctions and penalties. It specifically precludes faith of the religious kind. Muslims thus minded feel they can respond to this situation only by questioning the rule that confines religion to the sacred and removes it from the secular realm. Yet how can that questioning be credible when the solutions offered arise from a Muslim territoriality that departs but little from the norm of an outdated Christendom whose excesses and disasters forced Christians to abolish it and replace it with voluntarism?

A variety of issues are involved in that question, and they are considered below. What may be stated here is that Muslim scrutiny is no longer, if it ever was, restricted to a two-sided contest with Western secularism but implicates the centuries-long African pluralism in which Christian Africans are intimately involved. However, Muslim suspicions that such pluralism was hatched by a conspiratorial West are misplaced, for pluralism was the *entente cordiale* of the old Africa that predated, and anticipated, Muslim and Christian activity. A fresh opportunity, then, awaits the adherents of the two missionary faiths vis-à-vis the pluralist challenge of indigenous societies. Muslim and Christian Africans are already favored siblings in the African household but without the prodigal right or presumption to dispossess it or each other.

It should be stressed, however, that what Africa has experienced of the modern West is no trivial or passing fashion, because a truly ascendant fact of our time is the rise and triumph of the West alike in science, technology, and economic power. Everywhere else in the world people are astir with the forces and currents that the West has unleashed, and whether people have found fulfillment or disenchantment, the dream that lures them has the West written all over it. Given that fact, it is difficult to see how the West can be meaningfully sidelined in the emerging new world order. Nevertheless, there is a countermovement of ideas that rejects the West, or rejects the role the West has assumed in our world, and this countermovement is at present only a trickle, vigorous in spurts but generally sluggish in volume and range. Yet it is cutting for itself a deep channel among committed ranks of Muslims for whom the *Satanic Verses* controversy has unwittingly provided a rallying point. A sharp debate has been developing between conservative and liberal Muslims that questions whether temporal Islam with worldly jurisdiction, or ethical Islam concerned with personal choice, is the answer. The conservative position that religion without authority is worthless provokes the liberal response that religion without personal choice is, in its turn, meaningless, with the implication that religion and state law should be separated. Into that dichotomy, already complicated by the West's secular global ascendancy, Muslim Africa has brought its own pluralist experience. Although it is a distant Muslim corridor, Africa is still equally as important to the viability of the classical Muslim tradition of religion as sacred and secular as it is to the cogency of the liberal secular agenda. Africa offers the promise, and attendant hazards, of formulating and resolving this most crucial of debates for religious modernization. A conservative strand of the Muslim view is that Africa at present is being drawn into the dichotomy the West has made between church and state, between the sacred and secular. If the West succeeds in Africa with its worldview, then that will not spare Islam and its tradition of religion as sacred and secular. Whether or not this implies an inevitable clash of civilizations remains to be seen, as the following chapters will try to elucidate.

9

Religion and Politics
with Reference to Africa:
A Comparative Religious Critique

The modern West in its dramatic intrusion in Africa and elsewhere has been the bearer of two massive but uneven influences, one secular and the other religious. The secular influence has expressed itself in the autonomy of the national state, and the religious in the organization and extension of the missionary movement. Both influences have left an enduring legacy of a secular elite that maintains, and is in turn maintained by, the machinery of state bureaucracy and ecclesiastical jurisdictions that minister to their flocks. The uneven quality of these influences arises from the fact that state bureaucracy has primacy over the religious domain, with national sovereignty superior to ecclesiastical jurisdiction. This is the post-Enlightenment secular legacy that has competed with religion for the allegiance of Africans. The development and consequences of this uneven legacy, and its novel character, provides the subject of this chapter.

Although only relatively recently introduced in Africa, the secular national state has had a deep and lasting effect on African society. We should, therefore, examine its roots in the West in order to have a sense of the scale of the changes required by its establishment in Africa. As a dogmatic concept the national secular state is in part the legacy of Machiavelli and Bodin. In *The Prince* (published in 1515) Machiavelli establishes an absolute executive sovereignty as the supreme form of the state whose purpose is unity and order. Bodin, in his *République* (published in 1577), creates a state with uncontested power over citizens and subjects and is itself free of the constraints of the laws it enacts. The roots of the modern Western secular state and of the science of instrumental politics may be traced to these two authors and their historical contemporaries.[1]

Western political influence has not been confined to Western society but, as in Africa, has penetrated other societies. As Lord Hailey remarked in his monumental study of African conditions under colonial rule, "It is the singular fate of Africa that so many of its countries should be subject to the political control of one or other of the European Powers," though Lord Hailey took no notice of the nationalist movements that were active at his writing and which were questioning the basis of his confident assertions.[2] The existing state boundaries of Africa, for example, were created by Western colonial powers and inherited by the independent governments. These boundaries still provide the context of state jurisdiction in modern Africa, and, indeed, of religious identity.

Through the artificial colonial creation of tribes as an amalgamation of ethnic groups, and of nations as the fusion of tribes, states were established as the vehicle by which Africans could enter the twentieth century. The whole political apparatus of colonial and nationalist politics in Africa required setting aside Africa's own history, of its precolonial heritage, and blindly charging into a future of material fulfillment. In the context of the doctrine of the state as the machinery of progress and modernization, the denial of Africa's history, the charge of a dark continent of primitives without landmarks, produced the dialectics of Progress versus Tradition, of Science against Magic, with the vanguards of enlightenment ranged against the puppets of feudal privilege. The new discourse had the effect of compromising the modern African elites who were absorbed into the Western political heritage though they lacked any meaningful roots in it or, as Awolowo of Nigeria admitted,[3] in their own societies. They were in close enough proximity to colonialism to be drawn willy-nilly into the colonial orbit. However, precisely because of the relatively superficial nature of the assimilation of these new African elites and because they did not participate in the informed debate that should accompany the rise of national states, these elites became ineffective modernist brokers to their people. That provoked a crisis in the relations between state and society, in view of which we should scrutinize inherited political institutions and ideas. It is a process of reappraisal in which Muslims, too, have joined.

In his detailed discussion of the colonial context of church-state relations in Africa, Holger Hansen of Copenhagen, for example, described how the Berlin Congress of February 1885, which partitioned Africa among the colonial powers, stipulated freedom of religion and state neutrality as the appropriate framework for Western overlordship.[4] However, when applied to Africa, the European formulation of the relation of religion and politics would reveal glaring anomalies, the most significant being the lack of indigenous parallels to the Christian presuppositions of a laic state. Nevertheless, the colonial powers found a remedy in the several missionary organizations that were entering or had entered Africa. These organizations would be allowed to operate with the blessing of the state but without the state prescribing belief or enjoining practice, which is not the same thing as state indifference to religion for the obvious reason that religious affiliation often carried political implications. For example, if a local ruler converted to Catholicism, should his land and territories be incorporated into a Catholic missionary sphere or should they be broken up and offered to Baptists, Anglicans, Presbyterians, and others as well? Should the state afford similar protection and guarantees to Muslims? Apparently, at the Berlin Congress the German chancellor, Prince Otto von Bismarck, retreated from his original statement about the new colonial powers "favoring and aiding all religions" when Turkey, a Muslim state and a signatory to the convention, insisted that Muslim missionaries be included in that policy.[5]

Typically, the concordat was the instrument that prescribed church-state relations, assuring mutual benefit without harmful side effects; however, Muslims were insufficiently reared in the habit of separation to accept that arrangement. In the new colonial empires, it was discovered that a policy was needed to protect and contain Christian missions, and to do so on strictly impartial grounds so far as institutional religious interests were concerned. The question of freedom of religion was thus interpreted in terms of the right of institutional mission agencies and churches to establish themselves rather than freedom of religion as an individual matter without state involvement, though in Muslim areas the state would act as protector. Consequently, we have shades of territoriality surviving in the policy of institutional religious spheres of influence. This distinction had implications for administrative practice. The state would be neutral or indifferent in so far as the content of religious belief is concerned, but, when it came to acts and deeds, it would be active and participate in the work of religious agencies. Whether such state interest restricted or helped religious agencies, whether, for example, close cooperation in education and family life also meant control and dependence, is another question. Furthermore, if the state imagined that Christianity would play to a unitary idea of church and state, it was mistaken, for denominations were proof that there was no monolithic Christianity and that church membership implied no inclusion in a unified European religious community, for scarcely did such a thing exist. Sooner or later, a diverse African Christianity would emerge as the personal faith of individuals scattered among the tribes, however persistent collective ethnic loyalties may be.

In the general African view, religion and society are connected, even if not synonymous. The distinction between religion as private belief or as a subject fit only for study, and religion as public practice was a thoroughgoing Enlightenment distinction. However, it had no analogue in the radically different conditions of Africa, although educated African elites endorsed it. In contrast, missionaries were not too much out of step with African opinion on this matter. To the natural question, What is a Christian society? missionaries answered in terms of what was familiar to them: Victorian conformist morality and ethics mobilized behind a sympathetic colonial state. After all, the rule of good manners of Victorian sensibility sets only such standards as it can enforce, whatever the risk of cultural interference.

Thus to most missionaries, such as Robert Laws of Livingstonia in 1880, Robert Moffat of Kuruman, or the agents of the Blantyre mission, a Christian society was a desideratum, especially where Christian colonies composed of freed slaves could be set up to that end under white suzerainty. Yet the idea of such a society as a foreign political enclave, protected by European colonial power from without and governed by rules and regulations imposed by missionaries from within, was deemed an obstacle rather than a help to the service of the kind of Gospel that thrives from personal initiative.[6] In consequence, the special circumstances of Africa made such unthinking cultural transference all but impossible.

Let us pursue the subject and assess the religious aspect of the presence of the Western political heritage in Africa in three parts: The first, using some African examples, will examine the nature of the relationship between religion and politics, in particular, what religious interest there might be in political affairs and whether such interest is compatible with religious autonomy; the second will expound the Islamic formulation of the issue in terms of the rightful integration as well as proper separation of religion and politics; and, finally, the third will offer some reflections on the religious case for the inadequacy of the national state to serve as an absolute moral arbiter of human relations. The conclusion will be that the current ferment in religious circles in Africa, and elsewhere in the Muslim world, provides a useful context for reexamining standard Western suppositions on the principle of separation of church and state; we should therefore turn our critical eye back on the West and reassess what its successful expansion abroad has brought to other societies.[7]

An important thread runs throughout this discussion: Both national loyalty and religious loyalty appeal to, and have their source in, a commitment that is in the final analysis spiritual, so that an exclusive political definition of that commitment throws down a gauntlet to any religious commitment. In response, religious people have sometimes employed "holy nationalism"[8] to strengthen their cause, creating a debate on the issue.[9] Such a debate has opened the state to moral scrutiny and therefore to a qualification of its absolute claims. In view of such complex issues, we may argue that religion, in its critical realism about human nature, has a role in political renewal and social advancement. This argument can be extended by taking due cognizance of developments in Muslim thought, which shows a divergence from Western political practice.

On Origin and Tension

Any analysis of the impact of the secular state in Africa will result in two conclusions. One is that national, linguistic, or ethnic identity does not coincide with the boundaries of the state, and the state as presently constituted is unable to cope with the resulting complex political, economic, and military order. This problem has encouraged the creation of coalitions, alliances, and pacts between and across nations, including membership in international organizations. The other is the role religion plays in the relations between states and in issues of international security: There are often religious questions that go beyond national state jurisdiction. Given the persistence of religion as a force for change and identity or, on the negative side, as a force for obduracy and intractability, the modern national state often encounters religion in the course of seeking or constructing popular endorsement.

A potentially dangerous imbalance inheres in the relationship between religion and the national state, such as when ethnic nationalism is forged from the hard crust of ethnic custom and transmuted into the state instrument, and when the state in turn represents the unity of ethnic triumph and moral destiny. Under the right conditions, including when religion has been thoroughly domesticated as cultural identity, the ethnic state can become the opiate of the people, an intoxicating infusion of sentiments of national transcendence in defiance of logic and history. Our failure to recognize or understand the distinction, rather than the antipathy, between church and state tips the scales on the side of the sacralized ethnic state.

The crux of the case being presented in this chapter may be stated as follows: Those who have followed Machiavelli and Bodin in arming the sovereignty of the state in full panoply have also dissolved the separation of church and state by awarding authority to the state in religious matters. At the same time, the state, by being so absolutized, challenges religion in its own sphere. By proceeding on one front it must, in fact, proceed on another, much in the manner of the traditional square dance: moving three or four steps to the right anticipates as many to the left. In one pattern of political "absolutization" we elicit a contrasting pattern of religious "relativization." In Africa such gyrations have characterized much of the scene. In addition, it is clear that the absolutized state incurs a double jeopardy: It cripples the instrumental function of authority and infects religious motivation with tactical rewards. Thus has the versatile state stumbled on its own inflexible contradiction.

The conditions for the absolutization of political norms have their source in the theory of sovereignty. "Sovereignty," says Sir Ernest Barker, "is unlimited and illimitable."[10] As the definition of sovereignty expanded over time, it came to be applied to human relations in the notion of the liberator-state that may intervene to protect social groups from interfering with the principle of the free agency of their members. Marsiglio of Padua, a medieval writer who straddled the world of the middle ages and early modern Europe and as such was a precursor of Bodin, "asserted the primacy of law-making over all other expressions of state power; he insisted on the indivisibility of ultimate legislative authority."[11] Although it is clear that Marsiglio did not develop his ideas into a coherent theory of sovereignty, his emphasis on the formal right of the ruler to make laws provides support for the Machiavellian executive sovereign.

Two important elements may be said to persist in medieval writings about political authority, at least in writings about the medieval world in the advanced stages of its development.[12] One is the role assigned to reason and natural law, and the other is the concept of political obligation, especially how, if at all, dissent fits in with such obligation. The ruler is assumed to be beholden to norms of reason and justice, but, in fact, the circularity of thought involved makes those norms attributes of the sovereign. What you give with the right hand you take with the left. It was the veteran ideologue, the Abbé Sieyès, who, as guiding spirit of the French Revolution, made the national state assume an implacable doctrinaire posture when he wrote in 1789: "The nation exists before all, it is the origin of everything. Its will is always legal, it is the law itself." Who or what the nation is makes a difference here. Thus when the Abbé Sieyès' injunction is fused with Rousseau's General Will to become in effect the popular will, it entrenches an uncompromising nation state dogma that typically ignites into Chosen People activism once it is whipped up with racial or national fervor. Thus is spawned from both the left and right a veritable Leviathan that consumes all its opponents and rivals, the church included.

Given the benefit of hindsight, we may say the national state in its long and forceful expansion in Africa and elsewhere has thrived from its incestuous appetite and now appears to have reached the limits of its development. Consequently, we have reached a point where the task is to define the limits of the national state in terms of the new international order, human rights, social pluralism, and religious freedom—old questions, perhaps, but cast in a new light by unprecedented modern developments. The culture of political sacralization to which Muslim theocratic demands seem to lend support is appealing to a state that wants to bolster itself with metaphysical norms. However, when properly directed, current religious ferment in the Third World may be mobilized to check the excesses of the predatory state, as has happened in Ghana under Acheampong and in South Africa, with religion able to demonstrate, in however tentative or precarious a fashion, the limited nature of political sovereignty.

The secular, rational state thus conceived is not just the victim but an active protagonist in the religious controversy concerning its will and purpose. By absolutizing itself the state claims not only the power to organize life and command the obedience of men and women but to be itself what H. Richard Niebuhr calls "the value-center," consecrating its operative dealings with the henotheist faith of national loyalty.[13] It is a short step from there to the next, when the state becomes, in the words of ancient sacred monarchies, "the shadow of God on earth," followed by a third step when the state makes obligation a matter exclusively of its control.

Not merely content to restrain and arbitrate but wanting also to prescribe faith of a moral kind and conformity of an absolute nature, the omnipotent state in Africa has opened for itself a wide channel of power. Ideological advocates of the state who had used their theories to combat religious dangers have now inherited in the omnipotent state far worse hazards, only now magistrates have upstaged mullahs, commissars, and cardinals. With that change the state has attained a radical arbitrary posture for which a suitable motto might be, "If the state loses the confidence of the people, it shall dissolve the people and elect another." The idea of political stability is interchanged with that of the continuity of the state, bringing closer the day when, as Gladstone once described it, we have "the negation of God erected into a system of government."

My basic contention here is not born of a facile romanticism for a stateless society and of a Rousseauistic innocence, but rather of the conviction that the omnipotent state in Africa has been its own undoing, that it is riddled with fundamental contradictions. Such a state promotes a political metaphysic in place of religion. Dietrich Bonhoeffer used to complain that the modern world in which the church tries to minister has outgrown the metaphysical religious outlook of the Bible; "God as the working hypothesis" has been superseded in a "world come of age."[14] In fact, however, the religious metaphysic has been replaced with the political metaphysic, with political messianism the creed in which people place their trust. Thus, the otherwise natural convoy of religion and politics has been reduced to capture by the state, with citizenship its hostage.

In many countries in Africa, the capture of religion by the state was signaled by formal agreements. The Missionary Concordat of 1940 and the Statute of 1941, for example, created privileges for the Roman Catholic church in Portuguese Angola and Mozambique along the lines of the 1926 Missionary Accord. Under the terms of the Concordat the Portuguese state recognized the Catholic church as an official institution to promote the national and colonial aims of the state in the overseas territories, with financial provision for the church to that end. Cardinal Carejeira of Lisbon announced on national radio in May 1940 that the Concordat returned Portugal to its spiritual roots and would commence a process of inward national renewal and vigorous outward colonial expansion. Although Carejeira insisted that the Concordat did not create a state church, Antonio Salazar, the president of Portugal, was more candid, saying that the church would be subject to the higher requirements of national interest and public order, that the clergy would be "guaranteed" patriotic education, and that the state would be a party in the selection of the highest ecclesiastical authorities.[15] With particular reference to Africa, Salazar saw the Concordat as the completion of the Colonial Act whose purpose was to nationalize missionary work and harmonize it with colonial policy. In his address to the National Assembly in Lisbon, Salazar was in a heady mood about church and state as one harmonious ideal. "We return," he said effusively, "with the force and vigor of a reborn state to one of the greatest springs of our national life and, without abandoning our contemporary period with its material progress and the victories of civilization, we are in the upper spheres of spirituality—the same as eight hundred years ago."[16] Salazar was the impetus in the tidal wave of Portuguese immigration into Africa, which by 1974 numbered 350,000 in Angola and 200,000 in Mozambique, all of which bloated Portugal's Christendom pretensions. Thus, Salazar's version of Christendom rested on the colonial project as a unilateral construct, without any recourse to Africans. Portugal's future greatness would be the echo of historic Christendom, and the African colonies, though without exact parallels in the cohesive territoriality of classical Christendom, would nevertheless fit, or be made to fit, into an archetypal religious scheme. In this, as in so much else, Salazar was wrong, and the consequent unrest in Portugal's African empire, combined with progressive forces in the expanding European Community, would undermine Portugal's organic stability at home.

In retrospect, Salazar's colonial religious flirtations seem like rhetorical diversions when compared to the stripping that awaited the church in an independent Angola or Mozambique. On 11 November 1975, Angola declared its independence from Portugal, amidst a fractured armed liberation movement and the shreds of a divided society. The new MPLA government adopted Marxism-Leninism under a centralized party machinery as the vanguard of the revolution. Political militancy was at once declared the corrective to religion, a position that placed the party on a war path with the church. In December 1977, the official organs of the government announced that Catholics and Protestants could not become members of the party or the government. There was widespread harassment of religion, including the confiscation of property and the forcible taking of children from their parents for indoctrination. When the Catholic church responded to the situation, with Vatican Radio denouncing on 21 January 1978 the discriminatory measures against the church, the party answered back with charges of lies and conspiracy against the church. The secretary of the Party Central Committee, Lúcio Lara, cut to the chase with a long-running attack on the church, emphasizing its foreignness to Angola and thus, by implication, its traitorous character. To the church's criticism about imposing on Angolan society a foreign-born ideology like Marxism-Leninism, Lara answered that Christ was not born in Angola, either, thus exonerating the imported primacy of Marxism by the strategy of the proscribed foreignness of the church.[17] He warned opponents that the government had provided itself with the means to consider "as illegal and therefore [as] punishable any activity which places faith or religious belief in opposition to the revolutionary transformation of society."[18] The government moved against religious schools, taking them over and instituting a program of scientific socialism to shut down all access to information about Angola's long and distinguished religious history, beginning with King Afonso I (ruled 1506–1543).

The attacks on the church, and their tediously elaborate justifications in the theory of party supremacy, have led more than one commentator to conclude that Marxism-Leninism is actually a religion, even a church, and that it is competing with Catholicism or Protestantism for primacy. This is unconvincing and confuses—and rewards—political ideology with what it has plundered from religion. Thus the MPLA government produced what it called the Ten Principles of the Pioneers, deliberately modeled on the Ten Commandments, and, in case that was not obvious, ransacked the New Testament to identify a parallel set of what the party called Ten Commandments for Christian Youth.[19] The propaganda catechism of the MPLA government was an amalgam of expedient platitudes, and its wish to be compared to Scripture as a matter simply of comparing texts only proved forgery. The resemblance admits the difference. How else can we explain the hostility with which the government regarded religion? Thus in the torture and deaths of priests, sisters, and pastors, we have a pattern inscribed with the grim logic of political vengeance. It is small comfort to tell the religious faithful, who witness and survive these acts, that surveillance and repression are directed at them because of their kinship with the agents of political control. In one typical instance, a sister who survived a deadly ambush said that at the time Father Leandro Volken, a Swiss missionary, was killed in January 1983, the religious party was saying the rosary and meditating on the "sorrowful mysteries"—we have here not kin bonding but a state vendetta. A leading Protestant churchman was constrained to observe that although he himself would offer conciliation and cooperation, what the government required of religion was that it should remain a target for suppression.[20] Thus did the secular ideological state overturn the popular basis of Catholic piety to assert those of political monism. Politics as religion redeems no more than religion as politics.

The Christendom view of religion in which church and state were a unified though flawed institution was at work in other parts of Africa, too. In Ethiopia the Emperor Haile Selassie was crowned on 2 November 1930, in the cathedral in Addis Ababa, and the Ethiopian constitution formally recognized "the person of the Emperor as sacred, His dignity . . . inviolable and his power indisputable." In the 1955 Revised Constitution, after the Ethiopian Orthodox church was declared the established church with state backing, the emperor and the patriarch had thrones side by side in the cathedral in Addis Ababa, a value-added formula that was rooted in Ethiopia's national origin. The emperor was given the right of approval in the election and appointment of senior church officials and of attendance at Holy Synod meetings with veto powers over decisions there. Archbishop Basileyos, on his ordination and at his elevation to the patriarchate, swore an oath of loyalty to the emperor. He was given a place on the Council of Regency and on the Crown Council. Thus did the Revised Constitution effect the state takeover of the church and made the fit between government and religion exact. The Penal Code of 1957 recognized as national holidays the festivals of the Ethiopian church, followed by the Civil Code of 1960, which gave legal sanction to the church with respect to its dioceses, monasteries, and parishes.

These measures may also be seen as the "gelding of God," as the church's forfeiture of her maiden honor at the hands of an aggressive state. In our analysis of what happened in Ethiopia or Portugal, we should note that religion may become a state idea by the devious path of the state becoming a religious idea, that it is enough for Salazar to say it without Carejeira having to do so. Thus did the normal state boundaries expand to incorporate the church as a quasi department of government. Religion in turn became mixed up with the shifting fortunes of political expediency, allying itself with people who might be useful for short-term gain only and repulsing others whose long-term principles might cohere with those of religion but whose particular stand at the time made them oppose the state. For example, in 1960 there was an abortive left-wing coup in Addis Ababa, led by Germame Neway, who called for a program of nationalization of land, including land belonging to the church. After the coup was quelled, the church responded by demonstrating its loyalty to the state and declaring the coup leaders and supporters as antireligious traitors. However, the church could have benefited from a crystal ball then in view of the political storm that would engulf it after September 1974, when the emperor was overthrown in a Marxist coup.[21]

Following dramatic political changes in these states from the mid-1970s on, the governments of Angola, Mozambique, and Ethiopia swiftly moved to abolish preferment and to enact freedom of religion. Elsewhere in Africa it was a period of stormy relations as churches maneuvered for autonomy: In Ghana, there was the fateful confrontation between the church and the regime of General Acheampong; in Uganda, the clash between the churches and General Idi Amin, leading to the murder of Archbishop Lanani Luwum in 1977; and in Liberia, the coup d'état in 1980 of the late President Doe, which installed a military government that chose to make an example of the pastor-politicians who had ruled Liberia from the very beginning of the republic.[22] Similar tensions have existed in Zaire, Nigeria, the Sudan, Zambia, and Kenya. For example, in the tense atmosphere following the abortive coup attempt of August 1982, the churches in Kenya decided to respond to government attempts to introduce political indoctrination in schools. In September 1983 the churches published a document entitled, "Love, Peace, and Unity: A Christian View of Politics in Kenya," which stated that the churches should be true to their prophetic calling rather than merely do the state's bidding.

From all these complex situations we may draw the following conclusion: The results are the same whether religion is a state idea or the state is a religious idea. However church and state may be combined, an identical fate awaits them, for the reason that the mixing of church and state stakes everything on the temporal ground. The risk is that both sectors will get caught with tangled signals, that unrest will spread evenly between them even if unrest has only one origin. Each would be hoisted with the other's petard.

On another level, we may note that the call for political mobilization in Africa has made wide use of religious symbols, whether or not such symbols have received official sanction. This appropriation has led to a hybrid politico-religious culture, making familiar such phrases as "national redemption," "economic salvation," "political justification," "national regeneration," "seeking first the political kingdom," "sanctity of the state," "the supreme law of the state," and so forth. In a move calculated to muzzle the civil service, President Kwame Nkrumah of Ghana declared in 1962 that a civil servant "who sells information concerning his work is worse than a traitor and incurs an eternal curse upon his head."[23] The "eternal curse" was a code for political stigmatization, a fate carrying a serious threat. Nkrumah was on occasion more explicit, as when his Young Pioneers Movement adopted the Paternoster, the Lord's Prayer, for political catechism, substituting political vocabulary for religion. He intended the political takeover of religion as a matter of logical necessity. His effect on contemporary African youth, including myself, is hard to measure, so enormous was it.

In the hands of leaders of his ilk, then, the state assumed metaphysical connotations, with the single-party state becoming a monotheist secular absolute. Such a state was ideologically intolerant of pluralism, which excites all the bitter passion and iconoclastic fury monotheist crusaders reserve for polytheists, and brought the connection of religion and politics to the level of state monopoly. As a result, political life itself was transformed, with African leaders promoting themselves as anointed messianic champions.[24] One of the most successful contemporary figures of political messianism is General Mobutu of Zaire, who refers to himself as "the Father and god of the nation."[25] An American journalist in Africa recently observed of Mobutu that the Zairian leader aims at being omnipotent and omnipresent. His face is everywhere:

> His photograph hangs in every office in his realm. His ministers wear gold pins with tiny photographs of him on the lapels of their tailored pin-striped suits. He names streets, football stadiums, hospitals, and universities after himself. . . . He insists on being called "doctor" or "conqueror" or "teacher" or "the big elephant" or "the number-one peasant" or "the wise old man" or "the natural miracle" or "the most popular leader in the world." His every pronouncement is reported on the front page. . . . He bans all political parties except the one he controls. He rigs elections. He emasculates the courts. He cows the press. He stifles academia. He goes to church.[26]

The rhetoric of state power, however, is nearly in inverse proportion to the influence it exerts. In much of Africa political rhetoric has aroused feelings and expectations far in excess of realizable goals. People have responded with withdrawal, which leaders have alleged to be apathy resulting from colonial alienation. As messianic slogans have turned incandescent in the darkness, the bedazzled populations have also turned skeptical. Farmers, peasants, and workers in the mines and on the roads, rivers, and railways have bucked the system by holding back or falling to the highest bidder. Productivity has collapsed and with it state revenues. Parastatals have entered the scene and have combined economic incentives with political rewards to reverse the process, though the adopted measures have failed abysmally, with people seeing them as versions of state excess.

The assault of the state on its citizens has left people with a return to traditional values, however defined, as a last resort. However, even there the state has pursued the people, arrogating the right to define those values and to appropriate them for itself. Hence Mobutu's call for "African authenticity," including the dropping of European names and the adopting of African ones. Socialist doctrine in other parts of the continent has been assortedly upholstered in colorful communitarian values and stiffened with oriental lessons,[27] mostly lean-to ideas jacked up by party activists. A spiritual reaction has followed in which church leaders, backed by the rank and file, have taken up the cudgels. In response, the state has pretended that political obligation is a matter of its exclusive control, a state of mind requiring surrender and submission. It is as a state of mind that the churches have opposed the state bureaucracy.

As African and other political leaders have been quick to realize, religion and politics are intimately connected: They affect each other, draw on each other's insight, and make an identical appeal to trust and loyalty. Yet we appear to have inherited in Africa a Manichaean ideal, with the state as the embodiment of truth and goodness—a dichotomy that breeds political intolerance. It allows political leaders, when it suits their interests, to give religion an enclave, voluntary status, a secondary value vis-à-vis the primary truth-center of political action, although from the religious point of view "enclavement" may promote a liminal sense of superiority.[28] A notion has grown that politics impinge on religion in a superior way: that the state as the superior and ultimate representation of human reality will survive the demise of religion and, meanwhile, must actively work toward that end. The state has seized on its instrumental capability to press its right to limitless power. Consequently, in several well-known instances, religious people have responded with a counterchallenge, viewing the claims of political metaphysics as vestiges of genuine religious metaphysics. This religious case receives eloquent treatment in the Islamic tradition, and to that we now turn.

The Islamic Religious and Political Ferment

Representative Muslim scholars treat the issue of religion and politics without the sanguine notion that the public and private domain require separate and exclusive understanding. The Muslim counterargument, now the topic in media and print reports,[29] is symptomatic of the widespread disenchantment with the national state as a moral absolute. Early Muslim nationalists, however, had to run the gauntlet of orthodox suspicions that they were encouraging the usurping tendencies of the modern state. Thus in the constitutional debates preceding the establishment of the state of Pakistan, Muhammad 'Alí Jinnah, a founding father of Pakistan and a leading voice in the Constituent Assembly, in 1947 declared support for a secular, nonreligious basis for the new nation: "You may belong to any religion or creed or caste—that has nothing to do with the business of the state. . . . You will find," he added provocatively, "that in the course of time Hindus [will] cease to be Hindus and Muslims cease to be Muslims, not in the religious sense because that is the personal faith of each individual, but in a political sense as citizens of the State."[30] In a prophetic outburst against religious caviling, Jinnah insisted that "Pakistan is not going to be a Theocratic State ruled by priests with a divine mission."[31]

Yet religious sentiment, which legitimated the entire project of a separate state for Indian Muslims, would only be inflamed by Jinnah's assertions. Speaking to the same issue on a different occasion, Sádiq al-Mahdí, a veteran of Sudanese politics and more than once its prime minister, implicitly answered Jinnah's contention: "The concepts of secularism, humanism, nationalism, materialism, and rationalism which are all based on partial truths, became deities in their own right; one-eyed superbeings. They are responsible for the present Euro-American spiritual crisis. The partial truths in all these powerful ideas can be satisfied by Islam."[32] As this and other statements clearly suggest, the great ferment in the Muslim world today is proof of the riveting appeal of religion and politics for ordinary people. As Kenneth Cragg writes in his classic work, "The renewed and effective politicization of Islam is the most important single fact of the new century."[33] This politicization is at the level of the rank-and-file faithful and includes an overscrupulous populist reaction to the perceived religious menace of Europe and North America, regions that are also now home to significant Muslim communities.

Classical Islamic sources deny any strict distinction between religion and politics. The caliph (*khalífah*), the earthly sovereign, as the Prophet's successor, is charged with the "power to bind and to loosen," and is, furthermore, commanded to restrain people from bloodshed and to ensure their welfare in this world and in the future life.[34] Following the demise of the caliphate, the reformulation of Muslim political thought shifted the weight of opinion to the maintenance of the *sharí'ah*, the religious code, as the prerequisite of a viable community life. In the modern world of national states this reformulation has been practiced at the grassroots level, where it has introduced an ideology of populist legitimacy. This would suggest a shift in favor of the civil community, with the state representing, rather than replacing, popular appeal. Unlike the caliphate, the *Sharí'ah* is every believer's responsibility and comes within the terms of duties mandated not by the state but by the religious code. Since the *Sharí'ah* involves duties and obligations deemed incumbent on rank-and-file Muslims without respect to nationality, its introduction into ordinary life restricts state jurisdiction over the obedience of citizens whose "peoplehood" now has a primary religious basis to it. It explains why in several cases, it was the mullahs, imáms, and other *Sharí'ah* officials who led the movement to discredit the national state. As a famous African Muslim reformer put it, "Most people are ignorant of the *Sharí'ah*, and it is obligatory [therefore] that there should be, in every mosque and quarter in the town, a *faqíh* teaching the people their religion."[35] Thus did religious teachings acquire political significance.

In one sense Islam broke with the Aristotelian idea of "the good of the state [being] manifestly a greater and more perfect good" by making the "highest good" a religious one: A person's last end is happiness in God, which is as much a pursuit as it is "the gift of God." Knowledge of existing things helps in practical pursuits of many kinds, but perfection in the ethical life defines the higher happiness (*sa'ádah*).[36] The state itself is held to these norms. In another sense, however, Islam has extended the Aristotelian idea by positing the *ummah*, the religious community, as the indispensable foundation of human civilization. Aristotle's assertion, following Plato, that the human being is a "political being" (*zoon politikon*) is now expanded in the Muslim view that the human being is created for religious solidarity. Either way, whether it concerns the greater good of the state or the true end of human life, the religious foundation for the human enterprise is secured. In that sense Islam rejects the rigid separation of religion and politics to assert its stake in both realms.

Nevertheless, mainstream thought still supports at least a notional separation of religion and politics for eminently religious reasons. One general approach is the distinction Muslims draw between doctrinal stipulations and historical circumstances, between the external formulations of the jurists and the inner reality of life. As Gibb stressed, "Between the real content of Muslim thought and its juristic expression there is a certain dislocation,"[37] preventing us from being able to infer the reality from the outer form. Doctrinal formulation is not so much a historical transcript as a legal device serving a procedural and partial end. If we take this approach, then we may say that *Sharí'ah* supremacy is in terms of its juristic custody, of its being in the rightful possession of the guild of qualified jurists, rather than in terms of its comprehensive implementation.[38] In other words, it is the recognition of the proper sphere of *Sharí'ah* authority, not its sectarian application.

However, there is the other side to that view. Although doctrinal formulation compresses the diverse reality into a rigid mold, as Gibb describes it, it also serves notice that religious thought will not be "bound by outward formulae. It exerts a constant pressure, whose influence is to be seen in the unobtrusive reshaping of theory which, beneath an outward inflexibility, characterizes all branches of speculative activity in Islam, where Islam has remained a living organism."[39]

If this distinction between formal doctrine and the content of life is valid, it opens the way for affirmation of the religious sphere as nonidentical, though connected, with the political sphere. Religious activity is too bound up with everyday contingency to fit into the neat lines of formal doctrine, so that temporal Islam errs in seeking such a fit, and yet in its everydayness religion cannot be robbed of political significance either. The classical Muslim scholar, Sufyán Thaurí, referred to in the next chapter, emphasized this double theme by counseling religious scholars to maintain a prudent distance from political rulers, who, for their turn, should seek wise counsel from the religious scholars. Sufyán Thaurí intends to say that actions of political expedience must be qualified by moral norms, but moral norms must not be qualified by political expedience. Muslim scholars have argued, for example, that coercion is unworthy of religious integrity, basing their argument on a verse from the Qur'án to the effect that "there is no compulsion in religion" (*lá ikráha fí-l-dín*).[40] Thus, a prescriptive religious state conflicts with that scriptural injunction and, at another level, with the high ethical purpose of human felicity. In such a state many people, undoubtedly, would choose to join or remain in the religious fold for very sound religious reasons, but others would do so for reasons that would be very bad from a religious point of view: from fear of reprisal, hope of gain, or the force of blackmail—motives fatal to the spiritual pursuit. Similarly, it would make it impossible to treat minorities and other nonconformists, religious or other, with anything but expedient cynicism. Even the state could not survive for long if it made repression its only justification, for then repression would become the political means as well as the moral end of human conduct. Yet if means and end are thus interchanged, then expediency and moral truth would fuse and result in tyranny. Therefore, church and state should be separated obviously for practical mundane reasons but also for exalted religious ones.

The question of equal treatment for non-Muslims in an Islamic state has had a long and detailed examination, although attempts to assure critics that classical Islamic resources offer full guarantees have not been entirely persuasive.[41] Privileges conferred on minority groups in a prescriptive religious state soon carry the stigma of exclusion, with statutory safeguards becoming nothing better than inquisitional staging posts—society's handy valve for disgorging unassimilated elements in times of crisis. Even the majority under those circumstances would feel sucked in by the momentum of the engine of oppression directed at minority groups. Intolerance knows few scruples to discriminate between the stigmatized and the canonized. It will play the game both ways. This situation, therefore, forces us back to the sacred logic of distinguishing between religion and politics.

A Muslim writer who devoted considerable attention to this matter was Ibn Khaldún (d. 1406/07). Writing in 1377, Ibn Khaldún tried to summarize the views of his predecessors. He cautioned against the uncritical mixing of religion and worldly affairs lest we "patch our worldly affairs by tearing our religion to pieces. Thus, neither our religion lasts nor (the worldly affairs) we have been patching."[42] For Ibn Khaldún, religion is entangled at numerous levels with society, from having an established position at the center to being an unco-opted force. Thus religion has two senses: It is either a social ornament or a ruling ideology, useful or necessary.

The great insight of Ibn Khaldún consists in giving secular justification for the development of political institutions. However much he may defer formally to religion, he was astute enough a scholar to recognize theocratic claims as simplistic and lacking in historical realism. In essence, Ibn Khaldún argues that political society is founded on group cohesion, what he terms *solidarity*, '*asabiyáh*. He takes the prudent step of appealing to a *hadíth* from the Prophet, who is reputed to have said, "Learn your genealogies to know who are your near of kin." Aware of other traditions that have the Prophet abolishing kinship, Ibn Khaldún redeems himself by turning to the same source to find that the Prophet intended us to understand how "kinship only serves a function when blood ties lead to actual cooperation and mutual aid in danger—other degrees of kinship being insignificant."[43] In continuing with the defense of kinship, Ibn Khaldún asserts that the Prophet intended no neglect of group solidarity, but merely to inculcate its relative merit as a worldly arrangement vis-à-vis the higher obedience centered in revelation. In all this, Ibn Khaldún's project is the radical one of discerning sociological laws in collective historical institutions and hierarchies and in removing from all serious analysis any appeal to dogma. It is important to cite his own words on this point. According to him, rulership as such is not divine but is the outgrowth of social development. This is so because rulership

> is the natural end to which social solidarity leads. And this transformation is not a matter of choice but a necessary consequence of the natural order and disposition of things. . . . For no laws, religions, or institutions can be effective unless a cohesive group enforces and imposes them and without solidarity they cannot be established.

Social solidarity is, therefore, indispensable if a nation is to play the role which God has chosen for it. . . . For unless religious laws derive their sanctions from social solidarity they will remain totally ineffective.[44]

The importance Ibn Khaldún attaches to *'asabiyáh* brings the concept into deep affinity with modern notions of nationalism, in which a people, fired by sentiments of kin identity enclosed within stable territorial boundaries, establishes an effective community for the purpose. Such a community transcends the individual and expresses itself in the collective will to command, to prescribe for the present and future, to judge, reward, and punish. Ibn Khaldún says that kind of social solidarity is identical with the spiritual community. Therefore, "no religious movement can succeed unless based on solidarity."[45] Solidarity is the backbone of religion as it is of the state.

Such views have implications for political legitimacy, too, as Ibn Khaldún noted. He was at pains to point out that effective leadership is a matter not of revealed truth but of pragmatic competence. Good leaders are determined by the quality of their rule as seen by their subjects rather than by the purity of the ideals to which they subscribe. Governments are the just deserts of the societies in which they are found. Ibn Khaldún contends, "If such rulership is good and beneficial, it will serve the interests of the subjects. If it is bad and unfair, it will be harmful to them and cause their destruction."[46] Ibn Khaldún, writing here as a scholar, is not primarily concerned with spelling out the practical institutional arrangements by which harm may be determined and remedied,[47] but his insights would be compatible with our modern notions of democratic political liberalism, constitutional accountability, and participation. However, a theoretical limitation in his views is his failing to make the safety of citizens, what we speak of as human rights, a fundamental qualification of political obligation and state sovereignty. Be that as it may, he pioneered a methodology in which political society is sundered from any comprehensive doctrinal mooring and set amidst a pluralist social and historical context.

What is surprising is how, within his explanatory scheme, Ibn Khaldún could maintain religion as revealed truth. Two explanations may briefly be offered. One is that Ibn Khaldún is concerned with the civil status of "man," with human beings as members of the political community, when they enter into business and action, rather than as moral agents under God, when they are a subject of truth affirmation. The civil community is by its nature contingent, built as it is on intersecting plural interests, on the dynamic alliance of group solidarity and interest that would be effective in an instrumental, expedient sense, however inadequate in terms of any comprehensive moral norm. In this understanding the primary focus of historical study should be rational human interests that can be ordered and mobilized by a system of incentives, sanctions, and similar behavioral measures, without implying that historical study completes and exhausts the truth of being human. I am inclined to this view as the more important to Ibn Khaldún.

However, another explanation is offered by Sir Hamilton Gibb. According to Gibb, Ibn Khaldún used religion in two ways. The first is religion in the true or absolute sense, "when the whole will of man is governed by his religious conviction and his animal nature is held in check. Opposed to this is 'acquired religion,' a secondhand and relatively feeble thing, which saps his manhood and fails to control his animal impulses."[48] Gibb is convinced that religion in the first sense continued to occupy a central place in Ibn Khaldún's thought, as follows: statistically, human communities are disinclined to follow revealed truth for the conduct of affairs, and given this fact Ibn Khaldún would say that human society is locked into a grim cycle of rise and fall, "conditioned by the 'natural' and inevitable consequences of the predominance of its animal instincts. In this sense," Gibb avers, Ibn Khaldún's "pessimism has a moral and religious, not a sociological, basis."[49] This view may be related to Max Weber's assessment that Islam is almost by itself among the world religions in offering a practical orientation to political and worldly affairs.[50] We should repeat, however, that Ibn Khaldún's theory of history received its most cogent and explicit development from the preponderance of fact and practice, thereby implying the downgrading of theological speculation in favor of empirical observation. In his methodology, he was a pragmatist first and a moralist last, and so, it is still valid to question where religion stands after the dust has settled. If Gibb is right about Ibn Khaldún's moral and religious pessimism in contrast to his confident historical extrapolations, then we may say that his pessimism has its root in his idea of religion as a state enterprise, a theological limitation that cramped his historical view.

Ibn Khaldún understood religion as political dogma, which is evidently at odds with the kind of confident historical positivism he was pioneering. In that scheme, religion is not necessary to the understanding of historical change, although it must be if religion's political status is what is claimed for it. Thus, by the time he returned to religion, Ibn Khaldún had gone far enough to show he could get on without it, though he seems unprepared for that. Religion, he thinks, can be important only as political *ummah* rather than as personal faith based on persuasion and choice. His methodology requires no providence for historical understanding or consummation. He is disconcerted by this conclusion, and, accordingly, rouses himself and hurries back to religion to find he can only make rhetorical and anecdotal use of it. So he muses ruefully to himself about the flawed human capacity as the reason for religion not being as decisive in human affairs as it deserves. But what he saves of religion by that tactic is still too little too late, for religious rhetoric now slips into pessimism about humanity's animal impulses. Little did he realize that such a polarity of the human and divine denies any possibility of a vital contact point between history and providence. The historical record, filled with evidence of feeble animal impulses rather than with that of truth affirmation, predominates over divine primacy in faith and conduct, as material will predominates over spiritual ideal.

Thus Ibn Khaldún's otherwise penetrating insight fails near its religious elevation. To amend Emerson, while allowing an influx of divinity into his mind with his historical generalization, Ibn Khaldún flinched when it came to making the purpose of divinity congruent, in terms of effects, with the human striving for freedom and goodness, which affects the political realm without politics being driven into a theocratic shell. He secured the social levers of political change and felt with the same motion he must proceed against the enjoined pivot of religious truth. In spite of its brilliant originality, then, his schema, with its basis in the power of social scale, is too determinist to accede to any viable theory of political life grounded in spiritual truth.

The State: Source or Instrument? Christian Ruminations

The august counsels of Muslims demand an analogous response from Christians and others concerning the state.[51] The Islamic attitude indicates that the accepted principle of separation of church and state should come under close scrutiny.

In Western Christian thought, the fresh appraisal of the interconnection of religion and politics goes back to the origins of the modern state. Sir Thomas More (d. 1535), in his work *Utopia,* responded to the challenges of the "new economics" by speaking to the moral issues raised by the changes. To do this, he turned to the Sermon on the Mount and suggested that the interests of the worldly kingdom are not disconnected from those of the heavenly kingdom, an insight he deepened by closely reading St. Augustine's *City of God.* More felt that God's claims on us should oblige us to establish a City of Man such that God would be pleased to dwell within it.[52]

In his monumental work, *Of the Laws of the Ecclesiastical Polity,* Richard Hooker (d. 1600) made the first ambitious attempt to make the civil compact parallel to the religious community. In Hooker's scheme the state may safely be entrusted with the ecclesiastical polity, and he adduced reasons to that end. Hooker was a religious radical but a theological moderate. He accepted the rational law, or the light of reason/nature, as no less authoritative than divine injunction, but he rejected the antinomian strains of Puritan thought with its relentless anti-Catholic tendencies. Hooker would have nothing to do with the Barthianism of the Puritans, the theology that set a God of inscrutable will "over against" the "accursed nature of Man," as that dialectic creates a simultaneous extremism of the "right" and of the "left": Ask of any institution whether it is of God, in which case you will fall down and worship it, or whether it is of man, then you attack and destroy it. Unlike the majority of Puritans, Hooker was not searching for the true church and could never have prayed with John Donne, "Show me deare Christ, thy spouse."[53] His view of church and state is conditioned by his premise of Christianity as a "religion of the provinces," as Edward Gibbon would call it,[54] that is to say, as a religion that assimilates into the characteristics of national cultures.[55] Such pluralism was important to Hooker's thesis that the church belongs equally to this world and the next, which enabled him to secure natural law alongside Scripture as a necessary juridical source. Furthermore, Hooker, unlike the extreme Puritans, acknowledged and affirmed those who, because they are considered as heretics, idolaters, or otherwise wicked, might for that reason be excluded from the "sound" part of the church. Hooker believed that churches were "rather like diverse families than like diverse servants of one family," so that no "one certain form" of polity need be common to them all.[56]

All ages have their shibboleths, powerful generalizations that exert their influence beneath the surface of thought. Our age is no exception. The principle of the separation of powers, formulated in vastly different historical contexts, has been rigidified into the implacable doctrine of instrumental science. In that extreme form the doctrine denies the connection between the moral and the expedient and between means and ends. It goes further, however, by making separation the grounds for hostility between church and state. Yet many scholars in the West are critical of such an interpretation, a criticism echoed in practice throughout Africa, including Muslim Africa.

In this regard, the words of the American philosopher William Ernest Hocking are apt. In his work, *The Coming World Civilization,* he points to the great shibboleth of our age. "We rely," he argues, "on the political community to do its part in the making of men, but first of all to furnish the conditions under which men can make themselves."[57] But he goes on to say that "the state, purely as secular, comes to be regarded as capable of civilizing the human being, and in doing so of re-making him, training his will, moralizing him."[58] Yet the political community is seriously handicapped in enabling human beings to mature fully as moral agents. We need another realm for that:

> Human nature has indeed another mirror, and therewith another source of self-training. It is often the religious community—let us call it in all its forms "the church"—which has promised to give the human individual the most complete view of his destiny and of himself. It projects that destiny beyond the range of human history. . . . It provides standards of self-judgment not alone in terms of behavior, as does the law, but also in terms of motive and principle—of the inner man which the state cannot reach.[59]

Hocking contends we are unwilling to see the state as a partial mirror of truth, being inclined instead to concur when the state

> regards itself as the more reliable interpreter of human nature—dealing as it does solely with verifiable experience—and as a sufficient interpreter. . . . Outside the Marxist orbit, the prevalent disposition of the secular state in recent years has been less to combat the church than to carry on a slow empirical demonstration of the state's full equivalence in picturing the attainable good life, and its superior pertinence to actual issues. As this demonstration gains force the expectation grows that it will be the church, not the state, that will wither away.[60]

William Esuman-Gwira Sekyi (1892–1956) of Ghana, also known as Kobina Sekyi, expressed the continuity between religion and political affairs. Writing in 1925, Sekyi quoted an Akan proverb as follows, *Oman si ho na posuban sim,* "The company fence stands only so long as the state exists." He comments: "Now, our ancestors were above all things a religious people, with whom religion was no mere matter of form or weekly ceremony. Religion with our ancestors was interwoven with the whole fabric of their daily life; and therefore when the company system was established among them it was not without its religious concomitants."[61] Sekyi affirmed that religious loyalty was fundamental for state effectiveness without implying religion has only analogous value. Another wise saying of the Akan was, *Aban wo twuw n'dazi; wo nnsua no,* "Governments, too often heavily weighted with power, are to be pulled along the ground but not to be carried."[62] That saying suggests a need for a radical reappraisal of the church-state theme that goes beyond instrumental codes for public and personal conduct.

Summary and Conclusions

In new environments, transplanted phenomena tend to sit awkwardly: They beflatter themselves by exaggerating their own strengths and minimizing those of the host environment, when in fact the reverse is often the case. In the process, however, these transplant ideas and institutions bring to focus something of their essential character. The secular state in its expansion abroad has assumed this exaggeration and thus revealed, even in its triumphs, basic limitations in its nature. In the context of religion in Africa, in particular Islam, we find gaps in the operation of the national state, raising questions about its effectiveness. The proximity of religion and politics in practical situations discounts any rigid separation of the two. However, by the same token, an important distinction needs to be drawn between politics as instrumental and expedient and religion as a heritage of normative injunctions lest the state become above all sanctified and the church merely calculating. Ideally, there are as sound religious grounds as there are pragmatic ones for not confusing religion and politics, though in practice it is risky to attempt splitting the two. Crosscultural and interreligious issues and reflections in Africa and among Muslims may help shed light on the relation of religion and politics and thus help deepen our grasp of vital ground in the encounter between the two.

10

"The Crown and the Turban": Public Policy Issues in Christian-Muslim Relations, with Special Reference to Africa

Whatever one's attitude towards so-called fundamentalist Islam, there is no question that it is from that quarter that the major intellectual initiative has been launched to call for an uncompromising assessment of the comprehensive claims of secular political primacy over religion. The liberal mainstream abandoned that role when it staked its reputation on faith in human progress, with the secular state as necessary machinery. Human well-being in the liberal scheme requires the state instrument and, to a degree, that we be shackled to the state. Right-wing conservatism for its part seeks the capture of the state to mobilize market-driven individualism and the sanctity of personal property. Thus liberals and conservatives together reinforce state power from ostensibly opposite standpoints.

This double reinforcing secular ideology has provoked Muslim fundamentalism into attacking head-on modern confidence in political ultimacy, in the state as our finality. In this chapter I will search, through comparative analysis, for the religious underpinning of democratic liberalism and the connection between the political enterprise and the life of faith. I assess in this light Islamic objections to the notion of religion as only personal faith based on private persuasion and choice, however much such a notion might be fruitful of tolerance, pluralism, and the autonomy of the secular state. If religion is right in what it claims about the meaning and purpose of human life, then it cannot be banished from the public sphere, which is the Islamic contention—and it cannot, at the same time, be co-opted as a public commodity, which is the liberal democratic tendency.

To place Muslim objections to secular primacy in comparative historical context, we need to examine the roots of Western political secularism whose origins lie in the sixteenth-century crisis that overtook Christendom. The teaching of

Jesus about maintaining an appropriate separation between God and Caesar (Mk. 12:17; Mt. 22:21) provided the doctrinal remedy for those wishing to stop the damaging religious wars that wracked late medieval and early modern Europe. This teaching later came to be formulated as separation of church and state and given institutional expression. It has continued to inspire secular Europe by making freedom of religion an indispensable principle of political freedom. In the main, political authority was distinguished from confessional rules, with church membership no longer normative for national identity or political affiliation. Christianity then broke up into numerous groups and sects in a context that removed public sanction from religious differences and disagreements, resulting in Christianity abandoning any public role, except where being subsumed under the national state gave it that role. We should thus stress the crucial importance of the religious factor in giving rise to secularism, defined here as recognizing the separate and equally valid spheres of God and Caesar, or church and state. That separation is necessary for secularism, as well as pluralism, to thrive. Conversely, the fusion of the two retards secularism and pluralism.

Within this context we have seen the rise of modern Christianity and the missionary movement that effectively spread it. Cut loose from the Old World colonization movements of Spain and Portugal, the modern missionary movement made faith as a personal decision the basis of a new form of community and identity, which did not require converts to become members of a divine political system. However they may have regarded non-Christians, modern missions conceded all citizens to be equal in law. In that sense the modern missionary movement fostered pluralist religious practice within autonomous national communities. The denominations and confessions thrived within and across national and political boundaries, rather than being reduced to a single territorial designation, such as one church, one land, one faith, one race, one truth, or one tribe. In that sense, modern missions were an important secularizing force.

This situation, or something closely resembling it, is what characterizes Christianity in much of the West and in modern Africa, where in time the Western experience exerted itself, and we may say the contemporary Muslim encounter with Christianity is essentially an encounter with the religion as antitheocratic and pluralist in tendency. Consequently in the wake of the Christian retreat from theocratic politics we have a rising tide of Muslim demand for religion as a state idea. Canonical Islam has always conceived a political role for religion, whatever the ambivalence of modernist Muslim liberals.[1] However, what is new and different now is that Muslim temporal pressure is being brought to bear in numerous African states still struggling to hold their own against a significantly unamenable citizenry. In places in the West itself this temporal religious pressure is being increasingly felt as well, so that the issue is not simply a matter confined to distant and exotic societies. On this matter, as on so much else, Africans and Westerners face a common challenge and may, for that reason, benefit from common responsibility.

For example, current Muslim political activism in the West means immigrant Muslims are demanding "rights" that are not simply religious, narrowly defined, but also educational, legal, political, economic, social, and medical, including public health matters concerning abattoirs, matters that the Western rank and file have left in the hands of state and secular institutions.[2] Consequently, Westerners are caught in a bind in the face of Muslim demands: The logic of religious toleration, not to say of hospitality, requires making concessions to Muslims, whereas the logic of privatizing Christianity, of taking religion out of the public arena, disqualifies Westerners from dealing in any effective sense with Muslim theocratic demands.

We need caution here. For many people pluralism or multiculturalism has become a shibboleth of peculiar force, tending to displace any hard and serious thinking about particular and rival claims to truth and to encourage complacency among reasonable people. Complacent pluralism in this sense can blind us to the real opportunities of interfaith encounter, with platitudes replacing commitment and accountability. Espousal of pluralism can in fact be a disguise for religious retreat, a feeling that since there are so many religions, no one religion really matters in the end. Yet if the current global religious revival, including world Christianity, has any future, then the West in its current mood is likely to miss it. Yet few can escape the consequences of a religiously active world, including the West. In the global Islamic resurgence, for example, the West is necessarily implicated, even though the West's response has been to minimize the religious importance. The West is still surprised that Muslims show such little inclination to follow the secular path that it has confidently laid out. But the West may be forgiven for assuming that other cultures would follow where it leads, since for over two centuries now it has been the decisive culture of reference. Yet in matters of faith, human affairs are more subtle and complex. Thus have militant Muslims risen against an ideological secularism, for the idea seems riddled with religious compromise, as the West has proved.

Thus our Western brand of piety, with religion as a private individual matter, has blunted our grasp of genuine religious pluralism and left us with a strictly sociological and political view of it. The impact of technology and the information revolution, with their web of global interconnections at our fingertips, has also pushed, or allowed us to push, religion to the margins. Religion scarcely figures in the West's design of the new world order. Yet religion and technology in one sense correspond with a spiritual ideal: diverse expressions of faith and practice sustained in a cumulative global solidarity, with God at the center. Muslims are equally included in this new global horizon where technology has shaped the landscape. The field of religious encounter as defined by a nonprivatized transcendence is akin to the unpatrolled frontiers of cyberspace. However, religious claims have their source in timeless truths.

The question is, how do religions, especially proselytizing ones, impinge on the imperatives of a common humanity, and how can we harmonize the claims a tradition makes about itself with the demands of interfaith tolerance, so that a community's ownership of its tradition does not become in-bred and antiforeign? A major obstacle is the disincentive that religious privatization breeds. As it is, there are resources enough in most religious traditions to combine commitment with criticism, to make personal persuasion compatible with public scrutiny. If we are to hope for any progress in interfaith relations we must resist the view that our particular tradition is superior or else, because of a perceived convergence among religions, is progressively superfluous. Meanwhile, the pervasive language of religious privatization leaves us with the bland consensus of diplomatic politeness, a consensus that may save our manners but scarcely anything else. Thus religious privatization may foster a code of silence that is ultimately ineffective against indifference from the left or fanaticism from the right. We should explore here the limits of privatization against the challenge of political Islam and how we might meet the challenge.

Part of the difficulty is that religious privatization appealed to people grown weary from the bitter legacy of religious territoriality, even though with regard to Muslim demands they may be religiously tone deaf on account of it. However, even if privatization is unsatisfactory, the drive for freedom that led to it is central to religious pluralism and democratic liberalism. Thus, in the conclusion I argue that democratic liberalism and religious pluralism have their basis in the notion of religious freedom that sets so much store by persuasion and personal conviction, and that the converging of democratic liberalism with religious freedom invests religion with a public rationale, and on that basis we may promote interfaith relations in our time. Let us deal with the issue in three stages.

Stage I: Christianity and the Demise of Territorial Christendom

The church was never more involved in politics than during the era of the Holy Roman Empire, when faith and territory were joined as a principle of membership in church and state. Constantine secured the freedom of Christianity, not its establishment as an exclusive state religion. He saw himself as Pontifex Maximus, the visible earthly vessel of an all-too-misty divinity whose intuitive, malleable purpose he could attach to the robust will of the state. He claimed to be the colleague of the bishops of Nicea, but only as a "bishop of external affairs" and of those things in Christianity deemed useful and convenient. The real shift came with Charlemagne, who took Christianity out of the sacristy and established it as "Christendom," weaving it into the fabric of the state. In that scheme the political ruler was seen as God's appointed agent, the herald and instrument of God's mission. Thus political affairs and religious matters were two strands of one and the same reality. It follows from this view that church and state were united in purpose even though as institutions they represented different functions. Whereas the church reserved to itself custody of the absolute moral law, the state was concerned with enforcing the rules of allegiance and conformity that gave practical expression to the higher spiritual law. Conformity rather than personal persuasion was the chief end of religious activity under this corporate arrangement.

Christendom identified itself with territoriality in the sense of making religion a matter of territorial allegiance. Church membership was coterminous and interchangeable with territorial location, and territorial rule was established on, and made legitimate by, the ruler's professed religion.[3] Christian mission under these circumstances was inconceivable except as colonialism, the forcible swallowing up of the tribes as vassal subjects of, say, Ferdinand and Isabella, the earthly representatives of Christ. Thus were the Indians dispossessed in the *encomienda*, the distribution system in which by royal decree the tribes and their property were "given away" as the only way to evangelize them.[4] In Christendom, to evangelize was to colonize, and to colonize was to evangelize, though nothing broke down the walls of Christendom as effectively as the wider and later repercussions of European colonialism and Western missions. By the same token, Christians living in a territory ruled by a nonbeliever were considered resident aliens, even though prevailing conditions of peace and tolerance might reduce the necessity for embarking on acts of conscientious withdrawal, what Muslim sources refer to as *hijrah*.[5] Christendom prevented such situations from arising or proliferating, since religious integrity and territorial cohesion meshed, or were supposed to.

As an arrangement Christendom would work only if there continued to be a more or less homogenous, cohesive society apportioned into more or less stable social classes. Such homogeneity and cohesion became increasingly difficult to maintain in the face of growing pluralism and social mobility. Finally, with the rise of national ethnic consciousness, fueled by the drive for religious freedom, the formal structures of the Empire collapsed, to be lost irretrievably in the rubble of Napoleonic Europe, and Christendom as a territorial reality broke up into its constituent parts.[6]

For leading Christian thinkers of the time the demise of "Christendom" was a consummation the godly had devoutly wished for, because it allowed religion to become a matter of personal experience rather than of membership in a divinely designated race or church, as if heeding Emerson's wry sarcasm, "In Christendom where is the Christian?" In any case, religious faith prospered as the church was transformed from territoriality to voluntarism. Alexis de Tocqueville observed the shift to voluntarism in religious practice in America, saying it was a fact "that by diminishing the apparent [territorial] power of religion one increased its real [spiritual] strength."[7] John Locke turned to the principle of voluntarism in his *A Letter Concerning Toleration* (1689), in which he states that Christians as members of a "voluntary society" were those who came together for "the public worshipping of God in such a manner as they judge acceptable to Him, and effectual to the salvation of their souls."[8] The overriding concerns of such a society, he felt, ought to be spiritual and moral, "and nothing ought nor can be transacted in this society relating to the possession of civil and worldly goods." Such a religious arrangement allowed for the triumph of personal faith.

However, between that conception of religion and of the state Locke drew a neat, if overly formal, distinction. He gave to civil government the responsibility for ordering our material well-being, which includes "life, liberty, health, and indolence of body," as well as "possession of outward things, such as money, lands, houses, furniture, and the like."[9] Just as the church should not concern itself with the amassing of wealth and material possessions, so should government not concern itself with the salvation of souls.

This distinction between the nature of religion and of the state is not satisfactory either in detail or in principle, as Locke recognized, for he went on to observe that government should not be given authority over religion because "it appears not that God has ever given any such authority to one man over another as to compel anyone to his religion."[10] For Locke, as for many Puritan divines, religion was incompatible with state coercion, not simply because the state is a pretty blunt and oppressive instrument to use in delicate matters of faith, but because "though the rigor of laws and the force of penalties were capable to convince and change men's minds, yet would not that help at all to the salvation of their souls."[11] Politics is tied to conscience, but salvation is ballot proof.

Locke reasoned as he did because theological issues were paramount for him in the following sense: A soul that was compelled was a soul that had lost its religious worth, so that it would not be a legitimate subject for spiritual regeneration. He asserted: "True and saving religion consists in the inward persuasion of the mind, without which nothing can be acceptable to God. And such is the nature of the understanding, that it cannot be compelled to the belief of any thing by outward force."[12] Similarly, the political commonwealth would be a tyranny if nothing beyond compulsion held it together. Such a religious conception of the moral integrity of the human person was necessary to Locke's conception of the tool-making character of civil government. Religion and civil government, Locke continued, have an overlapping legitimate interest in "moral actions" that belong "to the jurisdiction both of the outward and the inward court; both of the civil and domestic governor; I mean both of the magistrate and the conscience."[13] In other words, religion as a voluntary society made possible the birth of the theory of limited state authority. In this complementarity of church and state we find the "good life" wherein "lies the safety both of men's souls and of the commonwealth."[14]

The Muslim challenge was not far from Locke's mind, and he considered how Muslims and others might be integrated into a society in which religion was not enforced, or enforceable. That form of Islam, he said, that represented a rupture with the tradition of voluntarism would be difficult if not impossible to assimilate, but only by force of circumstance, not on principle. The crucial test for Muslims, according to Locke, was whether they, too, would abjure the judicial and political weapon in religious life and accept that "nobody ought to be compelled in matters of religion either by law or force."

Atheism would present a no less troubling challenge. "Those that by their atheism undermine and destroy all religion, can have no pretense of religion whereupon to challenge the privilege of toleration."[15] This statement shows Locke is aware that the argument for religious toleration itself rests on a religious idea and that it is a contradiction in terms for people to repudiate religion while supporting tolerance and inclusiveness. That is why Locke insisted that neither atheist nor Muslim or any other "ought to be excluded from the civil rights of the commonwealth, because of his religion."[16] We may summarize Locke's reasoning to the effect that, on the one hand, moral integrity requires us to reject the use of the political instruments of Christendom in securing religious ends, whereas, on the other, we cannot surrender the religious ground concerning the liberty of conscience without making civil government in the narrow sense and religious toleration broadly conceived ultimate casualties. This is the sense in which we should understand the New England Pilgrims of 1620, whose brand of piety freed religion from political and territorial establishment and placed religiously inspired curbs on state supremacy. Thus, for example, did Roger Williams of Rhode Island argue that God had placed the Ten Commandments on two tablets. On one of these God wrote the laws regulating the divine-human relationship, and on the other were the laws dealing with the relationship of men and women among themselves. In that way, Williams concluded, we have a basis for the fundamental distinction between the divine jurisdiction and human tribunals. It would be improper to mix these two tablets, or confuse them, because to do so would imperil our souls and our political welfare. So the separate branches of church and state have a single theological root and, by extension, a common moral source.

Numberless other Western religious thinkers have given similar attention to the character of a free society and the proper relation within it of religion and politics. They separated the two by repudiating a theocratic state without jettisoning the religious ground as such. One seventeenth-century theologian insisted that religious persons of conscience cannot allow "a secular sword [to] cut in sunder those knots in religion which [it] cannot untie by a theological resolution."[17] The reason for this is that "to employ the [civil] magistrate in this kind of compulsion is a prejudice to the Lord Jesus, and the provision he has made for the propagation of the Church and truth."[18] Another writer who paid close attention to such matters, even though his fame rests in the impact of his scientific ideas, is Robert Boyle, with whom Locke was for a time closely associated. For him political authority could never be absolute and indeterminate lest it conflict with the higher authority of God. The political ruler should, therefore, be reminded that civil disobedience is an intrinsic right with which our Creator has endowed us. "For God being, as our only Creator, so the supreme governor of man, his laws are those of the truest supreme authority: and princes themselves being his subjects, and but his lieutenants upon earth; to decline their commands, whenever they prove repugnant unto his, is not so much an act of disobedience to the subordinate power, as of loyalty to the supreme and universal sovereign."[19] Milton declared himself to the same effect, namely, that if they turn to tyranny, kings and magistrates "may be as lawfully deposed and punished, as they were at first elected." Such political rights have their source in theological doctrine,[20] to wit, that men and women "were born free, being the image and resemblance of God himself," with government instituted among themselves "by common league to bind each other from mutual injury." Government is the servant of people, not their master, Milton asserted.[21]

In his trenchant observations on religion in American life, de Tocqueville argued for separation, saying that when a religion allies itself with government, "it must adopt maxims which apply only to certain nations. Therefore, by allying itself with any political power, religion increases its strength over some but forfeits the hope of reigning over all."[22] The compromise involved in bringing religion into alliance with partisan politics is fatal to the fundamental claims of religion, because "when it is mingled with the bitter passions of this world, it is sometimes constrained to defend allies who are such from interest rather than from love; and it has to repulse as adversaries men who still love religion, although they are fighting against religion's allies. . . . Alone, [religion] may hope for immortality; linked to ephemeral powers, it follows their fortunes and often falls together with the passions of the day sustaining them."[23]

Such teachings are the flaming sword by which this age has defended liberal democratic pluralism and religious freedom and under which we have conceived all human history as tending towards what R. G. Collingwood has called "the general development of God's purpose for human life."[24] The democratic liberal state is sovereign not because its laws are unquestioned or unquestionable but because of the rights of personhood established in natural and divine law. Democratic liberalism is a derived value, not itself the moral source. De Tocqueville affirmed a similar sentiment when he said that in a free, democratic society obedience and obligation are incumbent even on persons who do not believe and that persons who are free are to the same degree constrained to believe.[25]

Unfortunately, the development of Locke's ideas in one respect would not be fruitful for preserving the delicate balance between religion and government, for elsewhere he gave grounds for abandoning the primacy he gave to religion vis-à-vis government. Thus in his *Second Treatise on Civil Government*, he inserted private property rights under the rubric of the sacred, saying divine truth harmonizes here with "the voice of reason." Thus is justified the ultimate sanction of killing lawfully in defense of one's property. In the hands of his disciples, Locke's doctrine of property was given the explicit metaphysical status he implied for it. Thus did the American philosopher Richard Weaver write an impassioned defense of property rights, including the rights of capital, against the presumptions of social justice and of the rights of the laboring classes. He wrote: "When we survey the scene to find something which the rancorous leveling wind of utilitarianism has not brought down, we discover one institution, shaken somewhat but still strong and perfectly clear in its implication. This is the right of private property, which is, in fact, the last metaphysical right remaining to us. The ordinances of religion, the prerogatives of sex and of vocation, all have been swept away by materialism, but the relationship of a man to his own has until the present largely escaped attack."[26]

These words make clear how in a unitary secular order the moral law would be usurped for the ends of property and profit, and how banishing religion from the public realm would result in political territoriality as a sacred covenant for private wealth. Thus on secular grounds alone, separation, without the religious precaution, would enshrine interests and the instruments for defending them. Therefore, Locke's ideas on property, what he defines as "lives, liberties and estates," would make human beings, by reason of their labor, to belong first and last to themselves and not to God. That would blow a hole in the safety net of separation,[27] removing the distinction between property and religion.

These were decisive reasons why religion as territorial principle or state authority was opposed by many Christian thinkers, as well as by many non-Muslims today, including Christian Africans, though many such people feel encouraged by Islam's witness to divine justice in temporal affairs. It is, however, a question whether religion as personal faith only is adequate to the contemporary global situation with its rising Islamic challenge.

Stage II: Islamic Territoriality and the Countertradition

The late Ayátulláh Khumayní of Iran once complained that Muslims have been robbed of their heritage through the connivance of the West. Western agents, he charged, "have completely separated [Islam] from politics. They have cut off its head and [given] the rest to us."[28] The reference is to the creation in Muslim countries of the secular national state as the successor to the transnational Islamic caliphate. As we saw in the previous chapter, a similar complaint was made by Sádiq al-Mahdí, the Sudanese political leader who pilloried the secular national state for being the means by which antireligious forces entered non-Western societies and were fomented. He assured his bewildered coreligionists that Islam was the God-ordained answer for their undeserved ills.[29] Such sentiments have resonated with rank-and-file Muslims, in part because they invoke powerful religious symbols and in part because they exploit widespread popular disenchantment with Western-inspired economic programs. The religious objections to Western-style reforms have undercut the credibility of the state as an imported Western institution. Thus the appeal of religion reflects the disaffection with the West almost as much as it draws upon Islam's canonical tradition, or what is claimed for it.[30]

In terms of that tradition, modern Muslim views on political authority have their roots in the Prophet's own personal legacy in Medina and Mecca, where he established territoriality, *dár al-Islám,* as the handmaid of religious faith.[31] It was not long before the early Muslims were rallying round the political standard, "*lá hukm illá bi-illáhi*" ("no government except under God").[32] The words have echoed down to our day, refined and mediated by the mediaeval theologian Ibn Taymiyya (d. 1328) as a stringent theocratic credo. A contemporary Muslim writer cites an identical opinion from the second of the Four Righteous Caliphs, 'Umar ibn Khattáb (d. 644), to the effect that "There is not Islam without a group, no group without power (authority), no authority without obedience. If someone is made master on the basis of jurisprudence, this will be for their and his good, and if he is made master otherwise [say, by a secular constitution], this will be destruction for all of them."[33] However, it is from Ibn Taymiyya, among others, that modernist Muslim reformers in the last two hundred years have received their marching orders, from Jalál al-Dín Afghání to Sayyid Qutb and Ayátulláh Khumayní.

In view of Ibn Taymiyya's influence on modern critical Muslim assessments of the West, a few words are in order on his ideas. He spoke about the indispensability of God and the Prophet in political affairs, what he calls *siyásah iláhíya wa inába nubúwíya* ("divine government and prophetic vicegerency"). He contended:

> To govern the affairs of men is one of the most important requirements of religion, nay, without it religion cannot endure. . . . The duty of commanding the good and forbidding the evil cannot be completely discharged without power and authority. The same applies to all religious duties (holy war, pilgrimage, prayer, fast, almsgiving), to helping those who are wronged, and to meting out punishment in accordance with the legal penalties. . . . The purpose of public office is to further the religion and the worldly affairs of men (*isláh . . . dínahu wa-dunyahu*). . . . when the pastor exerts himself in proportion to his ability to further both, he is one of the most excellent fighters on the path of God.

"The exercise of authority," he concluded, "is a religious function and a good work which brings near to God, and drawing near to God means obeying God and his Prophet."[34] Thus authority is the possession of moral truth.

These are uncompromising words that impute territoriality to religious orthodoxy, words that would make Muslims discontented with a merely liberal pragmatic political ethic. Yet they are words that also make it difficult to coexist in a pluralist society. One way out of Ibn Taymiyya's rigid scheme is to make "the duty of commanding the good and forbidding the evil" (*amal bi-ma'rúf wa nahy 'an al-munkar*)[35] the basis for a theocentric view of the world rather than the justification for a theocracy. A theocracy would ironically still be the rule of mere earthen vessels, a limitation echoed in the Qur'ánic verse about intrinsic human weakness (30:54). Thus government *faqihs*, seduced by power, would dismay even dyed-in-the-wool stalwarts by the ease with which they add new, and not so subtle, inflections to the injustice of conjugation of the ill-omened verb "to corrupt." The twists of the turban may be politically more fraught than the religious sum of its folds.

A similar consideration has led many other Muslims to question whether even under Islamic territoriality it is wise to employ force and coercion to propagate religion. One early caliph, for example, agonized over the safety of religious truth when upheld by the instruments of the state. This was the Caliph al-Maʾmún, who declared in a public meeting in 830 that although under his rule many had converted to Islam for purely religious reasons, many others had done so from less honorable motives. "They belong to a class who embrace Islam, not from any love for this our religion, but thinking thereby to gain access to my Court, and share in the honor, wealth, and power of the Realm; they have no inward persuasion of that which they outwardly profess."[36] This view anticipates Locke's notion of the jurisdiction of the "outward and inward," and why territoriality offends conscience as much as it undercuts democratic pluralism, for if religion looks to political power for its ultimate defense, then it will find in that its sole vindication and reward, and, in time, its demise. We would, like the agonized caliph, be unable to determine the true from the spurious, sincerity from self-interest, or commitment from opportunism. Consequently, revealed law may not be domesticated into human schemes without direct risk to truth and the political scheme itself.

In an instructive piece of debate between two Muslim scholars on the need for a theocratic state, we find identical issues being raised. One of the scholars in question, Muhammad al-Kánemí (d. 1838), the ruler of Kanem-Bornu in West Africa, challenged the jihád leader, ʾUthmán dan Fodio (d. 1817), with regard to the use of the sword for religious ends. Al-Kánemí said the sword is too rough-and-ready a weapon to use in settling religious questions, especially questions between Muslims themselves, since they would attempt to resolve by *force majeure* what might be substantial matters of theology or even only differences of opinion. He insisted that Muslims must either settle for tolerance and mutual acceptance or else unleash a smoldering permanent war that would exempt, in his words, not even "Egypt, Syria and all the cities of Islam . . . in which acts of immorality and disobedience without number have long been committed." "No age and country," al-Kánemí cautioned, "is free from its share of heresy and sin,"[37] and any immutable division of the world between *dár al-Islám* and *dár al-harb* would fly in the face of this reality and reduce to ashes all sincere but inadequate attempts at truth and obedience. We could not find revealed truth in the blinding flames of fanaticism fed by short-fused *fatwas*.

It might be appropriate here to recall the words of Locke about religious triumphalism, for the point he makes is pertinent to the issues raised by al-Kánemí. Let us imagine, Locke argues, Christian missionaries, destitute of everything, arriving in a so-called pagan country and inserting themselves into the society by taking advantage of the kindness and hospitality of their so-called pagan hosts. The new religion then takes root in the country and spreads gradually. While Christians remain a minority they publicly espouse peace, friendship, faith, and justice for all. But at length they grow powerful and achieve substantial victory with the magistrate of the country converting and becoming a Christian. This fact emboldens the Christians to break all previous accords with the pagans on whom they turn, requiring them to repudiate their ancient religion and customs on pain of being dispossessed and reduced to servitude. Such a Christian religion, Locke concludes, would be merely "the pretense of religion, and of the care of souls," and would be "a cloak to covetousness, rapine, and ambition."[38]

That constructed tableau has an uncanny similarity to the condition of countless communities in Muslim Africa. To take one well-known instance of two hundred years ago, the Sarki, or king, of one West African pagan state, Gobir, woke up one day to find his Muslim guests had grown in number and confidence, had turned implacably militant, and were threatening his kingdom. They were in no mood for conciliation and concession. He had been too sanguine and now rued the day, he said, when he gave friendly sanctuary to Muslims. He later complained to his fellow kings that he had neglected a small fire in his country until it had spread beyond his power to control. Having failed to extinguish it, he was now burnt by it. "Let each beware," he lamented, "lest a like calamity befall his town also."[39] By then the flames were raging, and Locke is small comfort: the Sarki's warning had come too late.

In contrast to that way of religious proselytization, a whole religious vocation has developed among certain groups of Muslim West Africans that rejects political and military means for spreading and maintaining religious faith and institutions. One such group are the Jakhanké clerics, whose professional roots go back to medieval Africa through a cleric called al-Hájj Sálim Suwaré (hence the appellation "Suwarians" in some sources). I have described elsewhere their professional religious life. In received traditions al-Hájj Sálim is described as handing down teachings that represent a scrupulous disavowal of political and military coercion in religious matters and the repudiation of secular political office for the professional cleric, an astonishing position given the unambiguous rulings of the Qur'án and the jurists. Yet equally astonishing is the durability in Muslim West Africa of this pacific strain, whose antiquity and dispersed, mobile character have led scholars to offer a Semitic hypothesis as its origin. Indeed Jakhanké chronicles identify them as *Baní Isrá'ila* ("children of Israel"), which appears to lend at least conjectural credence to the Semitic theory.[40] At any rate, as professional clerics the Jakhanké people established educational centers as cells of influence among diverse ethnic groups, a clerical *cordon sanitaire* of mobility and dispersal from where they wafted the felicitous breath of pacific counsel. So distinctive was this tradition that local religious militants who defied it found themselves exposed to the virus of religious mutiny from within. Local populations that had come under the influence of clerical pacifism were so deeply affected that a theocratic dispensation was more disconcerting to them than the prospects of continuing pluralism.

This is not to say that pacific Muslim clerics did not clash with unamenable secular strongmen, for they did, but that clerical pacifism undermined the extreme program of a corporate theocratic state. The attempt was made many times in the nineteenth and twentieth centuries to create theocratic governments in Muslim West Africa, and each time it failed from the prevailing unfavorable qui-etist climate of opinion. Even the effort by European administrations to co-opt such pacific clerics into the colonial brand of political committedness by giving them chieftaincies foundered on the same pacific rock, with the clerics offering their sympathy, or even cooperation, but stopping short of becoming collabora-tors and active allies. In an era of total political mobilization that some colonial regimes preferred, such clerical independence was deemed an affront. It brought on the collision it was designed to avert and forced the clerics to reassess the her-itage in the light of new realities. In the example of one such stock-taking in 1911, the clerical leader who, along with his followers, was arrested at the point of a gun and sent into humiliating exile and imprisonment, spoke eloquently of clerical pacifism not simply in terms of personal survival but in terms of a long, self-con-sistent vocation. The French administrator and scholar, Paul Marty, who saw the relevant document, found it difficult not to be impressed by the argument. Marty said the leading cleric in question "formulated conclusions, stamped with the in-delible mark of loyalty, and remarked that his fidelity, had it not been born of nat-ural sympathy, would have been for him a necessity of the logic of history."[41] Marty described the attack on the pacific clerics as a St. Bartholomew's Massacre. Such conflicts were clearly painful personal setbacks, but scarcely a fatal loss for pacific credibility, or mobility, since the clerics conducted themselves with digni-fied restraint under violent provocation and then subsequently emigrated as haven-seekers.

The Málikí muftí of the Republic of Senegal, a seasoned child of the clerical peripatetic tradition, told me of his being invited from his country retreat in Casamance by the Senegalese president to travel to the capital to meet the king of Saudi Arabia. He declined on the principle that it would be tantamount to politi-cal sponsorship, which he would wish to reject. When he finally yielded it was as a courtesy to the royal visitor rather than as a concession to collaborating with po-litical office. He and clerics like him are happy to make their peace with political territoriality but are less willing to collapse religion into such territoriality. Admit-tedly, religious withdrawal, even with the clerical pacific principle at its heart, may not deal well enough with the problem of the doctrinaire ideological secular state, but it does sustain the moderate pacific counsels by which Muslim Africans have extended and deepened the tradition of genuine pluralism.

There is thus a large body of material in both Christian and Muslim traditions to support a public role for religion without requiring theocratic rule. Sufyán Thaurí, a classical Muslim writer, has a witty aphorism apt on this point. He wrote, "The best of the rulers is he who keeps company with men of [religious] learning, and the worst of the learned men is he who keeps the society of the king."[42] That is to say, religion and worldly affairs prosper together when political rules are qualified by moral principles, and they suffer when moral principles are qualified by political expedience. Ibn Khaldún defends this position, though in his case he was stepping forward with the same distrusted secular foot twice. He wrote: "The state whose law is based upon violence and superior force and giving full play to the irascible nature is tyranny and injustice and in the eyes of the law blameworthy, a judgment in which also political wisdom concurs. Further, the state whose law is based upon rational government and its principles, without the authority of the *Sharia*, is likewise blameworthy, since it is the product of speculation without the light of God . . . and the principles of rational government aim solely at worldly interests."[43]

In that statement Ibn Khaldún describes and criticizes the Hobbesian state, in which political sovereignty is the basis of moral jurisdiction, with people's rights being what is secured to them by the national political sovereign.[44] Yet his alternative of a religious state creates the situation in which religion as a fundamental personal matter is placed under state prerogative. Ibn Khaldún thus excoriates the power state only to reward it with jurisdiction over religion. In the Lockean view, by contrast, liberty is a principle of the people's God-given rights, rather than an indulgence granted by the sovereign national state. In that scheme, political rules may be effective without being sacred, and moral injunctions may produce practical fruit without being expedient. In neither case would people have to dance to the Vicar of Bray's tune in which the morality of taking the king's shilling is fixed at the king's bidding.

Stage III: The Roots of Controversy— Caesar Crowned and Turbaned?

The Muslim challenge and tradition examined in this brief account bring up the issue of how national secular state jurisdiction may find acceptance in the religious community. Muslims consider the *ummah* as a supranational community, one that transcends national identity. The reality, however, is that Muslims are not all assembled under one Islamic roof but are instead spread over many countries and subject to diverse and conflicting political jurisdictions. In virtually all cases, state authority has jurisdiction, however contested, over membership of the *ummah,* so that loyalty to the religious community would override or else conflict with the claims of territorial sovereignty. Yet modernist Muslims, modifying the fundamentalists, would compromise with the national secular state by holding it to standards of justice and respect for human rights or would otherwise settle for a benign liberal democracy with room for religious freedom. In its turn, the secular state, committed to toleration, would abjure the right to interfere with religion.

That liberal compromise commands wide support, bringing as it does religion into qualified association with the affairs of state, and making it possible for church and state to be united on a policy of coequality, instead of opposed in a mutually damaging adversarial relationship. Since religion stakes its reputation on moral commitment, the state cannot ignore it without risk of popular disaffection. For its turn, if religion is politically domesticated, political differences would escalate into major theological schisms. If the state intervenes to suppress or enjoin appropriate forms of religion, that would infringe its own liberalism. It follows, then, that liberalism and religious freedom share one foundation, though church and state function as a split-level structure. Thus a way must be found for them to cooperate in society while restricting the state in its invasive power to encroach on conscience and religion from turning expedient and partisan, as expressed in some of the Muslim fundamentalist debate.

In many significant cases, however, the secular state considers itself a competitor with religion for the moral ground, a competition that proves that the state is not neutral. The Leviathan national state, whose inauguration the Abbé Sieyès trumpeted with such confidence, is in its nature girded for combat against all irrational forces, especially organized religion. The Muslim instinct to distrust it is, therefore, understandable, though, with regard to Africa, such distrust should be mitigated by Africa's recent encounter with the Western secular Leviathan. Given that fact, Muslim (and, one should add, Christian) leaders in many parts of Africa sense all is not lost, so that, confronted with an ideological secularism and its iconoclastic view, they feel they can respond with a religious alternative. In Nigeria and the Sudan, for example, we have two cases where the ferment has created extreme public debate on the conflicting claims of religion and the state. More than academic, the debate in the two countries has produced political movements.

Thus was founded at Kaduna, Nigeria, the Supreme Council for Islamic Affairs in 1973, and thus, too, did Hassan al-Turábí's National Islamic Front, a radical Islamic movement, mastermind the 1989 coup d'état that installed Gen. Omar Hassan al-Bashir as head of state in the Sudan.[45] The Islamic revolution in the Sudan thus attempts to replace national state allegiance with religious obligation. As Turábí puts it, "Islam is becoming temporal,"[46] in other words, Islam is acquiring temporal power as an inevitable and necessary holy duty. In both countries Muslims have demanded the introduction of the *Sharí'ah* in public life, and in the Sudan the process has gone further with the implementation of parts of the *Sharí'ah* code. In Nigeria, by contrast, the plan has hit a major political snag. A proposal along the lines of the Sudan was voted down in Nigeria in April 1978 by the Constituent Assembly that met to draft a new constitution for the nation. The choice, as Muslims see it, is straightforward and unambiguous enough: either a state buttressed by the religious code, such as the *Sharí'ah* provides, or a secular state that is "godless." Muslims do not feel sanguine about a national state that has unrestricted access to unrivaled resources and power that it would use to uphold secular, "godless" aims and programs. On the pretext of religious neutrality, the secular state could cut off public funds for religious schools and institutions but allocate them to secular and atheist programs. Such a posture exposes the antireligious bias of the national secular state and shows, too, that political authority is setting itself above religion. Even when it professes neutrality towards religion, the secular state is in fact engaged in a contest with religion and is thus deeply entangled with it. Such views were canvassed in the national paper, *New Nigerian*, March to September 1977.

However, the *ummah* is unlikely to be the panacea doctrine claims for it: Ethnic, linguistic, and historical differences are too endemic to conform to its uniform rule. Besides, the present world security and economic system is too firmly invested in the secular state structure to survive the disarray involved in a shift based on a religious code. The secular state is attractive because of its capacity (and despite its limits) to absorb the great diversity and plurality of social and religious groups existing within its borders. The *ummah* as a religious community could not concede the secular principle of egalitarian individualism without self-contradiction. In this situation religion as temporal power would incur, and in turn incite, instability, injustice, and disaffection. Thus have Sudan's unassimilated southern tribes long constituted an obstacle both to Khartoum's policies of arabization (and islamization) and to the effectiveness of the unitary secular state. Such minorities, already persecuted, would also be stigmatized under the dispensation of the *ummah*. Nigeria has been faced with no less fundamental a choice.

In this sense, matters in Nigeria received a boost in 1986 from the Christian Association of Nigeria (CAN). An ecumenical grouping of Protestants, Catholics, and African Independent Churches, CAN was founded explicitly to respond to Muslims in general and to the military government's unpublicized decision to enroll Nigeria as a member of the Organization of Islamic Countries (OIC) in particular (on which more presently). CAN issued a statement protesting federal government backing for *Shari'ah* courts in north Nigeria and asking for an identical public status for Christianity. But CAN's strategy of demanding privileges for Christians comparable to those being offered to Muslims sets it on the Muslim side of the fault line, with Christians wheeling and dealing on a stage Muslims have constructed for their own purpose. For example, the Kaduna Branch of CAN published a statement asking the government to offset any concessions to the *Shari'ah* with similar concessions to Christians by establishing a Christian constitution based on ecclesiastical courts.[47] No wonder Muslims welcomed CAN's platform, forcing a catch-22 upon Christians by challenging them to say which they preferred, English Common Law, Ecclesiastical canon law, or secular law. The divisions among Christians, Muslims point out, are responsible for Christian confusion, contradiction, and indecisiveness towards the agenda of the secular state. And until Christians can make up their minds and decide either for transcendent truth or for secular humanism, Muslims, they feel, must carry the burden of the challenge.

However, Muslim confidence should be tempered by the realities of the world, because even in places where *qádí* courts have operated, the Islamic code has not been free of its share of corruption and exploitation, and Muslims who have had cause to resort to them have not always found relief or justice. With the *Shari'ah* becoming part of the political debate, Islam risks being reduced to a political enterprise in which the ultimate is turned into the expedient, and vice versa. Many

Muslim modernists say such a course risks irreparable damage to the claims for revealed truth. Such modernists see a tolerant secular state as less threatening than a theocratic state. For, after all, there is plenty of scope in a tolerant secular state for exercising the duties called for by Islam's ethical system with regard to *zakát*, economic probity, education, domestic tranquillity, marriage, care for widows, orphans, the poor and the sick, rearing of children, good neighborliness, honesty, forbearance, and so on. Modernists feel grievances in such matters are as much the consequence of internal failure and inadequacies as they may be of external infidel malice, and no amount of flaming *fatwas*, or infidel quarantine, can immunize against so endemic an infection.

All religious systems are equally vulnerable to the relentless incursions of temporal compromise and to the vagaries of human instrumentality even, or especially, where human stewardship is claimed in the service of revealed truth. The preface to The First Book of Common Prayer (1549), taking somber stock of what had overtaken a religion trapped in human systems, expresses the sentiment well when it says, "There was never any thing by the wit of man so well devised, or so sure established, which in continuance of time hath not been corrupted." Herein is echoed 'Uthmán dan Fodio's own painful musing in his poem, *Wallahi, Wallahi,* in which he bemoaned the corruption that had riddled the theocratic reform program he had initiated with the highest public ideals.[48] Religious truth cannot survive this corruption, for believers would become either cynics or Eliot's "hollow men," a presence without consequence. The only reasonable answer is to separate church and state, to desacralize the political instrument while safeguarding religion's independence.

These considerations prompt the following thought: Such separation need not deny the connection of ethics and politics, of church and society, of principle and precedent, or of faith and public order, a connection well described by Stackhouse as a "buffer zone" between church and state, between piety and power.[49] For example, religious ethics may provide for the maintenance and security of the public order in such matters as family life, the socialization of children, interpersonal trust, philanthropy, compassion, and humility without the public order being excluded from shared responsibility. However, in that partnership public agents might be tempted to sequester religion as expedient leverage only, taking short-term advantage of revealed injunctions that are the source and spring of ethical life. This analysis indicates that liberal arguments for distinguishing between public and private spheres would be hard to sustain purely on free-speech grounds, as Locke has cogently shown, for, however we define them, the private and public spheres are affected by identical rules of order, freedom, and responsibility. State institutions would be expected to observe standards of freedom, justice, honesty, truth, and decency no less than persons in community. In other words, the state in its nature distinguishes between right and wrong, punishes wrongful acts, and offers incentives for right conduct. It is not morally neutral. Even in the intimate domain of family life, for instance, the rule of safeguarding and promoting the welfare of children is no less valid when transferred to the public realm than when it is viewed in its natural sphere of parental responsibility. Thus, although separation defines the public and private domains, it does not abrogate the large area of partnership and overlap that turns out to be extremely fruitful for a humane and just society. There would be room in that partnership and overlap for absorbing Muslim ethical teachings and other values within an open, free, and pluralist community.

In spite of such considerations, the debate as it has been conducted in Nigeria has been a one-sided affair in which Muslims have taken the offensive and Christians have reacted with high-decibel slogans about pluralism and multiculturalism and with strategies of ecumenical unity striking for their ephemeral, tactical skittishness. If, by contrast, the example of Christendom and its disastrous consequences for genuine pluralism and multiculturalism were available to Muslims, it might calm passions and provide instructive lessons about the liabilities of religious territoriality in Africa or anywhere else. In that case, the secular state, shorn of its antireligious bias and conceived as a pluralist apparatus, might be less objectionable and might thus remove any conspiratorial odor from Christian support for such a state. It turns out, however, that events have preempted the issue, with the regime of General Ibrahim Babangida, which ruled Nigeria from 1985 to 1993, acting in 1989 to allow *Sharí'ah* court jurisdiction in the north, thus setting aside the position taken by Christians and endorsed in the decisions of the Constitutive Assembly.

International Muslim solidarity has aided and abetted national efforts and has distracted local Christian attempts to respond to Muslim initiatives. After several years as an observer, Nigeria in 1986 joined the OIC, which was set up following the meeting of the Third Conference of Islamic Foreign Ministers in March 1972. Its first secretary general was Tunku Abdur Rahman, who resigned as prime minister of Malaysia to assume that position. The OIC was registered with the United Nations in February 1974. A number of Islamic agencies was established within the OIC, whose religious character was spelled out in an official statement. This religious objective was described as the commitment "to propagate Islam and acquaint the rest of the world with Islam, its issues and aspirations."[50] The statement then went on to cite from the Declaration of the Third Islamic Summit of 1981, as follows: "Strict adherence to Islam and Islamic principles and values, as a way of life, constitutes the highest protection for Muslims against the dangers which confront them. Islam is the only path which can lead them to strength, dignity and prosperity and a better future."[51]

The statement in that form and in its fuller version proposes a frankly utilitarian political view of religion, with the unsettling theological implication that Islam seeks for its adherents political and judicial instruments for their protection and that only a temporary sacrifice need be involved in the process. Those who share in Islam's struggle, its *jihád*, will also share in its fruit, no more and no less.

The problem with this reasoning is that it does not seem to work in reverse: Many affluent and thriving communities, who are otherwise "lodged in this world in a goodly lodging" (16:43), claim no Scriptural credit for such advantage. By promising similar fruits to its adherents, religion, any religion, would be trafficking in double standards by placing the moral diacritic on political and economic goods but impugning those goods when their source is perceived to be the secular national state. If in the nature of the case the secular state or religion exists only to secure our material interest, that would make ends and means identical and make religion nothing more than mere everyday usefulness. Thus, if both state and religion have as their common end the single goal of being "lodged in this world in a goodly lodging," then the one would only be a duplicate of the other, and distinguishing between the two would defy even the most discerning. Religious pursuit and political interest would merge. We can avoid this situation only by drawing the distinction between church and state that moral principle and worldly expedience alike require. African states are embroiled in that struggle.

The OIC statement ended by quoting the Qur'án at 3:106, to the effect that Muslims "are the best nation ever brought forth to men, bidding to honour, and forbidding dishonour, and believing in God." The phrase "bidding to honour" is not sufficiently exact to reproduce the sense in the Arabic original of "commanding the good and fitting,"[52] a sense involving power and authority. "The duty of commanding the good and forbidding the evil," Ibn Taymiyya insists, as we saw, "cannot be completely discharged without power and authority." Member states of the OIC accept the binding authority of its charter, though the power and authority implied in the Qur'ánic verse it invokes might conflict with the sovereignty of national constitutions. At present the view has been expressed that the OIC lacks the power to hold member states accountable, even when it comes to the payment of dues. As it happens, this inadequacy in the structure of the OIC reduces its ability to challenge sovereign national states whose own internal domestic pluralism would, as in Nigeria, make doctrinal conformity difficult to enforce.

In terms of its historical origin, the OIC began as an organized Muslim response to the arson in August 1969 at the *Aqsá* mosque in Jerusalem under Israeli occupation, and in its original charter Jerusalem was designated as its *de jure* headquarters, with Jeddah being adopted *faute de mieux*. Before long, the activities of the OIC extended to numerous fields covering social, political, economic, media, publishing, educational, and intellectual activities. Membership in the organization is limited to sovereign nation states that are Muslim by definition, although several states with minority Muslim populations have joined, including Benin, Sierra Leone, and Uganda. However, somewhat inconsistently, India and Lebanon, which have significant Muslim populations, have not been allowed to join. They have been disqualified by the territorial rule, for their heads of government by practice are non-Muslim. In *territoriality* the religion of the ruler is the religion of the country, as we have remarked earlier. In other respects the OIC has applied stringent confessional criteria, from deciding on the venue of its meetings to granting economic assistance from its $2 billion development fund and awarding scholarships to Muslim candidates.

Although the OIC has agreed to work within the framework of the international security system in terms of explicit recognition of national state jurisdiction, it strives, in spite of that, to redirect the attention of member states to issues of international Muslim solidarity in terms of the primacy of the *Shari'ah* and the unity of the *ummah*, in other words, code and community. Indeed, the religious counsels it has invoked for its *raison d'être* commit it to appeal to Muslims without regard to state protocol. For example, in its founding charter the OIC declared that "jihád [is] the duty of every Muslim, man or woman, ordained by the *shari'ah* and glorious traditions of Islam," and called "upon all Muslims, living inside or outside Islamic countries, to discharge this duty by contributing each according to his capacity, in the cause of Allah Almighty, Islamic brotherhood, and righteousness."[53] Such appeals reveal the OIC's distrust of secular national states, even though publicly it says it respects and recognizes them. The ambivalence is also no doubt to be explained by the need to respond to Israel's dominance in the Middle East, as OIC's founding documents reveal.

Be that as it may, the OIC distinguishes itself from other international organizations, such as the United Nations, the European Community, the Organization of African Unity (OAU), and even the Arab League, by stressing its Qur'ánic identity as *ummah*. Yet the OIC as such has no independent sovereign power and relies on member states to carry out its decisions. It has, nevertheless, identified the secular character of modern states as the consequence of Western intellectual hegemony and therefore as something that is in tension, if not in conflict, with Qur'ánic norms and with the authentic Muslim aspirations they enshrine. By implication, Christian support or sponsorship of the secular national state is open to an identical objection.

The OIC issue has released a potent ferment of the fundamentalist debate and has thus caught Nigerians unawares. General Babangida announced in a news broadcast in August 1991 that Nigeria was suspending its membership in the OIC.[54] Yet, in spite of the fiasco, even here we have the possibility for interfaith understanding, because it can be said that the secular national state that is the butt of criticism among Muslims is also an issue for Christian Africans, and for them, as for their Muslim compatriots, the great stumbling block continues to be the idea of "secularism." It does not change very much to tinker with the notion and break it up into, say, "secularity," "secularism," and "the secular." For Christian Africans the secular state is the least of all possible evils, and for Muslims it is the worst of all available alternatives. Watched by Muslims, Christians are disinclined to side with the secular state as a "godless" institution,[55] but neither are they ready to buckle under Muslim pressure and endorse religion as state ideology because of what that would imply for minority groups in the community. For their part, Muslims are not reassured by the doctrinal minimalism of Christians and others who are willing to accept humanly constructed national constitutions for a secular state but refuse the role of revealed law in public affairs. Equally inconsistently, Christians plead for ethnic or cultural priority over any claim for religious primacy and yet insist that they speak also as religious people. Yet, how can religion count for anything when thus reduced to an ethnic decoy or a cultural filler? Here we see Ockham's razor dissected by the Muslim *sayf al-haqq*, the sword of God.

Historians of religion ought at this point to notice the special circumstances of an African Christianity that received from the mainline Western churches the tradition of an enlightened worldliness first preached by their eighteenth-century forebears. This worldliness furnished the basis for a "bland piety, a self-satisfied and prosperous reasonableness, the honest conviction that churches must, after all, move with the times. This—the concessions to modernity, to criticism, science, and philosophy, and to good tone—this was the treason of the clerics,"[56] in other words, the absolute liberal compromise. It is the principle of "finders, keepers, losers, weepers," whereby the church pleads its right to keep whatever it finds congenial in secular traditions, though such stolen property might taint its reputation. Christian reasonableness in this sense was a code for religion as the cultural helix that cuts and shapes religion as a social ornament. When the church entered confidently and uncritically upon the heritage of its secular captors it gave up its autonomy as the price for being included in the affairs of state. This created a peculiar situation: The church appropriated the national cultural enterprise as a devout vocation, fitting into Locke's idea of "the reasonableness of Christianity," though the idea of vocation with intrinsic religious merit was abandoned. Religion as cultural helix was corkscrewed into official submission, with the cultural coil guiding the religious axis. It would be difficult, as society became more materialist and pluralist, to maintain such a vital nexus of religion and culture. As Herbert Muller says of an earlier age, "As the commonplace was made holier, the holy became commonplace."[57] That development was unchallenged by the attendant scholasticism that constructed its system of human cognition with a built-in slight towards non-Western cultures.[58] The brilliance of its rational disputation exhausted itself in deductive reasoning, which permitted no new discovery and quenched even the slightest flicker of any interest in non-Western cultures. For the schoolmen of scholasticism, absorbed in dispute over the choice of horns in dilemmas, God disappeared in a blaze of verbal fireworks, and, as divinity floated away into the mists, it lost all connection with lived social practice, except, that is, in a gross, alien popular piety that had the universe infested with spirits, demons, sprites, and goblins.

As a consequence, from the intellectual captivity of the Gospel, cultural respectability resulted, with moral fervor and cultural devotion becoming synonymous. Thus was religion sequestered to become the national cult. Compromise does not have to be imposed to be fatal, and the church, relaxed and mellow, was trimmed with undue fuss and domesticated into the cultural matrix of its captivity, its solemn religious trunk pared down to remove all offense to good taste.

"There was much comfort and little anxiety in sermons purporting to prove that the course of a Christian life was easy, that reward for good conduct [i.e., conformity to the status quo] was sure and glorious, that God had commanded men nothing 'either unsuitable to our reason or prejudicial to our interest; nay, nothing that is severe and against the grain of our nature,' and that, on the contrary, 'the laws of God are reasonable, that is suited to our nature and advantageous to our interest.'"[59] Such justification, remarkable for its supreme, airy confidence, pulled religion by its roots from its social connectedness.

Historians struck by the survival in Christian Africa of vestiges of European influence will do well to remember that it was a scholasticized faith that came to Africa and that in its European form the church demanded little engagement with local priorities and attitudes. Jesus of Nazareth was swallowed up in abstract dogma, his earthly life refined as fuel for enlightened minds. Encountering such a religion, Africans soon discovered its inadequacies for the flesh and blood issues of their very different societies. The bracing religious commitment needed for creative cultural innovation and for a radical understanding of local social systems was at odds with Christianity as a system of human cognition, and the churches as transplants in Africa were too out of step with the African experience to enable people to decide what religious foundations to put in place for constructing a new society in new times. Thus, Muslims may be justified in thinking that Christians have abdicated from the religious center, confining themselves to the sidelines on the great issues of state and society. However, if Christians are mere rookies at the game of politics and state building, then it is hard to see how they could be charged with public responsibility for the policies of colonial regimes in Africa and for the enduring effects of those policies in postcolonial Africa, not the Christians trained in wielding Ockham's razor. Such theological minimalism is uncontroversial, content as it is with religion occupying a residual role in public life, where it subsists on political dole. It resulted in apathy in the face of maximal political participation, such as would be involved in setting up and running a state.

Furthermore, it is important to recognize the uncontroversial context of Muslims in modern African states not as the subjugated people of a colonial overlord but as masters of their own affairs, even where they are only a tiny fraction of the population. A similar context was obtained even under colonial rule, where Muslim life endured and thrived, in part because the muscle of secular colonial administrations could be harmonized with the momentum of a dynamic Islamic order to produce the Constantinian state and in part because, flowing from this logic, colonialism became the guarantor of the Pax Islamica, which discouraged Christian missionary activity or anything else that might offend Muslims. Colonialism became the Muslim shield and the riposte to the church's theological minimalism. In one example in British-administered Adamawa in Nigeria, the resident colonial officer presided over a meeting called by Muslims who headed the Native Authorities set up by the British. The meeting received charges from the Muslims against the Danish missionaries of the province for allowing the Classes for religious instruction to be taken by village catechists in mission schools. The meeting, held at Yola, the provincial headquarters, considered how these classes were in fact political platforms producing "young rebels," in other words, a class of young people not under the direct influence of the Muslim Native Authorities. The colonial administration backed Muslim demands, against missionary objections, for taking down the religious instruction classes,[60] which suggests that colonialism had become the Muslim shield and the guarantor of Islam as the public alternative to Christianity for Africans.

The examples are numerous: When in 1910 a traditional ruler of Bauchi Province converted to Christianity in what appeared a sincere act, the resident in charge objected and had him deposed because the ruler's authority depended on observing local rituals, which as a convert he had now forsaken. In another example, the colonial district officer upheld the decision by the Muslim chief to have Christian places of worship torn down—though he intervened after protest by the missionaries and prevented the chief from carrying out the demolition.[61] In yet another incident, the district officer felt that antimission feeling was getting out of hand after some mission boys were ordered flogged by the district head and his elders because some of the people associated with the mission had refused to be married under native custom and were thus flouting native authority.[62] One colonial officer, Fitzpatrick, expresses the widespread view that colonialism was the alternative to Christianity when he wrote, "The Christianised African in Kabba is presently a difficulty and is rapidly becoming a problem. To-day his attitude and his actions make it hard for the Native Administration to govern: tomorrow they may make it impossible."[63] This view led Fitzpatrick to launch an attack on mission Christianity, especially the Protestant form of it, as a subversive, dangerous influence on Africans. Christianity, he wrote in a fit of uncompromising candor, was "synonymous with idleness, impudence, inefficiency, with all that is meanest and worst in a native or any other polity."[64] Fitzpatrick's views were backed by his superiors, including the governor, Sir Hugh Clifford, who wrote that Native Administrations should receive the backing of political officers against Christian insubordination.[65] Barnes is more forthright, saying that administrators saw Christianity as giving African converts the temerity to presume that they could transcend "their status as members of a lesser race."[66] Thus the policy of indirect rule promoted the territorial interests of Islam as an effective block to Christianization with its tendencies, so inimical to religious territoriality and constituted authority, towards the separation of the religious and the secular and the emancipation of the individual. Missionaries there or elsewhere would plead forlornly and in vain for a role for educated youth in modern society, rather than their being stigmatized and subject to harassment and reprisal. Thus colonialism, while strengthening Muslim territoriality, reinforced the privatization of Christianity.

However, such historical cooperation has not removed all Muslim grievances, so that their need for transnational solidarity has pitted Muslims against the West as the source and guardian of the secular national state, a state that divides Muslims and sets at nought the just claims of the *ummah*.

Thus, in spite of differences of culture and language, and in spite of a common desire to succeed economically, such religious groups are, even in the West where they have chosen to immigrate, in the words of the legal manuals, "bound together by the common tie of Islam that as between themselves there is no difference of country, and they may therefore be said to compose but one *dár* [i.e., *dár al-Islám*, 'the abode of fraternal Islam']. And, in like manner, all who are not [Muslims], being accounted as of one faith, when opposed to them [i.e., Muslims], however much they may differ from each other in religious belief, they also may be said to be one *dár* [i.e., *dár al-harb*, 'the sphere of war and enmity']. The whole world, therefore, or so much of it as is inhabited and subject to regular government, may thus be divided" along these lines.[67]

De Tocqueville called attention to this strand in the Muslim tradition, noting how the refusal of Muslims to grant the principle of a separate jurisdiction in church and state makes the religion a liability in an enlightened, pluralist democracy,[68] since faith and the public interest must under those circumstances coincide. Consequently, the pursuit by radical religious activists of Islam's comprehensive doctrine perpetuates the difficulty.[69]

Our comprehension of this new reality must, however, keep abreast of moderate Muslim counsels concerning the anachronism of territoriality, and ecumenical groups need to come to a common mind about religious freedom, whether in Maiduguri, Manchester, or Medina. Religious toleration cannot survive by conceding the extreme case for religious territoriality, because a house constructed on that foundation would have no room in it for the very pluralist principle that would make the national secular state hospitable to religious voluntarism. The fact that such religious activity has grown and thrived under national state jurisdictions at a time when religious minorities established in religious territorial states have, if press reports are to be believed, continued to suffer civil disabilities shows how uneven the situation has become. As a prominent national political figure and television commentator put it, playing somewhat to the gallery with a bait of his own, "While Moslem minorities proliferate and prosper in Western societies that preach and practice freedom and tolerance, in nations where Moslems are the majority, Christians find the profession of the faith difficult, the preaching of the Gospel impossible."[70]

The substance of that view, shorn of its crowd baiting, is that a split-level structure in interfaith relations becomes untenable and poses a risk to democratic public institutions whose preservation demands that human rights be enshrined in the actions of the national secular state. Three points should be made here: a) religious toleration is an essential part of human rights and, thus, of democratic pluralism; b) it is necessary to separate church and state in order to protect human rights and to foster pluralism; and c) the matter cannot rest there, because religious toleration requires arguments that go beyond those of public usefulness.

Normative toleration as a safeguard of individual conscience is theological in the sense of being founded on the divine right of personhood, with obvious political implications. Although conscience, or the sanction for it, is not the concern of state jurisdiction, nevertheless, in its assumptions of moral agency, it touches inexhaustibly on the public order. Thus might religion produce fruits in projects of social welfare and their effects on public social ethics without religion turning into a mere expedient ethic, and thus, too, might state interest converge with religion without the state becoming a divine organ. They complement each other when church and state are separated, but each corrupts—and is in turn corrupted—when the other co-opts it.

This consideration leads to the following conclusion: Voluntary religious practice promotes ends that are constitutive of the values of a liberal democratic political community, though religion would be corrupted if it were co-opted merely as a tool of authority and politics turn tyrannical if it ceased to be morally accountable. In this regard the temporal Islam of conservative Muslims, in other words, the claim for a public sphere for religion, may be reconciled with the ethical Islam of liberal Muslims without yielding to theocratic extremism on the right or to prescriptive atheism on the left. Thus we may concede the point of Ibn Taymiyya that "the exercise of authority is a religious function" in the sense of accountability and subordination to the higher moral law, without granting that this requires establishing a theocratic order for the purpose. The political community is also the moral community, though the political and the moral, necessarily connected, are not identical. Truth is no less so even if it be politically inexpedient, while political expediency may serve the higher end without turning into the end itself. The political community, stretched to its extensive overlap with the moral law, cannot return to the exclusive dimensions of prescriptive atheism, so that, for example, when Ibn Khaldún (see Chapter 9) separates dogma and politics, truth and pragmatism, he expands the religious view while qualifying the political. Similarly, from the left we may agree with Locke when he argues for the "outward" and "inward" jurisdiction, with religion at the center, without going so far as to say that separation removes religion from any role in the political economy. A theocratic state in Ibn Taymiyya's terms would be no better than an ideological secular state in John Locke's terms, for in both God and obedience to Him would be reduced to tools of authority, with truth-seeking becoming a strategy for self-interest or group advantage, and vice versa. Separation of church and state, when taken to its logical extreme, would produce a doctrinaire secularism, aided and abetted by religious collusion, although without separation the situation may be reversed, yet identical consequences will follow, for then Caesar's political commissars will anoint themselves with the moral norms they confiscate from the church. As such, separation does not mean exclusion, and it does not imply as the alternative Hobson's choice of the state's absorption of the church. It only means that religion is so important that the state should take it seriously, and yet is too much so for the state to expropriate it, that although religion and politics are comprehended within the human scheme, religion exceeds the human measure by pointing beyond to the divine.

Conclusion

In view of growing signs of the pressure for temporal Islam, often expressed in terms of *Shari'ah* and political power, and in view of the utter inadequacy of the sterile utilitarian ethic of the secular national state in meeting this challenge, Christian Africans and their Western predecessors are faced with a question about supporting the pragmatist case for the secular state with moral principles. The state as the vehicle for tolerance, human rights, equality, and justice must now be conceived in terms that are hospitable to claims for truth. Too much is at stake in the survival of the state as a noncorporate, nondoctrinaire institution to allow it to fall victim to our Enlightenment scruples about not mixing religion and politics. The pragmatist liberal scruple that proceeds upon religion in the fashion of individual entitlement and free speech is in one sense the spoilt fruit of the original insight about keeping Caesar and God separate, about ensuring religious freedom against state power and jurisdiction. That insight became twisted into religion as individual entitlement and free speech, as a rights issue under state jurisdiction, in fact as a matter of private, individual choice without public merit. So Muslim critics are correct that rights without God are meaningless but mistaken to suggest that a religious state would do better, because under such a state rights would as a last resort spring from duress and intimidation, and that would just be another name for jungle power. If it is going to work, rights must presume an authority above and beyond individual or collective will, by general consent a transcendent tribunal that can support and adjudicate conflicting claims and interests. If we only have human authority as final arbiter of human rights, then there simply is no basis for saying one individual has rights of person and property against the multitude: Against the individual, the multitude's will is irresistible and final by reason merely of numerical preponderance. Human rights as such is meaningless in that environment precisely because the individual has been assured no God-given rights. Human rights must presume a public tribunal insulated from the tyranny of numbers by being grounded in faith in the divine right of personhood, a faith that fosters the twin culture of rights and obligations, of freedom and community. In this context, state capture of religion is bound to dismantle the machinery of civil society, so that in one move of state capture of religion the brakes are removed from political excess and in turn applied to freedom and commitment, in effect pressing political expediency into the service of a false absolute. All of that diminishes freedom and tolerance, two priceless and indispensable pieces of the apparatus of democratic liberalism.

Democratic liberalism seeks political sovereignty from the people rather than taking it to them, and so, to be successful, it rules and governs through consent. It is, therefore, a profound condition of its strength that religion flourish in it in the obvious sense of democratic liberalism using legitimate methods in the pursuit of ethical ends. "Despotism," de Tocqueville insisted, "may be able to do without faith, but freedom cannot. Religion is much more needed in [an egalitarian democratic society] than [in a privileged, aristocratic society]."[71] It is when the ties of political control are relaxed that those of religion are tightened, when freedom expands that personal responsibility increases with it, and that as men and women take control of their own affairs that they should be subject to the law of God. That much is clear on the political side of the equation. On the religious front, it is when religion yields territoriality that an inclusive territorial state can effectively emerge, and when religion demands territoriality that the state becomes sacralized and despotic. When people can enter into ultimate religious commitment, a commitment signifying the limitless possibility of human worth, they are equipped to conceive a separate, limited domain of political action, so that the norms of moral truth can be distinguished from the tactics of political compromise. Political sovereignty and state jurisdiction have their common foundation in the higher wisdom of the people's God-given rights, with religion the expression of that political axiom. Freedom is an act of faith.

Thomas Jefferson (1743–1826) appealed to this principle, invoking it as the last resort of democratic liberalism. "I have no fear," he affirmed, "but that the result of our experiment will be that men may be trusted to govern themselves without a master. Could the contrary of this be proved, I should conclude either there is no God or that he is a malevolent being." Jefferson fervently supported separation of church and state ("divided we stand, united we fall") not because he opposed religion, or his notion of it, but because he feared that government would use religion to bolster its despotic powers. Religion was at its best, he argued, when it did not feel the necessity to compel compliance, and, he might have added in the same breath, democratic liberalism was at its soundest when it allied itself to religion's spirit of freedom. John Dewey (1859–1952), for his part, comes to the issue with the instinct of a pragmatist, saying that those who are committed to democratic liberalism must "face the issue of the moral ground of political institutions and the moral principles by which men acting together may attain freedom of individuals which will amount to fraternal associations with one another."[72]

Religion thus constitutes the pillar upholding democratic liberalism, secured as it is on the consent of persons constrained by right rather than cowed by might. The state that can reach its people only through force will turn society into a battlefield, and religion allied with such a state becomes moral coercion, making salvation a political prerogative. We would be ill advised to abandon our faith in divinity on the basis of state fiat or to base it on the will of the collective, Rousseau's General Will, with its unrealistic assumption about innate human goodness and reasonableness. Instead, we should see that the notion of peoplehood, on which democratic liberalism depends, itself hinges on the doctrine of persons "born free, being the image and resemblance of God himself," as Milton expressed it, a view echoing the religious basis of peoplehood of classical Muslim thought, too.

At this stage we may redirect the Miltonian or Lockean view of religion and politics towards its modern day natural convergence with democratic liberalism in the following way. A liberal democratic state, however laissez-faire, must still impose laws and rules impartially on all citizens, and it is necessary to its success that such a state depend on a broad consensus concerning the fundamental constitutional axioms upon which laws and rules are based without a controversy about "beliefs" in each round of rule making. Thus disagreements may arise in society as to the material effects and consequences of rules but not about the fundamental axioms and their source in religion and tradition. For example, the axiom, "Thou shalt not kill," as a Scriptural injunction, would permit laws of murder to be promulgated and stipulated without the operative validity of those laws depending on prior assent to the authority of Scripture. Life is sacred because of divine affirmation, though the murderer or society need not affirm that to be subject to the law. In the law against suicide, for example, the point is poignantly made. Similarly, as a penal concept truth discovery and punishment are valid even if the criminal rejects confession and repentance as a religious duty. That these laws and rules may thus be detached from their source in religion and made impartially operative gives them their force. Thus liberal democratic regimes are concerned with those procedural tasks deriving from a Miltonian or Lockean doctrine even if in substance those tasks do not require avowal of the religious source. You do not have to bring up the roots to know the tree is sound.

Political realism and religious integrity thus have a common purpose in distinguishing between a Caesar crowned and a Caesar turbaned, and that purpose is to prevent constituted government from meddling with religion. Politics as a self-sufficient comprehensive system of values concerned primarily with public order is already too well equipped to tempt it further with jurisdiction over religion. In the power state religion is addictive, for transcendence is fodder to political despotism. Hence the caution that, although political liberalism can scarcely flourish without its foundational attachment in religious freedom, it will spoil from assuming political primacy over the religious domain. If it knows anything to do with religion, the impulse of secular liberalism is to "commodify" religion for short-term exchange, or, to amend de Tocqueville, government by habit prefers the useful to the moral and will, therefore, require the moral to be useful. By thus shortening the odds on the long-range, timeless truths of religion, the secular realm ends up removing the safety barrier against political absolutization and coming into conflict with George Herbert's religious rule that what "God doth touch and own cannot for less be told." Much of the church-state tension stems from the proximity of the two spheres, so that religion is too enmeshed in life not to profit, or suffer, from the state instrument, and vice versa, though marrying the two introduces an even greater risk of malignancy between them. Government with unlimited power will metastasize, leading to the adoption of injurious, despotic measures in the name of a prescriptive political code. At the same time, religion as a public order strategy will become just a power game. Ultimately, whether the state repudiates or co-opts religion, it ends up feeding off religion: Private piety as a liberal political concession is little different in restriction from the belligerent antireligious stance preferred by the atheist state. We need the prophylaxis of separation thus to tame the state and to create a public space for religion without religious differences becoming a public liability. In the contemporary global situation, such qualified separation also provides a crucial shield for pluralism and minority rights, enabling nonconformist groups and minority communities to play an assured role in the public sphere without fear or stigma.

Concerning the ultimate OIC case for the *ummah*, it may well be that, in principle, advocates of temporal Islam are right in their criticism of the national state as biased toward the secular metaphysic of the state as a moral idea, indicating that the secular state is not neutral towards the religious source of the moral idea but is actively at work to supplant it for self-serving reasons. The suspicion is that the state wishes to establish the public sphere as a religion-free zone so as to designate it as a religious no-go area. Yet this stringent criticism is reserved also for the doctrinaire state, now dressed in purple velvet, yet whose religious metaphysic gives no immunity from despotism, since the religious state is still the captivity of dogma in the service of expediency. The actions of the religious state ultimately can be guaranteed to spare not even its religious sponsors, either as agents implementing harmful laws or as the targets of such laws. That outcome is why religion and government between them should be united in requiring the safety net of separation, a separation in terms of coequal spheres of responsibility. Once we have secured that, then tolerance and pluralism can thrive, and with it religion, and especially politics, as a fundamental issue of personal choice within a culture of persuasion. All of which would ensure that minority status and religious or political preferences could possess public merit without necessarily carrying any stigma or reprisals, or the threat of any. Open and fair contest that does not exclude prayer, worship, and vocation would determine for the most part, or for the part that matters, what survives or does not survive of the ideas and values best deemed to advance our freedom and welfare.

Notes

Introduction

1. B. Lewis, *Race and Slavery in the Middle East: An Historical Enquiry,* New York: Oxford University Press, 1992, p. 3.

Chapter One

1. See, for example, J. Spencer Trimingham, *A History of Islam in West Africa,* London: Oxford University Press, 1962; and also Francesco Gabrieli, *Muhammad and the Conquests of Islam,* London: Weidenfeld and Nicolson, 1968.

2. H. T. Norris, *The Tuaregs: Their Islamic Legacy and Its Diffusion in the Sahel,* Warminster: Aris and Phillips, 1975.

Religious groups among the Berbers of North Africa, especially the Kunta shaikhly families, trace their genealogies back to 'Uqbah. A local Kunta historian writes that "the cradle of the Kunta is at Qayrawán, where there is the mausoleum of their ancestor, famous in Islam, 'Uqbah al-Mustajab b. Náfi', chosen by Alláh to conquer Ifríqiya as far as Ghana." A. A. Batran, "The Kunta, Sidi Mukhtár al-Kuntí and the Office of Shaykh al-Taríqa al-Qádiriyya," in J. R. Willis, ed., *Studies in West African Islamic History,* vol. 1, *The Cultivators of Islam,* London: Frank Cass, 1979, pp. 114–116, where the descendants of 'Uqbah are listed.

3. The clerical specialists among the Serakhullé, called the Jakhanké (in French sources "Diakhanké"), claim 'Uqbah as one of their ancestors.

4. Muhammad Bello, *Infáq al-Maysúr,* C.E.J. Whitting, ed., London: Luzac, 1957.

5. Jean Vuillet, "Récherches au sujet de religions professées en Sénégambie, anciennement ou à l'époque actuelle," *Comptes Rendus Mensuels des Séances de l'Academie des Sciences Coloniales* 7, no. 8, 1952, pp. 413–426. In this source the Fadiga and Kale Manding families claim descent from Jacob, which complements the different claim of the Fofana of their descent from Abú Bakr al-Siddíq, the companion and successor of the Prophet.

6. *Hadíths* were reported from the Prophet that said "There are no genealogies in Islam," and others forbade emulation and boasting over one's past ancestry. The Qur'án supports this idea by stressing that those most worthy of honor in the sight of God are those who fear Him most (*súrah* 49:13), rather than those whose lineage is the most famous or the most powerful. Al-Waqidi reported: "God has put an end to the pride in noble ancestry, you are all descended from Adam and Adam from dust, the noblest among you is the man who is most pious." Muhammad ibn 'Umar al-Waqidi (752–829), *Muhammad in Medina,* trans. and abridged by Wellhausen, Berlin, 1882, p. 338. See also Reuben Levy, *The Social Structure of Islam,* 1957; reprint, London: Cambridge University Press, 1965, p. 56.

7. Juana Elbein and Deoscoredes M. Dos Santos, "La religion Nago génératrice et réserve de valeurs culturelles au Brésil" in *Les Réligions africaines comme source de valeurs de civilisation, colloque de Cotonou, 16–22 Aout 1970,* Paris: *Présence Africaine,* 1972, pp. 156–171.

8. Elbein and Dos Santos, "Religion Nago génératrice," pp. 158 and 160, 164ff.

9. Ibid., pp. 160ff.

10. Pierre Verger, *Trade Relations Between the Bight of Benin and Bahia, 17th to the 19th Century,* Paris: Mouton and Ecole Pratique des Hautes Etudes, 1968; reprint, Ibadan, 1976, pp. 287, 288, 291ff.

11. In Islamic sources there are two chief inquisitors: al-Nakír (Nupe: Walakiri), who tests the faith of the departed, and Munkar, his companion. One of the four archangels, Azra'il (Nupe: Darayilu), carries the departed spirit to God. The Nupe do not know Munkar. Compare also with Mervyn Hiskett, *The Sword of Truth: The Life and Times of Shehu Usuman dan Fodio,* New York: Oxford University Press, 1973, p. 159.

12. J. Spencer Trimingham, *Islam in West Africa,* Oxford: Clarendon Press, 1959, pp. 56–57, 70, 77, 104–105, 106n., 118–119, 120. See also Siegfried F. Nadel, *Nupe Religion,* London: Oxford University Press for the International African Institute, 1954.

13. See Siegfried F. Nadel, *A Black Byzantium: The Kingdom of Nupe in Nigeria,* 1942; reprint, London: Oxford University Press, 1969, pp. 378–383.

14. Marcel Griaule, *Conversations with Ogotommêli: An Introduction to Dogon Religious Ideas,* London: Oxford University Press, 1975, originally published as *Dieu d'Eau: entretiens avec Ogotemmêli,* Paris: n.p., 1948.

15. Ibid., p. 183.

16. Claude Meillassoux, at the Sorbonne, told me that Islam was making inroads into Dogon country, although no serious attempt has been made to document this expansion. Conversation in Kinshasa, December 1976.

17. Germaine Dieterlen, "Mythe et organisation sociale en Afrique Occidentale," *J. Soc. Africanistes* 29, no. 1, 1959, pp. 119–138; (with Solange De Ganay) *La Génie des Eaux chez les Dogons,* Paris: Geuthner, 1942, among others of her works.

18. The priests of Ifa divination, called *babalawo,* remain prominent in Yoruba religion, and their divinatory authority and techniques have strongly influenced Muslim religious practices. Trimingham rightly observes in this respect that "Yoruba have little confidence in Muslim methods and refer contemptuously to Hausa diviners playing with the sand [Ar. *khatt,* geomancy]. They consult Muslim diviners only in connection with specifically Islamic ceremonies, such as the time for the payment of *iso-yigi* (bride price). African Islam does not have a special class, for divination is a clerical function, but diviners like the Hausa *mai-dúba* exist in all Islamic communities. A Hausa cleric diviner is not called *mai dúba,* though the practice is called *dúba.* The old terminology is not normally transferred but a new one invented, and a Yoruba cleric when divining is called *alafoshe.*" Trimingham, *Islam in West Africa,* p. 120.

19. Patrick J. Ryan, *Imale: Yoruba Participation in the Muslim Tradition,* Missoula, Montana: Scholars Press, 1979, p. 301. The ceremony of washing came to the Yoruba by way of the Hausa, among whom it is also called *wanka.* Islam is described in this sense as the religion of "washing," *wanka lisilenchi/lislami.* Trimingham, *Islam in West Africa,* appendix 1.

20. S. Johnson, *The History of the Yorubas,* London: Routledge and Kegan Paul, 1969, pp. 217–218.

21. Ibid.

22. Ryan, *Imale,* p. 328

23. Ibid., p. 319.

24. Alhaji M. S. Kasim, ed., *Songs and Prayers for Muslim Schools,* Ijebu-Ode, Nigeria: Council on Muslim Education, 1969.

25. Ryan, *Imale,* p. 263.

26. J.D.Y. Peel, *Ijeshas and Nigerians: The Incorporation of a Yoruba Kingdom, 1890s–1970s,* Cambridge: Cambridge University Press, 1983, p. 137.

27. Ibid., p. 165.

28. Ryan, *Imale,* p. 265.

29. Ibid., p. 348.

30. Ibid., p. 258.

31. Ibid., pp. 255, 310.

32. Ibid., p. 278.

33. Anthropological investigations into the ancient religions of the islamized Fulbé (or Fulani) and Hausa, for example, have uncovered a proportionately thin layer of material. See for example A.J.N. Tremearne, *The Ban of the Bori,* London: n.p., 1914, reprint, London: Frank Cass, 1968; Joseph Greenberg, *The Influence of Islam upon a Sudanese Religion,* New York: J. J. Augustin, 1946; and a slightly different work, Hampaté Ba and J. Daget, *L'Empire Peul du Macina,* Paris: Mouton, 1962. Also F. W. de St. Croix, *The Fulani of Nigeria,* Lagos: n.p., 1945; reprint, Farnborough, England: Gregg, 1972.

34. Ryan, *Imale,* p. 200.

35. William Bascom, "Yoruba Religion and Morality" in *Les Religions africaines comme source de valeurs de civilization: Colloque de Cotonou 16–22 Aout 1970,* Paris: Presence Africaine, 1972, p. 62.

36. Abayomi Cole addressed the meeting in Yoruba, paying particular attention to Olorun, the Yoruba High God. *Sierra Leone Weekly News* 9 Jan. 1889, and 12 Jan. of same year.

37. T.G.O. Gbadamosi, *The Growth of Islam Among the Yoruba: 1841–1908,* London: Longman, 1978 (in fact publication date was March 5, 1979).

38. Ibid., p. 198.

39. Ibid.

40. J. Olumide Lucas, *The Religion of the Yorubas,* Lagos: CMS Bookshop, 1948. This monograph, packed with information and local details and enhanced with superb illustrations and photographs, is still a splendid and valuable book in spite of its rather old-fashioned interpretation.

41. E. Bolaji-Idowu, *Oludumare: God in Yoruba Belief,* London: Longman, 1962.

42. John S. Mbiti, *Concepts of God in Africa,* London: S.P.C.K., 1982.

43. "Writers on the arts of sub-Saharan Africa have either ignored the influence of Islam or have treated the theme inaccurately. That they should ignore it is surprising. . . . Others have presumed that Islam would be bent on the destruction of the masking and figurative traditions so integral to the indigenous cultures and have described the religion and the arts as one that is invariably negative." René A. Bravmann, *Islam and Tribal Art in West Africa,* Cambridge: Cambridge University Press, 1974, p. 1.

44. Ibid., p. 28.

45. K. Carroll, *Yoruba Religious Carving,* London, 1967. Somewhat inconsistently Trimingham's book, *Islam in West Africa,* though utilized extensively by Bravmann, is not listed in the bibliography.

46. Bravmann, *Islam and Tribal Art,* ch. 3.

47. Ibid., p. 29.

48. Ibid.

49. Nehemia Levtzion, *Muslims and Chiefs in West Africa: A Study of Islam in the Middle Volta Basin in the Pre-colonial Period,* Oxford: Clarendon Press, 1968, pp. 65–66.

50. Levtzion gives the illuminating example of how the priest of a medicine shrine gave umbrage to Islam by himself praying twice a day, fasting three days during Ramadán, carrying a rosary, a Qur'án, and a bundle of Arabic manuscripts though he knew no Arabic himself. Levtzion, *Muslims and Chiefs,* p. 66.

51. Trimingham writes cogently of the pervasive influence of magic, witchcraft, and divination in much of Black Africa, emphasizing the enormous challenge these pose for the Muslim cleric. The Muslim Hausa practice magic (Trimingham, *Islam in West Africa* p. 115), the Fulbé/Tokolor clerics of Senegal specialize in it (p. 113), and the Muslim Manding also practice it (p. 114) as well as Muslims in western Guinea (p. 121) and the Temne of Sierra Leone (p. 122). The use of witchcraft and sorcery among the Hausa is connected to the no-

tion of *aiki,* meaning "deed" (Ar. *'amal*). *Aikin málam* is a spell to harm. A *malam* who practices magic is called *budeji* (or *ba bude*). "The Hausa have a vast catalogue of charms to harm." (p. 117) "Islam's cult of the supernatural is too deficient to satisfy many central Sudanese. Its clergy are powerless when confronted with the phenomena . . . and though they regard these cults as illegitimate and cannot islamise them they have been forced to recognize that they have a function . . . in society by their proved technique of healing," pp. 110–111.

52. See, for example, 'Abdulláh dan Fodio, *Tazyín al-Waraqát,* ed. M. Hiskett, Ibadan: Ibadan University Press, 1963.

53. See Murray Last's classic study, *The Sokoto Caliphate,* London: Longman, 1967, and Mervyn Hiskett, *The Sword of Truth: The Life and Times of Shehu Usuman dan Fodio,* New York: Oxford University Press, 1973.

54. E. W. Bovill, ed., *Missions to the Niger,* vol. 4: *The Bornu Mission 1822–25,* Hakluyt Society Series 2, vol. 130, London: Hakluyt Society, 1966, p. 679.

55. Ibid., pp. 669–670.

56. Ibid., p. 695. Clapperton also says elsewhere that the people believe in divination by the book, in dreams, and in good and bad omens. *Journal of a Second Expedition into the Interior of Africa,* London: Murray, 1829, p. 224.

57. See, for example, A.J.N. Tremearne, *Hausa Superstitions and Customs,* London: n.p., 1913; reprint, London: Frank Cass, 1970.

58. Yves Person, "Samori and Islam" in John Ralph Willis, ed., *Studies in West African Islamic History,* vol. 1, *The Cultivators of Islam,* 1979, p. 260.

59. Ibid., p. 261.

60. Louis Brenner, "Muhammad al-Amín-al-Kánimí and Religion and Politics in Bornu," in John Ralph Willis, ed., *Studies in West African Islamic History,* vol. 1, *The Cultivators of Islam,* 1979, p. 160.

61. See Trimingham, *Islam in West Africa,* pp. 38–39, 60, 109, 182n., and Mu'izz Goriawala, "Maguzawa," *Orita: Ibadan Journal of Religious Studies* 4, no. 2 (December 1970), pp. 115–123.

62. A. K. Ghazali and L. Proudfoot, "A Muslim Propaganda Play and a Commentary," *Sierra Leone Bulletin of Religion* 3, no. 2 (December 1961), pp. 72–79.

63. Trimingham, *Islam in West Africa,* pp. 44–45, 144–146. A Hausa Muslim woman, Baba of Karo, declared: "The work of *malams* is one thing, the work of *bori* experts is another, each has his own kind of work and they must not be mixed up. There is the work of *malams,* of *bori,* of magicians, of witches; they are all different but at heart everyone loves the spirits." Mary F. Smith, *Baba of Karo,* London: Faber, 1954, p. 222.

64. Robert Launay, *Beyond the Stream: Islam and Society in a West African Town,* Berkeley and Los Angeles: University of California Press, 1992, 154ff. See Chapter 5, following, for a discussion of this theme.

65. Kenneth L. Little, "A Muslim Missionary in Mendeland," *Man: Journal of the Royal Anthropological Institute,* September-October 1946, pp. 111–113.

66. The process is clearly elucidated in N. Levtzion, *Muslims and Chiefs,* and James F. Hopewell's short but acute thesis, *Muslim Penetration into French Guinea, Sierra Leone, and Liberia Before 1850,* unpublished Ph.D. dissertation, New York, 1958.

67. Uthmán dan Fodio was clearly perceived in such local religious terms, for even in his own lifetime he was transformed by popular piety into a cult hero, after the manner of Hausa *bochi* (also called *chigbe-jinchi*) or the Fulbé *bilejo,* the "medicine man." See Clapperton, *Second Expedition,* p. 206.

Chapter Two

1. J. Burckhardt, *The Civilization of the Renaissance in Italy,* New York: Mentor Book of the New American Library, 1961, p. 367.

2. Basil Davidson, *Which Way Africa? The Search for a New Society*, Baltimore, Md.: Penguin Books, 1964, p. 34.

3. Qur'án xvii:17–18; also vi:162–163: "My prayer, my ritual sacrifice, my living, my dying—all belongs to God,/the Lord of all Being."

4. Qur'án xxx:17; xx:130; xvii:80; xi:116; iv:104; ii:40. One Muslim authority comments on the later increase of this number. "The fact, however, that the prayers were fundamentally three is evidenced by the fact that the Prophet is reported to have combined these four prayers into two, even without there being any reason. It was in the post-Prophetic period that the number of prayers was inexorably fixed without any alternative to five, and the fact of the fundamental three prayers was submerged under the rising tide of the Hadíth which was put into circulation to support the idea that the prayers were five." Faslur Rahman, *Islam,* New York: Anchor Books, Doubleday, 1968, p. 33.

5. The Qur'ánic basis for *du'a* is in ii:182: "And when My servants question thee concerning Me—I am near to answer the call of the caller (*da'wah al-da'i*) when he calls to Me; so let them respond to Me."

6. "The advantage of appointing 40 days is that, on the completion of this period, the manifestation begins to appear" (Shiháb al-Dín al-Suhrawardí, *al-Awárif al-Ma'árif,* ed. and trans. Wilberforce Clarke, Calcutta: n.p., 1891, p. 43). Also al-Hájj Soriba Jabi, *Kitáb al-Bushrá: Sharh al-Mirqát al Kubrá,* Tunis: n.p., n.d.

7. All these types of prayers are known among Jakhanké clerics and were discussed at various meetings with al-Hájj Shaykh Sidiya Jabi and al-Hájj Soriba Jabi, among others.

8. René Caillie, *Travels Through Central Africa to Timbouctou and the Great Desert to Morocco Performed in the Years 1824–28,* 2 vols., London: H. Colburn and R. Bentley, 1830, vol. 1, pp. 266–268.

9. Ibid., p. 268.

10. Richard Jobson, *The Golden Trade; or, A Discovery of the River Gambia, 1620–21,* 1623; reprint, London: n.p., 1968, pp. 84–85.

11. Ibid., pp. 87–88. In Muslim canon law the worshipper may adopt as *qiblah* any direction if he or she is in any doubt about the exact location.

12. Jobson, *Golden Trade,* p. 21.

13. Mungo Park, *Travels in Africa: 1795–1797,* London: Everyman's Library, 1965, p. 249. The reference to spears might suggest that clerics were usually armed, but in fact such weapons as they had were carried either for ceremonial purposes or for self-protection, as clerics were normally exempt from bearing arms, see Jobson, *Golden Trade,* p. 99.

14. See, for example, Francis Moore, *Travels into the Inland Parts of Africa,* London: E. Cave, 1738, p. 102; Gaspard Mollien, *Travels in Africa to the Sources of the Senegal and Gambia in 1818,* London: H. Colburn and Co., 1825, pp. 147, 153; Park, *Travels in Africa,* pp. 32, 250.

15. Park, *Travels in Africa,* p. 208; see Paul Soleillet, *Voyage à Segou: 1878–1879,* Paris: Challamel, 1887, p. 460.

16. It is standard practice in much of Muslim Africa that the names for the days of the week are based on Arabic names, whereas the vernacular forms are retained for the calendar months whose associated rituals are Islamic, or at any rate islamized.

17. Al-Hajj Madi Hawa, field interview, Barrokunda, 17 November 1972.

18. Street 1971, pp. 18–19. For a thorough investigation of the phenomenon of dreams and dream-interpretation see Faraday 1972.The author appears to be in danger in this work of an over-concentration on the psychological significance of dreams, putting less emphasis on the social and practical side.

19. Cf. Ignaz Goldziher, *Muslim Studies,* trans. and ed. C. R. Barber and S. M. Stern, vol. 2, London: George Allen and Unwin, 1967–1971, p. 259ff.

20. Soriba Jabi, *Kitáb al-Bushrá,* p. 196. In the wider setting of saint veneration in Islam, the visit to the tombs of saints is also important, for it is widely held that "the saints cure

sickness and their prayers are always granted, every saint is a *mujáb al-du'a*" (Goldziher, *Muslim Studies,* vol. 2, p. 269).

21. 'Abd al-Rahmán Ka'ti, *Ta'ríkh al-Fattásh,* trans. O. Houdas and M. Delafosse, Alger: n.p., 1913; reprint, Paris: Librairie d'Amérique et d'Orient, Adrien-Maisonneuve, 1964, pp. 169–171, Ar. text pp. 90–91.

22. In Niokholo and Dental the descendants of al-Hájj Sálim considered themselves the inheritors of al-Hájj Sálim's *barakah* and guardians of his saintly relics. At Sillacounda in Niokholo, for example, the Suwaré clan retained custodial rights over the town, and in an emergency or change of political regime, they dug up the "amulets" that they believed contained the secrets of al-Hájj Sálim and used them to stabilize the town (Pierre Smith, "Notes sur l'organisation sociale des Diakhanké: Aspects particuliers à la région de Kédougou," *Bulletin et Mémoire de la Societé Anthropologie de Paris* 11, no. 8, pp. 263–302).

23. M. A. al-Hájj, "A Seventeenth-Century Chronicle on the Origins and Missionary Activities of the Wangarawa," *Kano Studies* 1, no. 4, 1968, p. 20. The phrase is *la'alli ajidu barakatuhu.*

24. Field-notes on site; Muhammad Khalífa Silla, grandson of Muhammad Sanúsí, Kounti.

25. Soriba Jabi, *Kitáb al-Bushrá,* p. 199.

26. Ibid.

27. Ibid.

28. John Spencer Trimingham, *Islam in West Africa,* Oxford: Clarendon Press, 1959.

29. Ibid. There was a widely circulated report that Shaykh Fanta Madi was a confidential seer to Dr. Kwame Nkrumah, the first president of Ghana. *West Africa,* 17 September 1979.

30. Trimingham, *Islam in West Africa,* pp. 90–91.

31. Ka'ti, *Ta'ríkh al-Fattásh,* p. 315.

32. Al-Bukhárí, *Sahíh,* text and tr., 9 vols., vol. 9, *Kitáb al-Ta'bír* (LXXXVII), New Delhi: Kitab Bhavan, 1987, p. 91.

33. See Faraday, 1972, pp. 167–73.

34. Trimingham, *Islam in West Africa,* p. 122.

35. 'Abd al-Ghaní al-Nábulsí, *Ta'tír al-Anám fí Ta'bír al-Manám,* vol. 1, Cairo: Dár al-Hayá al-Kitáb al-'Arabíyah, p. 2. The tradition cited as the Prophet's words in the latter half of the quotation has been preserved by al-Bukhárí (d. 870), *Sahíh,* 91:5. My translation throughout this passage.

36. Ibid., p. 3. Al-Nábulsí then gives a detailed list of how to recognize dreams that are false and those that are true. See also Duncan Black Macdonald, *The Religious Life and Attitude in Islam,* London: Darf, 1985, pp. 70–94; and Qur'án xxxix:43.

37. Ibid., p. 3.

38. Muhammad ibn Sírín, *Ta'bír al-Ru'yá,* Cairo: n.p., n.d., p. 3.

39. Al-Nábulsí, *Ta'tír al-Anám fí Ta'bír al-Manám,* p. 3.

40. Ibid.

41. See Gustave E. von Grünebaum and R. Caillois, *The Dream and Human Societies,* Los Angeles and Berkeley: University of California Press, 1966, *passim.*

42. Trimingham, *The Sufi Orders in Islam,* Oxford: Clarendon Press, 1971, p. 158, quoting al-Sanúsí.

43. *Miftáh al-Faláh,* vol. 2., p. 95.

44. This is Trimingham's distinction (*Sufi Orders,* p. 159), but this appears too rigid, although it would be right to say that visions occur during waking hours (and sometimes also in sleep), whereas dreams take place only in sleep. However, this is a slippery slope. See Fisher, H. J., "The Ivory Horn: Oneirology, Chiefly Muslim, in Black Africa," in *Conversion to Islam,* ed. Nehemia Levtzion, New York: Holmes & Meier, 1979.

45. Reported by Muhammad al-Murtadá, *Itháf al-Sáda,* vol. 1, p. 9, quoted in Trimingham, *Sufi Orders,* p. 33n. A conflicting tradition is reported by Grünebaum and Caillois, *Dream and Human Societies,* p. 16.

46. In a different tradition, it is said that Peter the Hermit, who canvassed the idea of the Crusades in medieval Europe, based support for the idea on a dream in which he heard the call to prepare for armed assault. C. Mackay, *Extraordinary Popular Delusions and the Madness of Crowds*, London: Richard Bentley, 1852; reprint, New York: Farrar, Straus and Giroux, 1932, p. 360.

47. Trimingham, *Islam in West Africa*, pp. 34–35.

48. Ibid., pp. 112–113.

49. Jobson, *Golden Trade*, p. 64.

50. Ibid., p. 64.

51. Ibid., p. 77.

52. The origin of the Mandinka word *safe* is unclear. The nearest Arabic word is *sifá'a*, meaning medicament, and with a slight vowel shift the Mandinka word can be derived. But this is all speculative.

53. Park, *Travels in Africa*, p. 28.

54. Paul Marty, *L'Islam en Guinée*, Paris: E. Leroux, 1921, p. 484.

55. Ibid., pp. 484–485.

56. Trimingham, *Islam in West Africa*, p. 103.

57. An instance cited by Fisher, "Hassebu: Islamic Healing in Black Africa," in *Northern Africa: Islam and Modernization*, ed. Michael Brett, London: Frank Cass, 1973, p. 28.

58. Ibid.

59. Harold W. Turner, *History of an African Independent Church: Church of the Lord (Aladur)*, vol. 1, Oxford: Clarendon Press, 1967, p. 9.

60. E. A. Ayandele, *Holy Johnson: Pioneer of African Nationalism*, London: Longman Publishers, 1970, pp. 356–357.

61. West African Islamic clerics generally, and the Jakhanké in particular, do not appear to make this kind of rigid distinction between religious healing and herbal or modern medicine. However, the *shuyúkh* of Mouride Brotherhood, for example, have resisted modern dispensaries because these challenge their control of healing procedures (Donal Cruise O'Brien, *The Mourides of Senegal*, Oxford: Clarendon Press, 1971, p. 232).

62. For faith healing in general see Fisher, "Hassebu," pp. 23–35.

63. In the sixteenth century, for example, the tomb of the *qádí* 'Uthmán Daramé was popular for this reason: any petitions brought there were always answered, and the sick healed (Ka'ti, *Ta'ríkh al-Fattásh*, p. 171).

64. O'Brien, *Mourides of Senegal*, p. 97.

65. Ibid., p. 105.

Chapter Three

1. As reported in E. W. Blyden, *Christianity, Islam, and the Negro Race*, London, 1887; reprint Edinburgh: Edinburgh University Press, 1969, 1971, pp. 319–320.

2. The abolition of slavery in the interior was undertaken by the French in their West African colonies beginning in 1905. In the Gambia, the Slave Abolition Ordinance was promulgated in 1906. However, the process was always a slow one. It was not until 1922 that the French finally suppressed public slave dealing in Morocco and c. 1930 that their control of the Saharan interior was sufficient effectively to end the trade. In Northern Nigeria, although abolition began in 1907, a new order was still required in 1936 to make the abolition mandatory. (See R. Brunschvig, "Abd," in *Encyclopaedia of Islam*, New Edition, Leiden: E.J. Brill, 1960, p. 39.)

3. Yusuf Fadl Hasan, *The Arabs and the Sudan*, Edinburgh: Edinburgh University Press, 1967, pp. 43, 46.

4. Hasan, *Arabs and the Sudan*, p. 43; also Washington Irving, *The Lives of the Successors of Mahomet*, Leipzig: n.p., 1850, p. 239.

5. Cited in Bernard Lewis, *Race and Slavery in the Middle East: An Historical Enquiry*, New York: Oxford University Press, 1992, p. 41.

6. See Mungo Park, *Travels in Africa: 1795–1797*, 1799; reprint, London: Everyman's Library, 1965, p. 222ff; Francis Moore, *Travels into the Inland Parts of Africa*, London: n.p., 1738, p. 29, for examples in Black Africa. Punishment for theft and insolvency as a source of slaves is of great antiquity, see, e.g. Leviticus 25:39; Deuteronomy 15:12; Exodus 22:2–4.

7. "Slaves by peaceful means tended, from an early date, to compete with the forcible method" (R. Brunschvig, "Abd," in *Encyclopaedia of Islam*, New Edition, Leiden: E. J. Brill, 1960, p. 32).

8. Ibid.

9. Ahmad Bábá (1556–1627), a Sudanic scholar, wrote a short treatise on slavery, the *Mi'ráj*, in which he argues forcefully that the reason and grounds for slavery are nonbelief, not the color of a person's skin, referring in this to the wide-scale practice of using color as a justification for enslavement. (See Bábá, 1977.) Over 300 years later Ahmad Bábá was quoted with approval by the nineteenth century Moroccan, al-Násirí, who said that in view of the serious doubt surrounding the true state of blacks enslaved it is better to presume their freedom until incontrovertible proof can be advanced to the contrary, and in that process the testimony of slave-dealers and traders should be dismissed a priori: they are tainted witnesses. He writes: "We would say that even if there were no more than a strong doubt in this matter . . . there would be . . . a case for preventive action, which is a principle of the Holy Law . . . sufficient to oblige one to cease having anything to do with an evil which is derogatory to honor and religion." (Text given in Hunwick, 1976.)

10. Ibn Khaldún, *Al-Muqaddimah: An Introduction to History*, vol. 1, Princeton: Princeton University Press in the Bollingen Series, ed. and trans. Franz Rosenthal, 2nd ed., 1968, p. 304.

11. Joseph Schacht, *An Introduction to Islamic Law*, Oxford: Clarendon Press, 1964, p. 127.

12. The *askiya* Dawúd of Songhay (reigned 1549–1583) gallantly rewarded the clerics of Timbuktu with numerous slave cargoes. When in one instance his generosity was repudiated he sought to redeem himself by granting further batches of slaves. 'Abd al-Rahmán Ka'ti, *Ta'ríkh al-Fattásh*, trans. O. Houdas and M. Delafosse, Alger: n.p., 1913; reprint, Paris: Librairie d'Amérique et d'Orient, Adrien-Maisonneuve, 1964, pp. 196, 198; Ar. text p. 106.

13. Cited in Lewis, *Race and Slavery*, p. 53.

14. Theophilus Conneau, *A Slave's Logbook; Or, Twenty Years' Residence in Africa*, [1854], New Jersey: n.p., 1976, pp. 69–70.

15. See Neil Baillie, ed. and trans., *Digest of Moohummudan Law: Containing the Doctrines of the Hanifeea Code of Jurisprudence*, [1869–1875], Lahore: Premier Book House, 1974, pp. 363ff.

16. Qur'án vii:4. Elsewhere an oblique reference can be found, ix:14. After the famous Battle of Badr, the Prophet ordered that some of the Meccan captives could secure their redemption on condition that each captive taught ten Medinan Muslims how to write, this at a time when the early Muslim recruits were mostly illiterate. Muir 1858/61: I, ix.

17. See Ibn Abí Zayd al-Qayrawání, *La Risálah: Ou épitre sue les éléments du dogme et de la loi de l'Islam selon le rite malikte*, ed. and trans. Léon Bercher, Alger: Éditions Jules Carbonel, 1952; English edition, trans. and ed. Joseph Kenny, *The Risálah*, Minna, Nigeria: The Islamic Educational Trust, 1992, pp. 220–230, 262, 272.

18. Imám Málik, *Al-Muwatta*, London: Diwan Press, 1982, p. 371.

19. Ibid., p. 372.

20. Ibid., p. 375.

21. Ibid., p. 378.

22. Ibid., p. 380. See also Joseph Schacht, *The Origins of Muhammedan Jurisprudence,* Oxford: Clarendon Press, 1950, pp. 279–280.

23. Malik, *Al-Muwatha,* p. 384.

24. Ibid.

25. Ibid.

26. Ibid., p. 385.

27. In actual fact such slaves have been sold. See Schacht, *Origins of Muhammedan Jurisprudence,* p. 173.

28. Ibid., p. 277.

29. Ibid. Qur'án iv:24.

30. Schacht, *Origins of Muhammedan Jurisprudence,* pp. 325–327.

31. Baillie, *Digest of Moohummudan Law,* p. 43.

32. Qayrawání, *The Risálah,* p. 179. In other legal schools the limit is two, in line with the principle that the slave is entitled to half the penalty of a free person in the penal code.

33. Qayrawání, 1945, p. 323. Also Qur'án iv:36; ix:60; xxiv:58. This sentiment was expressed by a local Mandinka Muslim to Dr. Blyden in Liberia, as we saw in the quote at the head of this chapter. "O man of understanding, be not arrogant over your slave or make yourself superior to him. Seek with kindness what God has decreed to you of profit from him" (Edward W. Blyden, *Christianity, Islam, and the Negro Race,* 1887; reprint Edinburgh: Edinburgh University Press, 1967, pp. 364–365). It is evident here that slavery is believed to be God's decree. Discretional manumission does not alter or weaken the force of the law recognizing it.

34. Al-Hájj Shaykh Sidiya Jabi, field interview, Brikama, 28 October 1972. Samori is said to have been enslaved himself in adolescence. Some traditions say that he bound himself to slavery to redeem his mother. (See John Hargreaves, *Prelude to the Partition of West Africa,* London: Macmillan, 1963, p. 244; also Yves Person, *Samori: Une Révolution dyula,* vol. 1, Dakar: Institut Fondamental de L'Afrique Noire, 1968–1970, *passim.*)

35. Pierre Smith, "Les Diakhanké: Histoire d'une dispersion," *Bulletin et Mémoire de la Societé Anthropologie de Paris* 11, no. 8, 1965, pp. 255–256.

36. Charlotte Quinn, "A Nineteenth-Century Fulbe State," *Journal of African History* 12, 1971, pp. 437, 438.

37. Al-Hájj Janko Darame, Jimara-Bakadaji, 12 November 1972. See p. 86ff. For Jakhanké opposition to Samori in Touba, see Person, "The Atlantic Coast and the Southern Savannahs," *History of West Africa,* vol. 2, ed. J.F.A. Ajayi and Michael Crowder, London: Longman Publishers, 1974.

38. Al-Hájj Shaykh Sidiya Jabi, field interview, Brikama, 28 October 1972.

39. Eleven thousand is the estimate given by Al-Hájj Soriba Jabi, field interview, Macca-Kolibantang, 9 October 1972; 12,000 by Ba Fode Jakhabi, field interview, Georgetown, 2 December 1972. The number is unexpectedly large but there is no reason to suspect deliberate invention.

40. *TKB* lists numerous concubines of Karamokho Ba and his successors.

41. *TKB:* folio 4.

42. Al-Hájj Shaykh Sidiya Jabi, field interview, Brikama, 28 October 1972.

43. Ibid.

44. Al-Hájj Mbalu Fodé Jabi, field interview, Marssassoum, 18 January 1973. Mbalu Fode was the grandson of Qutubo through his father Karamokho Madi, also known as al-Maghílí.

45. Al-Hájj Soriba Jabi, field interview, Macca-Kolibantang, 9 December 1972.

46. Ch. Monteil, "Le légende de Ouagadou et l'origine des Soninké," *Mémoire de l'IFAN* 23, 1953, p. 371.

47. Al-Hájj Soriba Jabi, field interview, Macca-Kolibantang, 9 December 1972.

48. Marty 1915/16: 280; Fisher 1970: 59n.

49. Richard Jobson, *The Golden Trade; or, A Discovery of the River Gambia, 1620–21, 1623*; reprint, London, 1968, p. 101.

50. Jean Suret-Canale, "Touba in Guinea—Holy Place of Islam," in *African Perspective,* ed. Christopher Allen and R. W. Johnson, Cambridge: Cambridge University Press, 1970, p. 68.

51. Al-Hájj Soriba Jabi, field interview, Macca-Kolibantang, 9 December 1972.

52. Al-Hájj Janko Darame, field interview, Jimara-Bakadaji, 11 December 1972. Many of these names were adopted by the slaves in recognition of their master's name. Sisekunda, for example, was owned by the Sise clerics. But names like Jallokunda indicate the Fula ethnic group from which the slaves originally came.

53. Al-Hájj Janko Darame, field interview, Jimara-Bakadaji, 11 December 1972.

54. Al-Hájj Mukhtár Jabi, field interview, Sutukung, 16 November 1972.

55. Muhammad Kebba Silla, field interview, Sutukung, 16 November 1972 (on tape). This source says that Karang Sambu Lamin was invited to a solemn community meeting as he prepared to leave Sutukung after a brief second visit. The meeting reminded him of an earlier promise he had made about adopting Sutukung as his home and held him to honor it. At that time Karang Sambu was teaching at Niamina-Jáfai.

56. Shaykh Farûqi Jakhabi, field interview, Sutukung, 16 November 1972.

57. Park, *Travels in Africa,* p. 16.

58. Durand, 1806, p. 44.

59. Reade, 1864, p. 582.

60. Park, *Travels in Africa,* p. 243.

61. Ibid., p. 18.

62. J. Bala Abuja, "Koranic and Modern Law Teaching in Hausaland," *Nigeria* 37, 1951, pp. 27–28. Also John Spencer Trimingham, *Islam in West Africa,* Oxford: Clarendon Press, 1959, p. 160.

63. Paul Marty, *L'Islam en Guinée,* Paris: E. Leroux, 1921, p. 135.

64. Ibid., p. 119.

65. Wilks 1968, p. 171.

66. Cf. Wilks 1968, p. 171. Al-Hájj Madi Hawa, now deceased, had numerous students from a fair distance, and not only the children of his three brothers but his own teenage brother have been fully occupied with education, a privilege some clerics in weak centers cannot enjoy.

67. Qayrawání, 1952, pp. 222–224. Upon default of payment such a slave forfeits his rights to emancipation and to the part of the sum already paid.

68. Kalámulláh Sise, field interview, Jimara-Bakadaji, 11 December 1972. Cf. Brunschvig, "Abd."

69. Kalámulláh Sise, *loc. cit.;* Isháq, 1956, pp. 114, 120. In Sháfi'í law the *zakát* is similarly not required of a slave (Chodjá' 1935, p. 17).

70. Brunschvig, "Abd."

71. Vincent Monteil, *L'Islam noir,* Paris: Seuil, 1964, p. 110.

72. Park says that at the ceremonies he attended it took two months and more for full recuperation. *Travels in Africa,* pp. 203–204.

73. This information comes from a public meeting in which the subject of the interview was Kalámulláh Sise, Jimara-Bakadaji. Perhaps as the result of a long process of conditioning, the slave families of Bakadaji are claimed to be the most ardent defenders of their own low caste status.

74. Notes are taken from a conversation with Mrs. Fatumata Sise, Serrekunda, February 1973. The example here refers to Bani-Kantora.

75. Al-Hájj Soriba Jabi, field interview, Macca-Kolibantang, 9 December 1972; also Qayrawání, 1945, p. 180.

76. Al-Hájj Soriba Jabi, *loc. cit.* According to this source, a slave master can compute on a daily basis and estimate the number of years a slave is likely to be in active service, and the sum arrived at that way is put to the charge of the slave.

77. Al-Hájj Soriba Jabi, *loc. cit.*

78. Qayrawání, 1952, p. 178.

79. This is based on the explicit ruling of the Qur'án iv:30.

80. Qur'án iv:3; also Qayrawání, 1945, p. 178. Concubinage (*istisrár*) is part of the same process as marriage of slave women (xxiv:32). The special provision in the law that recognizes the taking of an unlimited number of concubines removes the pressure for taking slave women as co-wives. The Qur'án, however, encourages the latter course, iv:28.

81. See also Park, *Travels in Africa*, p. 205.

82. Commenting on the society of Murzuq, which is known to be atypical, Nachtigal said that concubines were sometimes preferred to wives since the threat of resale acts as a check on fidelity. Nachtigal goes on: "If one considers that a slave girl, apart from the stronger motive for fidelity . . . is also by nature more industrious, more obedient, and less demanding, one cannot wonder that in these regions many prefer lawful concubinage, and in many houses where there are legitimate wives, the master's preference is to his slave girl." ([1879/89: I 102–03] 1974: I 95).

83. The *alkali* and others, field interview, Jimara-Bakadaji, 11 December 1972.

84. Isháq 1956: I 142.

85. Jobson, *Golden Trade*, pp. 87–88.

86. Moore, *Travels into the Inland Parts of Africa*, 29ff.

87. Park, *Travels in Africa*, p. 127.

88. Caillie, 1830: I 266–268.

89. Cecil Sitwell, 1893, pp. 190–192.

90. Colonial Office Records number CO/87/109, 6 January 1876, cited in Charlotte Quinn, *Mandingo Kingdoms of Senegambia*, Berkeley and Los Angeles: University of California Press, 1972, pp. 139–140.

91. The Slave Abolition Ordinance, Ref. 2/96, 1906, Records Office, Banjul.

92. In parts of Guinea, for example, the descendants of slaves still maintain their separate caste distinctions and their Fulbé patrons restrict them socially. See W. Derman, *Serfs, Peasants, and Socialists: A Former Serf Village in the Republic of Guinea*, Berkeley and Los Angeles: University of California Press, 1973, pp. 27–42ff.

93. Al-Hájj Soriba Jabi, field interview, Macca-Kolibantang, 9 December 1972. This may be a reference to the captives Mama Sambou presumably acquired during his military operations in Fogny, an area of Jola concentration. A story relates that the Jola gave him the name Sambou as a substitute for Shu'aibou because of a linguistic modification that still occurs in the Jola language.

94. Ba Fode Jakhabi, field interview, Georgetown, 2 December 1972.

95. Ba Fode Jakhabi, *loc. cit.*, says that while the French were making life difficult for the Touba Jakhanké, they were also taking similar actions against Muslim insurgents in Senegambia: Ma Ba, Lat Dior, Saer Mati Ba, Al-Bouri Ndiaye, all of them allies in a common cause against the French, Fode Kabba, and others. For this theme in Senegambian history, see Klein, 1972.

96. In a report in the *New York Times* slavery continues to be practiced in Muslim societies in Africa. See Charles Jacobs and Mohamed Athie, "Bought and Sold," (Op-Ed, 13 July 1994), for slavery in Northern Africa. See also letters to the editor, 30 July 1994. One correspondent testified: "Charles Jacobs and Mohamed Athie, in 'Bought and Sold' (Op-Ed, July 13), describe the existence of slavery in Mauritania and other areas of North Africa. I visited a Berber family in Mauritania in 1977, when I was a Peace Corps volunteer in neighboring Senegal. As we were served food by an elderly black man, my host said: 'He belongs to my father. His father belonged to my grandfather.' A number of people have flatly refused to believe this anecdote in the years since. None had spent time in Africa." Stuart F. Brown, Hollywood, July 21, 1994. For a comparative study of slavery see Patrick Manning, *Slavery and African Life: Occidental, Oriental, and African Slave Trades*, Cambridge: Cam-

bridge University Press, 1990, and Suzanne Miers and Richard Roberts, eds., *The End of Slavery in Africa*, Madison: University of Wisconsin Press, 1988.

Part Two

1. Cited in Christopher Harrison, *France and Islam in West Africa: 1860–1960*, Cambridge: Cambridge University Press, 1988, pp. 58–59.
2. Cited in Harrison, *France and Islam*, p. 59.
3. Cited in Harrison, *France and Islam*, p. 38.
4. Captain Frèrejean, a veteran of the French Mauritanian campaigns, in Harrison, *France and Islam*, p. 40.
5. Captain Lefebvre of the Niger campaign, in Harrison, *France and Islam*, pp. 46–47.
6. Governor William Ponty, writing in 1906, in Harrison, *France and Islam*, p. 55.
7. Cited in Harrison, *France and Islam*, p. 51.
8. Cited in Harrison, *France and Islam*, p. 52.

Chapter Four

1. Archives Féderales de Dakar (hereafter AFD), 7 G 99, Dossier no. 1: "Affaire Tierno Aliou ou le Oualy de Goumba," 1910–1912, p. 19.
2. Ibid., p. 6.
3. Paul Marty, *L'Islam en Guinée: Fouta Diallon*, Paris: E. Leroux, 1921, pp. 40–55.
4. John Spencer Trimingham, *The Sufi Orders in Islam*, Oxford: Clarendon Press, 1971, pp. 47–51, 84–90.
5. Ibid., p. 50. See also Annemarie Schimmel, *Mystical Dimensions of Islam*, Chapel Hill: University of North Carolina Press, 1975, pp. 250–251.
6. Ibn 'Ata'llah, *The Book of Wisdom*, ed. and trans. Victor Danner, in the series *Classics of Western Spirituality*, New York: Paulist Press, 1978.
7. John Spencer Trimingham, *A History of Islam in West Africa*, London: Oxford University Press, 1962, p. 159.
8. AFD, 7 G 99, Despatch no. 360 (15 April 1911), pp. 1–2.
9. Marty, *L'Islam en Guinée*, p. 478.
10. Ibid., p. 477.
11. Ibid.
12. Cited in Harrison, *France and Islam*, p. 78.
13. AFD, 7 G 99, Despatch no. 360 (15 April 1911), pp. 1–2.
14. Ibid.
15. Ibid.
16. Ibid., p. 4.
17. Ibid., p. 5.
18. See, for example, Thierno Diallo, *Alfa Yaya: Roi du Labé (Fouta Djallon)*, Paris, Dakar, and Abidjan: NEA, 1976.
19. Jean Suret-Canale, "Touba in Guinea—Holy Place of Islam," in *African Perspectives*, ed. Christopher Allen and R. W. Johnson, London, 1970, p. 71. Until now the fullest treatment of Tcherno Aliou's troubles is that by M. Verdat, "Le Ouali de Goumba," *Etudes Guinéennes* 3 (1949), pp. 3–66.
20. *L'A.O.F. Echo de la côte occidentale d'Afrique* (hereafter *Echo*), 20 September 1911.
21. Ibid.
22. AFD, Dossier no. 170: "Administrative Report of Kindia," 19 April 1911, p. 21.
23. *Echo*, 22 September 1911, p. 2.
24. Ibid.
25. Ibid.

26. Ibid., testimony of Ouri Monouna, pp. 3–4.

27. Text of treaty reproduced in Marty, *L'Islam en Guinée,* appendix 13.

28. *Echo,* 23 September 1911, p. 2.

29. Martin A. Klein, *Islam and Imperialism in Senegal,* Edinburgh: Edinburgh University Press and Stanford: Stanford University Press, 1968, pp. 169–170.

30. Lamin Sanneh, "Futa Jallon and the Jakhanke Clerical Tradition. Part I: The Historical Setting," *Journal of Religion in Africa* 12, no. 1 (1981), p. 53.

31. W. Derman, *Serfs, Peasants, and Socialists: A Former Serf Village in the Republic of Guinea,* Berkeley and Los Angeles: University of California Press, 1973.

32. *Echo,* 23 September 1911, p. 3.

33. AFD, 7 G 99, Dossier no. 132, 22 April 1912, pp. 1–2.

34. AFD, 7 G 63, Dossier no. 50, 21 August 1912. Estimates put the number of schools at no less than 3,000, with 15,000 pupils, of whom about 1,500 were adults. A similar number of children was at any given time under instruction at home.

35. Cited in Harrison, *France and Islam,* pp. 65–66.

36. Ibid., p. 43.

37. AFD, 7 G 87, Dossier. no. 18, 1912, p. 7.

38. AFD, 7 G 99, Dossier, no. 130, May 1912, p. 2.

39. Ibid., pp. 3–4.

40. Ibid., Dossier no. 132, 22 April 1912, p. 2.

41. Marty, *L'Islam en Guinée,* p. 59.

42. See the discussion of "enclavement" in Lamin Sanneh, "The Domestication of Christianity and Islam in African Societies," *Journal of Religion in Africa* 11 no. 1 (1980), pp. 1–12.

43. Marty, *L'Islam en Guinée,* p. 57.

44. Ibid.

45. Ibid., pp. 63–64.

46. Ibid.

47. Ibid., p. 65.

48. Ibid., p. 66.

49. Ibid.

50. Lamin Sanneh, *The Jakhanké Muslim Clerics: A Religious and Historical Study of Islam in Senegambia,* Lanham, Md.: University Press of America, 1989.

51. See the references to Turner and Honko in note 59. Also Humphrey J. Fisher, "Liminality, Hijra, and the City," in *Rural and Urban Islam in West Africa,* ed. Nehemia Levtzion and Humphrey J. Fisher, Boulder: Lynne Rienner, 1987.

52. Marty, *L'Islam en Guinée,* p. 61.

53. Ibid.

54. Ibid.

55. Ibid., p. 62.

56. Ibid., p. 63. Jean Suret-Canale observed in this connection that the *awliyá* had been diverted into establishing dissident chieftaincies in the tradition of the Hubbubé, but he has erred in treating Tcherno Aliou as such or in failing to recognize that the so-called *parvenu* class of *'ulamá* was different from the older scholarly class, whose members had become parasites of the discredited Fulbé *mawubé.* Suret-Canale, "Touba in Guinea," p. 73.

57. Boubacar Barry, "L'Expansion du Fuuta Jallon vers la côte et les crises politiques et sociales dans la Sénégambie méridionale au cours de la première moitié du xixéme siècle," unpublished MS, pp. 14–15.

58. Blyden as quoted, in ibid., p. 14.

59. Victor Turner, *The Ritual Process: Structure and Anti-Structure,* Ithaca: Cornell University Press, 1982. See also idem, *Dramas, Fields, and Metaphors: Symbolic Action in Human*

Society, Ithaca: Cornell University Press, 1983, especially the chapter "Metaphors of Anti-Structure in Religious Culture." For a critical assessment of ritual theory, see Lauri Honko, ed., *Science of Religion: Studies in Methodology,* The Hague: Mouton, 1979, pp. 369–427.

60. Fisher, "Liminality, *Hijra,* and the City," pp. 147–171.

61. Edward Wilmot Blyden, *Christianity, Islam, and the Negro Race,* 1887; reprint, Edinburgh, 1971, p. 206. Elsewhere in the same source (e.g., pp. 312–315) Dr. Blyden identifies "Samudu" as Almamy Samori, called by him "Imam Ahmadu Samudu." Thus, it would appear that the Hubbubé met their end at the hands of Samori.

62. Ibn Khaldún, *Al-Muqaddimah: An Introduction to History,* vol. 2, ed. and trans. Franz Rosenthal, Bollingen Series 43, 2nd ed., Princeton: Princeton University Press, 1967, pp. 295–296, 335.

63. Ibn Khaldún, *Al-Muqaddima,* text 2, p. 304, trans. Charles Issawi, *An Arab Philosophy of History,* London: Allen and Unwin, 1963, p. 69.

64. Ibn Khaldún, *Al-Muqaddimah,* text 1, p. 225, trans. Issawi, pp. 66–67.

65. Ibid., text 1, p. 228, trans. Issawi, pp. 67–68.

66. 'Abdalláh ibn Fúdí, *Tazyín al-Waraqát,* ed. and trans. Mervyn Hiskett, Ibadan: Ibadan University Press, 1963, p. 13.

67. Shiháb al-Dín al-Suhrawardí, *Al-Ma'árif,* ed. and trans. Wilberforce Clarke, Calcutta, 1891.

Chapter Five

1. André Gide, *Si le grain ne meurt,* cited in Ernest Gellner, *Muslim Society,* London: Cambridge University Press, 1983, p. 151.

2. Qur'án 2:258; 3:61; 6:51, 69; 17:111; 41:34; 42:7, 27; 45:18; 2:101, 114; 9:75, 117; 13:37; 18:25; 29:21; 32:3; 42:6, 30, 42; 4:77, 122, 173; 6:14; 18:16; 33:17, etc.

3. Ibid., 7:2; 11:22, 115; 13:17; 17:99; 18:48, 102; 25:19; 29:49; 39:4; 42:4, 7, 45; 45:9; 60:1.

4. Ibid., 3:27; 4:91, 138, 143; 5:56, 62, 84; 7:28; 9:23; 10:63; 60:9.

5. Ibid., 2:282.

6. Ibid., 61:11; 83:21, 28.

7. See, for example, Reuben Levy, *The Social Structure of Islam,* Cambridge: Cambridge University Press, 1957; reprint 1965, pp. 55–56. Qur'án 49:13. Baydáwí, *Anwár al-Tanzíl,* ed. H. O. Fleischer, vol. 2, Leipzig: F.C.G. Vogel, 1848, p. 276.

8. Qur'án 19:5.

9. Ibid., 50:15. The translation is that of A. J. Arberry, *The Koran Interpreted,* vol. 2, New York, Macmillan, 1969, p. 234.

10. Nehemia Levtzion, "'Abd Alláh ibn Yasín and the Almoravids," in *Studies in West African Islamic History,* ed. John Ralph Willis, vol. 1, London: Frank Cass, 1979, p. 80.

11. Al-Bakrí, *Kitáb al-Masálik wa'l-Mamálik* ("Book of Routes and Realms"), ed. M. G. de Slane, Algiers: A. Jourdan, 1913, p. 168. The most recent annotated edition is N. Levtzion and J.F.P. Hopkins, eds., *Corpus of Early Arabic Sources for West African History,* Cambridge: Cambridge University Press, 1981, p. 74.

12. For a brief but authoritative account of Ibn Tumart, see Duncan Black Macdonald, *The Development of Muslim Theology and Jurisprudence,* Beirut: Khayat Books, 1965.

13. For a good description of this subject in Muslim Africa, see Humphrey J. Fisher, "Dreams and Conversion in Black Africa," in *Conversion to Islam,* ed. Nehemia Levtzion, New York: Holmes and Meier, 1979, pp. 217–235.

14. J. Spencer Trimingham, *Islam in West Africa,* Oxford: Clarendon Press, 1959, pp. 66, 89–90.

15. Vincent Monteil, *L'Islam noir,* Paris: Seuil, 1964, p. 137.

16. On the Shádhiliyáh, see the previous chapter in this book on "Tcherno Aliou, the *Walí* of Goumba."

17. "Tcherno" is a Fula title meaning "scholar" or "learned teacher," although in this instance most of the personalities so identified were Manding rather than Fula.

18. Victor Turner, *The Ritual Process: Structure and Anti-Structure*, Ithaca: Cornell University Press, 1982. For a searching critique of Turner, see Humphrey Fisher, "Liminality, Hijrah, and the City," *Journal of Asian and African Studies* 20, no. 1 (1986): pp. 153–177, or "Liminality, Hijra, and the City," in *Rural and Urban Islam in West Africa*, ed. Nehemia Levtzion and Humphrey J. Fisher, Boulder: Lynne Rienner Publishers, 1987.

19. The term *sirr* occurs also in Súfí literature, where it is defined as "mystery," the infusion of the will of the *walí* with that of the All-Powerful. It became the intimate thought of the *walí* or *shaykh* to the extent he was under the divine influence. Some authorities go so far as to make it the germ of the soul. G. C. Anawati and Louis Gardet, *Mystique musulmane: Aspects et tendances—expériences et techniques*, Paris: Librairie philosophique J. Vrin, 1961, p. 226. Such pantheistic tendencies are slight in African Islam.

20. Paul Marty, *L'Islam en Guinée*, Paris: E. Leroux, 1921, p. 477; Trimingham, *Islam in West Africa*, p. 121.

21. On the *walí* of Goumba, for example, see Marty, *L'Islam en Guinée*, p. 477. In this connection mention should be made of the Jakhanké religious clerics, who saw themselves as standing firmly in the tradition of ethical moderation, an attitude that had a profound impact on the populations of Futa Jallon and beyond. Jakhanké clerics intervened in secular affairs to settle disputes, using their religious reputation to good effect in quiet diplomacy. L. Sanneh, *The Jakhanké Muslim Clerics: A Religious and Historical Study of Islam in Senegambia*, Lanham, Md.: University Press of America, 1989, pp. 101–102, 105, 115. A segment of the Jakhanké community spread to Kano in the fifteenth century during the reign of Muhammad Rimfa (1463–1499), who was so impressed by the saintly qualities of the Jakhanké clerical leader, 'Abd ad-Rahmán Jakhite, that he asked to be buried by the latter's graveside so that, in his own words, "I might inherit his *baraka*." (Sanneh, *Jakhanké*, p. 35).

22. Cited in Vincent Monteil, "Marabouts," in Kritzeck and Lewis, eds., *Islam in Africa*, ed. J. Kritzeck and W. H. Lewis, New York: Van-Nostrand, 1969, p. 89.

23. Fernand Dumont, *La Pensée réligieuse d'Amadou Bamba*, Dakar and Abidjan: Nouvelles editions Africaines, 1975, pp. 71–72.

24. Paul Marty, *Les Mourides d'Amadou Bamba*, Paris: E. Leroux, 1913, pp. 52–53. Cited in Donal Cruise O'Brien, *The Mourides of Senegal*, Oxford: Clarendon Press, 1971, p. 53.

25. Dumont, *La Pensée*, pp. 21–22.

26. O'Brien, *Mourides*, p. 143.

27. Ibid., p. 54.

28. Dumont, *La Pensée*, p. 85.

29. Ibid., p. 123.

30. Ibid., p. 88.

31. Ibid., p. 90.

32. Ibid.

33. Ibid., p. 95.

34. Ibid., p. 96.

35. Ibid., p. 112.

36. Ibid., p. 114.

37. Amar Sambe, *Diplôme d'études supérieures*, Faculté des Lettres, Université de Paris, 1964, p. 185. Cited in O'Brien, *Mourides*, p. 89.

38. O'Brien, *Mourides*, p. 85.

39. Ibid., p. 88.

40. Ibid., p. 85.

41. Ibid., p. 152.

42. Ibid., p. 165.

43. Sanneh, *Jakhanké*, pp. 147–184.

44. Tcherno Bokar Salifu Taal (c. 1883–1940), as quoted by Louis Brenner, *West African Sufi: The Religious Heritage and Spiritual Search of Cerno Bokar Saalif Taal,* London: Christopher Hurst, 1984, p. 114.

45. For example, O'Brien, *Mourides,* p. 302. O'Brien later revised his own position in "A Versatile Charisma: The Mouride Brotherhood 1967–1975," *Archives européenes de sociologie* 18 (1977), pp. 84–106.

Part Three

1. Ibn Khaldún, *Al-Muqaddimah: An Introduction to History,* vol. 3, ed. and trans. Franz Rosenthal, Bollingen Series 43, 2nd ed., Princeton: Princeton University Press, 1967, p. 304ff.

2. Milton, *Of Education.*

3. The Súdání Muslim leader and man of affairs, Dr. Hassan al-Turábí, speaks of Qur'ánic education as necessary for the legitimacy of governance in contemporary Muslim countries. "In the Sudan, Islamic Leader Talks of Tolerance," *New York Times,* 6 December 1994.

Chapter Six

1. This account is drawn from the author's experience in the Gambia, West Africa, in the 1950s.

2. John Spencer Trimingham, *Islam in West Africa,* Oxford: Clarendon Press, 1959, p. 38.

3. Members of the Tijániyya, a Súfí order founded in the eighteenth century by Ahmad al-Tijání. The order is widespread and popular throughout the Muslim areas of West Africa.

4. Member of the Qádiriyya, a Súfí order founded in the twelfth century by 'Abd al-Qádir al Jílání. This sect, too, is widespread throughout West Africa. Some rivalry exists between its adherents and those of the Tijániyya, which finds expression in West African politics as well as in religious attitudes.

5. The ninth month of the Islamic lunar calendar.

Chapter Seven

1. Cited in Mervyn Hiskett, "Problems of Religious Education in Muslim Communities in Africa," *Oversea Education* 32, no. 3 (October 1960), p. 119.

2. Haroun al-Rashid Adamu, *The North and Nigerian Unity: Some Reflections on the Political, Social, and Educational Problems of Northern Nigeria,* Lagos: Daily Times, 1973, p. 55.

3. Adamu, *The North and Nigerian Unity,* p. 57.

4. Selim Hakim, *Report: The Teaching of Arabic in Schools and Colleges in Nigeria,* unpublished MS, Ibadan, 1961, p. 6.

5. Hiskett, "Problems in Religious Education," p. 119.

6. Cited in Alhaji Sir Ahmadu Bello, Sardauna of Sokoto, *My Life,* Cambridge: Cambridge University Press, 1962; reprinted Zaria: Gaskiya Corporation, 1986, p. 29.

7. Bello, *My Life,* p. 31.

8. Adamu, *The North and Nigerian Unity,* p. 48.

9. Cited in ibid., p. 33.

10. See, for example, article by Murray Last, "Aspects of Administration and Dissent in Hausaland: 1800–1968," *Africa* 40, no. 4 (October 1970).

11. *Islam in Nigeria: A Report by Professor Mangin*, cited in Adamu, *The North and Nigerian Unity*, p. 16.

12. The point is developed in the chapter that follows, "Action and Reaction Among Freetown Muslims."

13. Humphrey Fisher, "Islamic Education and Religious Reform in West Africa," in *Education in Africa*, ed. Richard Jolly, Nairobi, Kenya: East African Publishing, 1969.

14. Ibid.

15. Among the objectives of Islamic centers in Belgium are educational facilities for Muslim children, to encourage research on Islam, organize lectures and studies, arrange conferences, undertake missionary activity, and act as a Muslim pressure group in relations with the Belgian authorities. This information comes from a special report drawn up at the time of the Belgian decision.

16. See the previous chapter, "A Childhood Muslim Education."

17. Details in Lamin Sanneh, *The Jakhanke Muslim Clerics: A Religious and Historical Study of Islam in Senegambia*, Lanham, Md.: University Press of America, 1989, p. 143ff.

18. J. Spencer Trimingham, *Islam in West Africa*, Oxford: Clarendon Press, 1959, p. 35.

19. Lamin Sanneh, *West African Christianity: The Religious Impact*, Maryknoll, N.Y.: Orbis Books, 1983, p. 144f.

20. A. R. Dehaini, *Report on Qur'án Schools in the Western State of Nigeria*, unpublished MS, Ibadan, 1965.

21. M. S. el-Garh, "Arabic in Nigeria: Why, When, and How To Teach It," seminar paper (unpublished), Ibadan, November 1970, p. 3.

22. Hakim, *Report*.

23. Dehaini, *Report on Qur'án Schools*.

24. Cited in el-Garh, "Arabic in Nigeria," p. 31.

25. See Chapter 8, "Action and Reaction Among Freetown Muslims," for details.

26. Ibid.

27. Proudfoot and Wilson, "Muslim Attitudes to Education," p. 92.

28. Sanneh, "Modern Education."

29. A famous example was when the Church Missionary Society (C.M.S.) college in Freetown, Fourah Bay College, employed Muhammad Sanusi and Muhammad Wakka to teach Arabic there in 1876. A little earlier, in 1845, the C.M.S. founded the Sierra Leone Grammar School on the principle of open access to all members of the Freetown community. Christopher Fyfe, ed., *Sierra Leone Inheritance*, London: Oxford University Press, 1964, p. 150.

30. Humphrey J. Fisher, *The Ahmadiyya*, London: Oxford University Press, 1963.

31. Sanneh, "Modern Education."

32. Hiskett, "Problems of Religious Education," p. 124.

33. Hakim, *Report*.

34. Musa Abdul, *A Report on Arabic and Islamic Studies in Secondary Schools in Nigeria*, unpublished MS, Ibadan, 1965.

35. John O. Hunwick, *Report on the Seminar on the Teaching of Arabic in Nigeria*, Ibadan, 11–15 July 1965, unpublished MS.

36. Selim Hakim, *Ta'lím al-Lughah al-'Arabiyyah fí Níjíriya*, Baghdad: n.p., 1966.

37. Selim Hakim, *al-'Arabiyyah al-Jadídah fí Níjíriya*, Ibadan: Longmans of Nigeria, 1966.

38. Hiskett, "Problems of Religious Education," p. 125.

39. See Fisher's chapter in Brown and Hiskett, 1975.

40. See Chapter 8.

41. El-Garh, "Arabic in Nigeria," p. 31.

42. "Kole Omotoso," *Cape Librarian*, February 1994, pp. 20–21.

43. Proudfoot and Wilson, "Muslim Attitudes to Education," p. 93.

44. Ibid.

45. Ibid.

46. Report in the *New York Times*, "Lagos Journal: Nigeria's Plan: Adopt the (250) Mother Tongues," 23 May 1991.

47. Vincent Cronin, *A Pearl to India: The Life of Robert de Nobili*, London: Rupert Hart Davis, 1959, p. 173.

48. M. H. Bakalla, *Arabic Culture: Through Its Language and Literature*, London and Boston: Kegan Paul International, 1984, p. 19.

49. See, for example, R. Santerre, *Pédagogie Musulmane de l'Afrique Noire*, Presse Universitaire de Montreal, 1975. See also Cheikh Amidou Kane, *Ambiguous Adventure*, London: Heinemann Publishers, 1963, which contains an excellent description of the Qur'án school and the impact of French Western education.

50. S. A. Jimeh, "A Critical Appraisal of Islamic Education with Particular Reference to Critical Happenings on the Nigerian Scene," *Nigerian Journal of Islam* 2, no. 1 (July 1971-January 1972), p. 37.

Chapter Eight

1. See Christopher Fyfe, *A History of Sierra Leone*, London: Oxford University Press, 1962, pp. 13ff, 114ff; P. Kup, *A History of Sierra Leone, 1400–1787*, Cambridge: Cambridge University Press, 1961.

2. *Sierra Leone Colonial Report, 1901*, London: H.M. Stationery Office, 1902, pp. 18–19.

3. The nucleus of the Aku may have been Yoruba Muslims, but it is obvious that their number included Creole Christian converts. I do not know of any satisfactory explanation of how in fact this Yoruba nucleus was able to preserve its language and culture on slave plantations, particularly if dispersal of slaves was a feature of plantation life. If Aku is taken to mean Yoruba and that in turn is taken to mean Muslim, how does one designate Yoruba Christians among the Creole population? Michael Banton hints at the difficulty in linguistic terminology when he writes: "Perhaps 5,000 Creoles would today describe themselves as Aku though the number who can speak Yoruba is much less." (*West African City*, London: Oxford University Press, 1957, p. 153.) In other words "Aku" in fact comprises more than Yoruba-speaking Muslims. In the Gambia Aku is used to describe the entire Creole community, Christian and Muslim, with the latter being distinguished as Aku-Marabout.

4. David E. Skinner, "Islam in Sierra Leone During the Nineteenth Century," unpublished Ph.D. dissertation, Berkeley, 1971, p. 142.

5. Skinner, "Islam in Sierra Leone," pp. 154–156.

6. The word "tamba" comes from a Mandinka phrase, *"tamba muru,"* meaning a "two-edged blade that a man cannot squarely grasp." It was applied to the Fourah Bay Muslim faction after a Mandinka mediation attempt failed. The factions became delicately poised for a confrontation. Leslie Proudfoot, "An Aku Factional Fight in East Freetown," *Sierra Leone Bulletin of Religion* 4, no. 2 (1962), p. 86.

7. Ibid.

8. Michael Banton, *West African City*, pp. 166–167. The word "geda" is Krio, meaning an assembly, gathering, or association, and indicates the eclecticism and aspirations of the founders.

9. Proudfoot, "Mosque-building and Tribal Separatism in Freetown," *Africa* 29, no. 4 (1959), p. 410.

10. Interview with Idriss Alamy, an official of the UAR Cultural Center, Freetown, April 1975.

11. Proudfoot, "Mosque-building," pp. 407–408.

12. Proudfoot, "Towards Muslim Solidarity in Freetown," *Africa* 31 (1961), p. 148.

13. Ibid., p. 155.

14. Ibid. During the visit in 1959 of Shaykh al-Hájj Cherri, an American Lebanese, generous support was received for projects launched by the Muslim Congress.

15. *The Ramadan Vision,* July 1947, p. 4.

16. Proudfoot, "Towards Muslim Solidarity," p. 151.

17. Ibid., p. 152.

18. Ibid.

19. Interview, Abbas Camba, Freetown, January-February 1975. A prominent street in the center of Freetown is named after Lamina Sankoh.

20. *Ramadan Vision,* 19 August 1944, p. 4.

21. Ibid., p. 8.

22. Proudfoot, "Towards Muslim Solidarity," p. 148.

23. *Op.cit.*

24. He dwelt on the Qur'ánic verse about man being a vicegerent of God (ii:28; xxi:105; xxxviii:25) and how man should be a partner with God in engaging in acts of creation in the world. Proudfoot, "Towards Muslim Solidarity."

25. *Ramadan Vision,* July 1947, p. 2.

26. Ibid.

27. Ibid., p. 3. Qur'án xxxiii:35ff (Flugel verse numbering).

28. *Ramadan Vision,* July 1947, p. 6.

29. Interview, Abbas Camba, Freetown, January-February 1975.

30. *Ramadan Vision,* July 1946, pp. 5–6.

31. Interview, Abbas Camba, Freetown, January-February 1975.

32. In actual fact the orchestra continued performing long after the cessation of publication of the *Ramadan Vision* in June 1948. It was run by the Fujalto Muslim Circle, a Fulani tribal association. The name "Fujalto" was derived from Futa Jallon and Futa Toro, where members of the Fulani tribal community originally came from. The orchestra was finally disbanded in 1969 after many of its members left.

33. Leslie Proudfoot and H. S. Wilson, "Muslim Attitudes to Education in Sierra Leone," *The Muslim World* 50, no. 1 (January 1960).

34. Information gathered from Idriss Alamy, interview, April 1975. I visited Magburaka where Ibrahim Kanu is buried in an unmarked grave in the school yard.

35. Kenneth Cragg, *Counsels in Contemporary Islam,* Edinburgh: Edinburgh University Press, 1965, p. 113ff.

36. Humphrey J. Fisher, *Ahmadiyya,* London: Oxford University Press, 1963, p. 179.

37. Idriss Alamy, interview, April 1975. A higher figure of 50 schools is given in a report of a meeting held at Kabala town on Sunday, 8 March 1970. It says in the same report that some 150 more schools were planned. The meeting was organized by the Muslim Propaganda Regional branch.

38. Idriss Alamy, interview, April 1975.

39. The head of the Islamic Institute in Magburaka was until recently Shaykh Faruq. The curriculum is heavily committed to traditional Islamic subjects.

40. Idriss Alamy, interview, April 1975.

41. The audit report claims that of this number only 414 had paid their fees and 5 more were allowed to continue in deferment of payment. A/1-70/71, Audit Report. Fees collected for the third term of the 1970/71 school year amounted to Le.5008:50 or £2504.25p sterling.

42. A mimeographed prospectus was being circulated. Some copies are kept in the files of Muslim Associations at the UAR Cultural Center.

43. Address given by Gibril Abdul Rahim to members of the Sierra Leone Muslim Community in Freetown, 12 July 1970, at the Islamiyah School. Mimeographed copies available.

44. Letter signed by Mr. A.B.S. Conteh and dated 8 October 1971. It was copied to the Ahmadiyah Missionary Movement in Sierra Leone.

45. The translation is my own. The play was not translated into English.

46. Abdul Karim Ghazali, "A Muslim Propaganda Play: De Man Way De Play Gyambul Wit God," *Sierra Leone Bulletin of Religion* 3, no. 2 (December 1961).

47. Proudfoot, "Towards Muslim Solidarity," 1961.

48. The petition was the result of a circular letter addressed to various *imáms* by Mr. Ola Koromah. The letterhead was the Sierra Leone Muslim Congress.

49. Proudfoot, "Towards Muslim Solidarity," pp. 153–154, where the association is reported to have cooperated closely with the Ahmadiyah Movement, but Fisher says only a couple or so of the Yoruba Muslims in Freetown joined the Ahmadiyah. Fisher, "Ahmadiyah in Sierra Leone," *Sierra Leone Bulletin of Religion* 2, no. 1 (June 1960), pp. 1–10. Also Proudfoot, "Ahmed Alhadi and the Ahmadiyah in Sierra Leone," *Sierra Leone Bulletin of Religion* 2, no. 2 (December 1960), pp. 60–68.

50. Fisher, *The Ahmadiyya*, p. 178.

51. Ibid.

52. Mr. Munir, Amir of the Ahmadiyah, interview, April 1975.

53. The offset press operated from their head office: 6 Back Street, Freetown. A bookshop selling these materials and school books and equipment was located at the same address.

54. Kamal Lotfy and Idriss Alamy, interviews, UAR Cultural Center, 8 April 1975.

55. It is said that the students complained about the practice of strict seclusion of women, which prevented contacts at their center. Kamal Lotfy and Idriss Alamy, interviews, 8 April 1975.

56. Information provided by the UAR Cultural Center and other sources.

57. Ibid.

58. Ibid.

59. I myself saw students from the Brotherhood schools on public parade at the Elizabeth Playing Fields in Freetown during the *Mawlid al-Nabí* celebrations on Monday, 24 March 1975. The precise figure was supplied by Idriss Alamy who used to be an auditor of the Brotherhood schools.

60. Article in the *Freetown Daily Mail*, 24 March 1975.

61. Ibid.

62. Ibid.

63. Ibid.

64. Information from the files of the Muslim Associations, UAR Cultural Center (with Idriss Alamy).

65. Ibid.

66. Idriss Alamy, interview, April 1975. See also *We Yone* newspaper, 11 June 1975, and the *Daily Mail* and *The Nation* of the same date.

67. The daily papers quoted in note 66.

68. Official files of the Muslim organizations, UAR Cultural Center. The names of the schools, with tribal affiliation in parenthesis, are Madrassah al Imaniyah (Temne), Nur al-Islam (Susu), al-Amariyah (Aku), Maqamat al-Islam (Temne), al-Almaniyah (Limba), al-Madinah al-Munawarah (Limba), Hayat al-Islam (Susu), Dar al-Hadith (all tribes), al-Salafiyah (all tribes), al-Huda (Loko), al-Rashad (Fula), Taqwa Falah (both mixed), and one school each in Kabala and Wellington.

69. Michael Banton, "Adaptation and Integration in the Social System of Temne Immigrants in Freetown," *Africa* 26, no. 4 (October 1956), p. 355.

70. One of the most ambitious ventures in this field was the Muslim Missionary Pioneers Association, organized and directed by a young convert from Christianity, al-Farid

Ibrahim Cole. It had been producing a number of mimeographed pamphlets called the "Islamic Education Series," devoted to a modern interpretation and defense of Islam.

71. A celebrated case of hair-splitting was the attempt by Ahmed Alhadi to define in highly legalistic language the separate functions of the Almamy and *imâm*, which ended by saying both officials have joint responsibility for the internal administration of their community. Proudfoot, "Aku Factional Fight," p. 8. A different matter involving litigiousness occurred in December 1970 and involved a check drawn on the account of Sir Banja Tejan-Sie, a Muslim who was then governor-general. The check was made out to Mr. L. S. Fofana and given to Arun al-Rashid, a pupil of the Muslim Brotherhood Secondary School at Berry Street of which Mr. Fofana was a former principal. It is not clear what the money was for, but al-Rashid cashed the check and with the money paid his school fees, presumably on the understanding that he was being supported by Sir Banja. This touched off a dispute leading to an inquiry. It erupted into a bitter feud with the Brotherhood school and the people connected with it as principals in the dispute.

Chapter Nine

1. For a summary of the views of Machiavelli and Bodin in the context of the modern national state see Sir Ernest Barker, *Principles of Social and Political Theory,* Oxford: Clarendon Press, 1951, p. 13ff.

2. Lord Hailey, *An African Survey: Revised 1956,* Oxford: Clarendon Press, 1957, p. 145.

3. See Basil Davidson, *The Black Man's Burden: Africa and the Curse of the Nation State,* London: James Currey, 1992, p. 107.

4. Holger Bernt Hansen, *Mission, Church, and State in a Colonial Setting: Uganda: 1890–1925,* London: Heinemann, 1984, p. 25ff.

5. Hansen, *Mission,* p. 26.

6. M. W. Waldman, "The Church of Scotland Mission at Blantyre, Nyasaland: Its Political Implications," *Bulletin of the Society of African Church History* 2, no. 4 (1968), pp. 299–310.

7. See Max Stackhouse, "Politics and Religion," *Encyclopedia of Religion,* vol. 11, ed. Mercea Eliade, New York: Macmillan, 1987, pp. 408–423.

8. The phrase occurs in Conor Cruise O'Brien, *God Land: Reflections on Religion and Politics,* Cambridge: Harvard University Press, 1987.

9. Among others, says Ninian Smart, the Christian or Buddhist "will have a certain ultimate skepticism about patriotism." The reason is that the nation state "has nothing truly transcendent," except, of course, a universal imperial urge. See Peter H. Merkl and Ninian Smart, eds., *Religion and Politics in the Modern World,* New York: New York University Press, 1985, p. 27.

10. Barker, *Principles,* p. 60.

11. Ewart Lewis, *Medieval Political Ideas,* vol. 1, New York: Cooper Square Publishers, 1974, p. 30.

12. See Charles H. McIlwain, "Mediæval Institutions in the Modern World," in *The Renaissance: Medieval or Modern?* ed. Karl H. Dannenfeldt, Series on *Problems in European Civilization,* Boston: D.C. Heath, 1959, pp. 29–34.

13. See H. Richard Niebuhr, *Radical Monotheism and Western Culture,* New York: Harper and Brothers, 1960.

14. Dietrich Bonhoeffer, *Letters and Papers from Prison,* London: SCM, reprinted 1971, pp. 286, 326, 381.

15. Lawrence W. Henderson, *The Church in Angola: A River of Many Currents,* Cleveland: The Pilgrim Press, 1992, p. 253.

16. Cited in Henderson, *The Church in Angola,* pp. 253–254.

17. Henderson, *The Church in Angola*, p. 357.

18. *Jornal de Angola*, 5 February 1978. Cited in Henderson, *The Church in Angola*, p. 357.

19. *Jornal de Angola*, 22 February 1976.

20. Henderson, *The Church in Angola*, p. 354.

21. See Andargachew Tiruneh, *The Ethiopian Revolution: 1974–1985*, Cambridge: Cambridge University Press, 1993, reprint 1995.

22. See David M. Gitari, "The Church's Witness to the Living God: Seeking Just Political, Social, and Economic Structures in Contemporary Africa," *Transformation: An International Dialogue on Evangelical Social Ethics* 5, no. 2 (April/June 1988).

23. Cited in Trevor Jones, *Ghana's First Republic: The Pursuit of the Political Kingdom*, London: Methuen, 1976, p. 52.

24. Echoes of this theme occur in David E. Apter, "Political Religion in the New Nations," in *Old Societies and New States: The Quest for Modernity in Asia and Africa*, New York: Free Press, 1963.

25. Cited in the *New York Times*, 14 April 1990.

26. See Blaine Harden, *Africa: Dispatches from a Fragile Continent*, New York: W.W. Norton, 1990; see also Thomas Callaghy, *The State-Society Struggle: Zaire in Comparative Perspective*, New York: Columbia University Press, 1984.

27. In imitation of China, the Malagassy President, Didier Ratsiraka, adopted what he called a "Red Book" *(Boky Mena)* program of state-directed policies in August 1975, marked by populist radical rhetoric. Its linchpin was the notion of *fokonolona*, the traditional village community *soi-disant*, but now conceived in agrarian revolutionary terms as a "territorial collectivity." The rural economy, supplying 80 percent of the country's export earnings, was shattered as a consequence, with the disaster being blamed on "compradore bourgeoisie." Ratsiraka resorted to the tactics of the secret police to combat disaffection; the Catholic church, however, stood its ground. See Mervyn Brown, *Madagascar Rediscovered: From Early Times to Independence*, Hamden, Conn.: Archon Books, 1979; see also "The Church and Christians in Madagascar Today," *Pro Mundi Vita Dossiers*, Africa Dossier 6 (July-August 1978).

28. "United or opposed to each other," writes Peter Merkl, "virulent nationalism and religious myths have been major political factors in modern history." See Merkl and Smart, *Religion and Politics*, p. 1.

29. The late Ayátulláh Khumayní of Iran, for instance, was quoted as saying that Muslims have been robbed of their heritage through the connivance of the West. See A. Rippen and J. Knappert, eds., *Textual Sources on Islam*, Manchester: Manchester University Press, 1986, pp. 191–192.

30. Cited in E.I.J. Rosenthal, *Islam and the Modern National State*, Cambridge: Cambridge University Press, 1965, p. 212.

31. Ibid.; see also Kenneth Cragg, *Counsels in Contemporary Islam*, Edinburgh: Edinburgh University Press, 1965, p. 21ff.

32. G. H. Jensen, *Militant Islam*, London: Pan Books, 1979, pp. 126–127; see also Cragg, *Counsels*, p. 115ff; and Rosenthal, *Islam*, pp. 138, 206.

33. Kenneth Cragg, *The Call of the Minaret*, rev. ed., Maryknoll, N.Y.: Orbis Books, 1985, p. 8; see also Cragg, *Counsel*.

34. See E.I.J. Rosenthal, *Political Thought in Medieval Islam*, Cambridge: Cambridge University Press, 1958, pp. 21–61.

35. Isma'íl A.B. Balogun, trans. and ed., *The Life and Works of 'Uthmán dan Fodio*, Lagos: Islamic Publications Bureau, 1975, p. 74.

36. Rosenthal, *Political Thought*, p. 13ff.

37. H.A.R. Gibb in *Studies on the Civilization of Islam*, collected essays, ed. Stanford J. Shaw and William R. Polk, London: Routledge & Kegan Paul Ltd., 1962, p. 148f.

38. See W. Montgomery Watt, *Islamic Political Thought: The Basic Concepts*, Edinburgh: Edinburgh University Press, 1968, pp. 102–103.

39. Gibb, *Studies*, p. 149.

40. Qur'án ii:256.

41. In the debates on the creation of an Islamic Constitution for Pakistan, a Congressman, B. K. Datta, observed in this connection that in such a state "minorities [have] an inferior status. The nation would remain communally divided into two houses, the minorities tasting neither democracy, nor freedom, nor equality, nor social justice, but being merely tolerated." See Rosenthal, *Islam*, p. 210.

42. A verse attributed to Abú al-ʿAtáhiyah and cited by Ibn Khaldún, *Al-Muqaddimah: An Introduction to History*, vol. 1, ed. and trans. Franz Rosenthal, Bollingen Series 43, 2nd ed., Princeton: Princeton University Press, 1967, p. 427.

43. Charles Issawi, *Arab Philosophy of History*. London: George Allen and Unwin, 1963, p. 104.

44. Issawi, *Arab Philosophy*, p. 137.

45. Issawi, *Arab Philosophy*, p. 133.

46. Khaldún, *Al-Muqaddimah*, vol. 1, pp. 328–329.

47. In an unflattering observation, Ibn Khaldún remarked on the unsuitability of intellectuals for political office. The intellectual life is afflicted with the same tendency for abstraction and idealization that affects the religious life. *Al-Muqaddimah*, vol. 1, p. 382f.

48. H.A.R. Gibb, "The Islamic Background of Ibn Khaldun's Political Theory," in *Studies on the Civilization of Islam*, collected essays, ed. Stanford J. Shaw and William R. Polk, London: Routledge & Kegan Paul Ltd., 1962, pp. 166–175.

49. Gibb, *Studies*, p. 174.

50. Max Weber, *The Sociology of Religion*, trans. Ephraim Fischoff, Boston: Beacon Press, 1963, p. 263.

51. Ninian Smart writes that the Christian or Buddhist, among others, "will have a certain ultimate scepticism about patriotism," for the reason that the nation-state "has nothing truly transcendent," except, of course, when it adopts a universal imperial destiny. Merkl and Smart, *Religion and Politics*, p. 27.

52. Alistair Fox, *Thomas More: History and Providence*, New Haven: Yale University Press, 1983.

53. Cited in C. S. Lewis, *English Literature in the Sixteenth Century*, in the *Oxford History of English Literature*, London: Oxford University Press, 1954, p. 454. For an abridged edition of Richard Hooker's work, see *Of the Laws of Ecclesiastical Polity*, ed. A. S. McGrade and Brian Vickers, New York: St. Martin's Press, 1975.

54. See Edward Gibbon, *The Decline and Fall of the Roman Empire*, 3 vols., New York: Modern Library, n.d., see especially chapters 14 and 15 of vol. 1.

55. Mojola Agbebi, a leader in the African Church movement in Lagos, Nigeria, made some acute observations on how the successful assimilation of Christianity into English life and culture justifies a corresponding process in Nigeria. The authors of the Anglican Book of Common Prayer, he notes, supported the view that "every country should use such ceremonies as they shall think best to setting forth of God's honor and glory," and consequently deny that they "prescribe anything but to their own people only." See his inaugural sermon, preached in 1902 and reproduced in J. Ayo Langley, ed., *Ideologies of Liberation in Black Africa: 1856–1970*, London: Rex Collings, 1979, pp. 72–77.

56. Lewis, *English Literature*, p. 455.

57. William Ernest Hocking, *The Coming World Civilization*, New York: Harper, 1956.

58. Ibid., p. 2.

59. Ibid.

60. Ibid., p. 3.

61. Kobina Sekyi, *The Parting of the Ways,* reproduced in J. Ayodele Langley, *Ideologies of Liberation in Black Africa, 1856–1970,* London: R. Collins, 1979, pp. 251–252.

62. Cited in F. L. Bartels, *The Roots of Ghana Methodism,* Accra: Methodist Book Depot and London: Cambridge University Press, 1965, pp. 241–242.

Chapter Ten

1. Isma'íl al-Farúqí (1921–1986) has written: "The Muslim is perpetually mobilised to bring about the actualisation of the absolute on earth." Cited in Kenneth Cragg, *Troubled by Truth,* Cleveland: Pilgrim Press, 1994, p. 127. See footnote 30 below.

2. John Locke, to be discussed presently, says that the secular magistrate may intervene in the slaughter of beasts only if "an extraordinary murrain" has threatened the stock of cattle. *A Letter Concerning Toleration,* Buffalo, N.Y.: Prometheus Books, 1990, p. 48.

3. For a succinct, lucid summary see Sir Ernest Barker, *Principles of Social and Political Theory,* Oxford: Clarendon Press, 1951.

4. Gustavo Gutiérrez, *Las Casas: In Search of the Poor of Jesus Christ,* Maryknoll, N.Y.: Orbis Books, 1993, p. 280ff.

5. The Muslim *jihádist,* 'Uthmán dan Fodio (d. 1817), wrote an exhaustive treatise on the legal and doctrinal foundations of *hijrah.* See his *Bayán Wujúb al-Hijrah 'Ala-l-'Ibád,* ed. and trans. F. H. El-Masri, Khartoum: Khartoum University Press and Oxford University Press, 1978.

6. In his *The Habsburg Monarchy: 1808–1918,* 1948; reprinted Penguin Books, London, 1990, A.J.P. Taylor examines some of the deeper social and political ramifications of the dissolution of the Holy Roman Empire.

7. Alexis de Tocqueville, *Democracy in America*, trans. George Lawrence, ed. J. P. Mayer, New York: Harper Perennial, 1966, p. 296.

8. Locke, *Toleration,* p. 22.

9. Ibid., p. 18.

10. Ibid., p. 19.

11. Ibid., p. 21.

12. Ibid., p. 20.

13. Ibid., p. 56.

14. Ibid.

15. Ibid., p. 64.

16. Ibid., p. 70.

17. A.S.P. Woodhouse, ed., *Puritanism and Liberty: The Army Debates (1647–9) from the Clarke Manuscripts,* London: J.M. Dent & Sons Ltd., 1974, p. 256. Richard Overton, another seventeenth-century Puritan thinker, expressed similar sentiments about the use of "human compulsive power or force" in religion. *Puritanism,* p. 332ff.

18. Woodhouse, *Puritanism,* p. 256.

19. Cited in Eugene M. Klaaren, *The Religious Origins of Modern Science,* Lanham, Md.: University Press of America, 1985, p. 144.

20. Augustine had written that there is an emperor in human affairs and a "King for otherworldly matters. There are a king for temporal life and a King for life eternal." Cited in Hugo Rahner, S.J., *Church and State in Early Christianity,* San Francisco: Ignatius Press, 1992, p. 136. Translated by Leo Donald Davis, S.J., from the German, *Kirche und Staat im Frühen Christentum,* Munich: Kösel Verlag, 1961.

21. John Milton, *The Tenure of Kings and Magistrates.*

22. Tocqueville, *Democracy,* p. 297.

23. Ibid., pp. 297–298.

24. R. G. Collingwood, *The Idea of History,* London and New York: Oxford University Press, 1946, p. 49.

25. Tocqueville, *Democracy,* p. 444.

26. Richard Weaver, *Ideas Have Consequences,* Chicago: University of Chicago Press, 1948. Cited in C.L.R. James, *American Civilization,* Cambridge, Mass., and Oxford: Blackwell, 1993, p. 243.

27. John Locke, *Two Treatises of Government,* ed. Peter Laslett, Cambridge: Cambridge University Press, 1963, and New York: Mentor Books of the New American Library, 1965.

28. Cited in A. Rippin and J. Knappert, eds., *Textual Sources on Islam,* Manchester: Manchester University Press, and Chicago: Chicago University Press, 1986, pp. 191–192.

29. Cited in G. H. Jensen, *Militant Islam,* London: Pan Books, 1979, pp. 126–127.

30. Nazih Ayubi argues for Islam as "a religion of collective morals," rather than as "a particularly political religion." Nazih Ayubi, *Political Islam: Religion and Politics in the Arab World,* London: Routledge, 1994, p. 120.

31. See W. Montgomery Watt, *Muhammad at Medina,* Oxford: Clarendon Press, 1962, still regarded as the definitive study of the subject.

32. An authoritative Muslim political tract put it as follows: "The [religious] law of the sultan is the [political] law of the country." *Usúl al-Siyásah* (*On the Fundamentals of Government*), reproduced in B. G. Martin, "A Muslim Political Tract from Northern Nigeria: Muhammad Bello's *Usúl al-Siyása*," in *Aspects of West African Islam,* vol. 5, ed. Daniel F. McCall and Norman R. Bennett, Boston: Boston University Press, 1971, pp. 82–83.

33. Cited in Yasir al-Mallah, "The Relationship of Religion to the State in Islam," *Al-Liqa' Journal* 3 (May 1994), p. 39. *Al-Liqa'* is a Palestinian review published in Jerusalem by the Center for Religious and Heritage Studies in the Holy Land.

34. Cited in E.I.J. Rosenthal, *Political Thought in Medieval Islam,* Cambridge: Cambridge University Press, 1958, p. 51ff.

35. Qur'án iii:104.

36. 'Abd al-Masíh ibn Isháq al-Kindí, *The Apology,* ed. and trans. Sir William Muir, London: S.P.C.K., 1887, pp. 29–30. Al-Kindí, himself a supreme controversialist, added that people turned to Islam in these circumstances, "some by fear of the sword, some tempted by power and wealth, others drawn by the lusts and pleasures of this life."

37. Text reproduced in Thomas Hodgkin, ed., 1960, *Nigerian Perspectives: An Historical Anthology,* London: Oxford University Press, 1960, p. 198ff.

38. Locke, *Toleration,* p. 50.

39. Muhammad Bello's correspondence with al-Kánemí, in Muhammad Bello, *Infáq al-Maysúr,* ed. C.E.J. Whitting, London: Luzac & Co., 1957, p. 131. Also cited in J. Spencer Trimingham, *A History of Islam in West Africa,* London: Oxford University Press, 1962, p. 199.

40. For a detailed study of the subject, see Lamin Sanneh, *The Jakhanké Muslim Clerics: A Religious and Historical Study of Islam in Senegambia,* Lanham, Md.: University Press of America, 1989. This is the first and only book-length study in any language.

41. Sanneh, *Jakhanké,* pp. 132–133.

42. Cited in Nizám al-Mulk, *The Book of Government for Kings* (*Siyásat Náma*), London: Routledge and Kegan Paul, 1960, p. 63. This work was written in the eleventh century.

43. Cited in Gibb, *Studies,* p. 173.

44. At the United Nations Human Rights Conference in Vienna in June 1993, the delegation of the People's Republic of China took the Hobbesian position that "no rights inhere in persons other than those accorded them by the state." As reported in Thomas Michel, S.J., "Differing Perceptions of Human Rights: Asian-African Interventions at the Human Rights Conference," in *Religion, Law and Society,* ed. Tarek Mitri, Geneva: World Council of Churches, 1995, pp. 131–137, esp. 132.

45. See the report in the *New York Times,* "A Fundamentalist Finds a Fulcrum in Sudan," 29 January 1992. Also William Langewiesche, "Turabi's Law," *The Atlantic,* August 1994, pp. 26–33.

46. Cited in Judith Miller, "The Islamic Wave," *The New York Times Magazine*, 31 May 1992.

47. Report in *Nigerian Tribune*, 21 October 1988.

48. See Mervyn Hiskett, "The Song of the Shehu's Miracles: A Hausa Hagiography from Sokoto," *African Language Studies* 12 (1971).

49. Max Stackhouse, *Public Theology and Political Economy*, Grand Rapids, Mich.: Eerdman's, 1987, p. 109.

50. Cited in *The Guardian*, 27 January 1986.

51. 'Abdulláh al-Ahsan, *OIC: The Organization of the Islamic Conference: An Introduction to an Islamic Political Institution*, Herndon, Va.: The International Institute of Islamic Thought, 1988, p. 19.

52. Qur'án iii:106

53. Cited in al-Ahsan, *OIC*, p. 60.

54. *Ecumenical Press Service*, 21–25 September 1991.

55. In a forthright statement supporting the establishment of a secular state in South Africa, Archbishop Tutu said that did not mean a "godless state." He declared: "A secular state is not a godless or immoral one. It is one in which the state does not owe allegiance to any particular religion and thus no religion has an unfair advantage, or has privileges denied to others. In some Muslim countries," he continued, "Muslim *Sharí'ah* law is enforced on all and sundry. We do not want to impose Christian laws on those who are not Christian, even if we are the majority." *Constitutional Talk*, Official Newsletter of the (South African) Constitutional Assembly, Supplement to *The Cape Times*, 12 July 1995.

56. Peter Gay, *The Enlightenment: An Interpretation*, vol. 1: *The Rise of Modern Paganism*, New York: W.W. Norton, 1977, p. 343.

57. Herbert J. Muller, *The Uses of the Past: Profiles of Former Societies*, London: Oxford University Press, 1952; reprint New York: Mentor Books, 1963, p. 277.

58. Richard Gray writes: "Most missionaries trained in the scholasticism of the first half of the twentieth century found it difficult to accept the legitimacy or even the feasibility of an African theology. This was true even of some of the most intelligent and sympathetic of missionaries. One of my most vivid recollections of the seminar on Christianity in Tropical Africa, organized by the International African Institute and held at Legon in 1965, was of René Bureau, fresh from presenting his brilliant, if Eurocentric, analysis of the impact of Christianity on the Duala, vehemently disputing with the Zaïrean, Vincent Mulago, the possibility of an African theology. 'Theology,' Bureau maintained, 'was a universal science, and one could not contrast African with Western theology.' We were all increasingly part of a universal, technological civilization founded on Jewish thought and Greek ideas, and another Western missionary maintained 'it was as unreal to talk of an African theology as of a lay theology.'" Richard Gray, *Black Christians and White Missionaries*, New Haven: Yale University Press, 1990, p. 72.

59. Gay, *Enlightenment*, p. 345, citing Archbishop John Tillotson in Norman Sykes, *Church and State in England in the Eighteenth Century*, London, 1934, pp. 258–259.

60. Niels Kastfelt, *Religion and Politics in Nigeria: A Study in Middle Belt Christianity*, London: British Academic Press, 1994, pp. 41–42.

61. Andrew E. Barnes, "'Evangelization Where It Is Not Wanted': Colonial Administrators and Missionaries in Northern Nigeria During the First Third of the Twentieth Century," *Journal of Religion in Africa* 25, no. 4 (1995), pp. 412–441, esp. 416.

62. Ibid., p. 417.

63. Cited in ibid.

64. Cited in ibid., p. 421.

65. Ibid., p. 422.

66. Ibid., p. 423.

67. Neil B. E. Baillie, ed. and trans., *Digest of Moohummudan Law: Containing the Doctrines of the Hanifeea Code of Jurisprudence*, 1869–1875; reprinted, Lahore: Premier Book House, 1974, pp. 169–170.

68. Tocqueville, *Democracy*, p. 445.

69. In a rambling polemic against the West, a U.S.-based Muslim fundamentalist group claims that for Muslims politics is a sacred duty, and Islamic fundamentalism must assume responsibility for it. "A Political Progress for Muslim America," produced by *Muslim America, Inc.*, Olympia, Wash.

70. Pat Buchanan, "The Global Ascent of Islam," *Colorado Springs Gazette*, 20 August 1989. Pat Buchanan was a Republican presidential candidate in 1992 and again in 1996.

71. Tocqueville, *Democracy*, p. 294.

72. John Dewey, *Freedom and Culture*, Buffalo: Prometheus Books, 1989, p. 125.

Bibliography

Abdul, Musa, *A Report on Arabic and Islamic Studies in Secondary Schools in Nigeria*, unpublished MS, Ibadan, 1965.

Abuja, J. Bala, "Koranic and Modern Law Teaching in Hausaland," *Nigeria* no. 37, 1951.

Abul-Fadl, Mona, *Where East Meets West: The West on the Agenda of the Islamic Revival*, Herndon, Va.: The International Institute of Islamic Thought, 1992.

Abun-Nasr, J., *The Tijaniyya: A Sufi Order in the Modern World*, Oxford: Oxford University Press, 1965.

Adams, C. C., *Islam and Modernism in Egypt*, London, 1933; reprint, New York: Russell and Russell, 1968.

Adamu, Haroun al-Rashid, *The North and Nigerian Unity: Some Reflections on the Political, Social, and Educational Problems of Northern Nigeria*, Lagos: Daily Times, 1973.

Aghnides, Nicolas P., *Mohammedan Theories of Finance*, New York: AMS Press, 1969.

Ahsan, 'Abdullah al-, *OIC: The Organization of the Islamic Conference: An Introduction to an Islamic Political Institution*, Herndon, Va.: The International Institute of Islamic Thought, Series no. 7, 1988.

Alao, Nurudeen, "Education in Islam: The Challenge of Numbers, Breadth, and Quality," in *Islam in Africa: Proceedings of the Islam in Africa Conference*, ed. Nura Alkali, Adamu Adamu, Awwal Yadudu, Rashid Motem, and Haruna Salihi, Ibadan: Spectrum Books Limited, 1993.

Alharazim, M. Saif'ud Deen, "The Origin and Progress of Islam in Sierra Leone," *Sierra Leone Studies*, old series no. 21, 1939, pp. 12–26.

Aminu, Jibril, "Towards a Strategy for Education and Development in Africa," in *Islam in Africa: Proceedings of the Islam in Africa Conference*, ed. Nura Alkali, Adamu Adamu, Awwal Yadudu, Rashid Motem, and Haruna Salihi, Ibadan: Spectrum Books Limited, 1993.

Ammah, R., "New Light on Muslim Statistics for Africa," *Bulletin on Islam and Christian-Muslim Relations in Africa* 2, no. 1, 1984, pp. 11–20.

Anawati, G. C., and Louis Gardet, *Mystique musulmane: Aspects et tendances—expériences et techniques*, Paris: Librairie philosophique J. Vrin, 1961.

Anderson, E., "Early Muslim Education and British Policy in Sierra Leone," *West African Journal of Education* 14, October 1970.

Anderson, J.N.D., *Islamic Law in Africa*, London: H. M. Stationery Office, 1954; reprint, London: Frank Cass, 1970.

Apter, David E., "Political Religion in the New Nations," in *Old Societies and New States: The Quest for Modernity in Asia and Africa*, New York: Free Press, 1963.

Arberry, A. J., *The Koran Interpreted*, 2 vols., New York: Macmillan, 1969.

Archives Féderales de Dakar, 7 G 99, Dossier no. 1, "Affaire Tierno Aliou ou le Oualy de Goumba," 1910–1912.

———, Dossier no. 170, "Administrative Report of Kindia," 19 April 1911.

Arinze, Francis A., *Sacrifice in Ibo Religion*, Ibadan: Ibadan University Press, 1970.

Arnaud, Robert, "L'Islam et la politique musulmane française en Afrique occidentale française, suivi de la singulière légende des Soninkés," *Bulletin du Comité d'Afrique Française, Renseignements Coloniaux*, 1911.

Asad, M., *Principles of State and Government in Islam*, Gibralter: Dár al-Andalus, 1980.

Ayandele, E. A., *Holy Johnson: Pioneer of African Nationalism*, London: Longman Publishers, 1970.

Ba, Hampate, and J. Daget, *L'Empire Peul du Macina*, Paris: Mouton, 1962.

Bah, Mohammad Alpha, "The Status of Muslims in Sierra Leone and Liberia," *Journal of the Institute of Muslim Minority Affairs* 12, no. 2, July 1991.

Baillie, Neil B. E., ed. and trans., *Digest of Moohummudan Law: Containing the Doctrines of the Hanifeea Code of Jurisprudence*, 1869–1875; reprinted, Lahore: Premier Book House, 1974.

Bakalla, M. H., *Arabic Culture: Through Its Language and Literature*, London and Boston: Kegan Paul International, 1984.

Bakrí, Al-, *Kitáb al-Masálik wa'l-Mamálik* ("Book of Routes and Realms"), ed. M. G. de Slane, Alger: A. Jourdan, 1913.

Balogun, Isma'íl A. B., trans. and ed., *The Life and Works of 'Uthmán dan Fodio*, Lagos: Islamic Publications Bureau, 1975.

Banton, Michael, "Adaptation and Integration in the Social System of Temne Immigrants in Freetown," *Africa: Journal of the International African Institute* 26, no. 4, October 1956, pp. 354–368.

_____, *West African City*, London: Oxford University Press for the International African Institute, 1957.

Barber, Bernard, and Michelle Jacobs, "The 'Miraj': A Legal Treatise on Slavery by Ahmad Baba," in John RalphWillis, ed., *Slaves and Slavery in Muslim Africa*, vol. 1, *Islam and the Ideology of Enslavement*, 125–159, London: Frank Cass, 1985.

Barker, Ernest, *Principles of Social and Political Theory*, Oxford: Clarendon Press, 1951.

Barnes, Andrew E., "'Evangelization Where It Is Not Wanted': Colonial Administrators and Missionaries in Northern Nigeria During the First Third of the Twentieth Century," *Journal of Religion in Africa* 25, no. 4, 1995.

Barry, Boubacar, "L'Expansion du Fuuta Jallon vers la côte et les crises politiques et sociales dans la Sénégambie meridionale au cours de la première moitié du xixème siècle," unpublished MS.

_____, "Senegambia from the Sixteenth to the Eighteenth Century: Evolution of the Wolof, Serer, and Tukulor," *UNESCO General History of Africa*, vol. 5, Paris: UNESCO; Berkeley and Los Angeles: University of California Press; Portsmouth, N.H.: Heinemann Publishers, 1992.

Bartels, F. L., *The Roots of Ghana Methodism*, Accra: Methodist Book Depot; London: Cambridge University Press, 1965.

Bascom, William, "Yoruba Religion and Morality," *Presence Africaine*, 1972.

Batran, A. A., "The Kunta, Sidi Mukhtar al-Kunti, and the Office of Shaykh al-Tariqa al-Qadiriyya," in *Studies in West African Islamic History*, ed. J. R. Willis, vol. 1: *The Cultivators of Islam*, London: Frank Cass, 1979.

Battúta, Ibn, *Travels in Asia and Africa*, trans. and ed. H.A.R. Gibb, 1929; reprint London: Routledge & Kegan Paul, 1957.

Baydáwí, *Anwár al-Tanzíl*, ed. H. O. Fleischer, vol. 2, Leipzig: F.C.G. Vogel, 1848.

Bello, Alhaji Sir Ahmadu, Sardauna of Sokoto, *My Life*, Cambridge: Cambridge University Press, 1962; reprinted Zaria: Gaskiya Corporation, 1986.

Bello, Muhammad, *Infáq al-Maysúr*, ed. C.E.J. Whitting, London: Luzac, 1957.

Benna, Umar G., "The Changing Patterns of Muslim Cities in Africa," in *Islam in Africa: Proceedings of the Islam in Africa Conference*, ed. Nura Alkali, Adamu Adamu, Awwal Yadudu, Rashid Motem, and Haruna Salihi, Ibadan: Spectrum Books Limited, 1993.

Betts, Robert Brenton, *Christians in the Arab East: A Political Study*, London: S.P.C.K., 1979.

Bickford-Smith, Vivian, "Meanings of Freedom: Social Position and Identity Among Ex-Slaves and Their Descendants in Cape Town, 1875–1910," in *Breaking the Chains*, ed. Nigel Worden and Clifton Crais, Johannesburg: Witwatersrand University Press, 1994.

Birks, J. S., *Across the Savannas to Mecca: The Overland Pilgrimage Routes from West Africa*, London: Christopher Hurst, 1978.

Bivar, A.D.H., "Arabic Calligraphy of West Africa," *African Language Review* 7, 1968.

Blasdell, R. A., "Use of Drum for Mosque Service," *Muslim World* 30, 1940.

Blasdoe, C. H., and K. M. Robey, "Arabic Literacy and Secrecy Among the Mende of Sierra Leone," *Man* 21, 1986.

Blyden, Edward W., *Christianity, Islam, and the Negro Race*, 1887; reprint Edinburgh: Edinburgh University Press, 1967.

_____, "The Koran in Africa," *Journal of the African Society* 4, January 1905.

Bolaji-Idowu, E., *African Traditional Religion: A Definition*, London: SCM Press, 1973.

_____, *Olodumare: God in Yoruba Belief*, London: Longman Publishers, 1962.

Bonhoeffer, Dietrich, *Letters and Papers from Prison*, London: SCM, reprinted 1971.

Bosman, William, *A New and Accurate Description of the Coast of Guinea, 1705*, 2nd ed., London: K. Knapton, 1721.

Bovill, E. W., ed., *Missions to the Niger*, vol. 4: *The Bornu Mission 1822–25*, Hakluyt Society Series 2, vol. 130, London: Hakluyt Society, 1966.

Bravmann, René A., "A Fragment of Paradise," *Muslim World* 78, 1988.

_____, *Islam and Tribal Art in West Africa*, Cambridge: Cambridge University Press, 1974.

Brenner, Louis, "Concepts of *Taríqa* in West Africa: The Case of the Qádiriyya," in *Charisma and Brotherhood in West African Islam*, ed. D. B. Cruise O'Brien and C. Coulon, Oxford: Oxford University Press, 1988.

_____, "Muhammad al-Amín-al-Kánimí and Religion and Politics in Bornu," in *Studies in West African Islamic History*, ed. John Ralph Willis, vol.1: *The Cultivators of Islam*, London: Frank Cass, 1979.

_____, *West African Súfí: The Religious Heritage and Spiritual Search of Cerno Bokar Saalif Taal*, Berkeley and Los Angeles: University of California Press, 1984.

Brenner, Louis, and M. Last, "Role of Language in West African Islam," *Africa* 55, no. 4, 1985.

Brown, Godfrey N., and Mervyn Hiskett, eds., *Conflict and Harmony in Education in Tropical Africa*, London: George Allen and Unwin, 1976.

Brown, Mervyn, *Madagascar Rediscovered: From Early Times to Independence*, Hamden, Conn.: Archon Books, 1979.

Brunschvig, R., "Abd," in *Encyclopaedia of Islam*, New Edition, Leiden: E. J. Brill, 1960.

Buchanan, Pat, "The Global Ascent of Islam," *Colorado Springs Gazette*, 20 August 1989.

Bukhárí, al-, *Al-Sahíh*, trans. Muhammad Muhsin Khan, 9 vols., New Delhi: Kitab Bhavan, 1987.

Burckhardt, Jacob, *The Civilization of the Renaissance in Italy*, New York: Mentor Book of The New American Library, 1961, p. 367.

_____, *Force and Freedom: An Interpretation of History*, New York: Meridian Books, 1955.

Caillie, René, *Travels Through Central Africa to Timbouctou and the Great Desert to Morocco Performed in the Years 1824–28*, 2 vols., London: H. Colburn and R. Bentley, 1830.

Callaghy, Thomas, *The State-Society Struggle: Zaire in Comparative Perspective*, New York: Columbia University Press, 1984.

Carroll, K., *Yoruba Religious Carving*, New York: Praeger, 1967.

Chittick, William C., *Faith and Practice of Islam: Three Thirteenth-Century Sufi Texts*, Albany: State University of New York Press, 1992.

"The Church and Christians in Madagascar Today," *Pro Mundi Vita Dossiers*, Africa Dossier 6, July-August 1978.

Clapperton, Hugh, *Journal of a Second Expedition into the Interior of Africa*, London: n.p., 1829.

Cole, Ibrahim, "Muslim-Christian Relations in Sierra Leone," *Bulletin on Islam and Christian-Muslim Relations in Africa* 1, no. 4, 1983.

Collingwood, R. G., *The Idea of History*, London and New York: Oxford University Press, 1946.

Conneau, Theophilus, *A Slaver's Logbook; Or, Twenty Years' Residence in Africa*, [1854], New Jersey: Prentice-Hall, Inc., 1976.

Conrad, David C., "Islam in the Oral Traditions of Mali: Bilali and Surakata," *Journal of African History* 26, 1985, pp. 33–49.

Conrad, David C., ed., *A State of Intrigue: The Epic of Bamana Segu According to Tayiru Banbera*, London: Oxford University Press for the British Academy, 1990.

Cooper, Frederick, "The Problem of Slavery in African Studies," *Journal of African History* 20, no. 1, 1979, pp. 103–125.

Cragg, Kenneth, *Counsels in Contemporary Islam*, Edinburgh: Edinburgh University Press, 1965.

_____, *The Call of the Minaret*, rev. ed., Maryknoll, N.Y.: Orbis Books, 1985.

Craton, Michael, ed., *Roots and Branches: Current Directions in Slave Studies*, Toronto: Pergamon Press, 1979.

Cronin, Vincent, *Pearl to India: The Life of Robert de Nobili*, London: Rupert Hart Davis, 1959.

Curtin, Philip, *Economic Change in Precolonial Senegambia in the Era of the Slave Trade*, Madison: University of Wisconsin Press, 1975.

Daily Mail, 11 June 1975.

Davidson, Basil, *The Black Man's Burden: Africa and the Curse of the Nation State*, London: James Currey, 1992.

_____, "West African Arabic Scripts," *West Africa* no. 2433, 18 January 1964.

_____, *Which Way Africa? The Search for a New Society*, Baltimore, Md.: Penguin Books, 1964.

Davis, David Brion, *Slavery and Human Progress*, Oxford: Oxford University Press, 1984.

Dawisha, A., ed., *Islam in Foreign Policy*, Cambridge: Cambridge University Press, 1983.

Deeb, M-J., "Islam and Arab Nationalism in Al-Qaddafi's Ideology," *Journal of South Asian and Middle Eastern Studies* 2, no. 2, 1978, pp. 12–26.

_____, *Libya's Foreign Policy in North Africa*, Boulder: Westview Press, 1991.

Dehaini, A. R., *Report on Qur'an Schools in the Western State of Nigeria*, unpublished MS, Ibadan, 1965.

Dennett, R. E., *Nigerian Studies*, London, 1910; reprint, London: Frank Cass, 1968.

Derman, W., *Serfs, Peasants, and Socialists: A Former Serf Village in the Republic of Guinea*, Berkeley and Los Angeles: University of California Press, 1973.

Dewey, John, *Democracy and Education: An Introduction to the Philosophy of Education*, New York: Macmillan Press, 1916, reprint, Free Press, 1966.

_____, *Freedom and Culture*, Buffalo: Prometheus Books, 1989.

Diallo, Thierno, *Alfa Yaya: Roi du Labé (Fouta Djallon)*, Abidjan and Dakar: NEA, 1976.

Dieterlen, Germaine, "Mythe et organisation sociale en Afrique Occidentale," *Journal de la Societé Africanistes* 29, no. 1, 1959.

Dieterlen, G. (with Solange De Ganay), *La Génie des Eaux chez les Dogons*, Paris: Geuthner, 1942.

Dilley, Roy M., "Spirits, Islam, and Ideology: A Study of a Tukulor Weavers' Song (Dillire)," *Journal of Religion in Africa* 17, no. 3, October 1987.

Dobbelaere, K., "Secularization: A Multi-dimensional Concept," *Current Sociology* 29, no. 1, 1981, pp. 11–12.

Donald, Leland, "Arabic Literacy Among the Yulanka of Sierra Leone," *Africa* 44, January 1974.

Dooling, Wayne, "'The Good Opinion of Others': Law, Slavery, and Community in the Cape Colony, c. 1760–1830," in *Breaking the Chains*, ed. Nigel Worden and Clifton Crais, Johannesburg: Witwatersrand University Press, 1994.

Doornbos, M., "Linking the Future to the Past: Ethnicity and Pluralism," *Review of African Political Economy* 52, 1991, pp. 53–65.

Duffy, James, *A Question of Slavery: Labour Policies in Portuguese Africa and the British Protest, 1850–1920,* Cambridge, Mass.: Harvard University Press, 1967.

Dumont, Fernand, *La Pensée réligieuse d'Amadou Bamba,* Dakar and Abidjan: Nouvelles editions Africaines, 1975.

Durand, Jean Baptiste, *Voyage au Senegal,* Paris: H. Agasse, 1802, English edition London: Printed for Richard Phillips by J.G. Barnard, 1806.

Earthy, E. D., "The Impact of Mohammedanism on Paganism in the Liberian Hinterland," *Numen* 2, 1955.

The Economist, "Islam and the West: A Survey," 6 August 1994.

Elbein, Juana, and Deoscoredes M. Dos Santos, "La religion Nago generatrice et reserve de valeurs culturelles au Bresil," in *Les Religions africaines comme source de valeurs de civilisation,* colloque de Cotonou, 16–22 Aout, 1970, Presence Africaine, Paris, 1972.

Eldredge, Elizabeth, and Fred Morton, eds., *Slavery in South Africa: Captive Labor on the Dutch Frontier,* Boulder: Westview Press and Pietermaritzburg: University of Natal Press, 1994.

Esposito, John, *The Islamic Threat to the West: Myth or Reality?* New York: Oxford University Press, 1990.

Fadera, al-Hájj Muhammad Fádilu, *Kitáb Tahdhíru Ummati 'l-Muhammadiyát min Ittibái 'l-firqati Ahmadiyát (A Warning to the Muslim Community on the Dangers of Following the Ahmadiyah Sect),* Dakar: n.p., n.d.

Fafunwa, A. Babatunde, *A History of Education in Nigeria,* London: George Allen & Unwin, 1974.

Faksh, M., "Concepts of Rule and Legitimation in Islam," *Journal of South Asian and Middle Eastern Studies* 13, no. 3, 1990, pp. 21–36.

Falconbridge, Alexander, *An Account of the Slave Trade on the Coast of Africa,* London: J. Phillips, 1788; reprint, London: Frank Cass, 1966.

Faraday, Ann, *Dream Power: The Use of Dreams in Everyday Life,* London: Pan Books, 1972.

Fasholé-Luke, Edward W., "Christianity and Islam in Freetown," *Sierra Leone Bulletin of Religion* 9, no. 1, June 1967.

Fisher, Humphrey J., "Ahmadiyah in Sierra Leone," *Sierra Leone Bulletin of Religion* 2, no. 1, June 1960.

_____, *The Ahmadiyya,* London: Oxford University Press, 1963.

_____, "Dreams and Conversion in Black Africa," in *Conversion to Islam,* ed. Nehemia Levtzion, New York: Holmes and Meier, 1979.

_____, "Hassebu: Islamic Healing in Black Africa," in Michael Brett, ed., *Northern Africa: Islam and Modernization,* London: Frank Cass, 1973.

_____, "Islamic Education and Religious Reform in West Africa," in *Education in Africa,* ed. Richard Jolly, Nairobi, Kenya: East African Publishing House, 1969.

_____, "The Ivory Horn: Oneirology, Chiefly Muslim, in Black Africa," in *Conversion to Islam,* ed. Nehemia Levtzion, New York: Holmes and Meier, 1979.

_____, "Liminality, Hijra, and the City," in *Rural and Urban Islam in West Africa,* ed. Nehemia Levtzion and Humphrey J. Fisher, Boulder: Lynne Rienner Publishers, 1987.

_____, "A Muslim Wilberforce? The Sokoto *Jihád* as Anti-slavery Crusade: An Enquiry into Historical Causes," in *De la traite à l'esclavage: Actes du colloque international sur la traite des Noirs, Nantes, 1985,* ed. Serge Daget, vol. 2, Nantes: Centre de recherche sur l'histoire du monde atlantique and Paris: Societé française d'histoire d'outre-mer, 1988, pp. 537–555.

_____, "Prayer and Military Activity in the History of Muslim Africa South of the Sahara," *Journal of African History* 12, no. 3, 1971.

Fisher, Humphrey J., and A. G. B. Fisher, *Slavery and Muslim Society in Africa*, London: Christopher Hurst Publishers, 1971.

Fitzgerald, Michael, "An African Brotherhood: Tijaniyya," *Encounter* (Rome) no. 167, July-August 1990.

Fitzgerald, Michael, and Jacques Lanfry, "The Ahmadiyya Community and Its Expansion in Africa," *Encounter* (Rome) 1, no. 2, February 1974.

Flügel, Gustave, *Corani Textus Arabicus*, Leipzig, 1883; reprint Farnborough, England: Gregg Press, 1965.

Fodio, Abdalláh dan, *Tazyín al-Waraqát*, ed. M. Hiskett, Ibadan: Ibadan University Press, 1963.

———, 'Uthmán dan, *Bayán Wujúb al-Hijra 'ala-l-'Ibád*, ed. and trans. F. H. El-Masrí, Khartoum: Khartoum University Press and London: Oxford University Press, 1978.

Forde, Daryll, *African Worlds*, London: Oxford University Press, 1954.

Fox, Alistair, *Thomas More: History and Providence*, New Haven: Yale University Press, 1983.

Freetown Daily Mail, 24 March 1975.

Fúdí, 'Abdalláh ibn, *Tazyín al-Waraqát*, ed. and trans. Mervyn Hiskett, Ibadan: Ibadan University Press, 1963.

Fyfe, Christopher, *A History of Sierra Leone*, London: Oxford University Press, 1962.

Fyfe, Christopher, ed., *Sierra Leone Inheritance*, London: Oxford University Press, 1964.

Gabid, Hamid al-, "The Organization of Islamic Conference (OIC) and the Development of Africa," in *Islam in Africa: Proceedings of the Islam in Africa Conference*, ed. Nura Alkali, Adamu Adamu, Awwal Yadudu, Rashid Motem, and Haruna Salihi, Ibadan: Spectrum Books Limited, 1993.

Gabrieli, Francesci, *Muhammad and the Conquests of Islam*, London: Widenfeld & Nicolson, 1968.

Galadanci, S.A.S., "Islamic Education in Africa: Past Influence and Contemporary Challenges," in *Islam in Africa: Proceedings of the Islam in Africa Conference*, ed. Nura Alkali, Adamu Adamu, Awwal Yadudu, Rashid Motem, and Haruna Salihi, Ibadan: Spectrum Books Limited, 1993.

Garh, M. S. el-, "Arabic in Nigeria: Why, When, and How To Teach It," seminar paper (unpublished), Ibadan, November 1970.

Gay, Peter, *The Enlightenment: An Interpretation*, vol. 1: *The Rise of Modern Paganism*, vol. 2: *The Science of Freedom*, New York: W.W. Norton, 1977.

Gbadamosi, T.G.O., *The Growth of Islam Among the Yoruba: 1841–1908*, London: Longman Publishers, 1978.

Gellner, Ernest, *Muslim Society*, London: Cambridge University Press, 1983.

Ghazali, Al-, *Taháfut al-Falásifah* [The Incoherence of the Philosophers], ed. and trans. Sabih Ahmad Kamali, Lahore: Pakistan Philosophical Congress, 1963.

Ghazali, Abdul Karim, "A Muslim Propaganda Play: De Man Way De Play Gyambul Wit God," *Sierra Leone Bulletin of Religion* 3, no. 2, December 1961.

Ghazali, A. K., and L. Proudfoot, "A Muslim Propaganda Play and a Commentary," *Sierra Leone Bulletin of Religion* 3, no. 2, December 1961.

Gibb, H.A.R., "The Islamic Background of Ibn Khaldun's Political Theory," in *Studies on the Civilization of Islam*, collected essays, ed. Stanford J. Shaw and William R. Polk, London: Routledge & Kegan Paul, 1962, pp. 166–175.

Gibbon, Edward, *The Decline and Fall of the Roman Empire*, 3 vols., New York: Modern Library, n.d.

Gitari, David, "The Church and Politics in Kenya," *Transformation: An International Evangelical Dialogue on Mission and Ethics*, July-September 1990.

———, "The Church's Witness to the Living God: Seeking Just Political, Social, and Economic Structures in Contemporary Africa," *Transformation: An International Evangelical Dialogue on Mission and Ethics* 5 no. 2, April-June 1988.

Goldziher, Ignaz, *Muslim Studies*, trans. and ed., C. R. Barber and S. M. Stern, 2 vols., London: George Allen and Unwin, 1967–1971.

Goody, Jack, "The Impact of Islamic Writing on the Oral Cultures of West Africa," *Cahiers d'Études Africaines* 11, no. 3, 1971.

Goriawala, Mu'izz, "Maguzawa," *Orita: Ibadan Journal of Religious Studies* 4, no. 2, December 1970.

Gouldsbury, M. D., *Expedition to Upper Gambia, August, 1881,* London: Public Records Office, Enclosure 1 in no. 17, 22 June 1881.

Grant, Douglas, *The Fortunate Slave: An Illustration of African Slavery in the Early Eighteenth Century*, London: Oxford University Press, 1968.

Gray, Richard, *Black Christians and White Missionaries*, New Haven: Yale University Press, 1990.

Green, J., "Islam, Religio-politics and Social Change," *Comparative Studies in Society and History* 27, pp. 312–322.

Greenberg, Joseph, *The Influence of Islam upon a Sudanese Religion*, New York: J. J. Augustin, 1946.

Griaule, Marcel, *Conversations with Ogotommêli: An Introduction to Dogon Religious Ideas*, London: Oxford University Press, 1975; originally published as *Dieu d'Eau: entretiens avec Ogotemmeli*, Paris: n.p., 1948.

Grünebaum, Gustave E. von, and R. Caillois, *The Dream and Human Societies*, Los Angeles and Berkeley: University of California Press, 1966.

The Guardian, 27 January 1986.

Gutiérrez, Gustavo, *Las Casas: In Search of the Poor of Jesus Christ*, Maryknoll, N.Y.: Orbis Books, 1993.

Haile, Getachew, "From the Markets of Damot to That of Barara: A Note on Slavery in Medieval Ethiopia," *Paideuma* 27, 1981, pp. 173–180.

Hailey, Lord, *An African Survey: Revised 1956*, Oxford: Clarendon Press, 1957.

Hájj, M. A. al-, "A Seventeenth-Century Chronicle on the Origins and Missionary Activities of the Wangarawa," *Kano Studies* 1, no. 4, 1968.

Hakim, Selim, *al-'Arabiyyah al-Jadîdah fî Nîjîriya*, Ibadan: Longmans of Nigeria, 1966.

_____, *Report: The Teaching of Arabic in Schools and Colleges in Nigeria*, unpublished MS, Ibadan, 1961.

_____, *Ta'lîm al-Lughah al-'Arabiyyah fî Nîjîriya*, Baghdad: n.p., 1966.

Hallam, W.K.R., *The Life and Times of Rabih Fadl Allah*, Elms Court, Ilfracombe, England: Arthur H. Stockwell Ltd., 1977.

Hansen, Holger Bernt, *Mission, Church, and State in a Colonial Setting: Uganda: 1890–1925*, London: Heinemann Publishers, 1984.

Hanson, John, and David Robinson, *After the Jihád: The Reign of Ahmad al-Kabîr in the Western Sudan*, East Lansing: Michigan State University, 1991.

Harazim, S. D. al-, "The Origin and Progress of Islam in Sierra Leone," *Sierra Leone Studies*, Old Series no. 21, 1939.

Harden, Blaine, *Africa: Dispatches from a Fragile Continent*, New York: W.W. Norton, 1990.

Hargreaves, John, *Prelude to the Partition of West Africa*, London: Macmillan, 1963.

Harrison, Christopher, *France and Islam in West Africa: 1860–1960*, Cambridge: Cambridge University Press, 1988.

Hasan, Yusuf Fadl, *The Arabs and the Sudan*, Edinburgh: Edinburgh University Press, 1967.

Hastings, Adrian, *The Church in Africa: 1450–1950*, Oxford: Clarendon Press, 1994.

_____, *A History of African Christianity: 1950–1975*, Cambridge: Cambridge University Press, 1979.

Haynes, Jeff, *Religion in Third World Politics*, Boulder: Lynne Rienner Publishers, 1994.

Henderson, Lawrence W., *The Church in Angola: A River of Many Currents*, Cleveland, Ohio: The Pilgrim Press, 1992.

Hilliard, Constance, "Zuhúr al-Basátin and Ta'ríkh al-Turubbe: Some Legal and Ethical Aspects of Slavery in the Sudan as Seen in the Works of Shaykh Musa Kamara," in *Slaves and Slavery in Muslim Africa,* ed. John Ralph Willis, 2 vols., London: Frank Cass, 1985.

Hiskett, Mervyn, *The Development of Islam in West Africa,* London: Longman Publishers, 1984.

_____, "The Islamic Tradition of Reform in the Western Sudan from the Sixteenth to the Eighteenth Century," *Bulletin of the School of Oriental and African Studies* 25, no. 3, 1962.

_____, "The Maitatsine Riots in Kano, 1980: An Assessment," *Journal of Religion in Africa* 17, no. 3, October 1987.

_____, "Problems of Religious Education in Muslim Communities in Africa," *Oversea Education* 32, no. 3, October 1960.

_____, "The Song of the Shehu's Miracles: A Hausa Hagiography from Sokoto," *African Language Studies* 12, 1971.

_____, *The Sword of Truth: The Life and Times of Shehu Usuman dan Fodio,* New York: Oxford University Press, 1973.

Hocking, William Ernest, *The Coming World Civilization,* New York: Harper, 1956.

Hodgkin, Thomas, "The Fact of Islamic History (II): Islam in West Africa," *Africa South* 2, no. 3, 1958, pp. 88–99.

_____, "Islam and National Movements in West Africa," *Journal of African History* 3, no. 2, 1962.

_____, "Islam, History, and Politics," *Journal of Modern African Studies* 1, no. 1, 1963.

Hodgkin, Thomas, ed., *Nigerian Perspectives: An Historical Anthology*, London: Oxford University Press, 1960.

Hogendorn, Jan S., "The Economics of Slave Use on Two 'Plantations' in the Zaria Emirate of the Sokoto Caliphate," *International Journal of African Historical Studies* 10, no. 3, 1977, pp. 369–383.

Hogendorn, Jan, and Marion Johnson, *The Shell Money of the Slave Trade*, Cambridge: Cambridge University Press, 1986.

Honko, Lauri, ed., *Science of Religion: Studies in Methodology,* The Hague: Mouton, 1979.

Hooker, Richard, *Of the Laws of Ecclesiastical Polity,* ed. A. S. McGrade and Brian Vickers, New York: St. Martin's Press, 1975.

Hopewell, James F., *Muslim Penetration into French Guinea, Sierra Leone, and Liberia Before 1850,* unpublished Ph.D. dissertation, Columbia University, New York, 1958.

Hopkins, J.F.P., and N. Levtzion, eds., *Corpus of Early Arabic Sources for West African History,* Cambridge: Cambridge University Press, 1981.

Horton, Robin, "African Conversion," *Africa: Journal of the International African Institute* 41, no. 2, April 1970.

_____, *Patterns of Thought in Africa and the West: Essays on Religion and Science*, Cambridge: Cambridge University Press, 1993.

Huntingdon, Samuel P., "The Clash of Civilizations?" *Foreign Affairs*, Summer 1993.

Hunwick, John O., "The Influence of Arabic in West Africa," *Transactions of the Historical Society of Ghana* 7, pt. 7, 1964.

_____, "Notes on Slavery in the Songhay Empire," in John Ralph Willis, ed., *Slaves and Slavery in Muslim Africa,* Vol. 2: *The Servile Estate*, 16–32, London: Frank Cass, 1985.

_____, "Religion and State in the Songhay Empire: 1464–1591," in *Islam in Tropical Africa*, ed. I. M. Lewis, London: Oxford University Press for the International African Institute, 1966.

_____, *Report on the Seminar on the Teaching of Arabic in Nigeria,* unpublished MS, Ibadan, 11–15 July 1965.

_____, *Sharí'a in Songhay: The Replies of al-Maghílí to the Questions of Askiya al-Hájj Muhammad,* London: Oxford University Press for the British Academy, 1985.

Ibn 'Ata'lláh, *The Book of Wisdom*, ed. and trans. Victor Danner, in the series *Classics of Western Spirituality*, New York: Paulist Press, 1978.

Ikenga-Metuh, Emefie, "Muslim Resistance to Missionary Penetration in Northern Nigeria, 1857–1960," *Mission Focus* 3, no. 2, 1986.

Ingham, K., *Politics in Modern Africa: The Uneven Tribal Dimension*, London: Routledge, 1990.

Irving, Washington, *Life of Mahomet*, New York: Lord Henry G. Bohn, 1850.

Ishaq, Khalil ibn, *Abrege de la loi musulmane selon le rite de l'imam Malek*, vol. 1: *Le Rituel*, trans. G.-H. Bousquet, Alger: Publications de l'Institut d'Etudes Orientales de la Faculte des Lettres d'Alger, 1956.

Isichei, Elizabeth, "The Maitatsine Risings in Nigeria, 1980–1985: A Revolt of the Disinherited," *Journal of Religion in Africa* 17, no. 3, October 1987.

Issawi, Charles, *An Arab Philosophy of History*, London: George Allen & Unwin, 1963.

Jah, al-Hájj U.N.S., "Christian-Muslim Relations: An Islamic Point of View," *BICMURA* 5, no. 4, 1987.

James, C.L.R., *American Civilization*, Cambridge, Mass., and Oxford: Blackwell, 1993.

Jensen, G. H., *Militant Islam*, London: Pan Books, 1979.

Jimeh, S. A., "A Critical Appraisal of Islamic Education with Particular Reference to Critical Happenings on the Nigerian Scene," *Nigerian Journal of Islam* 2, no. 1, July 1971-January 1972.

Jobson, Richard, *The Golden Trade; or, a Discovery of the River Gambia, 1620–21*, London; N. Oaks, 1623; reprinted London: Dawsons of Pall Mall, 1968.

Johnson, Marion, "The Slaves of Salaga," *Journal of African History* 27, no. 2, 1986, pp. 341–362.

Johnson, S., *The History of the Yorubas*, London: Routledge & Kegan Paul, 1921, 1969.

Jones, Trevor, *Ghana's First Republic: The Pursuit of the Political Kingdom*, London: Methuen, 1976.

Jusu, B. M., "The Haidara Rebellion of 1931," *Sierra Leone Studies*, new series 3, no. 4, December 1954.

Kane, Cheikh Amidou, *Ambiguous Adventure*, London: Heinemann Publishers, 1963.

Kasim, Alhaji M.S., ed., *Songs and Prayers for Muslim Schools, Nigeria*, reprint, Ijebu-Ode: Council on Muslim Education, 1969.

Kastfelt, Niels, "African Resistance to Colonialism in Adamawa," *Journal of Religion in Africa* 8, no. 1, 1976.

———, *Religion and Politics in Nigeria: A Study in Middle Belt Christianity*, London: British Academic Press, 1994.

———, "Rumours of Maitatsine: A Note on Political Culture in Northern Nigeria," *African Affairs* 88, 1989, pp. 83–90.

Ka'ti, 'Abd al-Rahmán, *Ta'ríkh al-Fattásh*, trans. O. Houdas and M. Delafosse, Alger: n.p., 1913; reprint, Paris: Librairie d'Amérique et d'Orient, Adrien-Maisonneuve, 1964.

Kerr, Malcolm, *The Arab Cold War: Gamal 'Abd al-Nasir and His Rivals: 1958–1970*, 3rd ed., London: Oxford University Press for the Royal Institute of International Affairs, 1971.

Khaldún, Ibn, *Al-Muqaddimah: An Introduction to History*, 3 vols., ed. and trans. Franz Rosenthal, Bollingen Series 43, 2nd ed., Princeton: Princeton University Press, 1967.

Khalidi, Tarif, "Islamic Views of the West in the Middle Ages," *Studies in Interreligious Dialogue* 5, no. 1, 1995.

Kindí, Abd al-Masíh ibn Isháq al-, *The Apology*, ed. and trans. Sir William Muir, London: S.P.C.K, 1887.

Klaaren, Eugene M., *The Religious Origins of Modern Science*, Lanham, Md.: University Press of America, 1985.

Klein, Martin A. *Islam and Imperialism in Senegal,* Edinburgh: Edinburgh University Press and Stanford: Stanford University Press, 1968.

Kokole, Omari H., "Religion in Afro-Arab Relations: Islam and Cultural Changes in Modern Africa," in *Islam in Africa: Proceedings of the Islam in Africa Conference,* ed. Nura Alkali, Adamu Adamu, Awwal Yadudu, Rashid Motem, and Haruna Salihi, Ibadan: Spectrum Books Limited, 1993.

"Kole Omotoso," *Cape Librarian,* February 1994, pp. 20–21.

Kreutzinger, Helga, *The Eri Devils in Freetown, Sierra Leone,* Vienna: Österreichische Ethnologische Gesellschaft, 1966.

Kumo, Suleimanu, "Shar'ia *[sic]* Under Colonialism—Northern Nigeria," in *Islam in Africa: Proceedings of the Islam in Africa Conference,* ed. Nura Alkali, Adamu Adamu, Awwal Yadudu, Rashid Motem, and Haruna Salihi, Ibadan: Spectrum Books Limited, 1993.

Kup, P., *A History of Sierra Leone, 1400–1787,* Cambridge: Cambridge University Press, 1961.

L'A.O.F. Echo de la côte occidentale d'Afrique, 20 September 1911.

Langewiesche, William, "Turabi's Law," *The Atlantic,* August 1994.

Langley, J. Ayo, ed., *Ideologies of Liberation in Black Africa: 1856–1970,* London: Rex Collings, 1979.

Last, Murray, "Aspects of Administration and Dissent in Hausaland: 1800–1968," *Africa* 40, no. 4, October 1970.

_____, *The Sokoto Caliphate,* London: Longman Publishers, 1967.

Launay, Robert, *Beyond the Stream: Islam and Society in a West African Town,* Berkeley and Los Angeles: University of California Press, 1992.

Law, Robin, *The Oyo Empire: c.1600–c.1836: A West African Imperialism in the Era of the Atlantic Slave Trade,* Oxford: Clarendon Press, 1977.

Lemu, B. A., "Islamisation of Education: A Primary Level Experiment in Nigeria," *Muslim Educational Quarterly* 2, 1988, pp. 70–80.

Levine, D., "Religion and Politics in Comparative Perspective," *Comparative Politics,* October 1986, pp. 95–122.

Levtzion, Nehemia, "'Abd Allah ibn Yasin and the Almoravids," in *Studies in West African Islamic History,* ed. John Ralph Willis, vol. 1, London: Frank Cass, 1979.

_____, *Muslims and Chiefs in West Africa: A Study of Islam in the Middle Volta Basin in the Pre-colonial Period,* Oxford: Clarendon Press, 1968.

Levtzion, Nehemia, and J.F.P. Hopkins, eds., *Corpus of Early Arabic Sources for West African History,* London: Cambridge University Press, 1981.

Levy, Reuben, *The Social Structure of Islam,* Cambridge: Cambridge University Press, 1957; reprint, 1965.

Lewis, Bernard, *Race and Slavery in the Middle East: An Historical Enquiry,* New York: Oxford University Press, 1992.

Lewis, C. S., *English Literature in the Sixteenth Century,* in the *Oxford History of English Literature,* London and New York: Oxford University Press, 1954.

Lewis, Ewart, *Medieval Political Ideas,* vol. 1, New York: Cooper Square Publishers, 1974.

Little, Kenneth L., "A Muslim Missionary in Mendeland," *Man: Journal of the Royal Anthropological Institute,* September-October 1946.

Locke, John, *A Letter Concerning Toleration,* Buffalo, N.Y.: Prometheus Books, 1990.

_____, *Two Treatises of Government,* ed. Peter Laslett, Cambridge: Cambridge University Press, 1963; New York: Mentor Books of the New American Library, 1965.

Lovejoy, Paul E., "Concubinage and the Status of Women Slaves in Early Colonial Northern Nigeria," *Journal of African History* 29, no. 2, 1988, pp. 245–266.

_____, "Problems of Slavery in the Sokoto Caliphate," in *Africans in Bondage: Studies in Slavery and the Slave Trade,* Madison: University of Wisconsin Press, 1986.

_____, *Tranformations in Slavery: A History of Slavery in Africa*, Cambridge: Cambridge University Press, 1983.

Lovejoy, Paul E., and Catherine Coquery-Vidrovitch, eds., *The Workers of African Trade*, Beverly Hills: Sage Publications.

Lucas, J. Olumide, *The Religion of the Yorubas,* Lagos: CMS Bookshop, 1948.

Lugard, Lady (*née* Flora Shaw), *A Tropical Dependency*, London: J. Nisbet, 1905; reprint, London: Frank Cass, 1964.

Lugard, Lord Frederick, "'Slavery in All Its Forms,'" *Africa* 6, no. 1, 1933, pp. 1–14.

Lynch, H. R., *Edward Wilmot Blyden: Pan-Negro Patriot*, New York: Oxford University Press, 1967.

Macdonald, Duncan Black, *The Development of Muslim Theology and Jurisprudence*, Beirut: Khayat Books, 1965.

_____, *The Religious Life and Attitude in Islam,* London: Darf, 1985.

Mackay, C., *Extraordinary Popular Delusions and the Madness of Crowds*, London: Richard Bentley, 1852; reprint, New York: Farrar, Straus and Giroux, 1932.

Málik, Imám, *Al-Muwatta*, London: Diwan Press, 1982.

Mallia, J., "Fundamentalists Rejoice but Sudan's Millions Starve," *The Guardian,* 15 July 1991.

Manga, Al-Amin Abu, "Resistance to the Western System of Education by the Early Migrant Community of Maiurno (Sudan)," in *Islam in Africa: Proceedings of the Islam in Africa Conference*, ed. Nura Alkali, Adamu Adamu, Awwal Yadudu, Rashid Motem, and Haruna Salihi, Ibadan: Spectrum Books Limited, 1993.

Manning, Patrick, *Slavery and African Life: Occidental, Oriental, and African Slave Trades*, Cambridge: Cambridge University Press, 1990.

Maranz, David E., *Peace Is Everything: The World View of Muslims and Tradionalists in the Senegambia*, Dallas: International Museum of Cultures, 1993.

Martin, B. G., *Muslim Brotherhoods in Nineteenth Century Africa*, Cambridge: Cambridge University Press, 1976.

_____, "A Muslim Political Tract from Northern Nigeria: Muhammad Bello's *Usúl al-Siyása*," in *Aspects of West African Islam*, ed. Daniel F. McCall and Norman R. Bennett, vol. 5, Boston: Boston University Press, 1971.

Martin, David, *The Religious and the Secular*, London: Routledge, 1969.

Marty, Paul, *L'Islam en Guinée: Fouta Diallon*, Paris: E. Leroux, 1921.

_____, "L'Islam en Mauritanie et au Senegal," *Revue du Monde Musulman* 31, 1915–1916.

_____, *Les Mourides d'Amadou Bamba*, Paris: Leroux, 1913.

Mason, John, "Paternalism Under Siege: Slavery in Theory and Practice During the Era of Reform, c. 1825 Through Emancipation," in Nigel Worden and Clifton Crais, eds., Johannesburg, 1994.

Mason, M., "Population Density and 'Slave Raiding'—The Case of the Middle Belt of Nigeria," *Journal of African History* 10, no. 4, pp. 551–564.

Masrí, F. H. El-, "The Life of Shehu Usuman dan Fodio Before the Jihad," *Journal of the Historical Society of Nigeria* 2, no. 4, 1963.

Mauny, R., *Tableau géographique de l'ouest africain*, Dakar: Institut Française d'Afrique Noire, 1961.

Mazrui, Ali A., "African Islam and Comprehensive Religion: Between Revivalism and Expansion," in *Islam in Africa: Proceedings of the Islam in Africa Conference*, ed. Nura Alkali, Adamu Adamu, Awwal Yadudu, Rashid Motem, and Haruna Salihi, Ibadan: Spectrum Books Limited, 1993.

Mbiti, John S., *African Religions and Philosophy*, London: Heinemann Publishers, 1969, 1985.

_____, *Concepts of God in Africa*, London: S.P.C.K., 1970, 1982.

_____, *New Testament Eschatology in an African Background,* London: Cambridge University Press, 1971.

_____, *Prayers of African Religion,* Maryknoll, N.Y.: Orbis Books, 1975.

McIlwain, Charles H., "Mediæval Institutions in the Modern World," in *The Renaissance: Medieval or Modern?* ed. Karl H. Dannenfeldt, Series on *Problems in European Civilization,* Boston: D.C. Heath, 1959.

McSheffrey, Gerald M., "Slavery, Indentured Servitude, Legitimate Trade, and the Impact of Abolition in the Gold Coast, 1874–1901: A Reappraisal," *Journal of African History* 24, no. 3, 1983, pp. 349–368.

Medhurst, K., "Religion and Politics: A Typology," *Scottish Journal of Religious Studies I* 2, no. 2, 1981, pp. 115–134.

Meek, C. K., *The Northern Tribes of Nigeria,* 2 vols., London: Oxford University Press, 1925.

Merkl, Peter H., and Ninian Smart, eds., *Religion and Politics in the Modern World,* New York: New York University Press, 1985.

Mews, S., ed., *Religion in Politics,* Harlow: Longman Publishers, 1989.

Miers, Suzanne, and Richard Roberts, eds., *The End of Slavery in Africa,* Madison: University of Wisconsin Press, 1988.

Miller, Joseph C., *Slavery: A Worldwide Bibliography, 1900–1982,* White Plains, N.Y.: Kraus International, 1985.

Miller, Walter, *Have We Failed in Nigeria?* London: Lutterworth Press, 1947.

_____, *Reflections of a Pioneer,* London: Church Missionary Society, 1936.

Milton, John, *Of Education,* in *Complete Poetry and Selected Prose of John Milton,* New York: Random House Modern Library, 1950, pp. 663–676.

_____, *The Tenure of Kings and Magistrates,* in Franklin Le Van Baumer, ed., *Main Currents of Western Thought,* New Haven: Yale University Press, 1978, pp. 351–353.

Miskin, Tijani, El-, "Da'wa and the Challenge of Secularism: A Conceptual Agenda for Islamic Ideologues," in *Islam in Africa: Proceedings of the Islam in Africa Conference,* ed. Nura Alkali, Adamu Adamu, Awwal Yadudu, Rashid Motem, and Haruna Salihi, Ibadan: Spectrum Books Limited, 1993.

Mitchell, Peter K., "A Note on the Distribution in Sierra Leone of Literacy in Arabic, Mende, and Temne," *African Language Review* 7, 1968.

Mitchinson, A. W., *The Expiring Continent,* London: W. H. Allen, 1881.

Moister, William, *Memorials of Missionary Labours in Western Africa, the West Indies, and the Cape of Good Hope,* London: John Mason, 1866.

Molla, Claude F., "Some Aspects of Islam in Africa South of the Sahara," *International Review of Mission* 56, no. 224, October 1967.

Mollien, Gaspard, *Travels in Africa to the Sources of the Senegal and Gambia in 1818,* 2nd ed., London: E. Cave, 1825.

Momoh, C. S., et al., eds., *Nigerian Studies in Religious Tolerance,* 4 vols., Ibadan: Shaneson C.I. Ltd., 1988–1989.

Monteil, Ch., *Les Khassonké,* Paris: Leroux, 1915.

Monteil, Vincent, *L'Islam noir,* Paris: Seuil, 1964.

_____, "Marabouts," in *Islam in Africa,* ed. J. Kritzeck and W. H. Lewis, New York: Van-Nostrand, 1969.

Moore, Francis, *Travels into the Inland Parts of Africa . . . with a Particular Account of Job Ben Solomon, Who Was in England in the Year 1733, and Known by the Name of the African,* London: n.p., 1738.

Moore, Kathleen M., *Al-Mughtaribun: American Law and the Transformation of Muslim Life in the United States,* Albany: State University of New York Press, 1994.

Morgan, John, *Reminiscences of the Founding of a Christian Mission on the Gambia,* London: Wesleyan Mission House, 1864.

Mourey, Charles, and Auguste Terrier, *L'Expansion francaise et la formation territoriale (L'ouvre de la Troisieme Republique en Afrique occidentale)* Paris: É. Larose, 1910.

Moyser, G., ed., *Politics and Religion in the Modern World*, London: Routledge, 1991.

Muir, William, *A Life of Mahomet*, 4 vols., London: Smith, Elder, and Co., 1858–1861.

Mulk, Nizám al-, *The Book of Government for Kings* (*Siyásat Náma*), London: Routledge and Kegan Paul, 1960.

Muller, Herbert J., *The Uses of the Past: Profiles of Former Societies*, London: Oxford University Press, 1952; reprint New York: Mentor Books, 1963.

Nábulsí, 'Abd al-Ghaní al-, *Ta'tír al-Anám fí Ta'bír al-Manám*, 2 vols., Cairo: Dár al-Hayá al Kitáb al-'Arabíyah, n.d.

Nachtigal, Gustav, *Sahara and Sudan*, vol. 1, trans. Humphrey J. Fisher, London: Christopher Hurst, 1974.

Nadel, Siegfried F., *A Black Byzantium: The Kingdom of Nupe in Nigeria*, 1942; reprint, London: Oxford University Press, 1969.

_____, *Nupe Religion*, London: Oxford University Press for the International African Institute, 1954.

The Nation, 11 June 1975.

Newland, C. H., "The Sofa Invasion of Sierra Leone," *Sierra Leone Studies*, old series 19, no. 4, December 1933.

The New York Times, 14 April 1990.

The New York Times, "A Fundamentalist Finds a Fulcrum in Sudan," 29 January 1992.

Nida, Eugene A., *Message and Mission*, New York: Harper and Brothers, 1960.

Nida, Eugene A., and William D. Reyburn, *Meaning Across Cultures*, New York: Orbis Books, 1981.

Niebuhr, H. Richard, *Radical Monotheism and Western Culture*, New York: Harper and Brothers, 1960.

Nizám al-Mulk, *The Book of Government for Kings* (*Siyását náma*), London: Routledge and Kegan Paul, 1960.

Noibi, D.O.S., "Muslim Youth and Christian-Sponsored Education," *Bulletin of Islam and Christian-Muslim Relations in Africa* 6, no. 3, pp. 3–25.

Noirot, E., *A travers le Fouta-Diallon et le Bambouc*, Paris: E. Flammarion, 1889.

Norris, H. T., *The Arab Conquest of the Western Sudan*, Oxford: Oxford University Press, 1986.

_____, *The Tuaregs: Their Islamic Legacy and Its Diffusion in the Sahel*, Warminster: Aris and Phillips, 1975.

O'Brien, Conor Cruise, *God Land: Reflections on Religion and Politics*, Cambridge: Harvard University Press, 1987.

O'Brien, Donal Cruise, *The Mourides of Senegal*, Oxford: Clarendon Press, 1971.

_____, "A Versatile Charisma: The Mouride Brotherhood 1967–1975," *Archives europêenes de sociologie* 18, 1977.

O'Fahey, R. S., "Slavery and Society in Dar Fur," in *Slaves and Slavery*, ed. John Ralph Willis, vol. 2, pp. 83–100.

Ogilby, J., *Africa, Being an Accurate Description . . .* , London: T. Johnson for the author, 1670.

Okunola, Muri, "The Relevance of Shar'ia [sic] to Nigeria," in *Islam in Africa: Proceedings of the Islam in Africa Conference*, ed. Nura Alkali, Adamu Adamu, Awwal Yadudu, Rashid Motem, and Haruna Salihi, Ibadan: Spectrum Books Limited, 1993.

Olayiwola, R. O., "Religious Pluralism and Functionalism Among the Ijesha-Yoruba of Nigeria," *Asia Journal of Theology* 6, no. 1, pp. 141–153.

Oloruntimehin, B. O., *The Segu Tukulor Empire*, London: Longman Publishers, 1972.

Olupona, J. K., ed., *Religion and Peace in Multi-Faith Nigeria*, Ile-Ife: Obafemi Awolowo University, 1992.

Onaiyekan, J., "Christians and Muslims: Human Rights and Responsibilities: The Nigerian Situation," *Islamochristiana* 9, 1983, pp. 181–199.

Onaiyekan, J., ed., *Religion, Peace, and Justice in Nigeria: Breaking New Grounds*, Communique of the Catholic Bishops' Conference of Nigeria, February, Ilorin, 1989.

Oseni, Z. I., "Islamic Scholars as Spiritual Healers in a Nigerian Community," *Islamic Culture* 62, no. 4, 1988.

Osman El-Tom, Abdullahi, "Drinking the Koran: The Meaning of Koranic Verses in Berti Erasure," *Africa* 55, no. 4, 1985.

Osuntokun, J., "The Response of the British Colonial Government in Nigeria to the Islamic Insurgency in the French Sudan and Sahara During the First World War," *Bulletin de l'Institut Fondamental d'Afrique Noire*, sér B, vol. 26, 1974 (janvier), pp. 14–24.

Owen, Nicholas, *Journal of a Slavedealer, 1746–57*, ed. E. Martin, London: G. Routledge and Sons, Ltd., 1930.

Oyelade, Emmanuel O., "Islamic Theocracy and Religious Pluralism in Africa," *Asia Journal of Theology* 7, no. 1, 1993, pp. 149–160.

———, "Sir Ahmadu Bello, the Sardauna of Sokoto: The Twentieth Century Mijaddid (Reformer) of West Africa," *Islamic Quarterly* 27, no. 4, 1983, pp. 223–231.

———, "Trends in Hausa/Fulani Islam Since Independence: Aspects of Islamic Modernism in Nigeria," *Orita* 14, no. 1, 1982, pp. 3–15.

Ozigi, A., and L. Ojo, *Education in Northern Nigeria*, London: Allen and Unwin, 1981.

Paden, John N., *Ahmadu Bello, Sardauna of Sokoto: Values and Leadership in Nigeria*, London: Hodder & Stoughton, 1986.

———, *Religion and Political Culture in Kano*, Berkeley and Los Angeles: University of California Press, 1973.

Park, Mungo, *Travels in Africa: 1795–1797*, London: Everyman's Library, 1965.

Parrinder, Geoffrey, *African Traditional Religion*, London: Hutchinson's University Library, 1954.

———, *Africa's Three Religions*, London: Sheldon Press, 1969.

———, *Religion in Africa*, Harmondsworth, England: Penguin Books, 1969.

———, *West African Psychology*, London: Lutterworth Press, 1951.

———, *West African Religion*, London: Epworth Press, 1969.

Parsons, Robert T., "Death and Burial in Kono Religion," *Sierra Leone Bulletin of Religion* 3, no. 2, December 1961.

Peel, John D. Y., *Aladura: A Religious Movement Among the Yoruba*, London: Oxford University Press for the International African Institute, 1968.

———, *Ijeshas and Nigerians: The Incorporation of a Yoruba Kingdom, 1890s–1970s*, Cambridge: Cambridge University Press, 1983.

Person, Yves, "The Atlantic Coast and the Southern Savannahs," *History of West Africa*, vol. 2, ed. Ajayi and Crowder, London: Longman Publishers, 1974.

———, "Samori and Islam," in *Studies in West African Islamic History*, ed. John Ralph Willis, vol. 1: *The Cultivators of Islam*, London: Frank Cass, 1979.

———, *Samori: Une Révolution dyula*, 3 vols., Dakar: Institut Fondamental de L'Afrique Noire, 1968–1970.

Piscatori, J. F., *Islam in a World of Nation States*, Cambridge: Cambridge University Press, 1986.

Porter, G., "A Note on Slavery, Seclusion, and Agrarian Change in Northern Nigeria," *Journal of African History* 30, no. 4, 1989, pp. 487–491.

Poston, Larry, *Islamic Da'wah in the West: Muslim Missionary Activity and the Dynamics of Conversion to Islam*, New York: Oxford University Press, 1992.

Proctor, J. E., *Islam and International Relations*, New York: Praeger, 1965.

Pro Mundi Vita Dossiers, "The Church and Christians in Madagascar Today," *Africa Dossier* 6, July-August 1978.

Proudfoot, Leslie, "Ahmed Alhadi and the Ahmadiyah in Sierra Leone," *Sierra Leone Bulletin of Religion* 2, no. 2, December 1960.

———, "An Aku Factional Fight in East Freetown," *Sierra Leone Bulletin of Religion* 4, no. 2, 1962.

_____, "Mosque-building and Tribal Separatism in Freetown," *Africa* 29, no. 4, 1959.

_____, "Towards Muslim Solidarity in Freetown," *Africa* 31, 1961.

Proudfoot, Leslie, and H. S. Wilson, "Muslim Attitudes to Education in Sierra Leone," *The Muslim World* 50, no. 1, January 1960.

Qayrawání, Ibn Abí Zayd al-, *La Risálah: ou épitre sue les éléments du dogme et de la loi de l'Islam selon le rite malikte*, ed. and trans. Léon Bercher, Alger: Éditions Jules Carbonel, 1952; English edition, *The Risálah*, trans. and ed. Joseph Kenny, Minna, Nigeria: The Islamic Educational Trust, 1992.

Quadri, Y. A., "The Qadiriyyah and Tijaniyyah Relations in Nigeria in the Twentieth Century," *Orita* 16, no. 1, 1984, pp. 15–30.

_____, "A Study of the Izalah: A Contemporary Anti-Sufi Organisation in Nigeria," *Orita* 27, no. 2, 1985, pp. 95–108.

Quinn, Charlotte, *Mandingo Kingdoms of Senegambia*, Berkeley and Los Angeles: University of California Press, 1972.

_____, "A Nineteenth Century Fulbe State," *Journal of African History* 12, 1971.

Raffenel, Anne, *Nouveau voyage dans le pays nègres*, 2 vols., Paris: Imprimerie et Libraraire Centrales des Chemin de Fer, 1856.

Rahman, Faslur, *Islam*, New York: Anchor Books, Doubleday, 1968.

Raji, R. A., "The Nigerian Association of Teachers of Arabic and Islamic Studies (NATAIS): An Appraisal of Its Effects on Muslim Minority Education," *Muslim Education Quarterly* 7 Winter, 1990, pp. 57–71.

The Ramadan Vision, Freetown, July 1947.

Rasmussen, Lissi, *Religion and Property in Northern Nigeria*, Copenhagen: University of Copenhagen, 1990.

Reade, W. W., *Savage Africa*, London: Smith, Elder, and Co., 1863; New York: Harper and Brothers, 1864.

Reeck, Darrell L., "Islam in a West African Chiefdom: An Interpretation," *Muslim World* 62, no. 3, 1972.

Reichardt, C.A.L., *A Grammar of the Fulde Language*, London: Church Missionary House, 1876.

Rippin, A., and J. Knappert, eds., *Textual Sources on Islam*, Manchester: Manchester University Press, and Chicago: Chicago University Press, 1986.

Roberts, H., "Radical Islamism and the Dilemma of Algerian Nationalism: The Embattled Arians of Algiers," *Third World Quarterly* 10, no. 2, 1988, pp. 567–575.

Roberts, S. H., *The History of French Colonial Policy: 1870–1925*, London: n.p., 1929.

Robertson, Claire C., and Martin Klein, eds., *Women and Slavery in Africa*, Madison: University of Wisconsin Press, 1983.

Robinson, David, "Beyond Resistance and Collaboration: Ahmadu Bamba and the Murids of Senegal," *Journal of Religion in Africa* 21, no. 2, May 1991.

_____, *The Holy War of 'Umar Tal: The Western Sudan in the Mid-Nineteenth Century*, Oxford: Clarendon Press, 1985.

Rodney, Walter, *A History of the Upper Guinea Coast: 1545–1800*, Oxford: Clarendon Press, 1970.

_____, "Jihad and Social Revolution in Fouta Djalon in the Eighteenth Century," *Journal of the Historical Society of Nigeria* 4, no. 2, 1968.

Rosenthal, E.I.J., *Islam and the Modern National State*, Cambridge: Cambridge University Press, 1965.

_____, *Political Thought in Medieval Islam*, Cambridge: Cambridge University Press, 1958.

Rubin, B., "Religion and International Affairs," *The Washington Quarterly* 13, no. 2, 1990, pp. 51–63.

Ruete, Emily, *Memoirs of an Arabian Princess from Zanzibar*, New York: Markus Wiener Publishing, 1989.

Ruxton, F. H., *Maliki Law*, London: Luzac, 1916.

Ryan, Patrick J., *Imale: Yoruba Participation in the Muslim Tradition*, Montana: Scholars Press, 1979.

Sahliyeh, E., ed., *Religious Resurgence and Politics in the Contemporary World*, Albany: State University of New York Press, 1990.

St. Croix, F. W. de, *The Fulani of Nigeria*, Lagos: n.p., 1945; reprint, Farnborough, England: Gregg, 1972.

Sambe, Amar, *Diplôme d'études supérieures*, Paris: Faculté des Lettres, Université de Paris, 1964.

Sanneh, Lamin, "The Domestication of Christianity and Islam in African Societies," *Journal of Religion in Africa* 11, no. 1, 1980.

_____, "Futa Jallon and the Jakhanke Clerical Tradition. Part I: The Historical Setting," *Journal of Religion in Africa* 12, no. 1, 1981.

_____, *The Jakhanké Muslim Clerics: A Religious and Historical Study of Islam in Senegambia*, Lanham, Md.: University Press of America, 1989.

_____, "The Origins of Clericalism in West African Islam," *Journal of African History* 17, no. 1, 1976.

_____, *West African Christianity: The Religious Impact*, Maryknoll, N.Y.: Orbis Books, 1983.

Santerre, R., *Pédagogie musulmane de l'Afrique noire*, Montreal: Presse Universitaire de Montreal, 1975.

Saul, Mahir, "The Quranic School Farm and Child Labour in Upper Volta," *Africa* 54, no. 2, 1984.

Sawyerr, Harry, "Do Africans Believe in God?" *Sierra Leone Studies* 15, December 1961.

_____, "Sacrificial Rituals in Sierra Leone," *Sierra Leone Bulletin of Religion* 1, June 1959.

_____, "The Supreme God and Spirits," *Sierra Leone Bulletin of Religion* 3, no. 2, December 1961.

Sayeed, Khalid Bin, *Western Dominance and Political Islam*, Albany: State University of New York Press, 1994.

Schacht, Joseph, *An Introduction to Islamic Law*, Oxford: Clarendon Press, 1964.

_____, *The Origins of Muhammedan Jurisprudence*, Oxford: Clarendon Press, 1950.

Schimmel, Annemarie, *Mystical Dimensions of Islam*, Chapel Hill: University of North Carolina Press, 1975.

Schlenker, C. F., *Collection of Temne Traditions, Fables, and Proverbs*, London: Church Missionary Society, 1861.

Searing, James F., *West African Slavery and Atlantic Commerce: The Senegal River Valley, 1700–1860*, Cambridge: Cambridge University Press, 1993.

Sekyi, Kobina, *The Parting of the Ways*, reprinted in J. Ayodele Langley, *Ideologies of Liberation in Black Africa, 1856–1970*, London: R. Collins, 1979.

Sesay, S. I., "Koranic Schools in the Provinces," *Sierra Leone Journal of Education* 1, no. 1, April 1966.

Shipton, Parker, *Bitter Money: Cultural Economy and Some African Meanings of Forbidden Commodities*, Washington, D.C.: American Anthropological Association, 1989.

Sierra Leone Colonial Report, 1901, London: H.M. Stationery Office, 1902.

Sierra Leone Weekly News, 9 January 1889, and 12 January 1889.

Sírín, Muhammad bin, *Ta'bír al-Ru'yá*, Cairo: Maktab 'Abbas 'Abd al-Salam Shagarun, n.d. (author d. 728).

Sitwell, Cecil, *South Bank Report*, Banjul, The Gambia: Public Records Office, Ref. 76/19, 1891.

Sivan, Emmanuel, *Radical Islam: Medieval Theology and Modern Politics*, New Haven: Yale University Press, 1985.

Skinner, David E., "Islamic Education and Missionary Work in the Gambia, Ghana, and Sierra Leone During the Twentieth Century," *BICMURA* 1, no. 4, October 1983.

_____, "Islam in Sierra Leone During the Nineteenth Century," Ph.D. thesis, Berkeley, 1971.

_____, "Mende Settlement and the Development of Islamic Institutions in Sierra Leone," *International Journal of African Historical Studies* 11, no. 1, 1978.

Slater, B., and R. Shultz, eds., *Revolution and Political Change in the Third World*, London: Adamantine, 1990.

The Slave Abolition Ordinance, Ref. 2/96, 1906, Records Office, Banjul.

Smart, Joko H. M., "Place of Islamic Law Within the Framework of the Sierra Leone Legal System," *African Law Studies* 18, 1980.

Smith, D. E., *Religion and Political Development*, Boston: Little, Brown & Co., 1970.

Smith, Jane Idleman, and Yvonne Yazbeck Haddad, eds., *Muslim Communities in North America*, Albany: State University of New York Press, 1994.

Smith, Mary, ed., *Baba of Karo*, New Haven: Yale University Press, London: Faber, 1954.

Smith, Pierre, "Notes sur l'organisation sociale des Diakhanké: Aspects particuliers à la région de Kédougou," *Bulletin et Mémoire de la Societé Anthropologie de Paris* 11, no. 8, 1965, pp. 263–302.

_____, "Les Dialchanké: Histoire d'une dispersion," *Bulletin et Mémoire de la Societé Anthropologie de Paris* 11, no. 8, 1965.

Snelgrave, William, *A New Account of Some Parts of Guinea and the Slave Trade*, London: J., J., and P. Knapton, 1734, reprinted London: Frank Cass, 1971.

Soleillet, Paul, *Voyage à Segou: 1878–1879*, Paris: Challamel, 1887.

Soriba Jabi, al-Hájj, *Kitáb al-Bushrá: Sharb al-Mirqát al Kubrá*, Tunis: n.p., n.d.

Stackhouse, Max, "Politics and Religion," *Encyclopedia of Religion*, vol. 11, ed. Mercea Eliade, New York: Macmillan, 1987.

Stibbs, Captain, "Voyage up the Gambia in 1723," in *Travels into the Inland Parts of Africa*, ed. Francis Moore, London: E. Cave, 1724.

Stock, Eugene, *A History of the Church Missionary Society*, vols. 2 and 3, London: Church Missionary Society, 1916.

Suhrawardí, Shihâb al-Dín al-, *al-'Awárif al-Ma'árif*, ed. and trans. Wilberforce Clarke, Calcutta: Government of India Central Printing Office, 1891. Reprinted London: The Octagon Press, 1980.

Suret-Canale, J., *L'Afrique noire: Occidentale et centrale*, Paris: Editions sociales, 1961.

_____, "Touba in Guinea: Holy Place of Islam," in *African Perspectives: Essays in Honour of Thomas Hodgkin*, ed. C. Allen and R. W. Johnson, Cambridge: Cambridge University Press, 1970.

Sweetman, David, *Women Leaders in African History*, London: Heinemann Publishers, 1984.

Swift, R., "Fundamentalism," *New Internationalist*, August 1990.

Tambo, David, "The Sokoto Caliphate Slave Trade in the Nineteenth Century," *International Journal of African Historical Studies* 9, no. 2, 1976, pp. 187–217.

Tangban, O. E., "The Hajj and the Nigerian Economy: 1960–1981," *Journal of Religion in Africa* 21, no. 3, August 1991.

Tauxier, L., *Moeurs et histoire des peulhs*, Paris: Payot, 1937.

Taylor, A.J.P., *The Habsburg Monarchy: 1808–1918*, 1948; reprint, London: Penguin Books, 1990.

Tibi, Basam, *Islam and the Cultural Accommodation of Social Change*, Boulder: Westview Press, 1990.

Andargachew Tiruneh, *The Ethiopian Revolution: 1974–1985*, Cambridge: Cambridge University Press, 1993; reprint 1995.

Tocqueville, Alexis de, *Democracy in America*, trans. George Lawrence, ed. J. P. Mayer, New York: Harper Perennial, 1966.

Tremearne, A.J.N., *The Ban of the Bori*, London: n.p., 1914; reprint, London: Frank Cass, 1968.

_____, *Hausa Superstitions and Customs*, London: n.p., 1913; reprint, London: Frank Cass, 1970.

Trimingham, John Spencer, *A History of Islam in West Africa,* London: Oxford University Press, 1962.

_____, *Islam in West Africa,* Oxford: Clarendon Press, 1959.

_____, *The Sufi Orders in Islam,* Oxford: Clarendon Press, 1971.

Trimingham, John Spencer, and Christopher Fyfe, "The Early Expansion of Islam in Sierra Leone," *Sierra Leone Bulletin of Religion* 2, no. 1, June 1960.

Turner, Harold W., *History of an African Independent Church: Church of the Lord (Aladura),* 2 vols., Oxford: Clarendon Press, 1967.

Turner, Victor, *Dramas, Fields, and Metaphors: Symbolic Action in Human Society,* Ithaca: Cornell University Press, 1983, especially the chapter "Metaphors of Anti-Structure in Religious Culture."

_____, *The Ritual Process: Structure and Anti-Structure,* Ithaca, N.Y.: Cornell University Press, 1982.

"Universal Islamic Declaration," *The Times,* London, 14 April 1980.

Vatikiotis, P., *Islam and the State,* London: Routledge, 1991.

Verdat, M., "Le Ouali de Goumba," *Études Guinéennes* 3, 1949.

Verger, Pierre, *Trade Relations Between the Bight of Benin and Bahia, Seventeenth to the Nineteenth Century,* Paris: Mouton and Ecole Pratique des Hautes Etudes, 1968; Ibadan edition, 1976.

Voll, J., and F. von der Mehden, "Religious Resurgence and Revolution: Islam," in B. Slater and R. Shultz, eds., *Revolution and Political Change in the Third World,* London: Adamantine, 1990.

Vuillet, Jean, "Récherches au sujet de religions professes en Sénégambie, anciennement ou a l'epoque actuelle," *Comptes Rendus Mensuels des Seances de l'Academie des Sciences Coloniales* 7, no. 8, 1952.

Waldman, M. W., "The Church of Scotland Mission at Blantyre, Nyasaland: Its Political Implications," *Bulletin of the Society of African Church History* 2, no. 4, 1968.

Walz, Terence, "Notes on the Organization of the African Trade in Cairo, 1800–1850," *Annales Islamologiques* 11, 1972.

Waqidi, Muhammad ibn 'Umar al- (752–829), *Muhammad in Medina,* trans. and abbreviated by Wellhausen, Berlin, 1882.

Warburg, Gabriel R., "Ideological and Practical Considerations Regarding Slavery in the Mahdist State and the Anglo-Egyptian Sudan: 1881–1918," Paul Lovejoy, ed., Beverly Hills, California: Sage, 1981.

Washington, Captain, "Some Accounts of Mohammedu-Sisei, a Mandigo of Nyani-Maru on the Gambia," *Journal of the Royal Geographical Society* 8, 1838.

Watt, W. Montgomery, *Islamic Fundamentalism and Modernity,* London: Routledge, 1990.

_____, *Islamic Philosophy and Theology,* Edinburgh: Edinburgh University Press, 1962.

_____, *Muhammad at Medina,* Oxford: Clarendon Press, 1962.

Weaver, Richard, *Ideas Have Consequences,* Chicago: University of Chicago Press, 1948.

Weber, Max, *The Sociology of Religion,* trans. Ephraim Fischoff, Boston: Beacon Press, 1963.

Weil, Peter M., "Slavery, Groundnuts, and European Capitalism in the Wuli Kingdom of Senegambia, 1820–1930," *Research in Economic Anthropology* 6, 1984, pp. 77–119.

West Africa weekly magazine, 17 September 1979.

Westerlund, David, ed., *Questioning the Secular State: The Worldwide Resurgence of Religion in Politics,* London: Christopher Hurst & Co, 1995.

We Yone newspaper, 11 June 1975.

Wilks, Ivor, "The Transmission of Islamic Learning in the Western Sudan," in *Literacy in Traditional Societies,* ed. Jack Goody, Cambridge: Cambridge University Press.

Willis, John Ralph, "*Jihád fí sabíl li-lláh*: Its Doctrinal Basis in Islam and Some Aspects of Its Evolution in Nineteenth Century West Africa," *Journal of African History* 8, 1967.

———, *The Passion of al-Hájj 'Umar: An Essay into the Nature of Charisma in Islam*, London: Frank Cass, 1989.

Willis, John Ralph, ed., *Slaves and Slavery in Muslim Africa*, 2 vols., London: Frank Cass, 1985.

Woodhouse, A.S.P., ed., *Puritanism and Liberty: The Army Debates (1647–9) from the Clarke Manuscripts*, London: J.M. Dent & Sons Ltd., 1974.

Worden, Nigel, "Between Slavery and Freedom: The Apprenticeship Period, 1834–8," in *Breaking the Chains: Slavery and Its Legacy in the Nineteenth-Century Cape Colony*, Nigel Worden and Clifton Crais, eds., Johannesburg: Witwatersrand University Press, 1994.

Worden, Nigel, and Clifton Crais, eds., *Breaking the Chains: Slavery and Its Legacy in the Nineteenth-Century Cape Colony*, Johannesburg: Witwatersrand University Press, 1994.

Wurie, A., "The Bundukas of Sierra Leone," *Sierra Leone Studies*, new series 1, no. 4, December 1953.

Wyndham, H. A., *The Atlantic and Slavery*, Oxford: Oxford University Press, 1935.

Yadudu, Auwalu Hamisu, "The Prospects for Shar'ia [sic] in Nigeria," in *Islam in Africa: Proceedings of the Islam in Africa Conference*, ed. Nura Alkali, Adamu Adamu, Awwal Yadudu, Rashid Motem, and Haruna Salihi, Ibadan: Spectrum Books Limited, 1993.

Yahya, Dahiru, "Colonialism in Africa and the Impact of European Concepts and Values: Nationalism and Muslims in Nigeria," in *Islam in Africa: Proceedings of the Islam in Africa Conference*, ed. Nura Alkali, Adamu Adamu, Awwal Yadudu, Rashid Motem, and Haruna Salihi, Ibadan: Spectrum Books Limited, 1993.

Yamusa, S., *The Political Ideas of the Jihad Leaders: Being a Translation, Edition, and Analysis of Usúl al-Siyása by Muhammad Bello and Diya al-Hukkum by Abdullahi b. Fodio*, M.A. thesis, Abdullahi Bayero College, Kano, 1975.

Yusuf, Bilikisu, "Da'wa and Contemporary Challenges Facing Muslim Women in Secular States—A Nigerian Case Study," in *Islam in Africa: Proceedings of the Islam in Africa Conference*, ed. Nura Alkali, Adamu Adamu, Awwal Yadudu, Rashid Motem, and Haruna Salihi, Ibadan: Spectrum Books Limited, 1993.

Zwemer, Samuel, *Arabia: The Cradle of Islam*, New York: F. H. Revell, 1900.

Zwemer, Samuel, ed., *The Mohammedan World of Today*, New York: Education Department of the Presbyterian Church in the U.S.A., 1908.

About the Book and Author

The Crown and the Turban: Muslims and West African Pluralism explores the historical and political dimensions of interreligious encounter in the context of a receptive and pluralist African environment. The Muslim tradition of uniting church and state was well established before the onset of European colonialism and was bolstered, and in turn complicated, by it, with secularism quickening the pace. In the contrasting and often parallel case of Christian expansion in Africa, a favorable climate was created for transmitting the Western secular tradition of separating church and state. The potential conflict of this secular tradition with Muslim practice has as one of its impacts a challenge in postcolonial Africa to separate the crown and the turban and to do so on the basis of theological arguments that can complement Muslim thought.

Lamin Sanneh is descended from the *nyanchos*, an ancient African royal house, and was educated on four continents. He went to school with chiefs' sons in the Gambia, West Africa. He subsequently came to the United States on a U.S. government scholarship to read history. After graduating he spent several years studying classical Arabic and Islam, including a stint in the Middle East, and working with the churches in Africa and with international organizations concerned with interreligious issues. He received his Ph.D. in Islamic history at the University of London. He was a professor at Harvard University for eight years before moving to Yale University in 1989 as the D. Willis James Professor of Missions and World Christianity, with a concurrent courtesy appointment as Professor of History at Yale College. He is a Visiting Fellow of Clare Hall, Cambridge. He has been actively involved in Yale's Council on African Studies. He is an editor-at-large of the ecumenical weekly, *The Christian Century*, and serves on the editorial board of several academic journals. He is the author of over a hundred articles on religious and historical subjects, and of several books, including *The Jakhanké Muslim Clerics: A Religious and Historical Study of Islam in Senegambia*, *West African Christianity: The Religious Impact*, *Translating the Message: The Missionary Impact on Culture*, now in its seventh printing, and *Encountering the West: Christianity and the Global Cultural Process*. For his academic work he was made Commandeur de l'Ordre National du Lion, Senegal's highest national honor. He is married with two children.

Index